Jesus in Johannine Tradition

Jesus in Johannine Tradition

Edited by
Robert T. Fortna and Tom Thatcher

Westminster John Knox Press
LOUISVILLE • LONDON

© 2001 Robert T. Fortna and Tom Thatcher

Scripture quotations from the New Revised Standard Version of the Bible are copyright © 1989 by the Division of Christian Education of the National Council of the Churches of Christ in the U.S.A. and are used by permission.

Book design by Sharon Adams
Cover design by Grand Design

First edition
Published by Westminster John Knox Press
Louisville, Kentucky

This book is printed on acid-free paper that meets the American National Standards Institute Z39.48 standard. ∞

PRINTED IN THE UNITED STATES OF AMERICA

02 03 04 05 06 07 08 09 10 — 10 9 8 7 6 5 4 3 2

Library of Congress Cataloging-in-Publication Data is on file at the Library of Congress, Washington, D.C.

ISBN 0-664-22219-6

Contents

Contributors

Paul Anderson teaches at George Fox University in Newberg, Oregon. He specializes in Johannine studies and is the author of *The Christology of the Fourth Gospel: Its Unity and Disunity in the Light of John 6*, a major study of the theology, sources, and composition history of FG.

John Ashton is a retired Fellow of Wolfson College at the University of Oxford. He specializes in Johannine studies and has written and edited numerous books and articles on the Gospel of John and the history of its interpretation, as well as a recent book on Pauline studies, *The Religion of Paul.*

Richard Bauckham teaches at St. Mary's College in the University of St. Andrews, Scotland. He specializes in the Gospel of John and New Testament Christology and has written on Revelation, James, and the theology of Jürgen Moltmann.

Johannes Beutler teaches at the Pontifical Biblical Institute in Rome. He specializes in Johannine studies and has written on the Gospel of John.

Craig Blomberg teaches at Denver Seminary. He specializes in the canonical gospels, and his numerous books and articles include studies of Jesus, the parables, the historicity of the canonical gospels, and more recently the Gospel of John.

Edwin Broadhead teaches at Berea College in Berea, Kentucky. He specializes in early Jesus traditions, Q studies, and the Synoptic Gospels, and has written on Q, Mark, and the Gospel of Thomas.

Ingo Broer teaches at the University of Siegen, Germany. He specializes in Jesus traditions and the canonical gospels and has written on the resurrection of Jesus, on Matthew, and on antisemitism. His most recent project is a two-volume introduction to the New Testament.

Gary Burge teaches at Wheaton College in Chicago. He specializes in Johannine studies, and his numerous books and articles include recent commentaries on the Gospel of John and 1–2–3 John.

Chrys Caragounis teaches at Lunds Universitet in Lund, Sweden. He specializes in ancient history, literature, and philology, as well as the canonical gospels and Pauline studies. He has written extensively on the Kingdom of God and the Son of Man as well as on Johannine themes. His most recent project, "A Diachronic and Acoustic Approach to the New Testament," explores the significance of later Greek for the interpretation of the NT.

Alan Culpepper is Dean of the McAfee School of Theology at Mercer University in Atlanta. He specializes in Johannine studies and has written on the Gospel of John, 1–2–3 John, and the history of Johannine scholarship.

April DeConick teaches at Illinois Wesleyan University in Bloomington, Illinois. She specializes in early Christian theology and noncanonical gospels, and has written on the Gospel of Thomas, the Dialogue of the Savior, the Gospel of Philip, and the recently discovered Gospel of the Savior.

Arthur Dewey teaches at Xavier University in Cincinnati. He specializes in the historical Jesus, Pauline studies, and oral-based literature and has written on the canonical and noncanonical gospels and Paul.

Joanna Dewey is the Academic Dean and Professor of Bible at the Episcopal Divinity School in Cambridge, Massachusetts. She specializes in oral traditions and the canonical gospels and has written on the gospels, their oral origins, and their interpretation as oral-based texts.

Tom Felton teaches at the Manukau Institute of Technology in Manukau, New Zealand. He specializes in statistics and has written on stylometry and the sources of the Gospel of John.

Robert Fortna formerly taught at Vassar College in Poughkeepsie, New York. He specializes in historical-Jesus studies and Johannine studies and has written on the sources of the Gospel of John, Johannine theology, and the historical Jesus. His most recent works include a commentary on Matthew.

Alan Kirk teaches at James Madison University in Harrisonburg, Virginia. He specializes in early Christian history and has written on Q and the Gospel of Peter.

Mark Matson is Academic Dean and Professor of Biblical Studies at Milligan College in Johnson City, Tennessee. He specializes in the canonical gospels and has written on Jesus, the Temple Incident, and the relationship between John and the Synoptics.

Gail O'Day teaches at the Candler School of Theology at Emory University in Atlanta and is the current editor of the *Journal of Biblical Literature*. She specializes in Johannine studies and has written numerous books and articles on the Gospel of John and Johannine theology.

Stephen Patterson teaches at Eden Theological Seminary in St. Louis. He specializes in early Christian history and the historical Jesus and has written on Jesus, the Gospel of Thomas, and the Nag Hammadi library.

John Perry teaches at Cardinal Stritch College in Milwaukee. He specializes in early Christian thought and contemporary faith and has written on the sacraments and modern theology.

David Rensberger teaches at the Interdenominational Theological Center in Atlanta. He specializes in Johannine studies and has written numerous books and articles on the Johannine Community, the Gospel of John, and 1–2–3 John.

Jeffrey Staley teaches at Pacific Lutheran University in Seattle. He specializes in postmodern hermeneutics, postcolonial studies, and Johannine studies and has written on the Gospel of John and literary and autobiographical criticism.

Tom Thatcher teaches at Cincinnati Bible Seminary. He specializes in oral traditions and Johannine studies and has written on Jesus traditions, the Gospel of John, and 1–2–3 John.

Christopher Tuckett is a Fellow of Wolfson College at the University of Oxford. He specializes in the Synoptic Gospels and Q studies. He has written numerous books and articles on Q and early Christian Jesus traditions.

Graham Twelftree formerly taught at All Souls College of Applied Theology in London and is currently the Senior Pastor of North Eastern Vineyard

Church in Adelaide, South Australia. He specializes in the ancient world and Jesus and has written extensively on miracles and exorcisms. His most recent work is a book on the historical Jesus.

Catrin Williams teaches at the University of Wales, Bangor. She specializes in rabbinic Judaism and Johannine studies and has written on the Gospel of John and "I am" sayings.

Walter Wink teaches at Auburn Theological Seminary. He specializes in early Christian thought, Gnosticism, and the historical Jesus and has written on Jesus, apocalyptic, the parables, and a wide variety of issues in contemporary ethics. His latest project is a forthcoming book on the Son of Man.

Sara Winter teaches at Eugene Lang College in New York City. She specializes in Pauline studies, Septuagint studies, and the historical Jesus and has written on Paul and early Christian history.

Abbreviations and Glossary

The following terms and abbreviations are used throughout the book with the meanings indicated.

aporia. Any break or disruption in a literary text. In Johannine studies, aporias are instances in which narrative or theological inconsistencies seem to appear between various sections of the Fourth Gospel. Such difficulties are sometimes seen as indicators that different sources have been woven together to produce the current text.

2 Bar. Second Baruch, or the Syriac Apocalypse of Baruch, a noncanonical Jewish apocalyptic work purporting to have been written by Baruch, scribe to the prophet Jeremiah, but actually written sometime between 150 and 60 B.C.E.

B.C.E. "Before the Common Era," referring to the centuries before the birth of Jesus. This term is preferred here over "B.C."

BD. The "Beloved Disciple," a character in the Gospel of John. This mysterious figure is present at the Farewell Address (John 13:23) and witnesses Jesus' crucifixion (19:26) and resurrection (20:2; 21:20). He is presented in John 21:24 as the source for the Fourth Gospel's information about Jesus (cf. 19:35). At some point it was apparently believed that this disciple would not die until Jesus returned (21:22–23). Because John 20:2 refers to the Beloved Disciple as the "other disciple," further references in the Gospel of John to "(an)other disciple" are sometimes taken as allusions to this character. Traditionally, the Beloved Disciple has been identified as the apostle John mentioned in the Synoptic Gospels and also as the author of the Gospel of John. More recently, considerable debate has surrounded the identity of this figure and his relationship to the historical Jesus and the Fourth Evangelist. The various authors in this volume take different positions on these issues.

Birkhat ha-Minim. The "Blessing/Curse Against the Heretics," a prayer added to the liturgy of the rabbinic synagogue at some point after the destruction of Jerusalem (70 C.E.). The precise date and purposes of this prayer are uncertain. Some scholars date the *Birkhat* in the mid-80s C.E. and believe that it was instituted as part of a broad attempt to expel Jewish Christians from synagogues and the Jewish community. Many Johannine scholars associate the references to excommunication in the Fourth Gospel (FG) with this new ordinance, suggesting that the Johannine Christians had been ejected from the Jewish community before FG was written.

Book of Signs. A term coined by C. H. Dodd to refer to chapters 2–12 of the Gospel of John. These chapters are called "the Book of Signs" because they narrate Jesus' public miracles, which John refers to as *sēmeia*.

canonical gospels. The New Testament books of Matthew, Mark, Luke, and John.

C.E. "Common Era," referring to the centuries after the birth of Jesus. This term is preferred here over "A.D."

crurifragium. The Roman practice of breaking the legs of crucifixion victims to hasten their death. John 19:31–37 mentions that Pilate ordered this done to Jesus, but the soldiers found him already dead. A similar episode is described in the Gospel of Peter.

current version. The final edition of a document. In these essays, "current version" refers to the various ancient gospels in the form in which they exist today, even if the current text is the endproduct of a process of writing and revising.

dependence. In discussing the composition history of a document, "dependence" indicates that a later author used an earlier document as a source of information. One might say, for example, that Matthew and Luke were "dependent on Mark" in producing their gospels. Many of the essays in this book discuss whether the Gospel of John was dependent on other known accounts of Jesus' life or teaching (the Synoptic Gospels, Q, Gospel of Peter, etc.).

Diaspora. The "dispersion" of members of the Jewish community from Palestine, beginning about the eighth century B.C.E., which extended Judaism to a worldwide religion by the time of Jesus. When used in association with a Jesus tradition, Diaspora usually characterizes that tradition as less ancient and less primitive, for it assumes a certain amount of time for the tradition to move from Palestine to the Hellenistic-Jewish context.

Didache. Abbreviated title of The Teaching (Greek: *Didache*) of the Twelve Apostles, a noncanonical work written between 80 and 120 C.E. and widely believed in the early church to reflect the teaching of the original twelve apostles of Jesus. The work is important to historical research in early Christianity because it reflects the views of the second-century church on Christian ethics, the sacraments, and church polity.

Eucharist. The sacrament of the "Lord's Supper," based on the account of Jesus' last meal with the giving of bread and wine in the synoptics. There is no explicit reference to this event in John.

Farewell (Discourse). Jesus' lengthy address to his disciples on the night before his arrest as recorded in John 13–17. This episode roughly corresponds to the Last Supper episode in the Synoptic Gospels but includes much more teaching and a footwashing.

FE. The Fourth Evangelist, author or final editor of the Gospel of John. In some essays, this term is equivalent to the name "John," and the pronoun "he" is used throughout in reference to the Fourth Evangelist.

FG. The Fourth Gospel, or Gospel of John.

GNT4. The *Greek New Testament*, 4th Edition (ed. Barbara Aland, Kurt Aland, et al., Stuttgart: Deutsche Bibelgesellschaft for United Bible Societies, 1993). This is the current standard text of the Greek New Testament. All direct citations of the Greek text of the Gospel of John, 1–2–3 John, or other NT books are taken from this edition.

Gos. Pet. The Gospel of Peter, a noncanonical gospel that tells the story of Jesus' passion and death. All citations of the Gospel of Peter in this book are taken from *The Complete Gospels* unless otherwise indicated.

Gos. Thom. The Gospel of Thomas, an early sayings gospel that records various teachings of Jesus but does not relate specific events from his ministry. All citations of the Gospel of Thomas in this book are taken from *The Complete Gospels* unless otherwise indicated.

Greek Solomon. The author of the Wisdom of Solomon, a book of Jewish wisdom purporting to be written by King Solomon but probably originating in Egypt in the first century B.C.E.

the historical Jesus. Jesus of Nazareth, a human being who lived in Palestine in the early first century C.E. This term distinguishes the life, ministry, and teaching of this person from the church's beliefs about him. The presentation of Jesus in various traditions was influenced by the tradition user's own theological and literary interests.

Jesus tradition. Any story about Jesus' life, ministry, or teaching that was circulated in oral or written form in the early church. The term "tradition" as used here does not imply the information is more or less primitive than that found in the extant written gospels.

the Jews. Common English translation of the Greek term *Ioudaioi*, which occurs frequently in the Gospel of John. In John, "the Jews" are often presented as hostile toward Jesus and his followers, and this presentation has been used throughout Christian history to justify antisemitism. There is considerable debate, however, as to whether John uses "Jews" to refer to all persons who subscribe to the Jewish faith. The editors use the common translation ("Jews") with no special formatting or punctuation. Of course, each essay will be informed by the author's individual opinion on this issue.

Johannine Christianity. That branch of Christian thought and fellowship with which the Fourth Evangelist was most closely associated.

Johannine Community. That group of people who formed the original audience of the Gospel of John. There is considerable debate as to whether this audience represented a specific body of people and Christian congregations, and what the history of such a group might have been.

Johannine Jesus. Jesus as presented in the Gospel of John, as distinct from the historical Jesus and the presentation of Jesus in other gospels. This distinction does not imply that any specific event or saying in the Fourth Gospel is unhistorical.

kerygma. The Greek word for "proclamation." In the context of Jesus traditions, *kerygma* generally refers to the use of Jesus materials in the oral preaching of the primitive church, specifically its evangelistic efforts. It is widely assumed that oral Jesus materials were adapted and developed in order to serve the needs of such preaching.

KOG. The "Kingdom of God."

logion/logia. The Greek terms for "saying" and "sayings." In the context of these essays, a logion is a saying of Jesus that circulated in oral or written tradition before the extant gospels were composed. Some logia may have circulated independently before being included in larger sayings collections.

Logos. The Greek term "Word." John 1:1 uses Logos in reference to the Christ. The term is therefore generally interchangeable in these essays with "the Johannine Jesus," that is, Jesus as the Fourth Evangelist interpreted him christologically.

LXX. The Septuagint, the standard Greek translation of the Hebrew Bible in use during the first century C.E. Most citations of the Hebrew Bible in the New Testament seem to have been taken from this translation.

midrash. An ancient rabbinic technique for interpreting and teaching the Hebrew Bible. Some authors here may use "midrash" to refer to any interpretation and application of the Hebrew Bible or of Jesus traditions by early Christians, including any such interpretations that may now appear in the written gospels.

noncanonical gospels. Early Christian works on the ministry, teaching, and/or death of Jesus that were not included in the New Testament canon by the Second Council of Carthage in 397 C.E. It should be noted that, while the canonical gospels evidence a fairly consistent view of Jesus' life and Christian theology, the noncanonical gospels represent a much wider spectrum of beliefs.

NRSV. The New Revised Standard Version. All citations of the Bible in this book are taken from this translation unless otherwise indicated.

NT. The New Testament.

oral tradition. Information that is transmitted by word of mouth within a society. When used in this book, the term refers to stories and sayings about Jesus that were told and retold in the contexts of oral preaching, teaching, and evangelism.

Paraclete. A transliteration of the Greek term *paraklētos*, which may be translated "Helper," "Comforter," or "Advocate." This is the typical name for the Holy Spirit in the Fourth Gospel.

par(s). "And parallel(s)," referring to passages within the canonical gospels in which similar events or teachings of Jesus are recounted.

pre-Easter. Refers to events involving Jesus, or the disciples' understanding of these events, in the period when he was still alive. The "pre-Easter Jesus" is synonymous with "the historical Jesus."

primitive. When used in reference to a specific source or strain of Jesus tradition, this term describes the views represented in that source or tradition as earlier than others and therefore chronologically closer to the historical Jesus. It is important to stress that "primitive" refers to the proximity of the *views* of a particular source to the historical Jesus. Some authors here will argue that certain sources and gospels that were written later than others nevertheless reflect an older view of Jesus or record of his activity.

Q. The hypothetical source that provided much of the sayings materials for Matthew and Luke. There is considerable debate on the nature and specific content of this source. Some authors here treat Q as a specific document that can be reconstructed with some level of certainty; some think of it more as a general collection of sayings that may have been oral and/or written; others doubt the existence of such a source.

redactor. A person who composes a book by combining information from several prior sources. Matthew and Luke, for example, are considered redactors because they seem to have borrowed material from Mark, Q, and other documents to compose their own gospels. When the term "final redactor" is used concerning the Gospel of John, it refers to that person who was responsible for the last stage of editing and composition that produced the current version of the Fourth Gospel.

sayings tradition. Another designation for Q, the hypothetical source that provided the sayings materials for Matthew and Luke. This source is sometimes referred to as "the Synoptic Sayings Tradition."

SG. The "Signs Gospel," a hypothetical source for the miracle stories and passion narrative in the Gospel of John. While many scholars have proposed a narrative source for the Fourth Gospel, "SG" refers specifically to the reconstruction introduced by Robert Fortna. The most recent text and translation of this hypothetical document appear in *The Complete Gospels*, 180–193.

Sir. Ecclesiasticus, the Wisdom of Jesus ben Sirach, a noncanonical book of Jewish wisdom purporting to have been written in Jerusalem between 190 and 175 B.C.E. and translated into Greek in Egypt around 132 B.C.E.

source. Any document or oral tradition that an author uses in writing a book. In this book, "source" implies that the author of a particular gospel drew information from previous written works or oral traditions about Jesus.

Synoptics. The Gospels of Matthew, Mark, and Luke. When this word is capitalized, it refers specifically to these three books as a group. The lower-case "synoptic" is used as an adjective to describe traditions, sources, or beliefs that are related in some way to the Synoptic Gospels.

Temple Incident. The occasion recorded in John 2 on which Jesus entered the Temple in Jerusalem and protested the sale of sacrificial animals and the exchange of currency. This term is preferred over "Temple Cleansing" because it does not presuppose a particular interpretation of this event.

tradition user. Any early Christian who used materials he or she had heard or read elsewhere to write or tell stories about Jesus. In most cases, the term refers to people who heard and repeated oral traditions about Jesus.

Wis. Sol. The Wisdom of Solomon, a book of Jewish wisdom purporting to be written by King Solomon but probably originating in Egypt in the first century B.C.E.

Introduction

Tom Thatcher

This book is about the Johannine Jesus tradition, the oral and written materials the Fourth Evangelist (FE) used to create the Gospel of John. Its purpose is not to outline that tradition or to establish its inner or outer limits, but rather to take a serious look at the issues and questions to be addressed in reconstructing the process that produced our Fourth Gospel (FG).

While a volume of this size could not contain even an abridged bibliography of studies into the synoptic Jesus tradition, there are relatively few serious works on the Johannine Jesus tradition. There are two reasons for this phenomenon, one theoretical and one methodological. First, since the days of Clement, most scholars have understood FG to be "a spiritual gospel," in some way consisting primarily of theological reflections rather than information from a living Jesus tradition. This has been the case whether one thinks of "John" as an apostle of Jesus, a nameless disciple, a member of a larger community of Christian storytellers, or an epitomizer of the Synoptic Gospels. The notion that FG was written later than the Synoptic Gospels, perhaps very late in the first century or even early in the second, has tended to carry a subtle implication that "John" is primarily a theologian with very little interest in traditions or history. Accepted views of authorship, then, have made the search for a Johannine tradition largely unnecessary from the very early days of biblical scholarship.

Theoretically, the authorship question should not have hindered the search for a Johannine tradition in the modern period, when so much attention has been given to early Jesus traditions and the formation of the Synoptics. The wave of interest in this topic in the last two centuries has, however, left the Fourth Gospel high and dry, largely for methodological reasons. Simply put, the tools of form, source, and redaction criticism, the primary means for identifying oral and written sources behind the books of the Bible, depend heavily

on the comparison of parallels between written documents. In general, scholars interpret close parallels among the extant gospels as evidence that their
authors appealed to common sources, oral or written. This approach has generated remarkable results, most notably the "Two-Source Theory" for the
composition of the Synoptics and the recovery of Q, a document that many
believe is the source for the sayings material in Matthew and Luke. FG, however, has very few close parallels with other extant gospels, and therefore cannot be easily studied in this way. Instead, Johannine source critics have been
forced to appeal to internal criteria, evidence from within the text itself that
oral or written sources have been used, and biblical scholarship has most often
regarded such criteria as too subjective to produce definitive results. In light
of these methodological obstacles, many scholars have concluded that FE's
sources are buried so deeply behind FG that there is no point to look for them.

Despite this general neglect, academic interest in the Johannine Jesus tradition has increased considerably in the last several decades. Recent studies in
this area may be divided into four categories, based on their conclusions about
the kind of materials FE used to create FG. These four models may be referred
to as the Oral Tradition Theory, the Written Source Theory, the Synoptic
Dependence Theory, and the Developmental Theory. Of course, most scholars combine elements from more than one approach when recreating the
background of the Johannine literature for exegetical purposes. Nevertheless,
at least one of these theories has had an impact on all contemporary studies of
FG and 1–2–3 John, including the articles in this book. A brief description of
each will set an appropriate backdrop for the essays to follow.

The Oral Tradition Theory

The Oral Tradition Theory suggests that significant portions of FG are based
on oral traditions that were available to the evangelist. C. H. Dodd (1963), for
example, argues that many sayings of Jesus in FG were drawn from a broad
oral tradition, some of which was also used by Matthew, Mark, and Luke.
Another major proponent of this approach is Barnabas Lindars (1971), who
believes that the dialogues of FG were developed from traditional sayings of
Jesus in the context of FE's oral preaching. A similar view has been taken more
recently by Tom Thatcher (2000), who argues that many of the dialogues and
speeches in the Fourth Gospel are based on a traditional oral form, the "riddle." In the broad sense, those who believe that FE is the apostle John, or some
other direct witness of Jesus, also fit into this category, since they believe that
the materials in the Fourth Gospel represent a disciple's oral preaching and
teaching. D. A. Carson (1991) is a prominent advocate of this position. All

FIGURE O.I THE ORAL TRADITION THEORY

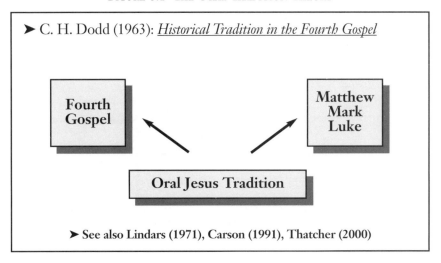

➤ C. H. Dodd (1963): *Historical Tradition in the Fourth Gospel*

Fourth Gospel

Matthew
Mark
Luke

Oral Jesus Tradition

➤ See also Lindars (1971), Carson (1991), Thatcher (2000)

these scholars believe that the present Fourth Gospel includes materials that were circulated orally before being directly incorporated into John's narrative. In general, they are skeptical of the existence of written sources for FG and particularly skeptical of attempts to reconstruct possible sources from the present text.

The Written Source Theory

The Written Source Theory suggests that large portions of the Fourth Gospel were drawn from one or several written sources, none of which exists today. The most significant recent proponents of this position are Rudolf Bultmann, Robert Fortna, and Urban von Wahlde. All three scholars suggest that portions of FG were adapted from a "signs source," a written document consisting of stories about Jesus' miracles. While scholars who take this position are divided on the specific scope and content of this source, most agree that it included the seven miracle stories of John 2–11, which were presented as "signs" of Jesus' messianic identity. Fortna (1988), whose theory is currently the most widely accepted among this group, also suggests that FG's narrative source, which he calls "the Signs Gospel," is based on two earlier documents, a miracle source ("SQ") and a separate passion story ("PQ"), which were joined together before FE's time.

FIGURE 0.2 THE WRITTEN SOURCE THEORY

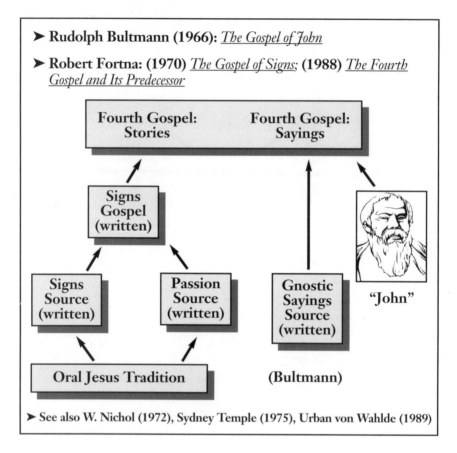

➤ **Rudolph Bultmann (1966):** *The Gospel of John*

➤ **Robert Fortna: (1970)** *The Gospel of Signs;* **(1988)** *The Fourth Gospel and Its Predecessor*

➤ See also W. Nichol (1972), Sydney Temple (1975), Urban von Wahlde (1989)

As Figure 0.2 indicates, there are also varying opinions within this camp about the origins of the Johannine sayings and discourses. Bultmann, for example, believes that the Johannine sayings were drawn from yet another written source, the *Offenbarungsreden*, a collection of "revelatory-discourses" with a bent toward Gnostic theology. Fortna, on the other hand, questions whether there were any pre-Johannine written sources for FG's discourse materials. Still others believe the speeches were entirely composed by FE himself as theological reflections on the signs. Scholars who adhere to the Written Source Theory generally believe that major portions of FG were drawn from written sources and that these sources can be identified within (and possibly reconstructed from) the current Gospel of John.

The Synoptic Dependence Theory

The Synoptic Dependence Theory is a variation of the Written Source Theory, but it has received so much attention in recent years that it deserves special consideration. Proponents of this position argue that FG is indeed based on written sources and that the primary written sources that can be identified are the Synoptic Gospels (Matthew, Mark, and Luke). This was the dominant theory of FG's composition throughout much of the modern period, and it remained popular during the early twentieth century through the influence of scholars such as B. W. Bacon (1910). This theory suffered a major setback, however, after the appearance of P. Gardner-Smith's *St. John and the Synoptic Gospels* in 1938. Scholars such as Bacon had focused on the few agreements between FG and the Synoptics as evidence of dependence, and then attempted to explain differences in terms of FE's unique theological or literary tendencies. Gardner-Smith, however, concluded that the differences between John and the Synoptics so outweigh the similarities that the theory is untenable. The few verbatim agreements could be explained under the premise that FE drew on the same "common store of Christian tradition" as the Synoptic evangelists (Gardner-Smith 1938, 88–91). Despite its brevity, Gardner-Smith's book had a dramatic impact on Johannine scholarship. In a 1992 survey, D. Moody Smith noted that "in the past three decades [1960–1990] there has been no major new commentary . . . in which the fourth evangelist's knowledge of the Synoptics has been presupposed" (1992, 69).

Even at the time Smith made this observation, however, the consensus was beginning to erode. The reemergence of the Synoptic Dependence Theory may be traced to the 26th Colloquium Biblicum Louvaniense in 1975. At this international conference, Franz Neirynck delivered a paper that proposed to identify the sources behind John 20:1–18 with the following caveat: if FG is found to reflect Matthew and Luke's editorial tendencies in recounting the resurrection story, then "we should have to conclude to the dependence [of FG] on the Synoptic Gospels themselves." Following this rule, Neirynck proceeded to argue that Luke 24:12 is "Luke's editorial composition," and that John 20:3–10 has been built up out of that verse. This case study allowed Neirynck to assert a general rule: "the Synoptic Gospels themselves are the sources of the Fourth Evangelist" (Neirynck 1977, 99–103). Because the resurgence of the Synoptic Dependence Theory was fueled by Neirynck and others associated with the University at Leuven (Belgium), those who subscribe to this position are sometimes referred to as "the Leuven School," although other notable scholars not associated with Leuven, such as C. K. Barrett and Thomas Brodie, have also taken this position.

FIGURE 0.3 THE SYNOPTIC DEPENDENCE THEORY

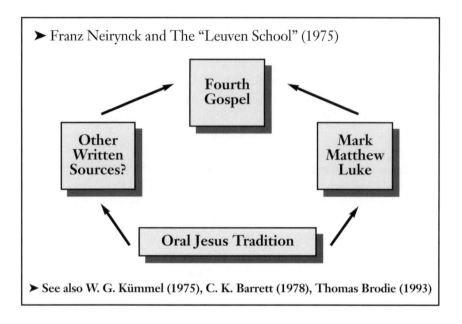

➤ Franz Neirynck and The "Leuven School" (1975)

Fourth Gospel

Other Written Sources?

Mark Matthew Luke

Oral Jesus Tradition

➤ See also W. G. Kümmel (1975), C. K. Barrett (1978), Thomas Brodie (1993)

The Developmental Theory

The Developmental Theory sees the current Fourth Gospel as the final stage in a long editorial process. While attempts to reconstruct this process vary, most depend on the type of reading popularized by J. Louis Martyn's *History and Theology in the Fourth Gospel*, which appeared in 1968. Martyn argued that John 9, the story of the blind man's healing and excommunication, can be read at two levels: as a narrative about Jesus and as a veiled reference to FE's personal experience. The key verse in this analysis is John 9:22: "the Jews had already agreed that anyone who confessed Jesus to be the Messiah would be put out of the synagogue." In Martyn's view, FE is here alluding to his own excommunication, which suggests that "the formal separation between church and synagogue has been accomplished in John's milieu. . . . What had been an inner-synagogue *group of Christian Jews* now became—against its will—a separated *community of Jewish Christians*" (Martyn 1979, 66). This experience led FE to alter his Jesus tradition in light of the changing needs of his community. From this point on, the Johannine tradition became more dualistic, and FE's Christology developed from a general Jewish messianism based on the Hebrew Bible into the higher presentation of Jesus as the divine Son of God that now characterizes FG (Martyn 1979, 102–107). The Johannine tradition, in other words, "developed" through FE's experiences, which led Robert Kysar (1975) to label this theory "the developmental approach."

Two notable proponents of the Developmental Approach, who have explored its implications for Johannine source criticism in detail, are Raymond Brown and John Painter. Brown's *The Community of the Beloved Disciple* (1979) traces the development of the Johannine Community from Palestine to the second century. Brown's hypothesis highlights theological tensions in FG as evidence of a series of revisions: "high christology next to low christology, realized eschatology next to final eschatology, individualism next to stress on community." These apparent inconsistencies reveal FE's "synthetic" thinking and continual editing of the tradition in light of community experience (Brown 1979, 51–54). John Painter also detects community history behind these anomalies and uses this history as a key to FG's compositional development. FG's dialogues, for example, evolved as FE "transformed the traditional [oral] stories into quest stories because he perceived the turmoil of human life as a quest and Jesus as the fulfillment of the quest." At each stage in the community's life the discourses were expanded to reflect FE's new theological concerns (Painter 1993, 212).

Proponents of the Developmental Approach differ in their understanding of the base material at the earliest stage of this evolution. Brown believes that the Johannine tradition began as "a body of [oral] traditional material pertaining to the words and works of Jesus" (Brown 1966, 1.xxxiv–xxxv). Painter largely follows Brown's reconstruction of the community's history and suggests three major stages in the development of FG: a base oral tradition, three written editions published by FE, and a final redaction that produced the present version of FG. Painter stresses that the oral tradition at the first phase of this process cannot be reconstructed from the present text of FG (Painter 1993, 28, 66–79). By contrast, Martyn, who was Robert Fortna's doctoral adviser, argues that a distinct, apparently written signs source underlies all subsequent editions of FG (Martyn 1978, 28–32).

Our Assumptions

While most studies of the Johannine Jesus tradition showcase one of the four theories described above or their variants, this book hopes to reflect the tension among them. For this reason, the editors have solicited a series of essays by authors who represent many differing perspectives. Each author has been selected on the basis of expertise in his or her respective area of specialization, not on the basis of his or her presuppositions. For this reason, a number of the

FIGURE 0.4 THE DEVELOPMENTAL THEORY

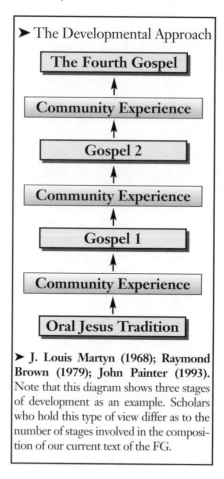

➤ The Developmental Approach

The Fourth Gospel

↑

Community Experience

↑

Gospel 2

↑

Community Experience

↑

Gospel 1

↑

Community Experience

↑

Oral Jesus Tradition

➤ **J. Louis Martyn (1968); Raymond Brown (1979); John Painter (1993).** Note that this diagram shows three stages of development as an example. Scholars who hold this type of view differ as to the number of stages involved in the composition of our current text of the FG.

authors in this volume are not normally associated with Johannine studies. All, however, have agreed to direct their discussion toward the Johannine Jesus tradition and to explore that tradition from the perspective of their own disciplines.

Despite this attempt at objectivity, the selection and arrangement of articles in this volume will indicate that the editors have proceeded under two working assumptions. First, we presuppose that the early Christian storytellers who preserved and used primitive Jesus traditions made no attempt to be unbiased in their presentation. As a consequence, their selection and presentation of traditional materials was heavily shaped by their respective ideologies and social contexts, creating the wide diversity of portraits of Jesus in the extant gospel literature. Second, the editors presuppose that the Gospel of John originated from social and ideological conditions different from those that produced the Synoptics. FE's ideology may have been closer to the ideology of the noncanonical authors than to that of the other canonical evangelists in some ways. The Gospel of John may therefore resemble the other canonical gospels at some points, but at other points may more closely resemble noncanonical gospels. We state this as a general principle, not as an evaluation of FG's relationship to any other specific document.

It is also important, and perhaps more important, to stress what the editors of this volume do *not* presuppose. We have no working assumptions regarding the identity of the author of the Fourth Gospel: whether that person was or was not "John" or another disciple of Jesus; Jewish or non-Jewish; literate or nonliterate; whether one or several persons were involved in the production of the current text. Nor do we presuppose the existence of any specific written source or sources behind the Fourth Gospel, whether the Synoptics or other sources that are now lost. As a corollary, we do not presuppose that any specific portions of FG were composed orally. We also make no presuppositions as to whether the current text of FG is or is not the product of a series of revisions. Finally, we do not presuppose that the Gospel of John is or is not a valuable source of information about the historical Jesus, or whether it is more or less valuable than other sources, canonical or noncanonical. At the same time, the individual contributors to this volume will have presuppositions about each of these issues, and they have been encouraged to proceed from the perspective of their personal assumptions.

A brief explanation of the format of this volume is appropriate. All contributors were asked to avoid "history of research" and detailed interaction with other scholars, and to focus instead on the creative presentation of fresh ideas. In this spirit, they were also asked to avoid footnotes wherever possible. Citations of, or references to, other works are therefore incorporated directly into the text in parentheses. This reference system directs the reader to the master bibliography at the end of the book by indicating the author, date, volume number (where a multivolume work), and page number of the citation in question. For example, the reference "(Painter 1993, 212)" refers the reader to p. 212 of the book written by John Painter in 1993 that is listed in the bibliography. The reference "(Brown 1996, 2. 415)" refers the reader to page 415 of volume 2 of the work by Raymond Brown.

Unless indicated otherwise, all citations of scripture are from the New Revised Standard Version, and all citations of noncanonical works are from *The Complete Gospels* (ed. Robert J. Miller, Sonoma, Calif.: Polebridge, 1994).

Part 1

The Fourth Gospel and Jesus

Although this book is not immediately concerned with the historical Jesus, it is impossible to discuss the composition history of the Fourth Gospel (FG) without addressing the relationship between the author of that book and its main character. The essays in Part 1 discuss this relationship. The articles fall into two broad categories, depending on the direction from which the author has chosen to approach the connection between John and Jesus. One group offers new insights on traditional questions such as the identity of the Fourth Evangelist (FE), the relationship between that person and the Beloved Disciple, the relationship between the Gospel of John and the Synoptic Gospels, the provenance and date of FG, the history of the community that first read FG, and other issues that address the historical context in which FG was written. The second group of essays approach the relationship between John and Jesus more broadly, attempting to define key points in FE's theology that shaped his presentation of Jesus, to discover whether or not he had a "historical interest" in Jesus and what that might have meant to him, and to address biases in the methods modern scholars use to reconstruct the background of the Johannine literature. Of course, both types of concerns are blended in some way by all the authors in this section; the distinction depends on the main emphasis of the article in question.

Regardless of their primary emphases, all the authors in this section have been asked to address the relevant questions not from a purely historical perspective but also in terms of the ways in which the relationship between the Fourth Evangelist and Jesus may have influenced the presentation of Jesus in the current text of FG. As a result, the essays attempt to situate FE not only in time and space but also ideologically. This is done first by examining FE's kerygma, his proclamation about Jesus, and then more broadly by asking questions such as, How many years and how many miles separated FE from Jesus? In what ways did FE's beliefs and experience differ from those who wrote other gospels—Matthew, Mark, Thomas, Peter—and in what ways were they same? In what ways were FE's beliefs closer to the life and message of Jesus, and at what points was he farther away? And, most importantly, how has all of this affected the way in which John tells his story about Jesus?

While the authors of the essays in this section were assigned specific topics and given general guidelines for their studies, they were also allowed complete freedom to develop the issues according to their own beliefs and conclusions. As a result, the reader will notice significant differences between the articles in both the questions that are raised and the methods for answering them. This diversity reflects the wide range of contemporary opinions about key issues regarding the authorship of the Gospel of John.

The Fourth Evangelist's Kerygma

1

The Messiah Who Has
Come into the World

The Message of the Gospel of John

DAVID RENSBERGER

It is a remarkable fact that the Gospel of John can be, and has been, used to support widely varying understandings of who Jesus is and of what Christianity is. Evangelical Christians, for example, often look to John 3:16, "For God so loved the world that he gave his only Son, so that everyone who believes in him may not perish but may have eternal life," as the simplest and clearest statement of what they believe and proclaim. Christians whose faith and practice center on the sacrament of the Eucharist, on the other hand, might be more likely to find central meaning in John 6:53–55: "Very truly, I tell you, unless you eat the flesh of the Son of Man and drink his blood, you have no life in you. Those who eat my flesh and drink my blood have eternal life, and I will raise them up on the last day; for my flesh is true food and my blood is true drink." Christians who understand salvation and eternal life as the restoration of humanity's originally intended participation in God, made possible when the Son of God took on human nature, may look to such passages as John 17:3: "[T]his is eternal life, that they may know you, the only true God, and Jesus Christ whom you have sent." Christians of a "liberal" or liberation orientation are likely to think of John 8:32: "[Y]ou will know the truth, and the truth will make you free"; and John 13:34: "I give you a new commandment, that you love one another. Just as I have loved you, you also should love one another."

In one way or another, John lends support to each of these understandings of Christianity. Indeed, taken as a whole and as it stands, it supports *all* of them simultaneously. I do not believe that this is accidental. The Fourth Gospel

(FG) is not only subject to differing interpretations, it seems to invite them deliberately. Three well-known characteristics of FG may be noted as contributing to this "invitation." First, the Fourth Evangelist (FE) expresses much of what he has to say about Jesus by means of symbols and images, calling him "the bread of life," for instance, or "the light of the world," or "the true vine" (John 6:35, 48; 8:12; 9:5; 15:1, 5). Such imagery is inherently flexible and open to diverse understandings. Second, FE often uses statements that are deliberately ambiguous and are even misunderstood by characters in the story. For example, in John 2:18–22, Jesus says, "Destroy this temple, and in three days I will raise it up." His opponents naturally think of the Temple in Jerusalem, where they are all standing; but the narrator tells us that Jesus was speaking of his own body, and mentions that even his disciples only understood this after he was raised from the dead. Third, FE makes statements that simply conflict with one another. Jesus is said to be "the good shepherd" but also the gate through which the shepherd leads the sheep (John 10:1–18). He is said to be one with God, his Father (John 10:30); yet the Father is greater than he (John 14:28) and is indeed his God (John 20:17). The Logos or Word, made flesh in Jesus, was *with* God in the beginning, and yet at the same time *was* God (John 1:1). After one particularly convoluted and self-contradictory assertion, Jesus asks, "Do you believe this?"—as if acknowledging that it might well be impossible to believe, or even understand. Martha of Bethany makes the right response, however: "Yes, Lord, I believe that *you* are the Messiah, the Son of God, the one coming into the world" (John 11:25–27). What seems to be desired is not an abstract doctrinal affirmation but a response to Jesus himself.

How are we to understand this complexity, not to say contrariness? It is possible to analyze FG with a view to distinguishing various sources, editings, and time frames within it, as numerous of the essays in this volume will make clear. But it is also possible to assume that the Gospel of John made sense to someone, whether author or redactor, precisely as it stands now; and that that "someone" is at least as likely to have been fully aware of, and even intentional about, these difficulties as simply to have blundered into them. FG's paradoxical, ironic, contradictory, ambiguous, and symbolic language is essential not only to its mode of communication but also to what it has to communicate. The Fourth Gospel is intricate, manifold, and even enigmatic because its author perceived the central truth that he wished to convey as intricate, manifold, and enigmatic. No other gospel is so concerned about truth, but the truth that is John's message is anything but a simple verity that could be captured in a single, one-sided dogmatic formulation. FG supports differing understandings of Christianity because it means to show that Christianity, like Christ himself, cannot be nailed down, but will always rise free and ascend to the place from which it came—and that those who believe will ascend with it.

Believe what, though? What is this truth that the Fourth Evangelist wants his readers to apprehend and make their own through its paradoxical text? We may look first, of course, to the well-known purpose statement in John 20:31: the book was written "so that you may believe that Jesus is the Messiah, the Son of God, and so that by believing you may have life in his name" (my translation). That seems simple enough; and it is pretty much this declaration that Martha makes in response to Jesus' challenging question about a much more complex and difficult statement. All of FG's convoluted narratives, discourses, and images, then, are apparently to be understood in light of this formulation: Jesus is the Messiah and the Son of God. These titles themselves, however, are far from transparent or self-evident, as may be seen even from the debates about their significance within FG (John 5:17–18; 7:25–31, 40–44; 10:30–39; 12:32–34; 19:6–7). It would be at least equally correct, in fact, to say that this formulation is to be understood in light of what is said by and about Jesus throughout the book. What FE means by calling Jesus "Messiah" and "Son of God" must be grasped by considering the things that he presents Jesus doing and saying, and by the Gospel's own statements about him. "Messiah" and "Son of God" sum up what John claims Jesus to be, but the summary may not substitute for the full claim. Moreover, the titles, on the one hand, and the narratives, discourses, and images, on the other, must always be allowed to interpret one another.

The Gospel of John associates both "Messiah" and "Son of God" with the concept of Jesus' "coming" or "being sent by God" into the world. The point is that Jesus does not simply originate within human society or even the created universe ("the world" can mean both of these in the Johannine literature), but enters it from outside, from the divine realm ("heaven" or "above"). This essay will explore the meaning of John's claims about Jesus as Messiah and Son of God, who has been sent by God and has come into the world.

When Martha of Bethany confesses her belief in Jesus, she says that he is "the Messiah, the Son of God, the one coming into the world" (John 11:27). This expression could, if carefully interpreted, be understood within the framework of common Jewish eschatological expectations. The messiah, the ultimate anointed king of Israel, might be thought of as God's Son in the same sense that the king of Judah and even Israel as a whole can be given this title in the Hebrew Bible (Ps. 2:7; Hos. 11:1): as one designated and favored by God for a special role in the world. He would "come into the world" in the sense of appearing in it, or perhaps as coming from heaven where the eschatological events and actors have been prepared beforehand. Taken in this sense, the phrase does not imply divinity or ontological equality with God.

FE does present Jesus as fulfilling the eschatological role of messiah, but expands this concept in the direction of Jesus' divinity. As messiah, Jesus is indeed Israel's true king, acclaimed as such by his earliest followers and by the crowds on Palm Sunday, and crucified as such by Pontius Pilate (John 1:49 [accompanied by "Son of God"]; 12:13; 18:33–39; 19:3, 12–16, 19–22). In this last connection, note Jesus' assertion that his kingship is "not of this world," that is, has a different origin and nature from ordinary human kingship, a fact demonstrated by his followers' refusal to fight. It is part and parcel of this that Pilate, who displays his contempt for both Israel and its king by crucifying Jesus, thereby provides him with his ironic enthronement, his "glorification" as messiah (see John 12:23–26; 17:1). The Johannine Jesus also takes on the role of prophet (4:19, 44; 7:52; 9:17), and indeed of *the* prophet, the eschatological prophet foretold by Moses (7:40; based on Deut. 18:15–19). Though the text at one point makes Jesus' signs (miracles) a criterion for his messiahship (7:31), signs are also naturally associated with prophets, and John connects the two eschatological roles in 6:14–15: following the feeding of the five thousand, "[w]hen the people saw the sign that he had done, they began to say, 'This is indeed the prophet who is to come into the world.' When Jesus realized that they were about to come and take him by force to make him king, he withdrew again to the mountain by himself." It is in his capacity as prophet that Jesus tells Pilate that, while the title "king" may be used by Romans and Jews, Jesus' own claim is that he "came into the world to testify to the truth" (18:37). As messianic king and prophet, then, Jesus rules without violence, suffers a shameful death that is his glorification, performs signs, and above all testifies to the truth, to the divine reality from which he came into the world.

It is in the portrayal of Jesus as having "come into the world" that FE bends the concept of the messiah in the direction of divinity. If anyone might expect the messiah to be "coming" (4:25; 7:27, 31) or to "come into the world" (11:27), it nevertheless sounds a bit different for Jesus to speak of *himself* as having "come into the world" to testify to the truth (18:37). Then when he declares, in a final public speech summarizing the significance of his words and deeds, "I have come *as light* into the world, so that everyone who believes in me should not remain in the darkness" (John 12:46; italics added), we seem to have entered another realm of thought entirely. No merely human prophet or king, even a messianic one, could claim to come into the world as light. Elsewhere, too, Jesus claims to be "the light of the world" (8:12; 9:5). In another passage, one whose markings are so unclear that scholars debate whether the speaker is Jesus addressing Nicodemus or the narrator addressing the reader, we again read of the light coming into the world—and being rejected, a rejection that is the world's condemnatory judgment (3:19). Similarly, Jesus declares in John 9:39 that he came into the world to bring about a judgment, "so that those who do not see may see, and those who do see may become blind." In fact, at the very beginning of FG, in a passage that provides the key for understanding all that will follow, we read that the light that enlightens every human being, the Logos through whom the world was made, came into the world and went unrecognized and unwelcomed, although those who did welcome it became children of God (1:9–13).

In these texts, the messianic language has become mythological; it tells of events that fall outside the usual reach of human historical experience, events that are foundational for human relationship with the divine. Jesus came into the world, not simply in the sense of being born into it like everyone else, but from elsewhere, from outside the world, "from above." This origin seems to set him apart from other people, and those who belong to the world simply fail to recognize that Jesus does not (John 7:28–29; 8:23–24). That Jesus "comes from above" is not just a statement about his origin, however. Over and over again, FE emphasizes that Jesus has been *sent* from God (e.g., 3:17, 34; 4:34; 5:36–38; 6:38–39; 7:16–18; 12:44–50; 15:21–24). He has a specific mission to perform, a set of tasks to carry out, and when this mission is completed, he returns to God who sent him (7:33–34; 13:1–3; 16:28; cf. 6:62; 19:28–30). Indeed, his means of returning to God, his death on the cross and his resurrection/ascension, are an essential part of his mission.

It is in this connection that FE takes up the early Christian claim that Jesus' crucifixion was the result of a definite divine plan. Indeed, FE goes further than any other New Testament author in saying that God commanded Jesus to lay down his life, and that Jesus' death at the hands of Pilate and the Jewish authorities was a willing act of obedience on his part. Jesus lays down his life for his friends, like a good shepherd laying down his life for his sheep (see John 10:11–18; 15:13; 18:4–8). John the Baptist, in a contrasting image, calls him "the Lamb of God who takes away the sin of the world" (1:29). Yet the Fourth Evangelist does not develop a theory of atonement, or of any other specific relation between Jesus' death and the forgiveness of sins. Even the expression "lamb of God" does not clearly lead in this direction, since lambs are not used as sin offerings in the Hebrew Bible. Jesus' death is for the benefit of those who believe in him, but FE leaves the details of this benefit vague, perhaps intentionally so (see 14:2–3, 12; 16:5–7). God sent Jesus into the world with a mission that included laying down his life for the sake of human beings; but like "light" and the other symbols in FG, this image of self-sacrifice is allowed to evoke a broad range of responses in the readers.

As messiah, God's eschatological redeemer sent to the people of Israel, Jesus' mission involves bringing about many of the expected eschatological blessings. These blessings include the Last Judgment, the resurrection of the righteous dead to life eternal, and the outpouring of God's Spirit (cf. Ezek. 36:26–27; 37:11–14; 39:29). So it is that FG (alone among the canonical gospels) presents Jesus not only promising the coming of the Spirit to his disciples, but actually giving them the Spirit on Easter day (7:37–39; 14:15–17, 25–26; 15:26; 16:7–15; 20:22). So also the Johannine Jesus asserts that those who believe in him have already passed from death to life, and so are not subject to the Last Judgment. God has given over judgment to the Son, and Jesus carries out this judgment by his presence, his words, and his works in the world, which cause the world to undergo its judgment by the way it responds to him. Thus both judgment and the power of raising the dead to life belong to Jesus (John 3:17–21; 5:19–30; 8:15–16, 26; 9:39; 12:31, 44–50). Whether one considers the passages that speak of a resurrection on the last day (6:39–40, 44, 54; 12:48) as an earlier layer of futuristic eschatology overwritten by FE's strongly realized eschatology, or as a later redactional reversion to the standard futuristic eschatology of the church, or as a promise to carry out an act that has in essence already been accomplished, it is clear that the eschatological weight in FG falls on the coming of Jesus himself. The realization of eschatological blessings occurs in him and in the believers' response to him: "I am the resurrection and the life. Those who believe in me, even though they die, will live, and everyone who lives and believes in me will never die" (John 11:25–26). Not only does Jesus himself rise from the dead, but he offers that resurrection life to all who believe in him, not only as a hope for the last day, but as a present experience. For believers, eternal life starts now. The Messiah has come into the world, and with him have come the Spirit, the resurrection, and a gift of life that means the judgment has already occurred.

This gift of life that Jesus brings requires further exploration. First, though, there is one other eschatological expectation that must be mentioned. With the Messiah should come the Kingdom of God (a term that occurs in John only in 3:3, 5), an era of restored relationships between human beings and God, and among humans themselves. Righteousness should prevail, and injustice and oppression should have no more place. FG has a version of this eschatological blessing as well, in the new commandment that Jesus gives his disciples: love one another (John 13:34–35; 15:9–17).[1] Though this is not a commandment to love their enemies, as found elsewhere in the canonical gospels (Matt. 5:44; Luke 6:27, 35), it still poses a radical challenge, for two reasons at least. First, Jesus calls this a *new* commandment, not because it is unheard of (it certainly resembles Lev. 19:18), but because it is the Messiah's eschatological commandment, the basic structuring principle for human relationships in the new, messianic era. Not competition, whether for honor, goods, or power, but love is to be the basic characteristic of the new social group created by the coming of the Messiah and the response of believing in him. If at first glance this commandment seems too trite, too sentimental, to make any radical difference in human life, we should simply consider the nature and experience of those few communities and individuals in Christian history who have actually attempted to carry it out. Second, the disciples are to love one another *as Jesus has loved them*. It is not just a matter of warm feelings, but of actions, of "giving up one's life for one's friend"—a commonplace image that could not remain an abstraction or an improbable worst-case scenario for a group that claimed the Messiah had actually been crucified. The commandment of mutual love is not a piece of romantic yearning or an outcome of social and cultural evolution. It is the radical restructuring of interpersonal and social relationships within the community of those who believe the Messiah has come, the unavoidable complement of their equally radical claim that death itself has been overcome by eternal life.

The expression "eternal life," used so often in FG, sums up what Jesus the Messiah and Son of God came into the world to give to human beings. It is not surprising that two of the best-known verses in John are 3:16, which says that God sent the Son into the world so that everyone who believes in him might have eternal life, and 10:10, where Jesus says, "I came that they may have life, and have it abundantly." What does this gift of life signify? "Eternal life" does not simply mean "unending life, everlasting life." Certainly it does mean that; but "eternal life" basically means "the life of eternity," or better, "the life of the world to come." It means a life that is *characterized* by eternity, by the divine world, the world of God that transcends the world of this life. "Eternal life," then, refers not only to quantity but to quality. That is why FE can declare that this kind of life begins now, at the moment of belief. It is not a life that begins after death and extends indefinitely, but a life that already shares in the life of God now.

This life is in Jesus' power to give, and the gift is received by believing in him. But once again, this is not simply a matter of signing on to a doctrinal formulation. In John 17:3, we read, "This is eternal life, that they know you, the only true God, and the one whom you have sent, Jesus Christ" (my translation). If eternal life is *knowing* God and Jesus, then it is a relationship with the divine, a relationship of intimacy and love that FE calls "abiding" (or simply "being") in Jesus, and, through Jesus, in God (14:20; 15:1–10; 17:20–23). Belief in Jesus, the belief that God did indeed send him into the world, means abiding in him, a continuous engagement with him, an ongoing knowing and being known, loving and being loved, that brings, and indeed is, eternal life. It is in this relationship that the believer knows God, and Jesus can bring this relationship about because he makes God known. His mission, the reason God sent him into the world, was to bring life. It was not simply to be crucified, though that is part of the means by which he brings eternal life (6:51). Most fundamentally, Jesus brings life into the world by bringing the knowledge of God.

He does this by speaking God's words and doing God's deeds. Jesus defines his mission in the world in the following terms: "I have come down from heaven, not to do my own will, but the will of him who sent me" (John 6:38; cf. 5:30; 17:4). To do this is his very food (4:34). The deeds that he does—by this FE seems to mean particularly Jesus' miracles, his "signs"—are proof that God sent him, precisely because they are God's deeds. Jesus does nothing on his own, but only what he has seen God doing and what God has told him to do (4:34; 5:19–20, 36; 9:3–4; 10:24–25, 37–38). The same is true of his teaching, which consists, not of his own words, but of the words that he has heard from God and which God has commanded him to speak (7:14–18; 8:26–29; 12:49–50; 14:24). For this reason, seeing Jesus is seeing God, believing Jesus is believing God, and rejecting Jesus is rejecting God (12:44–50; 14:6–11; 15:22–24; cf. 13:20). Jesus makes God known by doing God's deeds and speaking God's words. This implies that believers gain a knowledge of what God is like by observing Jesus. Jesus performs only seven miracles in FG, but they are distinctive in being *life-giving* acts. There are none of the exorcisms that are so common in the Synoptics. Instead, Jesus provides food and drink (2:1–11; 6:1–13); he heals people who are paralyzed, blind, and dying (4:46–54; 5:1–9; 9:1–7); and at the climax of his ministry, he brings Lazarus back from the grave itself (11:38–44).[2] These works of life-giving love and power demonstrate that Jesus is a window to God, and they give a glimpse through that window to the character of God. Likewise Jesus' commandment to love one another makes known not only God's will but also God's nature because the disciples' love is to be an imitation of Jesus' love, which in its turn is modeled on the love of God (15:9–12; cf. 1 John 4:7–18). By doing God's deeds and speaking God's words of love and life, Jesus reveals God, making it possible not only to know about God but to know God, and so to have eternal life.

There is one further, deeper aspect to Jesus' giving of life. His miracles, his crucifixion, and his resurrection give life, not only because *God* sent him into the world to do them, but because God sent *him* into the world to do them. We return here to the characterization of Jesus as the Son of God. Since a son does what his father does, when his father allows and commands him to do it, the Son of God has the power to give life to the world just as God does (John 5:19–21; 17:1–2). But there is more than filial imitation involved. The Son enters the world like bread from heaven, bringing the divine power that nourishes and sustains and keeps the world alive (6:33). Jesus' power to give life is not simply that of a human miracle worker specially gifted by God, but that of the divine Life Giver, the force that constantly imbues the universe with life, who has now entered the world in the flesh of Jesus of Nazareth.

This brings us to the heart of the paradoxical claim made by the Fourth Evangelist: Jesus, the Messiah, the Son of God who came into the world, was a fully human being who ate, drank, walked, wept, bled, and died; yet this human being, this flesh, was the Logos, the divine Son of God, who existed with God, and was God, before the creation, the One through whom the creation received its being and its life (John 1:1–4). "The Logos became flesh": whether or not the specific formulation of John 1:14 has an antidocetic intention, it (like 20:31, but with greater intensity and deeper paradox) succinctly expresses what the rest of FG puts into narrative, discourse, and imagery. As with 20:31, the succinct formulation can point to, but cannot substitute for, the stories and speeches, and the stories and speeches find their interpretive key in this formulation. Jesus can make God known because in him we encounter the unique being who "is in the bosom of the Father" (1:18, my translation). The Logos, the word and wisdom of God that underlies and pervades the structure, life, and existence of the universe, understood as a being with a distinct yet not independent existence, became the flesh known as Jesus of Nazareth. In this way, the divine wisdom that is always present everywhere in the created world (Wis. Sol. 7:22–8:1) entered it afresh. Jesus brought the presence of God into the world in a new and unprecedented way. In him, the Logos encountered the world that it had made, yet met with rejection, precisely because this unanticipated irruption could not be accommodated by the world's set ways and established powers. The rejection of the incarnate Logos meant the death of Jesus, and, turning the paradox over once again, through his very death the world was offered eternal life.

This is not a concept that can be grasped or expressed by dogmatic reasoning alone; it requires the aid of poetry and paradox, redundancy and self-contradiction. John is what it is because someone conceived of this inconceivable paradox, believed that it was the truth, and created this paradoxical text as the most appropriate form to express it. The Messiah, the Son of God, has come into the world, and the story of his coming is as simple and as complex as the event itself.

Notes

1. The NRSV of John 15:17, "I am giving you these commands so that you may love one another," somewhat oddly renders a common Johannine idiom in a way not used elsewhere in that translation. The more usual "I am giving you this command: that you love one another" is surely to be preferred.
2. Only the walking on the water (John 6:16–21) falls outside this pattern. As in Mark 6:30–52, and very likely in the traditions prior to both Mark and FG, this story is attached to the feeding of the five thousand. In John, Jesus' reassuring "It is I" becomes a moment of divine self-revelation, as in 4:26; 8:58; 18:5–6, and elsewhere. This series of seven miracles does not include the miraculous catch of fish in 21:4–6 (a chapter that was probably appended in a revised edition of John); but this miracle also represents, among other things, Jesus' provision of life-sustaining food.

2

The Gospel of John

Reading the Incarnate Words

GAIL R. O'DAY

The Gospel of John has intrigued readers from the moment it was written. Centuries of readers have been drawn to its language and have been simultaneously comforted and confused, encouraged and enraged by what they find there. The first known commentary on a New Testament book was an exposition of John by Heracleon (160–180 C.E.), an expert teacher of Gnosticism. For Heracleon, the Fourth Gospel (FG) provided the biblical warrants for Valentinian Gnosticism's distinctive cosmogony and anthropology, and the Johannine picture of Jesus supported his understanding of the role of the Gnostic Savior. Ironically, we now know of Heracleon's commentary only by fragments preserved in the works of those who opposed him. Irenaeus (180 C.E.) uses FG against the Gnostics and finds within its pages the warrants for the "Rule of Faith." Origen (ca. 200–250 C.E.), in his commentary on John, devotes page after page to Heracleon, expressing overt disagreement but also a grudging respect for Heracleon's biblical erudition. All of these writers, and many more, argued for their very divergent Christian perspectives from the same pages of the Fourth Gospel.

The Fourth Gospel was appealed to by Montanists and by advocates of Nicene orthodoxy, by allegorists and by such masters of hortatory encouragement as John Chrysostom. Why did FG play a prominent role in the interpretive strategies of such a wide range of early Christian interpreters? Part of the answer to John's prominence lies in the early church's assessment of its apostolic authorship, the popular view that the book was written by one of the twelve disciples, John son of Zebedee. The assumption of an apostolic pedigree moved FG into prominence in early christological and ecclesiological debates and made it a powerful resource for orthodox interpreters in their theological battles with Gnosticism. But the attribution of apostolic authorship to FG is a largely formalist answer to the question "Why John?" Apostolic authorship also was attributed to Matthew, Mark, and Luke, yet these books were not read in as varied ways across the wide theological spectrum of early Christianity. "Why John" specifically, and not those other "orthodox" gospels?

A more promising answer to the "Why John?" question lies in the theological and literary character of the Fourth Gospel itself. The vast array of early Christian thinkers and writers who were attracted to FG as an essential conversation partner may have recognized in this Gospel and its author a kind of interpretive predecessor and model. The Fourth Evangelist (FE) was also an early Christian thinker and writer, who moved seamlessly from telling the story of Jesus to expounding its theological and spiritual meanings. In this second move, he came close to his later commentators' own interpretive enterprises.

The early church's awareness of FE's combination of story and theology is made explicit in a famous quotation from Clement of Alexandria (190s C.E.): "Last of all John, perceiving that the external facts had been made plain in the gospel, being urged by his friends and inspired by the Spirit, composed a spiritual gospel" (in Eusebius's *Ecclesiastical History* 6.24.7). Clement's statement is most often used in modern scholarly debates with concerns far different from his own: to dismiss the historical value of the Johannine evidence by referring to it as the "spiritual gospel" or to bolster arguments for FG's dependence on synoptic traditions. In other words, Clement's remarks tend to be read more for what they say negatively about FG than as a positive statement about the nature of this particular gospel's witness. The positive side of Clement's remarks, however, has the longer-term significance, because in making this observation Clement perfectly captures the narrative and theological dynamics of FG. Clement recognized that the Gospel of John poses a decisive question about the interrelationship of history, theology, and interpretation. He does not say that the external facts are of no matter to FE, but instead identifies a crucial characteristic of FG: that the external facts *as facts alone* do not make this Gospel move. Rather, FE writes a gospel story that tells the "internal facts" as well.

Story (or *historia*, to use a term common in the first centuries of Christian exegesis) and theological interpretation are inseparably intertwined in the Fourth Gospel. The stylistic characteristics that most markedly distinguish FG from the narrative style of the Synoptics embody this intertwining. The "I am" sayings that are a distinctive trait of Jesus' speech in John; FG's rich metaphors and images; the poetic language of the Prologue (John 1:1–18); the theological reflections of the Farewell Discourse (John 13–17); Jesus' repeated statements about his unity with the One who sent him into the world, the One who loves him; the repeated identification of God as Jesus' Father—all these tell more than the "external facts." All ask readers, in the very moment of reading the story, to ponder who Jesus is and who God is. These various narrative techniques contribute to FG's theological elasticity, because they invite the reader to read for more than just the events. They invite the interpreter to join the Fourth Evangelist in identifying what this story means for those who read it.

The Fourth Gospel's various literary techniques have a common theological goal: to open up the world of the gospel story to the world of the reader's own experience. Because the questions Jesus asks his conversation partners also become questions for the reader, FG's dialogues and conversations draw the reader into the stories as a participant. FE makes frequent use of irony and symbolism, literary devices that ask the reader to discover the deeper meaning of an expression. At times, the narrator comments directly on a story to ensure that the reader is grasping its significance (John 7:39; 8:27; 11:51–52; 12:33; 18:32; 19:35). The confessional language of the Prologue, which affirms, "We have beheld his glory" (1:14), blurs the line between author and audience by including the reader in the first-person plural pronoun ("we"). The Gospel of John opens up the Jesus story to the reading community's own experience so that readers can discover the presence of God in Jesus for themselves. It is small wonder, then, that Heracleon could see in the Samaritan woman of John 4 a paradigm of Gnostic anthropology and cosmogony, while Origen saw in her a paradigm of the Christian's spiritual growth, and Chrysostom saw in her the tireless disciple whom he calls his congregation to imitate.

The Prologue

The opening verses of FG are an excellent example of the distinctive narrative and theological world this Gospel creates. Much more straightforward beginnings are to be found in the other canonical gospels: the terse announcement in Mark 1:1 ("The beginning of the gospel of Jesus Christ [son of God]"); the genealogical orientation of Matthew 1:1 ("The book of the genealogy of Jesus Christ, son of David, son of Abraham"); the rhetorically polished and conventionally proper introduction of Luke 1:1–4 ("Since many have undertaken to set down an orderly account of the events that have been fulfilled among us . . . I, too, have decided, after investigating everything from the first, to write an orderly account"). But for the Fourth Evangelist, something other than straightforward narrative is required, because to relate the events of the Jesus story is not enough. FE places the Jesus story into the context in which that story makes sense for him, the larger story of God, and signals that context with the words "In the beginning." From that context, FE is able to introduce the relationship between God and the Word that is crucial to everything else that follows:

> In the beginning was the Word, and the Word was with God and the Word was God. (1:1)

John 1:1 points to what the reader needs to know to understand the story that is about to be told. It is a "prologue" in the true sense, in that it sounds the introductory note that anticipates what is to follow, but it is only half the introduction. The rest follows:

> [T]he Word became flesh and lived among us. (1:14)

When these two verses (John 1:1 and 1:14) are read together, the distinctive character of FG's theological world begins to take shape. John 1:1 announces and affirms the presence of the Word with God "in the beginning," outside the reckoning of time and place. John 1:14 then announces and affirms the reshaped presence of the Word completely within the reckoning of time and place. The movement of the Word from God's sphere (1:1) into the human sphere (1:14) by means of the incarnation, the making-flesh of the Word, positions Jesus to provide humanity with access to God in ways never before possible through the relationship between God and the Word. Yet instead of engaging in speculation about the nature of this relationship, as writers would do in the christological controversies of later centuries, FE allows elasticity to this relationship through the language of incarnation. And before the Prologue is completed, the terms of the metaphor for this relationship will shift, from incarnate "Word" and "God" to "only-begotten (Son)" and "Father" (1:18).

Through this language, FE cuts through the externals of the story to show readers what is really being acted out before their eyes. A helpful metaphor for thinking about the literary and theological dynamics of the Prologue can be borrowed from the work of geologists. In the Prologue, FE provides a geological cross section of the terrain of the Gospel. John 1:1–18 displays the surface level of the story, provided by the references to John the Baptist (1:6–8, 15), but also displays the composition of the other layers of the terrain to show the substructure that is at work within and under what is visible on the surface. In this way, the Prologue provides readers with all that they need to know about the heart (or "core," to stay with the geological metaphor) of FE's theological affirmations.

Thus, the Johannine Jesus does not reveal God simply by speaking God's words and doing God's works, although that is part of it (John 5:19–20, 30; 10:25, 37–38; 12:48–49). It is rather that Jesus *is* God's Word. Jesus' words and works, his life and death, form an indissoluble whole that provides full and fresh access to God. FE weaves together narrative and theology in an attempt to open up the wonder and mystery of the incarnation as fully as possible, so that his readers can know themselves to be the recipients of Jesus' gifts. As a result, the Prologue does not fit conventional storytelling techniques, which is one reason that its presence at the beginning of FG has generated extensive scholarly conversation about its origins and its relationship to what follows. Yet its presence at the beginning of the story perfectly fits FE's purposes. The Prologue uses language—Word, light, dark, flesh, glory—that can only be comprehended if the reader moves beyond the level of the "external facts" to the theological realities that the "external facts" incarnate.

The interpretive puzzle and delight of the Gospel of John comes from the fact that the movement between and among its many levels of meaning is not usually accompanied by explicit markers that say, "Now we move from the level of narrative to the level of theological meaning." This is because the theological reality of the incarnation—that God is made known in the life, ministry, and death of the incarnate Word, the Son—is the shaping hermeneutical principle of the creation of this Gospel. FE simultaneously tells a story and tells other than a story. The narrative style of FG re-incarnates the theological reality behind the Gospel: that the Word became flesh and dwelt among us. Story and interpretation intertwine in FG because human and divine, flesh and glory, intertwine in Jesus (see O'Day 1986).

The incarnation, then, provides a hermeneutical principle that can guide interpreters as they move through the various levels of meaning generated by FG. From the perspective of the incarnation, we can look at the theological touchstones of this Gospel—Christology, ecclesiology, pneumatology, and eschatology—to see FE's working vocabulary for parsing the incarnation in a gospel narrative.

John's Theological Touchstones[1]

The pivotal role of the incarnation in FG helps to clarify the relationship between theology and Christology. Ultimately, this Gospel is concerned with God: the good news is the revelation of God in Jesus. To focus exclusively on Jesus is to miss FE's central claim. John celebrates what Jesus reveals about God, not what Jesus reveals about himself. Christology redefines theology—Jesus decisively changes how one talks about and knows God—but Christology does not replace theology.

The interrelationship of theology and Christology in FG is clearly seen in the names FE uses for God. God is referred to as "the one who sent me [Jesus]"

(John 4:34; 5:38; 8:29) and as "the Father" (5:17; 6:45; 14:16). Both of these titles highlight God's relationship with Jesus. "The one who sent Jesus" identifies God as the One from whom Jesus' mission to the world originates (3:17). This identification of God points to the union of God's and Jesus' work in the world. By speaking of God as Father and Jesus as Son, FE calls attention to the love and familial intimacy between them. Indeed, this familial intimacy is one of the central theological metaphors of the Fourth Gospel. At 1:12–13, for example, FE notes that all who receive Jesus and believe in him become "children of God."

All of FG's other theological concerns also derive from its theology of the incarnation. For example, its ecclesiology, its understanding of the life of the faith community, is expressed succinctly in Jesus' "new commandment": "Just as I have loved you, you also should love one another. By this everyone will know that you are my disciples, if you have love for one another" (John 13:34–35). The full expression of Jesus' love is the gift of his life (see 10:11, 14, 17–18; 15:12–15), the crowning moment of the incarnation (19:30). To love one another as Jesus loves is to live out the love of the incarnation, to show in one's own life the fullness of love that unites God and Jesus. FE's image of the faith community derives from his understanding of the relationship between God and Jesus.

FE's pneumatology, his understanding of the Spirit, also derives from his understanding of the relationship between God and Jesus. By definition, Jesus' crucifixion marks the end of the incarnation, because death is the end of human, enfleshed life. If the revelation of God is lodged decisively in the incarnation, what happens after Jesus dies? Is the revelation of God so temporally bound that it is only available to those who knew the historical Jesus? FE resolves this theological dilemma through the Paraclete. "Paraclete" is the transliteration of the Greek noun *paraklētos*, the noun FE uses to speak of the Spirit. This noun can have many meanings—"the one who exhorts," "the one who comforts," and "the one who helps"—all of which FE seems to employ in his discussion of the identity and function of the Spirit in the life of the faith community. The Spirit/Paraclete will remain in the community after Jesus dies and returns to God ("And I will ask the Father, and he will give you another Paraclete, to be with you forever," John 14:16; see also 14:26). The Spirit/Paraclete will continue the revelation of God begun in the incarnation: "He will glorify me because he will take what is mine and declare it to you" (16:14; see also 14:26; 16:13, 15). The Spirit thus makes it possible for succeeding generations of believers to come to know the God revealed in Jesus.

FE's eschatology, too, is shaped by his understanding of the incarnation. Because God is fully revealed in Jesus, Jesus' advent into the world brings the world to a moment of crisis and decision (John 3:16–21). One does not have to wait for a future revealing of the fullness of God's glory and God's will for the world or for eternal life to be bestowed. Both are available now in Jesus: "Very truly, I tell you, anyone who hears my word and believes him who sent me has eternal life, and does not come under judgment, but has passed from death to life" (5:24); "And this is eternal life, that they may know you, the only true God, and Jesus Christ whom you have sent. I glorified you on earth by finishing the work that you gave me to do" (17:3–4). The eschatological judgment is whether one can recognize the glory of God in the flesh of Jesus. Jesus' death, resurrection, and ascension (together his "hour") also enact this eschatological judgment. Jesus' death, the full expression of his love, reveals the character of God (14:31; 17:24); Jesus' victory over death reveals the impotence of the ruler of the world (e.g., 12:31; 14:30; 16:11); Jesus' ascension belongs to the eschatological judgment because when he is reunited with God "with the glory that I had in your presence before the world existed" (17:5), his work of revealing God is completed (16:10).

The Incarnation as Hermeneutical Principle

All of FG's theological vocabulary, then, can only be understood in relationship to the incarnation. When cut off from the incarnation, FE's language world is open to wide-ranging interpretations, as the Gnostic commentaries demonstrate. For example, in almost every instance in which Heracleon looked for a symbolic meaning in FG, he correctly took his cue from the text. Jesus' conversation with the woman at the well (John 4) clearly has symbolic meaning. The whole chapter is constructed around misunderstanding, irony, and metaphor. Even on the surface level of the story, Jesus means one thing by "living water" while the woman takes "living water" to mean something quite different (4:10–15). When Jesus asks the woman to go call her husband (4:16–18), at the very least this exchange is ambiguous, and the gap in meaning creates an opening for interpretation. Yet when Heracleon took these openings and saw in them the perfect demonstration of the Gnostic Demiurge and the Pleroma, he was reading only for the glory of Christ and not for the inseparable intertwining of glory and flesh. Heracleon's readings stand only if one ignores the grip of the incarnation on John's literary and theological perspectives.

When it is abstracted from the flesh-bound, and hence crucifixion-bound, reality of the incarnation, FG's multilayered language is open to a myriad of interpretations. But when FG's multilayered language is grounded in the inescapable reality of the incarnation, this hermeneutical principle places controls on the infinite regress of this Gospel's theological elasticity.

The importance of recognizing the incarnation as the shaping literary and theological principle behind FG is not simply a means of discounting ancient Gnostic interpretations of John. Rather, it also suggests a means by which contemporary interpretations of the Fourth Gospel can be assessed. Any reading of Johannine spirituality, for example, that focuses exclusively on an individualistic interpretation of FG or on a body/spirit divide needs to be assessed by the reality of the incarnation and found wanting. Readings of FG that focus on the image of the beloved community without attending to the relations between the Johannine Community and Judaism also depart from the hermeneutical principle of the incarnation, because they read for the glory of the community without attending to its particular incarnations. Interpretations of FG that read its Christology in isolation from its theology or its ecclesiology also risk separating the glory from the flesh.

To say that the incarnation is the final arbiter of meaning in FG is not to come down on the side of a fixed or absolute meaning, but is rather to name the source of this Gospel's remarkable interpretive elasticity. As noted above, even Heracleon, who moved far afield in his readings from the perspective of the incarnation, correctly noted the openings for the interpreter's imagination that are inherent in the literary style of FG. The incarnation is itself fluid and elastic, articulated by FE in the language of Word-become-flesh, in the language of Son of the Father, in the metaphors of the bread from heaven or the good shepherd. In the litany of christological titles in John 1:35–51 and the broad metaphorical range of the "I am" sayings, one sees an openness of literary and theological expression embodied within the narrative itself. The incarnation is a nonnegotiable theological, even ontological, reality for FE that is nonetheless expressed in a variety of negotiable literary forms. The intertwining of flesh and glory, divine and human in the incarnation is what drives the combination of "external facts" and spiritual gospel noted by Clement. The Gospel of John both embodies and recreates the incarnation in the words of the story it tells.

Note

1. The following five paragraphs appear in a slightly different form in Gail R. O'Day, *The Gospel of John: Introduction, Commentary, and Reflections* (NIB; Nashville: Abingdon Press, 1995). They are used here by permission.

The Fourth Gospel and Jesus

3

Situating John's
Gospel in History

GARY M. BURGE

In the last ten years, many of the assumed conclusions of Johannine studies
have experienced remarkable upheaval. Questions concerning such "assured
results" as the Fourth Gospel's (FG) Signs Source or John's relation to the synoptic tradition now find themselves occupying center stage. Even the date of
FG has been revisited, pressing the origins of the Johannine tradition to the
period before the First Jewish War (pre–66 C.E.). It appears that John A. T.
Robinson's neglected book *The Priority of John* (1985) has come into vogue
when scholars like Berger (1997) can argue that FG was the first gospel written. Voices that once viewed FG as secondary, late, and steeped in Hellenistic
thought do not dominate discussions the way they once did. As one consequence of this trend, arguments that dissect FG to identify layers of redactional activity today seem less compelling.

As part of this new day in Johannine studies, in a 1987 lecture at Princeton
Seminary, Martin Hengel professed his belief that the Fourth Evangelist (FE)
was a resident of Jerusalem and an eyewitness of Jesus' death who reflected on
Jesus' story and perfected his account early. This disciple founded a "school" or
community somewhere in Asia Minor that flourished from 60 to 110 C.E., and
his witness grew to become the critical link between this group of believers and
the historical Jesus (Hengel 1989). To my mind, Hengel has situated the Fourth
Gospel where it belongs. The earliest traditions in FG stem from the era before
the catastrophic war with Rome, and FE assumes that his readers understand
that they are receiving an eyewitness record that bears considerable personal

authority. There is no doubt that the Beloved Disciple (BD) figures seriously in this equation. BD is both a historical figure and an ideal disciple, someone who sees Jesus, understands the significance of what he sees, and bears this testimony to his community. FE also assumes that his readers understand the complexities of Jewish traditions and their setting in Jerusalem, a Jerusalem that has not yet been disturbed by upheaval and conquest. Each narrative in FG employs concepts and imagery that are best interpreted through the lens of Judaism's faith. This commitment suggests a community that was well versed in the Hebrew Bible and that appreciated the nuances of Jewish religious life.

Here, then, are two assertions worth defending: 1) FG is historically early and thus can make a genuine claim to having access to a historical record about Jesus, and 2) FG fits within the conceptual framework of the Hellenized Jewish circles of first-century Palestine. While these two assertions may seem unsensational, in recent discussion many scholars have argued that this assessment does not represent FG's situation. This has particularly been the case with those scholars who have emphasized the role of a "Johannine Community" in the composition of FG. It will therefore be necessary, before proceeding to outline my view of FG's situation in more detail, to address the arguments of the "school approach."

For some time it has been popular to posit a "school" or community that was founded by the Beloved Disciple and carried on his understanding of discipleship. Some scholars who have taken this approach are led to argue that FG tells us more about the history of this Johannine Community than about events from the life of Jesus (Brown 1979; Martyn 1979). John 4, in this view, is a parable of Samaritan relations with the Johannine Community. Nicodemus (John 3) becomes a symbolic figure representing a *type* of character within the Johannine world, a man whose investment in the status quo of Jerusalem's religious life has paralyzed him with "fear of the authorities" (John 12:42–43). And the apparent rivalry that surfaces between the Beloved Disciple and Peter (18:15; 20:1–10; 21:20) is taken to be symbolic of a rivalry between the Johannine Community and the "great church" identified with the work of Peter. Nicodemus, Joseph of Arimathea, and those like them who fear "the Jews" and will not become public disciples are, from this perspective, foils for Johannine Christians whose discipleship is being criticized (19:38f.; 12:42f.).

The community approach, then, situates FG and its stories in an ecclesial framework, where historical perspective has either been naively lost or carefully jettisoned in order to speak to later generations. The task of the modern interpreter is therefore to reconstruct the thought and life of the Johannine church through the artful *deconstruction* of FG's narratives about Jesus. A significant example of this effort can be found in the work of Raymond Brown, who not only sees FG's narratives as reflecting the church's interests but also believes that even the sequence of stories in the Fourth Gospel tells us something about the history of the Johannine church (1979, 25–58). For example, it is no accident, according to Brown, that FG introduces Samaritans early in the text (John 4), since Samaria is likely the home of the originating Johannine community with its antitemple views.

I have no complaint with the notion that a Johannine Community existed and that the concerns of this community inspired the construction and shape of the Fourth Gospel. But if this perspective leads us to conclude that FG has lost touch with the historical events of Jesus' pre-Easter life it must be rejected. While it is true that every gospel was influenced by the needs of its original audience, it does not follow that this influence negated a historical appreciation for Jesus' life. Passages such as John 2:22 indicate that FE is writing with a historical perspective in mind: in *another*, earlier time Jesus said something that could only be understood in the present time (the author's time). Indeed, FE writes so that his readers can make sense of Jesus' words, but he does not write to obliterate any commitment to that "other time," that historical time that stands at a distance from him, that time whose story must be recalled and interpreted with the aid of the Spirit (14:26; 16:12–13). It therefore seems inappropriate to situate FG in a church context that does not respect historical distance or that does not understand the importance of historical recitation for faith. In fact, this very theme drives much of the argument of 1 John: newly inspired teachings in the community that do not cohere with *what was in the beginning*, with the historical record, do not merit the community's trust. The Johannine Community has witnessed what happens when theological development is not moored in historical objectivity. And the appeal of this important letter is that new prophetic voices that contradict this objective mooring must be abruptly challenged.

Finding an Interpretive Locus
for the Fourth Gospel

Locating the context within which FG was written is a matter of detective work. Some have attempted to answer the question with far greater specificity than the evidence warrants. Nevertheless, if we look at this Gospel carefully we can draw some conclusions about its likely life setting. What sort of community or communities stand behind FG? What sort of conceptual framework did they have? What social world can we glimpse by reading between the lines of its stories? In order to open this line of inquiry, we will explore four issues: 1) the Fourth Evangelist's relationship to Judaism, 2) FE's sense of commitment to history, 3) FE's relationship with other Christian communities in the eastern Mediterranean, and 4) FE's understanding of the work of the Spirit in forming his community and unveiling the deeper things about Jesus.

John and Judaism

The days of reading John's Gospel as a response to Gnosticism or Hellenistic mysticism are over. Not only have these suggestions proven untenable, but the Gnostic myth of redemption that Bultmann and others employed as the conceptual key to FG has turned out to be a fiction (W. D. Davies 1996). Far more promising avenues of research have probed the conceptual world of Philo and the forms of Judaism living on the fringes of Israel's life, such as the Qumran community. In these contexts we begin to see the sort of religious language that FE knows well, and we also see that someone steeped in this type of Jewish religious tradition could have framed arguments like those we find in FG. Of course, this is not a Judaism that is isolated from Hellenistic thought. Jews who were faithful to the synagogue read the LXX and were conversant with Hellenism. FE lives where these two worlds, Judaism and Hellenism, merge.

The most important clue to the relationship between FG and Judaism is the theological outlook used by the Fourth Evangelist as he builds stories about Jesus. Here we do not have an amateur storyteller who stands in Hellenism and attempts to write a Jewish story whose setting is foreign to him. FE is deeply indebted to Judaism for his basic understanding of what Jesus has accomplished. The discourse of John 5, for instance, and FE's exploitation of that discourse's christological implications, turns on a rabbinic appreciation of the meaning of the Sabbath. The feeding miracle in John 6 closely parallels the Synoptics, but it is also forged anew as a comparison with and commentary on the biblical story of Moses in the wilderness. The same can be said for FE's treatment of the Feast of Tabernacles (John 7–9) and Hanukkah (chap. 10). In each case, subtleties arise in the symbolism of the text that one would least expect of an outsider: water and light, wrongful shepherds, Jesus' location in the Treasury. These symbols are subtle clues to deeper theological meanings that would be best appreciated by an audience familiar with synagogue life and the Jewish festival year.

The same argument can be made concerning FE's use of the Hebrew Bible. Sometimes he, like Matthew, cites OT texts overtly (see John 12:38–40); on other occasions he alludes to some OT reference in a way that only an "insider" would understand. Simply put, FE has absorbed the theological categories of the OT and brought these to bear on his description of Jesus' work. His treatment of the Good Shepherd (John 10) and the Vine and the Branches (chap. 15) make clear reference to OT concepts without citing any specific text from the Hebrew Bible. Similarly, John 1–4 employs the Jacob stories (Genesis 25–35; 46–50) in ways that a non-Jewish reader would likely miss. Likewise, FE's treatment of the encounter between the resurrected Jesus and Mary in the garden (John 20) evokes remarkable images of Jewish lore (a garden, spices, lost love, a man and a woman). All of this is to say that FG is a gospel written for an audience that is expected to understand and appreciate nuances strictly anchored in the Jewish religious world. This is a world that understands the meaning of "the land" in Jewish thought, what it means to have an "inheritance" there, and how Jesus' promise to make a "place" for his followers exploits these ideas (chap. 14). This is a world that knows Jerusalem and its Temple, that understands the holiness code and the law. It recognizes the irony when Jesus at Tabernacles offers living water in the midst of an autumn drought and Jerusalem's great water ceremony (7:37–39).

FG's strong connections to the conceptual world of Judaism highlight one of its deeper paradoxes: while FE carefully interprets Jesus for a Jewish audience, he nevertheless finds himself in harsh conflict with the very Judaism he is trying to engage. FE refers to certain characters in the story as "the Jews" over sixty times, and in many cases this term distinguishes these characters from others in the story who are also clearly Jewish (see John 1:19; 2:13; 3:25). Martyn understands these references and the reference to expulsion from the synagogue at John 9:22 as allusions to FE's own experience of excommunication after the imposition of the *Birkhat ha-Minim* ("blessing against the heretics") promoted at Jamnia after 85 C.E. But this conclusion is not necessary, for tense relations between Christian and Jewish communities existed long before this date. Luke attests to it (Acts 6–8), and Paul refers derisively to "the Jews" who persecuted believers in Judea (1 Thess. 2:14). Conflict with opponents is likewise threaded through every aspect of the synoptic story. But this conflict is described in FG with more intense language, which suggests that FE's community may consist of Jewish believers who have left the synagogue and now find themselves in heated debate with their former group. It is hard to say if they have abandoned Judaism altogether, since the Jewish theological and cultural setting is still their interpretive framework. In any case, they now see themselves primarily as followers of Christ, and this designation has permanently severed the tenuous continuity they enjoyed with their Jewish roots.

John and the Historical Jesus

The Fourth Evangelist everywhere takes pains to underscore that his gospel is a reliable record, based on eyewitness testimony, of what happened during Jesus' lifetime. The overt purpose of FG is to present this testimony in a persuasive and

compelling way that will generate belief (John 20:30–31). FE provides incidental details in his narrative that must be taken either as symbols or as reminiscences
of historical information forgotten by others. For example, he sometimes notes
the hour when things happen (1:39; 4:6, 52; 18:28; 19:14; 20:19) and supplies
small descriptive details such as the character of a burning fire (18:18; 21:9) or
the quantities that accompany miracles (2:6) or deeds (19:39).

At the core of the Johannine Community's life was an eyewitness source,
the enigmatic Beloved Disciple, to whom the community could point with
confidence (John 19:35). BD leads the way among those who have seen and
heard and touched (1 John 1:1–4). Of course, the identity of this "beloved disciple" has long been a matter of controversy. Some have even denied that such
a person existed, arguing instead that BD is an idealized character who models faith. But Charlesworth's 1995 study of FG's authorship, the most exhaustive to date, shows the weaknesses of this symbolic view and demonstrates that
FE thinks of the Beloved Disciple as a real person who validates the historical
message of his gospel. BD is well known to his community, which explains why
he can remain anonymous in FG. It thus makes best sense to see the Beloved
Disciple as the "author" or source of FG's traditions.

The testimony of the Johannine church is thus anchored in what has happened in history: what has been *seen* is the basis of what can be preached ("we
have seen and testify that the Father sent his Son as the Savior of the World"
[1 John 4:14]). John 1:14 makes this clear: the word became flesh and *we saw
his glory*. FE's use of the aorist tense here with the plural ("we saw") is an
attempt to place himself among the earliest eyewitnesses. This is why one vital
function of the Spirit/Paraclete is remembrance (14:26), so that the historical
events of Jesus' life may be recalled successfully (Burge 1987, 210–214). FE
even supplies hints within his gospel that events in Jesus' life were remembered
at a later time (John 2:22; 12:16). Jesus likewise urges the disciples to "remember" so they will be strengthened in the future (16:4).

The author of the Fourth Gospel sees himself standing at an important
juncture. He has seen Jesus-in-history, and his gospel is an attempt to place in
writing what he has witnessed so that others removed from these events may
benefit (John 20:31). This historical situation explains the not-so-surprising
accuracy of FG in matters of geographical detail. The author knows Jerusalem
and the Temple well. In fact, he writes with the comfortable assumption that
his readers will also understand the Temple, because it may have been standing when his gospel first circulated.

John and New Testament Churches

Scholars have often atomized the early Christian communities that stand
behind the canonical gospels. It has become fashionable, for example, to refer

to the "Matthean Community" and the "Markan Community," when in fact we have no evidence that these communities existed beyond the respective Gospels themselves. It is simply a hypothesis that a community existed behind the social and ethical commands of these writings. The Johannine Community—if it existed—is often assumed to have lived in relative isolation, independent of the historical and theological accountability of the wider church in the Mediterranean world and free to rewrite its story of Christ along personal lines. A typical study by Jerome Neyrey (1988) employs the high Christology of John as a cipher to describe the community's isolation, estrangement, and final revolt from the synagogue that gave it birth.

But the assumptions behind such reconstructions are enormous. It is far better to acknowledge the widespread mobility and communication channels available in the first century and to conclude that the early Christians communicated with one another vigorously. The New Testament suggests that Christian leaders moved from place to place with remarkable frequency—simply note Paul and his colleagues Timothy, Titus, and Tychicus, or others who appear in more than one place, like Peter, Barnabas, Mark, Silas, Apollos, Philip, Aquila and Priscilla, Andronicus, Junia, and Agabus. The first century offered a speed and safety of travel not seen before. It could take as little as eight days to sail from Ephesus to Syrian Antioch on a Roman grain vessel. Along with these advances in travel, letter writing was apparently a habit in the early church. Not only can we point to Paul's correspondence, but from the second century there are extant letters from Polycarp, Ignatius, and Dionysius of Corinth. Letters imply not only content but messengers: men and women who carried them from one church to another and talked about their experiences and told stories, thus linking the different Christian communities (Bauckham 1998, 9–48). If we are right that perhaps 10 to 15 percent of the Roman Empire was literate, much of the work of a courier such as Phoebe was the oral communication of what she had seen and heard.

The importance of these facts for understanding the Johannine Community should be clear: FE knew what other Christians were saying and reading. The Fourth Gospel was not their first exposure to the story about Jesus. This approach touches on the debate concerning FG's relationship with the Synoptics: did FE use Matthew, Mark, and/or Luke as sources for his own gospel? A more valuable question, however, does not inquire about FE's *sources* but rather about his *intended audience*. Bauckham (1998, 147–171) and others have made a compelling case that FE wrote to *accommodate* readers of Mark, a gospel that may have already had a wide "hearing" among Christians. From this perspective, parenthetical remarks in FG serve as aids to readers who may have known Mark already. For example, John 3:24 explains that John the Baptist "had not yet been thrown into prison" when Jesus' disciples were baptizing in Judea, and yet this would only be a problem if one had already read Mark 1, where the prophet is imprisoned early (1:14). John 3:24, then, functions to explain that the events of John 1:19–4:43 fit between Mark 1:13 and 1:14. Another example of such a parenthetical remark appears at John 11:2. Here the audience is told that Jesus has come to the home of Mary in Bethany, "the one who anointed the Lord with perfume and wiped his feet with her hair." The anointing in question, however, does not occur until the next chapter. The knowledge presupposed in John 11:2 is found exclusively in Mark 14:3–9, and FE's reference identifies a character the reader knows from elsewhere (Mark) but has not yet met in FG. Of course, one could conclude from this that FG is in some way dependent on Mark as a source, but it is equally reasonable to view John's Gospel as a complement to Mark.

These clues are vital to our understanding of the "situation" of FG. The Gospel of John did not spring from an eccentric, isolated community but instead was fully immersed in the wider conversation of Christians around the Mediterranean world. The historical claims central to Luke 1:1–4 may like-wise have been central to FE as he thought about his gospel circulating in the larger world of Christian discourse. And if this is true—if the Gospels were produced in full awareness of the existence of other similar written gospels—the traditional dating of FG may need revision. Thompson (1998) has sug-gested that the Gospels were written within several years of each other and in full awareness of one another, a process that likely began well before the out-break of the First Jewish War.

John and the Spirit

Thus far I have suggested that we should situate the Gospel of John in a com-munity of Christians whose cultural framework is principally Jewish, whose lives were shaped by the cultural world of Hellenistic Judaism before the destruction of Jerusalem (70 C.E.), and who were living in conversation with other churches in the Mediterranean. The Gospel of John was penned in the first instance to provide a compelling eyewitness historical portrait of Jesus Christ for this context. In fact, the literary design of FG presents "evidence" for Jesus and invites the reader to decide whether to join those who believe and walk in the light.

But the Fourth Evangelist does not attempt to offer a raw historical portrait of Jesus. Instead, John's Gospel provides us with a Spirit-led interpretation of the traditional stories about Christ. The Spirit does not simply come into the community to recall basic facts of history (John 14:26) but rather to give the community a deeper insight and interpretation of those facts (16:12ff.). One major difference between FG and the Synoptics is that FE articulates more pre-cisely his own understanding of the work of the Spirit in the interpretive process. FG suggests that the Spirit both contributes to the community's understanding of Christ (John 3:34; 7:37–39; etc.) and plays a key role in personal discipleship. Followers of Christ experience both the personal indwelling, empowerment, and transformation of the Spirit (3:1–15, 31–34; 4:7–26; 14:16f.) and the recollection of Jesus' words by the Spirit's power (14:26), along with personal illumination and teaching (1 John 2:25–26). Indeed, in FG the Spirit can lead the believer into truths not before disclosed (16:12–13). In the Synoptics, the chief function of the Spirit is the defense of the persecuted (Mark 13:11), a doctrine that FE also promotes (John 15:26). But even in this instance, FE sees the work of the Spirit as revelatory, supplying words of witness as they are needed. Revelation and persecution are wed in FE's two titles for the Spirit, the "Paraclete" (a legal term) and the "Spirit of Truth."

FE's unique emphasis on the role of the Spirit reveals yet another element in the situation of the Fourth Gospel and its community. The experience of the Spirit, prominent in the life of the church and in the polemics of 1–2–3 John, was a crucial test for faithful discipleship (1 John 4). FE has made the Spirit into the alter ego of Jesus, so that fidelity to the resurrected Jesus must incorporate some experience of Jesus-in-Spirit. Within the pages of FG, this emphasis explains FE's careful critique of both baptism and the Eucharist in light of the Spirit. Baptism requires more than water to be efficacious, and it must be joined to the Spirit (John 3:5). Similarly, wine and bread are insufficient if they do not evoke a reality found in the Spirit (6:63). Likewise, Christian worship must be directed in a manner that concentrates less on form and more on its Spirit experience (4:24). This prominent feature of Johannine thought no doubt has contributed to the character of the Fourth Gospel as well. FG is not just a historical recitation, but a Spirit-inspired interpretation probing deeper meanings of Christ that were barely understood by Jesus' original audiences. At the same time, however, this continuing revelatory work does not compromise the historical tradition. Rather, it focuses the tradition and concentrates our attention on aspects of it we would not have seen before. Like an icon, FG stylizes the images of Christ for our benefit and devotion while still recognizing the historic realities that rest behind the portrait.

The Situation and Growth
of the Fourth Gospel

In this essay, I have attempted to rediscover the original situation that gave birth to the Fourth Gospel. In the process, I have considered four issues that affect our understanding of that situation: FG's relationship to first-century Judaism, FG's relationship to the historical Jesus, FG's relationship to the broader Christian movement, and FE's understanding of the role of the Spirit. Our analysis has suggested that a claim to historicity lies at the center of the Fourth Gospel's theological outlook. FG's incarnational Christology lays a groundwork for the importance of history as a medium of revelation: God entered the world of time and space to disclose himself. FG's record of Jesus' life assumes that what its pages record about Jesus in history is not only trustworthy but of critical theological value. This commitment to history allows us to suggest that FG originated in the earliest strata of early Jewish Christianity in Palestine. FE's use of the OT and his understanding of Jewish imagery and argument are clues to this Jewish setting. Moreover, FE's insistence on an "eye-witness" source fits this same historical commitment. But FG also emerged from a community that had evolved, and whose gospel had evolved along with it. Later debates with "the Jews" forged the vocabulary of its rhetoric. And ongoing conversations with other Christians who knew the Synoptics helped shape FG's story so that it could be appreciated by a wider audience. But this evolution and insight, this deepening of Jesus' portrait, is not based solely on FE's historical research. It comes, instead, from the guidance of the Holy Spirit. The Johannine Community lived with the tension of both *revelation historicized* in Jesus and *revelation experienced* through the dynamic work of the Spirit.

If this Johannine Community and its gospel witnessed evolution and change, can we propose specific stages in its history? I do not believe that the Gospel of John came to life in one writing. Scholars from Bultmann to Fortna have attempted to uncover layers of tradition and redaction in FG that betray something of the text's composition history. While an exact delineation of these sources is likely beyond our grasp, every scholar senses that FG offers hints of its history, tantalizing bits of data that point to stages of literary development. In my view, the Fourth Gospel as we now have it evidences four strata of composition that represent broad periods in the history of its development.

Stratum One

The earliest stratum of FG derived from stories about Jesus that came to the community from the Beloved Disciple. One can make a defensible argument that BD was a member of the circle of Jesus' apostles (see Burge 1992). This explains FE's emphasis on eyewitness testimony, his Jewish cultural framework, and his easy assumptions about Jewish festival and Temple traditions. We could date this stratum to well before the First Jewish War (pre–66 C.E.).

Stratum Two

At this stage, the material from John 1:19 to the end of chapter 20 was put in written form as a single story. The catalyst for this writing was no doubt the struggles between FE's fledgling community and the synagogue. The tense and polemical nature of this relationship framed the original literary structure of FG, the trial motif, and a judicial framework was projected at this point onto the entire story of Jesus' life and ministry. Jesus is on trial from the first day: evidence is given; judgments are made; audiences are divided. The reader is invited to make the same decision as Jesus' judges in chapter 18: "I find no case against him" (18:38). Essentially, FE's struggles at this stage are with the "world," a place of unbelief and darkness where hostility is commonplace.

At this stage of composition, FE appears to have been in conversation with other religious communities. The followers of John the Baptist receive special treatment at John 3:22–30, and since their allegiances to the Baptist must be challenged so too their claims about John must be corrected (1:19–34; 3:31–36; 10:41). True disciples of the Baptist will recognize Jesus and come follow him (1:35–42). In addition, FE is aware of others in his world: Samaritans (John 4) and perhaps even Jews who would like to become disciples but who fear the authorities (12:42–43). The presence of these surrounding communities gave shape to the emphases and character of the narratives in the present version of FG.

Stratum Three

The three letters of John signal a complete change in setting. Conflicts previously waged externally now become internal as members of the church once thought to be faithful leave the community (1 John 2:18–21). The high Christology of FG and its emphasis on pneumatology have fueled a christological heresy led by charismatic teacher-prophets. This spiritual elitism spurns commands about ethical behavior and leads to chaos. First John in particular corrects misinterpretations of FG and confronts these schismatics. With its many links to this letter, the Johannine Prologue (John 1:1–18) was likely developed at this time.

Stratum Four

The death of the Beloved Disciple, the community's founder, brought a crisis. John 21:20–23 describes the dilemma of his death, and in 21:24 we find his disciples and the final editors of FG disclosing their identities ("This is the disciple who is testifying to these things and has written them, and *we* know that his testimony is true"). These followers no doubt edited the Gospel to produce the text that we possess today. They added the Prologue (1:1–18) as an overture to the great theological themes of FG and also added chapter 21, employing a resurrection story passed down by their great teacher. As a final gesture of devotion, they named their departed founder "the beloved disciple"—a person everyone would at once recognize, whose memory was deeply venerated by all.

The Fourth Gospel continues to intrigue because its situation in history is so elusive. The community that gave it shape could point to its founder with pride and know that it had a trustworthy eyewitness connection to the story of Jesus. And yet this community also knew intense struggle both with the world and within its own walls. These experiences forged its worldview, as well as the way it began to see the character of Jesus, his ministry, and his death.

4

What Can a Postmodern Approach to the Fourth Gospel Add to Contemporary Debates About Its Historical Situation?

Jeffrey L. Staley

To most critical readers, it appears obvious that the text of the Fourth Gospel (FG) underwent a number of editings or redactions prior to attaining its present canonical form. Beyond the notable additions of John 5:4 and 7:53–8:11 (which are clearly non-Johannine interpolations, as indicated by the manuscript tradition), John 21 also appears to be an addition to the book. Many scholars view chapter 21 as an appendix for a number of reasons, not the least being that the book seems to reach its natural conclusion at 20:30–31. Furthermore, John 21 uses words not found elsewhere in FG and seems to answer some of the unresolved questions of chapters 13–20 regarding the relationship between the Beloved Disciple and Peter. Beyond chapter 21, most scholars accept the possibility that some or all of the Prologue (John 1:1–18), and perhaps also John 5–7 and 15–17, betray evidence of major editorial work. However, aside from these generally accepted editorial additions or revisions there is little agreement. Scholars debate, for example, whether the order of John 5 and 6 was reversed at an early stage of writing. Was Jesus' symbolic destruction of the Temple (John 2:13–22) pushed back from a later position in the narrative into Jesus' early ministry in order to make the resurrection of Lazarus the event that immediately precipitates Jesus' arrest and death? Was an independent collection of miracle stories (the "Signs Source") incorporated into the book? And was chapter 12 introduced as a bridge between this "book of signs" and a "book of glory"?

Today, scholars are not nearly as willing to take dogmatic stands on such redactional issues as they were fifty or more years ago. On the one hand, the

mid-twentieth-century discoveries of the Dead Sea Scrolls and the Nag Hammadi library, and more recent archaeological excavations in Jerusalem and
Galilee, have made for much more interesting hypotheses regarding the different possible social contexts of the Johannine editors. On the other hand,
these discoveries have also made it increasingly difficult to reconstruct neatly
first-century Judaism and to place the history of the Fourth Evangelist's (FE)
community within this complex milieu. One cannot simply say that FG is Jewish or Greek, Palestinian or non-Palestinian in origin. Furthermore, a wide
variety of studies in the social sciences, orality, feminism, and literary theory
have raised serious questions about the very nature of historical criticism as it
is usually practiced by New Testament scholars, with their hypothetical editors, sources, and social contexts. In our postmodern era, issues related to the
status of the interpreter and "his" ideological commitments have challenged
the historical positivism of past reconstructions of the Johannine Community
and its texts and have pointed out the tenuous nature of those theories.

This is not to say that Johannine scholars—even postmodern ones like
myself—have lost their zest and appetite for historical questions. Indeed, it is
precisely the unchallenged assumptions of historical Jesus research (e.g., "the
Fourth Gospel tells us virtually nothing about the pre-Easter Jesus") and
recent narrative-critical interpretations of the book (e.g., "the focus of our
attention will be on the text as it now stands") that have brought back to the
forefront of Johannine research questions regarding the connection between
FG, its author(s), its sources, and the historical Jesus. But as Gary Philips and
Danna Fewell have recently pointed out,

> we might frame source criticism of the New Testament . . . as an eth-
> ical concern. The face of Jesus within the folds of the text speaks and
> calls on us to speak, to uncode all the names surrounding it, evoking
> it, touching on it, making it appear. The quest for "original" sources
> and the "historical" Jesus would draw its first breath not from its sta-
> tus foremost as a distanciated historical exercise that uncovers layers
> and facts of textual history, as important as that may be, but from the
> desire to preserve the face of Jesus, to keep it from becoming a
> metaphor or, better, a mere mirror of our own particular, religious,
> ideological, or cultural interests. (Phillips and Fewell 1997)

So the larger question is, having once isolated and exposed the "face of
Jesus" in the editorial layers of FG, what do we do with that face? Could FG
suddenly reclaim its place in the Christian canon as a viable witness to Jesus
once scholars successfully kept its "face of Jesus" from just "becoming a
metaphor"? Would FG's authoritative claim to an apostolic vision of Jesus'
mission somehow be reconfirmed if historians took pains to separate their
research from the "mere mirror of [their] own particular, religious, ideologi-

cal, or cultural interests"? Or would historians instead simply affirm that, like the Synoptics, FG is also "somehow rooted in events related to the life of Jesus"? And would they then insist that it is important to say "rooted in events related to the life of Jesus" and "somehow" without defining either term too narrowly?

The Significance of Historical Origins

Having identified a few editorial stitches in FG does not mean that scholars are agreed on the issue of how to attach significance to such sutures. For example, narrative critics may "see" evidence of editorial work in a text yet remain uninterested in tying to it any historical or communal event. Here, postmodern hermeneutical and philosophical issues begin to intrude upon contemporary biblical interpretation: *Does the quest for origins, or exposing a process of evolution in the formation of the Johannine text, exhaust the significance and meaning of that text?*

All aspects of critical thinking, including the canons of source criticism, share at their core certain presuppositions about the relationship between the objects under investigation. For example, when John 3:22–26 and 4:1–2 are read together, they seem to contradict each other: the first passage states explicitly that Jesus baptized people during his ministry while the second says that Jesus did not actually baptize people, but instead his disciples did the baptizing. This is an obvious point of contrast. But is the contradiction between these passages "solved" by a hypothesis that proposes multiple editings of the text, or by a theory of literary genius or authorial stupidity, or by a theory of rhetorical effect?

One can imagine a "premodern" person seeing an individual who is having difficulty walking and noticing that the person is in pain. This premodernist may then detect that one of the person's legs is significantly larger than the other: one leg, we might say, contrasts with the other. It is similar enough to the other leg to be recognized as the typical human ambulatory appendage, but why is it different? Although the premodernist may not think explicitly in such terms, he or she may "theorize" about the historical origin of the difference between the individual's two legs, much as source critics note differences in the texture of John 3:22–26 and 4:1–2 and then theorize that these differences have their roots in an editorial prehistory. The premodernist may conclude that the person with the swollen leg fell down and twisted it; or perhaps the person was bitten by a poisonous animal; perhaps an evil spirit attacked the person because of some irresponsible act on their part.

My point is that many of the observed similarities and differences between objects in our world are really rooted in their shared prehistory and can be explained by delineating that prehistory. Modern medicine, with its understanding of symptoms; the biological sciences, with their analyses of fossil records; geology, with its theories of sedimentary rocks; and cosmology, with its theories of the universe's origins, all share this common historical orientation. Things that are similar might be related to each other while their differences may have arisen from past events. In all these situations, whether we are thinking of ordinary human experiences or scientific theories, the observed differences between things are generally understood to be rooted in events of the past. And delineating that past (no matter how theoretical) establishes an authority and a "reason" for why things have come to be the way they now are. The same applies to the apparent "differences" in the text of FG—its aporias, its disjunctions and apparent narrative breaks, may represent a prehistory and an evolution of the text as it moves toward its final canonical form.

But a postmodern sense of contrast and difference is not tied to historical questions of origins nearly as closely as source and redaction criticism are tied to them. For example, a contemporary, postmodern skyscraper in downtown Seattle, Atlanta, or New York City may have adapted architectural elements from modernist, rococo, and neoclassical styles without having been built in three different architectural eras or by three different architectural firms. Here, the juxtaposition of styles and motifs and the jarring, clashing textures reflect difference and contrast without presupposing any historical priority between the elements of the building. In other words, the "rhetorical effect" of the building is more important in this case than the precise historical origin of any one of its peculiarities. It is entirely possible to view the text of FG in the same way one might look at the postmodern skyscraper. That is, one may grant the historian the point that FG has a compositional prehistory without granting the peculiarities of that history any particular authority—even if we could be sure what that history was. Were we to adopt this mode of analysis, as in the example of the postmodern skyscraper, the rhetorical effect of FG's editorial seams would become the central focus of the postmodern interpreter's attention and the locus of "authority" rather than the history of the text's origins.

Let me be perfectly clear about this latter point. As a postmodern interpreter of FG, I do not wish to deny the importance of the historical questions raised by the past 150 years of Johannine scholarship. But the twenty-first-century New Testament scholar with a postmodern sense of texts can and must challenge the traditional historicism of Johannine scholarship. It is especially important to do so when traditional reconstructions of FG's origins and its community are so tenuous that they stretch historical credibility to the breaking point, or when the prehistory of the text and its "origins" function merely as a rhetorical ploy to absolutize and authorize particular interpretations of that text. For this reason, I am quite skeptical of scholarly attempts to develop a hypothetical trajectory for the history of the Johannine Community—its loves and hates, its geographical movements, and its social formation—from FG and 1–2–3 John. And texts outside the New Testament canon—whether "Gnostic" or otherwise—are even more difficult to connect with a particular phase of the Johannine Community.

So while it is quite reasonable to assume that FG has undergone a process of development and expansion (or shortening?), one is on surer historical grounds when investigating questions related to *the type of audience FG creates for itself*. Here, I think, we can make some historical and rhetorical judgments that are open to verification. In the analysis that follows, I will simply lay out some of the key places where FG seems to be grounded in pre-Easter Jesus traditions and then move on to discuss the sort of audience the text constructs from these basic traditions to see if that audience could actually match one of those that have been proposed by Johannine historical critics.

Pre-Easter Jesus Traditions in FG

There are a number of elements in the Gospel of John that seem to reflect pre-Easter Jesus traditions. Some of these Johannine traditions are validated by multiple attestation (i.e., similar information appears in Mark, Q, or Paul's letters), while others fit the criteria of difficulty (i.e., it is unclear why FE would have invented such information, as it does not reflect the expectations of the day or his own theological position). We can divide these traditions into two general categories: traditions about Jesus' followers and traditions about Jesus. With respect to the Johannine *traditions about Jesus' followers*, the following may be pre-Easter in origin: some of Jesus' followers had first been followers of John the Baptizer (John 1:35–51); Jesus selected twelve of these followers (all males?) for a special role, perhaps as a symbolic gesture (6:67); people named Peter, Thomas, Andrew, Philip, Nathaniel, and "the other Judas" were among Jesus' followers; going slightly beyond the pre-Easter phase, Mary Magdalene was the first follower to have a post-Easter revelation of Jesus (20:11–18).

Similarly, some Johannine *traditions about Jesus* have a high likelihood of being pre-Easter in origin: Jesus' and John the Baptist's prophetic activities overlapped and were in competition with each other (John 3:22–30); Jesus was from Nazareth and had brothers (7:1–10); Jesus was a charismatic who healed on the Sabbath (5:1–9; 9:1–14); he traveled through Samaria at least once in his lifetime (4:4ff.); he understood himself to be "sent from God" and spoke of God as his "father" (5:36–38; 8:42–55); he may have been to Jerusalem more than once, and his public activity may have lasted more than one year; Jesus disrupted Temple activities around the year 27 C.E. (2:13–22); was accused of being demon-possessed and of misleading the masses as a false prophet (7:45–52; 8:48); and was crucified before Passover during Pontius Pilate's prefecture in Judea (18:28; 19:13ff.).

These lists, of course, are not complete, and they obviously assume that much of FE's portrait of Jesus is either historically doubtful or simply inaccurate. But since some of the Johannine "inaccuracies" are also found in the Synoptics, they do not particularly undermine FG's historicity. For example, I doubt that Jesus actually walked on water, multiplied loaves and fishes, turned water into wine, or raised Lazarus from the dead. I doubt that Jesus met one-on-one with Pilate, the Samaritan woman, or Nicodemus, and had the memorable conversations with these people recorded in FG. I doubt that Jesus' disciples were, in Jesus' lifetime, excluded from synagogues for affirming him to be the Christ. I do believe that Jesus could have said things like "the father and I are one" in a spirit trance, an altered state of consciousness that is a common cross-cultural phenomenon. But this does not necessarily mean that Jesus had an absolutely unique relationship to God—an ontological unity of "substance" with the Father.

So where does this leave us? If the above Johannine Jesus traditions may be considered "authentic," what were their sources? If most of the book does not reflect historical reminiscences from the era of the historical Jesus, then what historical situation does it reflect? Like the Synoptic Gospels, the Gospel of John reflects the historical situation(s) of its author(s). But what are the clues to that situation? Has the author been cast out of the synagogues, or been cast out of the Johannine Community, or mourned the death of the Beloved Disciple? If so, can any of these circumstances be correlated with specific historical situations in first-century Judaism (if such a thing as "first-century Judaism" existed)? And, if the author's situation included excommunication from the synagogue, then what was a "synagogue" in the first century and could "being cast out" reflect the *Birkhat ha-Minim* of the later rabbinic world (85 C.E.)? What would it mean to be excluded from "the Jewish community" in first-century Judea or Galilee or Samaria? And if such problems exist in reconstructing the possible Jewish context of FE, concepts like exclusion from the Johannine Community or the death of the Beloved Disciple are even more difficult to chart historically, since the only data we have to work from are the Johannine documents themselves, which are notoriously lacking in explicit historical references. How would we even begin to reconstruct these scenarios?

Such questions, in my estimation, are largely unanswerable given our present meager resources from the first century. I believe, however, that we can make some helpful observations regarding FG's probable rhetorical audience without waiting for a new archaeological discovery to confirm our proposals.

A Two-Tiered Witness Motif
and Its Historical Implications

One of the most notable features of the opening chapter of FG is the manner in which Jesus gathers his first disciples. Not only do some of these followers come from the circle of John the Baptizer, but they also meet Jesus *through the agency of some other person* (see John 1:35–51; 4:39–42; 12:20–23; 21:7). This peculiarly Johannine motif of meeting Jesus through an agent is not found in the Synoptic Gospels, where association with Jesus normally comes instead through direct personal contact with him. More importantly, this motif of agency is found in distinct segments of FG that are often viewed as coming from three major redactional periods. Many scholars believe that John 1:35–51 was the original opening of the narrative and that this story reflects traditions from the original community of Johannine Christians whose roots lay with John the Baptizer's group. The middle period of the community is represented by its Samaritan and Gentile mission, which is reflected in the narrative at John 4:39–42 and 12:20–23. Finally, the latest period of the community is evident in the role of the Beloved Disciple (BD), who becomes crucial to the survival of the community as it faces internal conflict (13:23–30; 17:20; 21:7). Yet the theme of meeting Jesus through an agent appears in all three of these sections of FG.

If redaction critics are correct to conclude that FG reflects forty to fifty years of editing, it is remarkable that the current text also reflects an unusual rhetorical unity on the themes of "authority" and "witness." For example, Jesus' earliest disciples follow him not because he calls them, but rather because John the Baptizer says, "Behold the Lamb of God." The next two pairs of followers come to Jesus in the same way, through the agency of some other person (Peter through Andrew and Nathaniel through Philip). The same idiosyncratic motif appears later in the stories of the Samaritan mission and the Gentile mission. In the former case, the men of Sychar "believed in him because of the woman's testimony" (John 4:39). In the latter case, the Greeks come to Philip, who then goes and tells Andrew, both of whom then go and tell Jesus that there are Greeks who want to meet him (12:20–22). Finally, when BD appears on the scene in the Farewell, Peter can get to Jesus only by talking to the one who reclines on Jesus' breast (13:23–25). Similarly, at John 21:7 it is BD's recognition of Jesus ("It is the Lord") that motivates Peter's early morning plunge into the Sea of Galilee. The historical, christological, and ecclesiological importance of this rhetorical strategy is confirmed by its appearance in Jesus' final prayer: "I ask not only on behalf of these, but also on behalf *of those who will believe in me through their word*, that they may all be one. As you, Father, are in me and I am in you, may they also be in us, so that the world may believe that you have sent me" (17:20–21; italics added). Thus, a two-tiered motif of witnessing is reflected in the three major redactional stages in FG's composition history, a motif that corresponds to FE's estimation of Jesus' earthly purpose. Throughout FG, no one comes to Jesus without the assistance of another person.

In reflecting on the significance of this universal motif, it is interesting to note that the Signs Source from which much of the narrative material in FG may have been drawn (assuming for the moment that such a source existed) evinces a similar rhetorical strategy in its narrative style. For example, the first three signs in the source exhibit a uniquely Johannine strategy for portraying how the reader/hearer comes to know that a miracle has taken place: the reader learns about the significance of something Jesus has done from a character in the story. In the first sign, the wedding at Cana (John 2:1–11), the reader discovers that the water has turned into wine through the chief steward's experience of tasting a surprisingly good vintage. Here, a third party becomes the unsuspecting witness who confirms for the reader the powerful deed of Jesus. In the second sign, the healing of the royal official's son (4:46–54), it is the slaves, who know nothing of Jesus' previous words, who tell their master that his son is well. Here again, a third party (the slaves) has become the unsuspecting witness who confirms Jesus' powerful deed to the reader. The third sign, the healing of the paralytic (5:1–17), is told in the more traditional manner of synoptic miracle stories. This time the narrator functions as the primary witness by simply stating, "At once the man was made well, and he took up his mat and began to walk" (5:9). On this occasion, there is no immediate third-party character through which the miraculous event is filtered, although the Jews do function later on as inadvertent witnesses to Jesus' powerful deed ("It is the Sabbath; it is not lawful for you to carry your mat" [5:10]). Like the chief steward and the royal official's slaves before them, the Jews have no idea that a sign has been performed, yet their words function as a testimony for the reader of FG to Jesus' miraculous deed.

There is, however, an interesting difference between the secondary witness motif as it is found in the Signs Source and the two-tiered witness motif as it is found in the current text of FG. In the Signs Source, all the secondary witnesses apparently have had no previous encounter with Jesus, which means that they are ignorant of their roles as witnesses to Jesus' power. They witness certain events without knowing the peculiar circumstances surrounding them and therefore cannot come to the conclusion that these things are "signs" of anything about Jesus. But in John 1:35–51, 4:39–42, 12:20–23, and 21:7, all those who witness about Jesus have previously met Jesus and formed a notion of his identity. They are therefore witnesses for Jesus even though, at least in the first two passages, they have not seen Jesus do any powerful deeds.

The manner in which the reader of FG comes to know that these signs have taken place and the manner in which the first disciples come to Jesus both correlate nicely with Jesus' final words to Thomas: "Blessed are those who have not seen and yet have come to believe" (20:29). "Believing without seeing" has been the reader's experience on a number of occasions throughout FG, since the reader, in at least the first two signs, "sees" nothing of the miracles themselves but instead learns of them only through the reports of characters who have seen them. It is only through the words of the unsuspecting bystanders that the reader knows that anything unusual has happened.

My point here is that the Signs Source exhibits a strategy remarkably similar to the one isolated earlier in the three "formative redactional periods" of the Johannine Community. Readers are invited to play a role like that of Peter and Nathaniel or the Samaritans and the Greeks: to believe and follow even though their experience of Jesus is mediated through other, sometimes questionable, witnesses.

I would like to think that the two-tiered witness motif described above reflects a unified rhetorical strategy on the part of the Fourth Evangelist. That is to say, whatever the sources and prior history of the present text of FG, one person was able to mold it all together into a cohesive whole that reflected that one person's unique relationship to the Johannine Jesus tradition and the apostolic community. Furthermore, the cohesive perspective on "witness" reflected in the current text of FG seems to suggest a certain historical point of origin, for this perspective seems to reflect a community that is at least two generations removed from its founding events (the generation of Jesus and BD and the generation of "those who believe having not seen").

A Two-Tiered Witness Motif and Its Cultural Implications

Some biblical scholars, however, might construe my two-tiered witness motif quite differently. For those with a bent toward cultural anthropology, this motif might not appear to be unusual or unique at all. It could, in their view, simply reflect the patronage system that pervaded the ancient Mediterranean world, a system that made exchanges of power and authority possible when inequality and difference were the norm in interpersonal relationships. From this perspective, FG's two-tiered witness motif should not be construed as a peculiar characteristic of the Johannine Community. For just as Jesus is a "client" or "broker" for his patron father who "sends" him (John 7:28–29; 12:44; 17:25) to "do his will" (4:34; 5:30), so also the disciples function as brokers or clients for their patron Jesus. Not surprisingly, Jesus sends his clients to do his will (13:16, 20; 17:18; 20:21). And just as Jesus introduces God, his "father," to his disciples and friends, the disciples introduce their friends and interested strangers to Jesus. In a more overt, political way, Pilate is also a broker ("friend") for his patron, Caesar (19:12), as are the chief priests for Pilate (11:47–50; 18:3, 12–14, 28). Finally, on a different level, characters in the Signs Source sometimes function as unsuspecting witnesses, mediators, or brokers for the reader, who is forced to trust the characters' limited experiences in order to "see the signs" within what otherwise would appear to be ordinary events.

But this conclusion would mean that FG's witness motif cannot function as evidence of a unique missionary strategy in the Johannine Community. Nor does the witness motif reflect a peculiarly Johannine Christology. Rather, it is evidence of a widespread Mediterranean patronage system that can be found in other texts inside and outside the New Testament canon. In support of this interpretation, one could note that many characters in FG are quite sensitive to the inequality of power relations. For example, the socially elite "royal official" (John 4:46–47) pointedly asks Jesus to come and heal his son. And while the socially inferior Samaritan woman makes a similar demand (4:15), her request only comes after Jesus has already broken other social barriers with her (4:7–9). No other Johannine characters make the kinds of straightforward requests that these two characters do. Jesus' mother does not (2:3), nor do the lame man (5:7) or Jesus' female friends, Mary and Martha (11:3). One could argue, then, that the two-tiered witness motif I have attached to historical developments in the Johannine Community is simply one part of a more deeply embedded cultural phenomenon, the ancient Mediterranean patronage system. But if this is the case, we must ask, Does this witness motif reflect a specific historical situation related to the time of FE, or is the motif just part of a broader, social phenomenon of Mediterranean culture? And further, Are we even able to develop the tools needed to distinguish between specific historical events and broader social phenomena when the data related to this ancient community are so meager?

A Postmodern Reassessment
of the Johannine Historical Situation

What is clear from this discussion is that FG, which most scholars date from the end of the first century, shows a remarkable rhetorical unity for a text that is purportedly the product of a composition history of fifty years or more. Either the rhetorical unity of the text reflects a single authorial voice, or its sources and traditions were so heavily reworked over the years that it is now virtually impossible to detect the historical progression of a community behind the text.

However, if FG's historical situation or authorial unity are impossible to establish, its rhetorical situation seems much easier to analyze. Here, a postmodern sense of text and rhetoric can make the strong argument that, regardless of the text's prehistory or origin, its rhetorical structure forms an audience whose trust is predicated on the authority of go-betweens: clients and mediatory figures. But whether this rhetorical effect reflects an actual historical experience in the life of the Johannine Community is beyond the pale of historical investigation. In fact, while it may be interesting to speculate about this issue, a postmodern sense of history will not attach any undue burden of authority to that hypothetical point of origin. For "origins" always presume that power relations are at work, power relations that suppress other possible origins in their very act of explication. Discussions of origins, whether in the "hard" sciences or the "soft" sciences, always reflect elements of their own ideological construction. All theories of origin are historically conditioned and rhetorically produced. So when all is said and done, the postmodern historical critic will look at the various reconstructions of the Johannine Community, the Johannine Jesus, and the Jews and other characters in FG and ask, Whose interests are being served by these historical reconstructions? Why have the points of origin for this text been set at these junctures and not others?

I have argued that a careful reading of FG reveals a two-tiered witness motif that pervades all its supposed levels of sources and redactions. According to this motif, persons come in contact with Jesus through the agency of others. This could imply that the book was written at a time when the community was wrestling in some way with the loss of an authoritative connection (a broker or client) to the historical Jesus. But I am postmodern enough to pose these additional questions to myself: What ideological constraints make me push for this reading of FG over all others? Why should my quest for FG's origins focus on such a narrow reading of the two-tiered witness motif when anthropological studies of the ancient Mediterranean world suggest that this motif might simply reflect a widespread cultural phenomenon?

My goal in this essay has been to show that a postmodern approach to questions of the Johannine historical situation is not necessarily ahistorical or uninterested in issues relating to the community's origins and development. As I have sought to argue, the literary motif of "two-tiered witnessing" may in fact have its origins in a specific historical moment within the community. However, what a postmodern approach does bring to the conversation is a healthy respect for the ways in which ideological concerns get translated into historical hypotheses, which sometimes in turn become consensus views. In this light, the history of Johannine scholarship is as much in need of critical analysis as is the history of the Johannine Community or its Jesus tradition.

5

The Eyewitness of History

Visionary Consciousness in the Fourth Gospel

ARTHUR J. DEWEY

What was the historical interest of the Fourth Evangelist (FE) in Jesus of Nazareth? Obviously this question mingles two worlds: the ancient world of FE and our postmodern world. Our investigation will therefore cross many boundaries. Not only shall we move beyond the notion of "history" as an archive of facts, but we shall also reconsider what constitutes the very act of "remembering" for FE. In one sense, the historian of religion betrays a modern agenda in attempting to assess FE's "historical" concern. Nevertheless, this inquiry can be very fruitful, and in the process we may well pick up something of FE's interpretive horizon. To do so, we must ask what concerns guided FE's story of Jesus and whether the way in which FE used Jesus tradition enables us to see beyond our interests to his concerns.

The cumulative research of the Jesus Seminar suggests that the historical Jesus figures minimally in the composition of the Fourth Gospel (FG). But this assessment may not be the most fruitful entrance into the question of FE's historical interest in Jesus, for a "historical interest" and "historicity" must be sharply differentiated. We shall look, therefore, at the matter of "eyewitness" in FG to see if we can detect another way of describing FE's historical interest in Jesus. In order to do so, I will use John 19:31–37 as a test case. A detailed consideration of this episode will reveal some surprising relationships in FG, which will in turn provide a profile of how FE "remembers" through an eyewitness. Indeed, the force of this investigation will cause us to reconsider what is meant by "history" and to suggest that FE was creatively engaged in what should be called a "visionary consciousness." An "eyewitness" for FE is not a simple observer of raw data. Rather, through enlisting the symbolic presence of the Paraclete (Spirit), FE provides the means for every reader to become an active participant in the epiphany of the death of Jesus.

John and the Historical Jesus

Much recent research has argued that FE had little concern with the historical Jesus. The findings of the Jesus Seminar are notable here. Of FG's 851 verses (minus the non-Johannine 7:53–8:11), only three verses (18:13b; 19:16; 19:18a) were judged to be "undoubtedly" from the historical Jesus (0.35 percent), while four more verses (4:44b; 18:12b; 18:28ab; 19:1) were judged "probably" from the historical Jesus (0.47 percent). Fifty-seven verses were categorized as "possible but not historically probable" (2:13–16a; 4:46b; 4:47b–54; 5:2–9; 11:33–44; 12:1–6; 12:24–25; 13:20; 18:1–3a; 18:3c; 18:28c; 19:19; 19:25; 20:1–2; 20:11–18). In other words, only 6.6 percent of the total number of verses in FG may have, at best, some vague connection to the historical Jesus. Less than 1 percent of the entire Gospel of John won the consensus of the Seminar as material likely to have come from the historical Jesus (Funk 1993, 401–470; 1998, 365–495).

In more concrete terms, the Seminar concluded that the following information from FG may somehow reflect historical events from the life of Jesus. It is certain that Jesus of Nazareth died by crucifixion in Jerusalem under Pontius Pilate. It is also certain that Annas was the father-in-law of Caiaphas (John 18:13). Slightly less certain is the possibility that Jesus was a disciple of John the Baptist and gathered some of his own followers from the Baptist's movement (John 1:19–42). Jesus is also believed to have said that "a prophet has no honor in the prophet's own country" (John 4:43). The Seminar concluded that Jesus' arrest and flogging probably occurred. In a number of cases, the Seminar determined that certain events narrated in FG might have happened but cannot be accepted as probable. The Temple Incident (John 2) and the Bethany anointing (John 12) were judged problematic at best, and the healings of the official's son (John 4:46–54) and the paralytic (John 5:1–9), as well as the raising of Lazarus (John 11), also failed to win a consensus. The scenes of the women at the cross and at the tomb (including Mary Magdalene's solitary encounter in John 20) were also found to be of questionable authenticity. The paradoxical sayings of 12:24–25 were likewise voted possible but not definite.

In sum, in evaluating the historicity of FG, the Jesus Seminar concluded that Jesus was a former disciple of John the Baptist who attracted some of John's followers. This uneducated man, unwelcome in his own town, was arrested, flogged, and suffered a Roman execution. To move beyond this—to include the healings, Temple Incident, anointing at Bethany, the garden scene, the women at the cross, and the empty tomb episodes—is to step into considerably less certain territory. Such findings go a long way from the usual distinctions scholars make between FG and the Synoptic Gospels. It is not simply that the Johannine Jesus doesn't speak in parables but that there is hardly anything that the Johannine Jesus does or says that convincingly reflects the life of the historical Jesus.

But while the sustained analysis of the Jesus Seminar helps yield part of the picture of the historical Jesus, it does not directly address the question of our investigation. Our task takes up where the Seminar left off. To determine FE's historical interest in Jesus, we shall have to look at what the author actually offers us. How does FE construct this interest in Jesus? And we must also be aware that a prior question is embedded in our attempt to describe FE's historical interest: How do we determine FE's understanding of "history"? It may well be that we shall find "history" among the 93.4 percent of FG's verses that the Seminar judged to be secondary and not attributable to the historical Jesus.

The matter of "eyewitness" in FG is crucial to FE's understanding of "history." It is usually assumed that FE used a historical tradition that existed prior to his Gospel. Brown, for example, considers that there must have been witnesses to the death of Jesus, although there may have been considerable reshaping of the eyewitness accounts during the handing down of the tradition (Brown 1994, 1.14). Others have suggested that a Signs Gospel may have been one of the sources for FG. But something more than FE's sources is at stake here. Many commentators believe that there exist certain facts (some of them unique) "behind" FG. This is due not only to significant differences between FG and the Synoptic Gospels but also to the apparent "eyewitness reports" in FG. John 21:24 is paramount here. In this appended chapter to the Gospel of John, the redactor attests to the trustworthiness of the "disciple's" witness. This "disciple" has testified and written his testimony down (21:24). The disciple in question is identified only as "this one" (*houtos*), apparently referring to the disciple described as the one "loved most" by Jesus at 21:20. In John 20:2 the disciple whom Jesus loved most is also called the "other disciple." This "other" or "beloved" disciple plays a key role in FE's sense of "witness."

A Test Case of Johannine "Eyewitness"

Perhaps the most significant passage on the Beloved Disciple's "witness" appears at John 19:35–37, which highlights the truthfulness of BD's testimony about the "water and blood" that flowed from Jesus' side. These verses strongly resemble 21:24. A comparison of the passages reveals that, while 21:24 is an assertion *about* some earlier testimony, 19:35–37 *is* the apparent testimony. In fact, John 21:24 has been understood as a rewriting of 19:35 (Brown 1966, 2.1127). It should also be noted that the perfect tense appears twice in 19:35 ("this disciple *has seen* [*heōrakos*] and *has testified* [*memartureken*]"); but not at all in 21:24 ("testifies," *marturon*; "wrote," *grapsas*). There is an emphasis on some sort of written testimony in 21:24 while at 19:35 an oral accent is underscored ("says," *legei*). How are we to understand the meaning of this "eyewitness"? Does 19:35–37 preserve an ancient tradition that goes back to the historical Jesus, to the very moment of his death? Could we have here a counterweight to the skeptical conclusions of many modern interpreters? If not, how do we make sense of this material? Would we have to characterize it as fiction and, therefore, without significance for our investigation of FE's historical interest? A detailed analysis of this passage will move us toward the answers to these questions.

John 19:31–37 forms a distinct section in the Johannine passion narrative. The Jews initiate action by asking Pilate to perform the *crurifragium* (breaking the legs of crucified victims) to finish off the condemned and remove them before the Sabbath begins. The soldiers proceed to break their legs, but coming to Jesus last of all they find him already dead. Nevertheless, one soldier pierces his side with a lance. There follows the assertion of eyewitness testimony and then two scriptural citations. John 19:38 begins a new section, telling of the burial of Jesus' corpse. The Johannine composition of 19:31–37 becomes evident when one notes that the entire crucifixion scene in FG is constructed as a chiasmus (A–B–C–D–C′–B′–A′):

A 19:16b-19   crucifixion site; two other victims; death inscription cited
  B 19:20–22   Jews, Pilate
    C 19:23–24   crucifixion site; Jesus' clothes; scripture citation
      D 19:25–27   crucifixion site; Jesus' mother; Beloved Disciple
    C′19:28–30   crucifixion site; Jesus' thirst; Jesus' death; scripture mentioned
  B′19:31   Jews, Pilate
A′19:32–37   crucifixion site; *crurifragium*; scripture cited

From this outline we can see that John 19:31–37 actually includes two scenes in the larger passion sequence of FG. FE has constructed 19:31, the discussion between the Jews and Pilate about killing the crucified victims quickly, to provide the reason for the action of 19:32–37 (breaking their legs), where the intent of the Jews is ironically worked out. John 19:32–37 not only frustrates the attempt to get rid of the troublesome Jesus but also provides ironic insight, for the events become revelatory in the eyes of the witness and through the words of scripture. While some commentators see nothing intrinsically improbable with the scene, others have debated whether there might have been redactional insertions (such as vv. 34b–35).

In order to evaluate further the tradition history of John 19:31–37, it will be helpful to compare FE's account with other versions of the *crurifragium*. While there is no parallel to John 19:31–37 in the Synoptic Gospels, the Gospel of Peter has a similar scene:

> [1] And they brought two criminals and crucified the Lord between them, but he himself remained silent, as if in no pain. And when they set up the cross, they put an inscription on it, "This is the king of Israel." [3] And they piled his clothing in front of him; then they divided it among themselves, and gambled for it. [4] But one of those criminals reproached them and said, "We're suffering for the evil that we've done, but this fellow, who has become a savior of humanity, what has he done to you?" [5] And they got angry at him and ordered that his legs not be broken so he would die in agony. (Gos. Pet. 4:1–4)

While some have dismissed Gospel of Peter's account as secondary and therefore unworthy of serious consideration (Brown 1994, 2.1317–49), it is difficult to conclude that this section is dependent on FG—even in a "confused" state. There is no residue of distinctive Johannine language. Nor is there any divergence from the main action, such as the FG scene that shifts the focus away from the crucifixion site by having the Jews go to Pilate (John 19:20–22). On the other hand, one can argue that FE drew on Peter in this instance (Crossan 1995, 141); Gospel of Peter 4:4 may well be part of the earliest layer of this fragmentary Gospel (A. Dewey 1998, 62). If FE knew Peter, we can note that he follows Peter's order of events except for the *crurifragium*. The order of events is as follows: crucifixion between two criminals (4:1); the inscription (4:2); division and gambling for clothing (4:3); the criminal's defense of Jesus (4:4); not breaking Jesus' legs (4:5); giving a drink to Jesus (5:2); Jesus' death (5:5b). FG follows this order exactly except for the bone-breaking reference, which FE puts after the death of Jesus. Such a move fits the redactional tendency of FG. FG follows Peter in not having any mockery of Jesus during the crucifixion, in contrast to Mark 15:27–32 and parallels, but adds the scene in which the Jews go to Pilate to protest the death inscription and request its removal (John 19:21–22). But if FE knew this portion of Peter (or an earlier edition thereof), then we can no longer consider the FG material as pure eyewitness, for FE would be constructing this scene from an earlier source. Indeed, the discrepancies between the Gospel of Peter and FG would suggest a significant revision of the earlier material.

That FE's account of Jesus' death is indeed a development of earlier material

is further evident from the role scripture plays in the narrative. Many scholars
would suggest that the earliest layer of traditions concerning the death of Jesus
was created by historicizing OT prophecies, and that this prophetic tradition
was later developed into a single extended story through the narrative pattern
of "The Suffering and Vindication of the Innocent One" (see Crossan 1995,
1; A. Dewey 1990, 108). If this is the case, then what we find in John 19:31–37
must represent an advanced stage in the development of the passion story. For
here the citations of scripture are connected directly to the developing narrative tradition, thereby augmenting it and causing further interpretive growth.
As the previous outline indicates, "what is written" has a decisive part to play
in FE's construction. The ironic inscription on the cross ("Jesus of Nazareth,
the King of the Jews") provides the climax to the first scene and brings the Jews
in protest to Pilate. Scenes C and C' move along "in fulfillment of scripture."
Scene A' ends with a double citation that builds on the citation in Scene A and
adds what appear to be prophetic applications of scripture. Furthermore,
Scene B is replayed in Scene B' when the Jews return to Pilate to request the
quick removal of the victims. In the latter scene Pilate yields to their request,
which, in turn, has additional ironic twists.[1] Brown has suggested that the
scripture citations in John 19 did not give rise to the episode but were added
later to bring out its theological depth (Brown 1994, 2.1179). But it is equally
reasonable to suggest that the Beloved Disciple's testimony in v. 35 is a later
insertion into a scene that had already been generated from the scriptural quotations in vv. 36–37.

Some would defend the veracity of John 19:35 by pointing to the presence
of the Beloved Disciple at the foot of the cross at 19:25–27. It is commonly
held that BD is also the "witness" referred to in 19:35. Brown, for example,
asserts that attempts to identify "that one" who testifies as FE, Jesus Christ, or
God fail to make sense. Since no other disciple has been mentioned at the foot
of the cross, "that one" (ekeinos) must refer to BD. And while Brown can
declare that 19:25–27 (where Jesus tells BD to care for his mother) symbolically represents the relationship between men and women within the Johannine Community, he continues to insist that BD was a real person who was
actually present at the crucifixion. Any attempt to explain BD's "witness" as a
symbolic dramatization suited to FE's theological purpose is, in Brown's view,
"implausible." He adds that such interpretations are "highly speculative" and
more the result of the "interpreter's ingenuity than of the evangelist's plan"
(Brown 1970, 2.936–944). In truth, Brown's reading is a desperate attempt to
retain the historicity of the Johannine crucifixion scene. If such eyewitness testimony about the death of Jesus were available, how is it that this witness finds
no parallel in any of the other gospels? For this reason, many scholars conclude that both references to the Beloved Disciple at the foot of the cross,
19:25–27 and 19:35, are FE's own creations.

Anticipatory Memory

The above reading of John 19 obviously suggests that FE's definition of "eye-witness testimony" would not be in line with the modern understanding of that term. It seems clear that FE's crucifixion story, the very point where the validity of the Beloved Disciple's witness is stressed, has been developed from other sources in line with certain OT prophetic themes. If this is the case, what does FE mean when he says that BD "witnessed" these events? To answer this question, it will be necessary to analyze other passages in FG that address the issues of "seeing" and "remembering," and to observe how these experiences connect with scripture.

"Seeing" in FG

The first mention of the "beloved" or "other" disciple comes in John 1:35–40. Both Andrew and the "other" disciple are challenged by Jesus to "come and see" (v. 39). This scene comes directly after John the Baptist declares in the first person that he had seen and testified (perfect tense; v. 34), a declaration which mirrors 19:35a. It should be pointed out that the Baptist states that he utters these words under the impulse of the "one who sent him to baptize with water" (v. 33). His ability to see "the spirit coming down" upon Jesus connects with this divine impetus. Thereupon, he "saw and testified."

The notion of "seeing Jesus" continues to be a complicated affair in John 12:20–28. The simple request by some Greeks to see Jesus receives a response that is hardly simple. First, Jesus says that the "time" (*hōra*) has come for the glorification of the Son of Man (v. 23). As is well known, "glorification" in FG points to the revelatory aspect of the death of Jesus. The proverbial saying about the death of a kernel of wheat promising a great harvest continues to underline Jesus' fate. Verse 25 adds a paradoxical saying that twists the meanings of "death" and "life," and the next verse implicates the person addressed by reading in the fate of Jesus. Finally, verses 27–28 appear to be a Johannine revision of the Gethsemane scene (cf. Mark 14:36). In sum, the quest to "see" Jesus here meets a layered response. The various oblique sayings, centering around the death of Jesus, appear to unpack the depths of potential meaning behind "seeing" him.

In the resurrection material we see a further nuancing of the notion of "seeing." Upon "seeing" inside the empty tomb, BD "saw and believed" (both aorist tense; John 20:8). The following verse (20:9) is not clear at first glance. What did BD "see and believe" if the disciples "did not understand the scripture, that he must rise from the dead"? It would seem that BD had "seen" that Jesus, as Son of the Father, had returned to the Father. The Johannine version of Jesus' fate appears to enter here. Curiously, even here there is an

66 Arthur J. Dewey

anticipatory sense to this "seeing": it still awaits further connection with the scriptures.

Finally, in John 20:29 we find the emphasis now placed on those who come to believe without seeing. This is not in the same league as the previous passages. The intent here appears to be to establish a legitimate connection with the later generations of the community, Johannine Christians who have believed in Jesus even though they never saw him alive. As elsewhere in FG, "seeing" here is not a matter of physical contact, but rather of insight into a deeper understanding (cf. John 9:41).

Memory and Scripture

The three passion predictions in FG carry a distinct nuance. John 3:14, playing on the image of Moses lifting up the bronze serpent for all to see and be healed, focuses on the "elevation of the Son of Man" so that, by believing, people can have real life. In John 8:28, Jesus declares that when he is "elevated" people will know that "I Am." The death of Jesus thereby becomes a means of revealing the divine name (*ego eimi*). Finally, in John 12:32–34 Jesus declares that, when "lifted up," he will be the focal point for all. In sum, instead of predicting the fate of Jesus, the Johannine passion sayings throw the audience forward in anticipation. By the time one comes to the death scene, the audience has been tutored into seeing Jesus' death as a revelation of God.

The Temple Incident in John 2 is distinct not only because of its early placement in the narrative. Unlike the parallel in Mark 11:17, where Jesus himself refers directly to scripture to explain his actions, the Johannine version has an editorial sidebar (2:17) that describes the disciples being "reminded" of the words of scripture (Ps. 69:9). The next three verses present the Jews' challenge and Jesus' response, which becomes the occasion for further editorial elaboration. After Jesus had been raised from the dead, the disciples, remembering his words, came to "believe the scripture" and what Jesus had said (2:22). "Memory" in this case is quite complex, entailing a curious juxtaposition of the sacred writings and the words of Jesus.

In the scene detailing Jesus' entrance into Jerusalem, we find not only embedded scriptural citations (John 12:13, 15) but also another editorial remark quite similar to 2:22: "His disciples did not understand these things at first; but when Jesus was glorified, then they remembered that these things had been written of him and had been done to him" (12:16). In this instance, however, what has happened is "matched" with the sacred writings. This echoes John the Baptist's testimony, where he connects his own act of baptizing with the divine signal of the Spirit's descent (1:33).

John 7:39 provides an editorial comment on the saying of Jesus (quoting scripture) in verse 38. Here the narrator wants to make clear that the "living water" to which Jesus refers is the Spirit. But it is important to note that the narrator also reminds the audience that the Spirit had not yet arrived because Jesus hadn't been glorified. Thus, there is a direct connection between the emergence of Spirit and the revelatory death of Jesus. Even Jesus' quotation of scripture is not comprehensible before this focal event.

The Johannine Paraclete, promised during the Farewell Address of Jesus (John 13–17), has distinct characteristics. It is a spirit of truth (14:17), causing the community to remember all that Jesus said (14:26; cp. Mark 13:11). "That" (*ekeinos*) spirit will testify about Jesus (15:26) and glorify (reveal) him (16:14). The Paraclete becomes the agent of memory, the spur generating the community's meaningful recollection of Jesus. The presence of the Paraclete justifies new and different understandings of Jesus as the community puts together the words and deeds of Jesus in juxtaposition with the sacred writings.

The "Witness"

Returning now to John 19:31–37, we can determine some significant fault lines. Verse 31 is clearly a Johannine construction, repeating, as noted above, 19:20–22. Verses 32–33 connect with the scriptural citation in verse 36, while verse 34 is tied in with the scripture in verse 37. One can see the possibility that the events in verses 32–34, the nonbreaking of Jesus' legs and the piercing of his side, were created to stress that Jesus' death fulfilled the scriptures cited in verses 36–37. This leaves verse 35, the statement concerning the legitimacy of BD's "witness." This verse appears to be a distinctive Johannine insertion: the perfect verbs recall 1:34; the verse brings in vocabulary from the Paraclete passages; the phrase "[its] his testimony is true" sounds very much like an editorial addition; the phrase "that [one] he knows that his [its] testimony is true" leads into the purpose of the testimony, namely, that the reader "may also believe," which is also FE's overall purpose in writing (John 20:30–31). Further, FE has made a definite advance over the way the synoptic evangelists connect events with scripture. Instead of simply historicizing scriptural citations, FE has placed verse 35 between verses 32–34 and verses 36–37. We have once again a combination of scene and sacred writing, but in this case verse 35 functions as the linchpin of this imaginative act. It declares that this combination of scene and scripture is revelatory, as we have seen anticipated in FG (John 2:22).

As for the identity of the "one who saw this [and] has testified," "that one" is not the Beloved Disciple found in 19:25–27. Rather, "that one" must be the Paraclete, who arrives at the moment of Jesus' glorification and reminds the reader of the truth of the revelation. The text, in effect, mirrors the creative recollection of scene and scripture in the mind of the audience. It deliberately delivers a mimetic presentation: anyone who closely follows the text can do what the text is doing. Each reader can connect these things in memory and become, thereby, a "witness" to Jesus.

For these reasons, we must conclude that FE does not share the modern definition of an "eyewitness" as an observer of a situation. Instead of a detached viewer, the Johannine eyewitness is someone who connects with the transmission of the Johannine tradition. Here we can begin to see the force of the use of the perfect tense in 19:35a: the vision and the testifying *have begun and continue to be in full effect*. The Johannine Paraclete is a projected symbol of visionary consciousness that allows what happened (Jesus' death) to become eventful for every believer. The scriptures speak loudly to those who have come to see this creative possibility.[2]

The Historical Interest
of the Fourth Evangelist

How does the writer of FG see "history"? It is as much *how* he sees as what he sees. The "how" for him involves participation in a historical event that is not over. Indeed, "history" becomes meaningful when the deeds of Jesus (in this case, his death) and scripture come together in remembrance. The one who "sees" the events is the Paraclete, not the Beloved Disciple (perhaps that is the cautionary note of John 20:9?). The recollection or rehearing of all the echoes in FG helps the reader/listener understand the message. Thus, the eyewitness account is not a simple report given by an individual. Rather, it is a revision through memory, enlisting both the Gospel story and the resources of Jewish scripture. The effect of this is that the eyewitness to the past is happening *now*. It is an ongoing eyewitnessing—open to all who come to share FE's collaborative vision.

The dilemma is often raised whether an event is an "eyewitness account" or a "fiction." But this dilemma is predicated on a modern concept of history and the role of the eyewitness in historical reporting. From this perspective, the interpreter might presume a prior layer of tradition before the composition of FG. This assures us that the canonical gospels have some sort of historical basis—a kernel of historical "truth." Such historical truth is usually identified through the limp argument that something which is not implausible and carries a general verisimilitude might have really happened. Unfortunately, this usually means that the historian of religion is begging the question, presuming rather than determining the facticity of the material under consideration. The presupposition of some earlier foundational source material behind FG may be only that—especially if one is presuming some sort of factual basis. It curiously discounts the layers of tradition that have their own structure and agenda. It may overlook the necessity to see how the scriptural citation tradition got started and continued to grow. In short, such a presumption is a reflection of the modern imagination that does not ask about the texture and development of the text. What is the very nature of the evidence? To say something is plausible only means that it is possible, not that it happened. Moreover, one may well miss the way in which the ancient writer imagined or saw history.

So, if one asks if John 19:31–37 actually happened, the answer usually given starts with the presumption that this is the eyewitness account of the Beloved Disciple. But that begs the question whether BD was even present at the death of Jesus. It avoids asking broad questions about the nature of the evidence that is available, and instead moves directly to the particular facets of the case: Was there any such matter of *crurifragium* or a piercing of Jesus' side? One standard answer is that these elements of the story are historically plausible. Therefore, the rash conclusion comes: it is historical. But, if this is the only instance of the piercing of Jesus' side, how certain can one be? If the bone-breaking material is taken over from the Gospel of Peter, then there has been a decided revision. This line of questioning may lead to the opposite conclusion: because these events did not occur, they are a fiction. And this in turn leads to historical meaninglessness. Such conclusions will be reached if one sticks solely to the "facts," to a view of historical reconstruction that does not take into consideration that the evidence might demand more work. What if the meaning of "eyewitness" in FG is not some sort of simple report? And what if FE's understanding forces us to revise how we understand the writer's vision of history (and creative consciousness)?

We have argued that John 19:31–37 is not a simple observation of events involving Jesus. If the Gospel of Peter was used by FE, then it is not a question of eyewitness in the modern sense. The notion of eyewitness in FG takes on a distinctive character: an eyewitness "sees," but it is a multifaceted envisioning. Just as the miracles of Signs Gospel have been adapted and turned into epiphanies of an incarnate deity by FE, so also the function of the Baptizer in FG turns now upon his revelatory role. The death of Jesus is *the* focal point of FG. The three Johannine passion predictions anticipate this revelatory vision. An eyewitness has to be there at the crucifixion site. For the meaning of the death of Jesus only comes to light through this active envisioning—through the eyewitness.

Visionary Consciousness and the Creation of Experience

The ancients did not have words for the notion of the creation of experience. This does not mean that they were not creative. But there had to have been some sort of divine breakthrough for the ancient reader to understand that a change had occurred in one's understanding, a dramatic change in significance, in meaning. The presence of the divine signals for the ancient mind what we today would term a "transformation of consciousness." This transformation was then projected onto their world of meaning.

The eyewitness of FG was the eyewitness of history, but for FE "history" was not something given and finished. Instead, the presence of the Paraclete allowed FE to see the concussive effect of event and tradition. An eyewitness is one who has made the connection. For the first century, this was tantamount to declaring that consciousness could be visionary and that historical interest was found precisely in that creative chemistry of remembrance.

Notes

1. Only Scene D has no explicit connection with what is "written," nor with the Jews and Pilate; it provides instead the center point of the story, focusing on the self-giving ideal of mother and son in the face of death.

2. FG is not alone in speaking of eyewitnesses. First Corinthians 15:3–8 provides witnesses to the postmortem visions. Yet it seems that it is the later NT works (Luke–Acts, John, 2 Peter) that are concerned with eyewitnesses. This may well be due to the issues emerging toward the end of the first century. It has been long argued that the question of eyewitness surfaced due to the deaths of the original generation of disciples. Moreover, the delay of the expected Second Coming may have triggered some doubt among the communities. In addition, the rising Gnostic debates over the true successor of the apostolic witnesses may have been the occasion for the Johannine language.

    On the other hand, such ecclesial and political questions, although very important, may be a red herring for understanding the notion of "eyewitness" in FG. The concern over authoritative leadership and succession may well be a later phenomenon. We must resist reading the agenda of the second and third centuries into the first. On the other hand, the Gnostic claim of delivering the resurrection vision from teacher to student may have some connection to what we are investigating in John. Yet, we must be careful not to conclude that this second-century debate determines the Johannine understanding of "eyewitness." In fact, it might have been the Johannine sense of "eyewitness" that is reflected in the subsequent debate over authentic resurrection visions.

6

The Historical
Reliability of John

Rushing in Where Angels Fear to Tread?

CRAIG L. BLOMBERG

The last twenty years have generated the so-called "third quest of the historical Jesus," which has recovered a substantial optimism concerning the historical reliability of the main contours of the Synoptic Gospels and has placed Jesus squarely within an early first-century Palestinian Jewish milieu. For slightly longer, "the new look on John" has equally stressed the Jewish backgrounds of the author, audience, and issues involved with the Fourth Gospel (FG). But for the most part, these two bodies of scholarship have not intersected. When they have, the obvious differences between John and the Synoptics have led many to conclude that they cannot both be historical. If the overall synoptic portrait of Jesus is largely reliable, then John has created a theological and literary interpretation of Christ that much less closely corresponds to the actual Jesus of history. Or, with a minority of scholars, if a number of the places John goes his separate way show signs of authenticity, then John's picture must be accepted at the Synoptics' expense. I have elsewhere addressed in book-length form the broad question of the historical reliability of the gospels, and I, too, focused primarily on the Synoptics, with only one chapter that sketched out some possibilities for appreciating FG's historicity (Blomberg 1987). With even less space available in this essay, I will briefly summarize and update some of my findings.

Introductory Considerations

Although critical scholarship widely rejects John the apostle, son of Zebedee, as author of the Fourth Gospel, current study increasingly acknowledges the

71

author to be a Jew steeped in accurate knowledge of the customs of Judaism and the topography of Palestine at the time of Jesus. One detailed, recent study of this "Johannine question" concludes that the author is the "Beloved Disciple" of John's narrative, a Palestinian Jew, an eyewitness to Jesus' ministry, and an old man writing to the Ephesian church at the end of the first century, precisely as the dominant strand of early church tradition alleges (Hengel 1989).

In fact, the classic arguments of B. F. Westcott for apostolic authorship based on the internal data of FG—"John" is a Jew, a Palestinian, an eyewitness, an apostle, and the son of Zebedee (1908, x–lii)—have never been convincingly refuted. One of the main reasons for not equating the apostle John with the author of FG is his apparently greater knowledge of Judea than of Galilee and his access to the high priest's courtyard (John 18:15). But this underestimates the amount of contact a well-to-do fisherman with relatives of priestly lineage could have had with Judea and powerful circles within that province. This point has been made well by James H. Charlesworth (1995, 55–57), who, ironically, argues for Thomas as the Beloved Disciple, a view almost without parallel in church history. Yet Charlesworth does not present Westcott's full argument, or any of its detailed, contemporary elaboration by Domingo Munoz Leon (1987, 403–492), so he can hardly be said to have disproved traditional claims of authorship. We must allow, therefore, for the very real possibility that the primary author of this Gospel relied on his own memory for a considerable amount of its material, even as its form may reflect decades of homiletical use and stylization.

Now, apostolic authorship in no way precludes other kinds of tradition-critical development. Rudolf Bultmann's (1971) famous hypotheses of a signs source, discourse source, and passion source, edited and overlaid by the corrections and substantial rearrangements of an ecclesiastical redactor, have largely and correctly fallen on hard times. The stylistic unity and the coherence of the sequence of the twenty-one chapters as they stand is pervasive. The Fourth Evangelist (FE) may well have used sources, but it is doubtful if we can reconstruct them. At the same time, the references in John 21:24–25 to "we" and "I" who attest to the veracity of the Beloved Disciple's witness most naturally suggest one final stage of redaction. And the discussion of the fates of Peter and "John" in the preceding verses (vv. 20–23) makes good sense on the assumption that the Beloved Disciple had recently died. But these verses cohere with the "rivalry" between the two disciples throughout both chapters 20 and 21. And almost everyone agrees that chapter 20 is an integral part of the whole Gospel, even while many relegate chapter 21 to a later redactor. So it is worth considering if the entire book may have gone through final editorial work just after the Beloved Disciple's death, with 21:24 preserving the conviction that the redactor has remained faithful to the contents and truthfulness of what that disciple initially wrote.

In addition to authorship and sources, the question of literary genre bears heavily on historicity. On the one hand, FG supplies more incidental references to details of time, place, appearance, and emotion than do the Synoptics, which naturally suggests eyewitness testimony or historical verisimilitude. For example, only from the Fourth Gospel do we learn of Christ's multiyear ministry. But we discover this information primarily from FE's references to Jesus journeying to the various Jewish feasts in Jerusalem. His purpose in recording these references is theological—to demonstrate Jesus as the fulfillment of the rituals and institutions of Judaism—an aim that itself requires that Jesus was indeed in Jerusalem on these occasions and said something like what is attributed to him there. But the ability to reconstruct a chronology of the life of Christ is a derivative byproduct that did not demonstrably motivate FE and thus was not likely fabricated.

On the other hand, several studies have noted that FE's style of history or biography is more akin to Greek drama, so that we should allow for an element of artistic license as he recounts the words and deeds of Jesus. This is particularly significant for interpreting the long discourses of Jesus in John. While longer than all but Matthew's five famous sermons of Christ in the Synoptics (themselves regularly assumed to be composite in nature), each exhibits an internal coherence that suggests careful composition and unity but perhaps as an "abstract" of much longer discourse and debate. Yet all these features fall well within the range of acceptably accurate historiography or biography by ancient Jewish and Greco-Roman criteria. It would be anachronistic to foist modern standards of precision on ancient texts (for further discussion see Blomberg 1993, 27–55).

The Differences between John
and the Synoptics

For many scholars, here is the real heart of the problem. It may be acceptable theoretically to allow that the author of the Fourth Gospel could have been in a position to preserve accurate historical information and that the process of composition and the literary genre chosen do not make it impossible to recover a significant amount of this information. But surely the Gospel of John is just too different from the Synoptics to accept both. As a partial reply, we may briefly expound four arguments.

First, the current generation of scholarship has indisputably demonstrated the theological and stylized nature of the Synoptics. They are every bit as selective and paraphrastic in what they report as FG, and they regularly rely on thematic as well as chronological outlines. Mark organizes the first half of his Gospel (Mark 1:1–8:30) by presenting brief units that collect together material of like form or content; Matthew alternates between narrative and discourse so that each consecutive pair of subsections presents parallel themes, while Luke organizes his information geographically to have Jesus minister exclusively in Galilee, then Samaria and Judea, and finally in Jerusalem. This outline sets up an inverted parallelism with Luke's structure for Acts, which describes selected early Christian ministry moving outward from Jerusalem to the ends of the earth (Acts 1:8). Thus a primary reason the Synoptics do not contain material from FG that we might assume would have been included if it actually happened (e.g., the resurrection of Lazarus—John 11) is that it simply does not fit into their outlines (see Blomberg 1997, 115–117, 126–129, 140–145).

Conversely, while the case for FG's literary independence from the Synoptics seems to be firmly established, FE clearly presupposes his audience's familiarity with a relatively detailed summary of the life of Christ, perhaps even the Gospel of Mark itself, and chooses to supplement rather than repeat the majority of this information (Bauckham 1998, 147–171). Thus we learn of Jesus' public ministry prior to the major period of his itinerant teaching in Galilee (John 2–4; but cf. Luke 4:44), his numerous trips to Jerusalem at festival times (John 5–11; but cf. Mark 14:49, 58), and extensive additional teaching in and around the upper room on the last night of his life (John 13–17).

The Synoptics' portrait of Jesus has often been taken to be closer to the historical Jesus simply because we have three accounts that are more similar than dissimilar to one another. But precisely because of their literary interrelationship, when the Synoptics triply attest something they count only as one independent witness. It is far more likely, if one could reconstruct a more fully-orbed life of Christ using a modern historical genre with contemporary standards of precision, that in many respects it would appear as close to (or as far from) the common synoptic portrait as that of the Fourth Gospel (cf. John 21:25). Second, there *are* Johannine distinctives that seem further removed from Jesus' Jewish milieu precisely because FE masterfully models the early Christian practice of contextualizing the gospel. Mark 10:24 and 30 demonstrate that "Kingdom of God" and "eternal life" could be used synonymously, so it should not surprise us to find the Synoptics using the former term more often while FE prefers the latter. Here the Synoptics may preserve a more "literal" translation of Jesus' words, but FG faithfully represents Jesus' intention by employing an expression that was meaningful in the world of Greco-Roman thought in ways that speaking of God's theocratic kingship (a distinctively Jewish concept) was not.

Or, again, consider the famous "Johannine thunderbolt" (Matt. 11:25–27; Luke 10:21–22). When Jesus in Q praises his Father for hiding spiritual truths from the seemingly wise and learned but revealing them to "children," when he speaks of God's good pleasure and how the Father has committed to him all

things and how no one knows the Son but the Father and those to whom the
Son chooses to reveal him, he uses language and articulates a significant cluster of themes that are pervasive in the Fourth Gospel but otherwise rare in the
Synoptics. Clearly one of FG's major emphases is to portray Jesus as akin to
divine Wisdom, a concept rooted in Proverbs and intertestamental Wisdom literature and thus both thoroughly Jewish and conceivable on the lips of Jesus
(see esp. Witherington 1995). But *sophia* (the Greek word for "wisdom") also
played an important role in the emerging Gnosticism that seems to have threatened the Johannine Community. So, if it is plausible to imagine Jesus speaking
this way more often than the Synoptics disclose, it is equally reasonable to imagine the Fourth Evangelist wanting to preserve larger quantities of this teaching
to counter the heterodox conviction that anyone or anything other than Jesus
himself embodies God's unique self-revelation. The differences between Jesus'
and FE's environments probably account also for the noteworthy omission of
Jesus' parables. FE obviously knows that Jesus regularly employed metaphor;
C. H. Dodd's attempts to discern kernel parables at the heart of many of Jesus'
discourses in John remains largely persuasive—for example, the apprentice's
son (John 5:19–20), the good shepherd (10:1–5), or the grain of wheat (12:24)
(1963, 366–387). But the closest generic parallels to the full-fledged parables of
the Synoptics come without exception in Jewish literature, including more than
two hundred parables from the earliest era of the rabbinic writings (the first
three centuries C.E.). Especially when one recognizes an opacity as well as a
transparency to these parables, it is not as surprising that FE did not choose to
include them for his primarily Greek audience in Ephesus.

A similar approach may explain the omission of the exorcisms. FE clearly articulates a theology of the devil (see esp. John 8:31–59) but probably recognizes that,
unlike Jesus' Palestinian world that apparently knew of other true, divinely
empowered, Jewish exorcists (Matt. 12:27), his Greco-Roman context believed
in opposing the devil primarily via means more magical than miraculous.

Third, numerous Johannine distinctives emerge directly from FE's theo-
logical agenda. It cannot be coincidental that FG says more about John the
Baptist and Jesus' relationship with him and more about Jesus' teaching on
"Maundy Thursday" than do any of the Synoptics, yet nowhere in FG does
the actual baptism of Jesus or institution of the Lord's Supper appear. The
Johannine Christians can scarcely not have known about these "sacraments";
John's deliberate omission seems best explained as a protest against a growing
institutionalization of the church at the end of the first century, complete with
an overemphasis on the spiritual value of baptism and the Eucharist. After all,
in the 90s we are a scant thirty years away from the ministry of Ignatius, complete with the monarchical episcopacy that his letters reflect.

Theology obviously accounts for FG's dramatically high Christology as well. This may be the single biggest difference with the Synoptics that prevents some from acknowledging a pervasive historical interest in the Fourth Gospel. Yet, on the one hand, we must not underestimate the high christology of the Synoptics—a person who is presented as virginally conceived, accepts worship, forgives sins, transcends the eternal Torah with his teaching, determines people's eternal destinies on judgment day, works miracles as demonstrations of the in-breaking Kingdom and the arrival of the messianic age, and who professes a uniquely intimate relationship with God is hardly the conventional militaristic and merely human messiah of important strands of intertestamental Jewish expectation (esp. the Psalms of Solomon; see Witherington 1990). And Richard Bauckham has recently stressed how from the earliest creedal elements in the Epistles through to the Gospel of John, the first Christians directly linked Jesus with Yahweh's divine identity in ways that contradict evolutionary hypotheses of a slow-developing early Christology (Bauckham 1999).

On the other hand, we must not overestimate how directly the Fourth Gospel equates Jesus with God. The seven distinctive "I am" sayings all involve metaphor (bread of life, light of the world, etc.), and even the famous declaration "Before Abraham was, I am" (John 8:58) is ambiguous enough to make it uncertain whether Jesus is alluding to the divine name of Exodus 3:14 or to Yahweh's numerous "I am he" statements in Isaiah. That various groups of Jews attempted to stone Jesus (John 8:59; 10:31) does not mean that they took him to have claimed to be Yahweh; the definitions of blasphemy were more fluid before 70 C.E. (Bock 1998). But the Johannine Jesus clearly did cross a certain perceived boundary in usurping divine prerogatives (John 10:33).

The cluster of christological confessions in John 1:41, 45, and 49 almost certainly reflect misguided enthusiasm on the part of the first disciples along the lines of conventional Jewish messianic expectation; as late in the narrative as 16:29–30 the disciples will claim that only now do they understand Jesus' true identity for the first time. Nor does Jesus' self-revelation to the Samaritan woman in 4:26 contradict his pattern of reluctance to reveal himself to the Jewish leaders in the Synoptics. It is precisely because of the distinctive Samaritan hope for a *Taheb* (more of a "teacher" or "restorer" than a military king) and because of all the ways this woman contrasts with the Jewish leaders in her powerless, outcast role that it is appropriate for Jesus to declare himself to her but not to others. And it must not be forgotten that FE's high Christology probably stems from his desire to begin from a position of common ground with his docetic opponents (cf. esp. Schnelle 1992); the climax of his Prologue (John 1:1–18) is not his opening gambit ("the Word was God"—v. 1) but his announcement of the incarnation (v. 14—"The Word became flesh").

A final reply involves the cautious use of a form of historical harmonization that is often unjustly ridiculed. For example, Maurice Casey's recent *Is John's Gospel True?* (1996, 4–29) begins by exploring the divergent accounts of the

Temple Incident in John and the Synoptics and the apparently discrepant chronologies of the Last Supper. Like many, Casey concludes that these "contradictions" are real and demonstrate the extent to which FE was prepared to play fast and loose with history. He pours scorn on writers like Carson, Morris, and me who suggest that plausible harmonizations are still possible. But even if we take FE on its own, we must conclude that "the day of preparation" (*paraskeue*) in John 19:31 and 42 refers to "Friday" as the preparation for the Sabbath, not for the initial Passover meal, so that the standard critical hypothesis that sees Jesus' death in the Fourth Gospel taking place *before* the beginning of Passover must give two different meanings to the same word in the same context. While 13:1 could suggest that FE thinks that the Thursday night meal precedes the Passover, it seems equally likely, after having said it was just before a certain feast and then referring to a solemn meal, that John intends his readers to understand that meal *as* the Passover. And while it is true that no known references exist for "Passover" referring solely to a meal during Passover week later than the initial one, 18:28 may simply be referring to the entire week-long festival as a whole (Carson 1991, 590).

As for the Temple Incident, Casey fails to mention that I give equal credence to the view that John has thematically relocated this passage as a headline to the first major section of his Gospel (Blomberg 1987, 171) On the other hand, reading FG on its own would suggest that John intends a straightforward chronological sequence here (cf. John 2:23 with 3:22), and the reference to building the Temple for forty-six years (2:20) points to a date in 28 C.E. (Josephus, *AJ* 15.380), which cannot be the date of Christ's death (30 or 33 C.E.) on anybody's system! Whether we then favor FG at the expense of the Synoptics is another matter, but it cannot fairly be claimed that the proposed harmonization violates standard historical methodology.

Interlocking between John and the Synoptics

This last issue illustrates another oft-neglected feature of the "John vs. the Synoptics" debate known as "interlocking": texts in the Fourth Gospel that presuppose information that FE does not supply but that appears in the Synoptics, or vice versa (Morris 1969, 40–63). For example, only the Synoptics narrate the false allegation at the Sanhedrin trial that Jesus threatened to destroy the Temple (Mark 14:58 par.), while only FG describes a statement of Jesus before the Jewish leaders susceptible to such misinterpretation (John 2:19). And if indeed the two incidents were separated by at least two years, it becomes much clearer how his words could have been so misconstrued.

Other examples of FG providing data that illuminate synoptic events may be briefly noted. The call of the first disciples seems very abrupt and unmotivated in Mark 1:16–20 pars., but if several of the Twelve had prior exposure to Jesus, especially in conjunction with the Baptist's ministry (John 1:35–51), their ready response becomes more intelligible. The Messianic Secret theme, especially in Mark, has puzzled many, and a standard explanation has often involved an appeal to Jewish expectations of a regal or militaristic messiah, but the genuine danger of Jesus being forced to become an earthly king appears only in John 6:15. John 11 offers helpful detail to account for the close relationship presupposed between Jesus and Mary of Bethany in Luke 10:38–42, which otherwise stands out strikingly with him allowing her to assume the formal posture of a disciple learning from a rabbi, contra dominant Jewish tradition. And John 11:45–57, 18:31, and 19:12 all provide needed rationale to explain details of the synoptic passion narrative that otherwise appear unmotivated: the depth of Caiaphas's hostility toward Christ and vendetta to see him executed, the reason the Jewish leaders would involve Pilate, and a motive for Pilate eventually succumbing to the demands of the Jews.

In even more instances the Fourth Evangelist presupposes knowledge of a synoptic-like *kerygma* on the part of his readers. He introduces John without calling him the Baptist or ever actually describing his ministry of baptism; in 1:26 John himself refers to it as if it is already understood. In 3:24, the author explains that a certain conversation occurred before John was imprisoned, but nowhere in FG does he narrate that imprisonment (but see Mark 6:14–29 pars.). In 11:2 he introduces Mary of Bethany as the same woman who had poured perfume on the Lord and anointed him with her hair. But he will not relate this story until 12:1–8. Perhaps this is mere foreshadowing, but it reads more naturally as a way to distinguish this Mary from the others well known in early Christianity, with FE realizing that his listeners would have already heard her story. Indeed, Mark 14:9 explicitly declares that Jesus promised that her behavior would be recounted as part of that common *kerygma* preached wherever the Gospel was proclaimed. Finally, the passing references to Jesus' trial before Caiaphas in John 18:24 and 28 are so brief as to be meaningless, unless one already knows something of the account that Mark 14:53–65 narrates in much more detail.

There is no question that conservative scholars have proposed improbable harmonizations of seemingly discrepant biblical parallels in their eagerness to avoid declaring a text in error. But harmonization, even of the straightforward "additive" kind (two texts each give partial treatment of a fuller original), is a standard tool of historians who would reconstruct what most likely happened in antiquity, so the method may not be jettisoned simply because of periodic abuse (Blomberg 1995b, 135–174). When one observes repeated, clear examples of the interlocking between John and the Synoptics, one actually is encouraged to consider whether harmonization may not best deal with other more ambiguous texts as well.

Criteria of Authenticity

Considerable methodological improvements have been made recently in the standard criteria of authenticity used in NT scholarship. Instead of four separate criteria—dissimilarity, multiple attestation, Palestinian environment, and coherence—we may now profitably speak of two foundational criteria: (1) multiple attestation within and outside the canon (when sources have genuinely been demonstrated to be independent of each other), including attestation of themes and forms as well as words and events (Thiessen and Merz 1998, 116–117); and (2) double similarity and dissimilarity from both conventional early first-century Judaism and later post-Easter Christianity (Wright 1996, 131–133). But a full-scale application of these criteria to the Gospel of John, passage by passage, has yet to appear. I hope to produce something along these lines in a forthcoming work; here I can only sketch sample applications.

John 2:1–11 narrates one of the Fourth Gospel's unique miracle stories—Jesus' turning water into wine. Yet form-critically, it is a gift-miracle, matching the feeding of the five thousand, the only miracle to appear in all four canonical gospels (Mark 6:30–44 pars.). In terms of its symbolism, like many of the nature miracles, it closely parallels the meaning of a synoptic parable or metaphor with similar imagery, in this case Jesus' teaching on new wine demanding new wineskins (Mark 2:21–22 pars.; Blomberg 1986, 327–359). Thus by the expanded definition of multiple attestation, this miracle is precisely the type of thing we should expect the historical Jesus to have performed.

Similar arguments may be advanced for the authenticity of the miracles in John 5:1–15 and 9:1–12. The healing of the invalid by the pool of Bethesda in the former passage closely resembles both the form and content of the healing of the paralytic in Mark 2:1–12 pars., with Jesus giving the identical command, "Rise, take up your bed and walk," in both episodes (John 5:8; Mark 2:11). Both passages also meld healing with controversy; in the one case about the Sabbath (a characteristic issue of division between Jesus and the Jewish leaders throughout the Synoptics as well); in the other case about Jesus' authority to forgive sins. The two events are clearly separate, and there is little possibility of FG's direct, literary dependence on the Synoptics, but the similarities are sufficient to vouchsafe the authenticity of the Fourth Evangelist's account. So also the healing of the man born blind in John 9 parallels the frequent healings of blind men in the Synoptics, even down to the use of spittle on the eyes and the need for a "second stage" of the miracle (cf. Mark

8:22–26). And both Mark and John, in their own ways, juxtapose reflection on the comparison between physical and spiritual blindness and sight (Mark 8:27–33; John 9:13–41).

The double similarity and dissimilarity criterion is profitably applied to Jesus' dialogue with Nicodemus (John 3:1–15). The setting and contents are thoroughly Jewish—a leading Pharisee interrogates the upstart Jesus in Jerusalem, and Jesus replies by alluding to the spiritual cleansing of Ezekiel 36:24–36, but in an unprecedented way by requiring even the "holiest" within Israel to undergo a new birth. The text has been precious and influential in Christian history, but already in its second generation people were wrestling with how to treat those "born" into the faith and holding up Nicodemus as a model convert, whereas in this text the dialogue ends with his simply not understanding (Blomberg 1995a, 1–15). The lengthy dialogues between Jesus and the Jerusalemites in John 7–8 may be similarly analyzed. His two central claims to offer living water and light for the world (7:27–28 and 8:12) mesh perfectly with the timing and contents of the Tabernacles' water-drawing ceremonies and service of darkness in the Temple (after the previous days' candelabra-lighting ritual; cf. *Sukkah* 5:1–4). But his personal claims astound and divide the leaders and crowds alike. Later Christians would pick up on this "high Christology" but often lose sight of the pervasive theme of Christ's subordination to the Father, as Jesus repeatedly stresses that he is merely an agent who does the will of the one who sent him (7:16–17, 28; 8:14–19, 26–29, 42, 50, 54). The latter theme was not likely a later fabrication, but it is inextricably intertwined with Jesus' other claims in ways that suggest the whole passage is both unified and authentic.

One final illustration considers a text in which FG clearly adds material to a shorter narrative that is paralleled in the Synoptics—Jesus' bread-of-life discourse after the miracles of the loaves and the walking on water (John 6:25–59). Here we are indebted to Peder Borgen's famous analysis (1965) of the discourse as a tightly unified midrash on the Old Testament texts discussed. What is often not noted, because of the compartmentalization of scholarship, is that the form is very similar to the proem midrash of several of Jesus' parables in the Synoptics (e.g., Luke 10:25–37; Mark 12:1–12 pars.). The Jewish form and contents support authenticity even of John's unique material. But, once again, Jesus' claims are unprecedented. And later Christian theologizing quickly focused on possible eucharistic overtones in verses 53–58, notwithstanding the fact that verse 63 suggests that Jesus himself may have been protesting against the anticipated institutionalization of the church, as indeed happened at the end of the first century, moving in the directions of sacramental regeneration. The appropriate combinations of double similarity and double dissimilarity are once again present.

Final Reflections and Conclusions

Space prohibits treatment of numerous other important topics. FE's familiarity with the customs of Judaism and the topography of Palestine, especially Jerusalem, have been regularly noted. The occasional, apparent exceptions to this accuracy can in fact be plausibly explained in ways that do not validate charges of historical error (see Carson 1991; Bruce 1983; Morris 1995). A growing appreciation for FE's literary artistry explains other anomalies—for example, his use of irony in presupposing that his audience knows what some of the Jewish leaders do not, namely that Christ was born in Bethlehem in Judea rather than in Galilee (7:42, 52). It is hardly plausible that any prominent Christian by the end of the first century would not have known of Jesus' birthplace!

J. Louis Martyn's (1979) famous "two-level" reading of the Fourth Gospel raises another important cluster of questions that bear on historicity. There is no question that FE writes with an eye on the circumstances of his community, selecting and tailoring his material to address external Jewish polemic and internal incipient Gnosticizing. But FE also leaves numerous signs that he is not confusing pre-Easter history with post-Easter theology when he includes remarks like 2:22: "After he was raised from the dead, his disciples recalled what he had said. Then they believed the Scripture and the words that Jesus had spoken" (cf. 7:39; 12:16; 16:12–13).

As for the supposed anachronism of Jews excommunicating Jewish Christians from the synagogue during Jesus' lifetime (John 9:22 and 12:42), a situation that has been said to prevail only after the curse on the heretics (*Birkhat ha-Minim*) introduced into the synagogue liturgy in the late first century, two lines of reply must be pressed. First, a growing number of scholars argues that no such curse was ever invoked empire-wide at one fixed time. Second, if even the broadest contours of the Synoptics and Acts are accepted as historical, Jesus and the first disciples experienced the greatest hostility from limited, local, and informal actions by various Jewish authorities. Given Jerusalem as the center of the most conservative Judaism of Jesus' day, it is not at all implausible that small-scale policies of disfellowshipping should have begun here, especially as the hostility mounted that would eventuate in Jesus' crucifixion. And the Fourth Gospel itself observes that this will primarily occur after his death (16:2).

Additional discussion needs to supplement the main points we have considered. Apostolic authorship does not guarantee an accurate memory, while the conservative nature of Jewish oral tradition makes it quite possible that a second-generation author could have penned FG in a historically reliable fashion. For all the differences between John and the Synoptics, we must not overlook a large number of similarities not discussed here (see Blomberg 1987, 156–159). Given all the examples of "interlocking," we must leave room for the view that certain pairs of apparent parallels not discussed in this essay (e.g., John 4:43–54 and Matt. 8:5–13 par.) are actually separate but similar episodes that FE may have partially stylized to draw attention to the similarities. They do not, however, allow us to assume the radical redactional freedom on his part that would be the case if both narratives reflected the same incident. For all of the Hellenistic parallels that can be drawn, and for all of the stylistic freedom that FE used to impose his own consistent, linguistic stamp on his material, there is no pericope in the Fourth Gospel that does not reflect early first-century Jewish background of the type one would expect from information about the historical Jesus. Johannine scholarship has increasingly recognized this and focused on putative early Jewish-Christian stages and even Palestinian locations of the Johannine Community. But the time has come for Johannine scholars to push back one stage further and ask the question many students of the Synoptics have raised of Matthew, Mark, and Luke: Does an origin with the unique genius of the historical Jesus not account for the bulk of John's material better than a Jewish-community formulation in the early church, which was subdivided into numerous subjectively identified strata?

To be sure, John 14:26 and 15:26 suggest that the Fourth Evangelist believed he was inspired by the Spirit to recount these events, and such perceived inspiration undoubtedly gave him certain freedoms to retell things as he presently understood the significance of the past. But if this freedom extended to the actual invention or falsification of history, he would scarcely have described the Spirit's ministry as not only "teaching the disciples all things" but also reminding them "of everything I have said to you" (14:26). And the pervasive themes of "witness" and "truth," made all the more poignant by the Hebrew "lawsuit" form in which they appear to be couched (Harvey 1976), are very hard to square with an approach to the composition of the Fourth Gospel that finds John playing fast and loose with history, *by the standards of his day*, and believing this to be theologically acceptable.

7

Knowledge of Palestine
in the Fourth Gospel?

INGO BROER[1]

Now in Jerusalem by the Sheep Gate there is a pool, called in
Hebrew Bethzatha [Bethesda], which has five porticoes.

(John 5:2)

Christians of the first three centuries had practically no interest in the geographical sites of Jesus' activity and therefore were not concerned with the exact
settings of the traditional stories that made their way into the NT gospels. This
is clear in Mark 9:2, where the evangelist names the mountain of the transfiguration only in very general terms yet gives a precise temporal notice ("after six
days"). The same is true of the mountain where the risen Christ appears to the
eleven disciples in Matthew 28:16. Even in the case of Jesus' tomb, there is little concern for location. While the women see where Jesus is buried and can find
the place again on Easter morning (Mark 15:47; 16:1ff.), the evangelists nowhere
indicate where this place was—apart from the general mention of a garden in
John 19:41. In view of the gospels' relative lack of interest in concrete geographic
data, it is surprising that in the latest canonical gospel, John, there are a number
of details that reveal some interest in the places of Jesus' deeds and that reflect a
surprisingly exact knowledge of Palestinian geography. This is especially surprising in view of the particularly theological aim of the Fourth Gospel (FG),
which hints at symbolic worlds more often than the Synoptics and so gives an
impression even more "detached" and remote from Jesus than they.

In the literature on FG one finds a widespread opinion that the Fourth Evangelist (FE) evidences a precise knowledge of Palestinian places and Jewish customs, which some have used to support the notion that FE was familiar with
Palestine. Passages in FG often held to show such a knowledge of places and

customs include 1:28, 44; 2:6, 20; 3:23; 4:4–9, 20ff., 46–52; 5:2ff.; 6:1, 23; 7:2, 22ff., 37ff.; 10:22, 40; 11:54. Martin Hengel, for example, refers to Aramaic terms, names, and "astonishingly accurate geographical, historical and religious details, and . . . interesting information about Jewish customs and festivals" (1989, 110). Raymond Brown, in his commentary on John, writes of 4:51ff., "In going to Capernaum from Cana one must go east across the Galilean hills and then descend to the Sea of Galilee. The twenty-mile journey was not accomplished in one day, so it is the next day when the servants meet the official who had already begun the descent. These indications suggest that the author knew Palestine well" (1966, 1.191). And on 5:14 Brown says, "The pool [of Bethesda] lay just north-northeast of the temple area—another indication of the evangelist's knowledge of Jerusalem in the days before the Roman destruction" (1966, 1.208).

In response to Brown's reading, however, we must ask whether FE depended on an exact knowledge of the place. Did FE really know that the pool mentioned in John 5:2 was near the Temple, or does this reference reflect a more general literary motif based on broad generalities? Ancient towns were not big; there were usually temple installations, and the Temple of Jerusalem was widely known. Or, if this piece of information about the pool is indeed accurate, could it have come to the evangelist from another source? In any case, the healing in John 5:2 does include concrete details that raise questions about their historicity and their importance for FG.

John 5:2 and Ancient Jerusalem

Whether John 5:2 reflects FE's personal knowledge of events from the life of Jesus (as Brown suggests), or only goes back to traditions on which the author depends, is variously discussed in the scholarly literature. Quite a few authors attribute the healing story to a source (see Schnackenburg 1971, 117), but Hengel traces the remarks about places and customs to FE:

> [P]articularly in Jerusalem (but also in Samaria and even in Galilee) [FE] hands down astonishingly accurate geographical, historical and religious details, and adds interesting information about Jewish customs and festivals. . . . Probably these translations, interpretative remarks and geographical details had been part of the oral teaching of the author, who explained even Aramaic names to his audience. . . . As these notes relating to Judaism and his mother-country are very numerous . . . superficial experiences from a journey are no better an explanation than the unprovable hypothesis of an originally non-Johannine Jewish-Christian basic document (1989, 110).

The following examination of this problem assumes that John 5:2–9a is a traditional story. In 5:9b, as in 9:14, the motif of the Sabbath—the cause of the following dispute with "the Jews" (5:9b–6:1)—has obviously been added. Since

FE is especially interested in Jesus' stay in Jerusalem, we might ask if he has also added the mention of Jerusalem in 5:2. But it is verse 1 that introduces Jerusalem and the Jerusalem story that follows, chapter 4 having taken place in Galilee. So we have to assume that the extensive description of place in 5:2 was already to be found in FE's source. The question of reliability of the data of 5:2–9a is therefore a question of the reliability of the source(s) of FG and of the possibility that this source was of Palestinian provenance.

Sheep Pool or Sheep Gate?

One cannot attempt to analyze the statements in John 5:2, nor ask about FE's underlying knowledge of the place described, without addressing the text-critical problems this verse presents. In the first place, variants among the different manuscripts make it impossible to tell whether the adjective in 5:2a that derives from the noun "sheep" modifies the word "pool" that follows, or whether the author has simply omitted the noun that the adjective "sheep" modifies. If the latter, the noun to which the term "sheep" refers must be supplied to make sense of the phrase "whose name in the language of the Jews is Bethesda." The first solution to the puzzle can be found in the NEB: "Now at the *Sheep Pool* in Jerusalem there is a place with five colonnades. Its name in the language of the Jews is Bethesda." Here "sheep" modifies the pool at which the healing occurred, which is also called "Bethesda." The NRSV adopts the other alternative: "Now in Jerusalem by the *Sheep Gate* there is a pool, in Hebrew called Beth-zatha, which has five porticoes." Here the noun "gate" has been supplied by the translators and attached to the adjective, so that FE refers to both a gate *and* a pool in Jerusalem and calls the pool "Bethesda." The NRSV reading is justifiable because such a "sheep gate" did exist in Jerusalem. As a third possibility, FE may have two pools in mind, the "sheep pool" and the "Bethesda pool" ("in Jerusalem by the Sheep Pool there is a pool called Bethesda"). The question of which translation should be preferred is obviously important in determining the author's knowledge of Jerusalem's geography.

On this issue, Jeremias wrote in his widely influential study of 1966, "a decision as to which [translation] is the right one can be reached with certainty, predicated upon the fact that not one ancient writer, translator or pilgrim author has found a mention of a Sheep Gate in John 5:2. On the contrary, the ancient tradition unanimously speaks of the Sheep Pool. It is undoubtedly in this sense that John 5:2 must be understood" (pp. 10ff.; also Küchler 1999). Yet against this solution it seems necessary to raise two objections. First, must we really read "at the sheep pool" as Jeremias argues? As he correctly notes, there is no evidence that FE's phrase was understood to mean "at the sheep gate" in early Christian literature. In fact, such an interpretation is not found before the Middle Ages (Küchler 1999). But the third-century Christian authors no longer had precise geographic knowledge of first-century

Jerusalem (as we shall see later when discussing the question of the porticoes around the pool), and therefore the third- and fourth-century understanding of the text cannot determine what FE intended to say. Second, and more important, the adjective in question occurs three times in the LXX and exclusively in the expression "sheep gate" in reference to Jerusalem (Neh. 3:1, 32; 12:39). At the same time, it appears only once in all pagan literature before the end of the first century C.E.[2] Therefore, is not an association with the Sheep Gate self-evident when any adjectival use of "sheep" appears in connection with a place in Jerusalem?

Moreover, the emphatic notice of the Jerusalem locale speaks against the translation "at the sheep *pool*." The narrator of John 5:2 clearly intends to call special attention to a known place and its situation—in contrast to most of the other NT stories. But that demands the reading "at the sheep gate"—at least according to our understanding—since apart from John 5 there is no evidence, before or apart from Christianity, of a "sheep pool" in Jerusalem. And among the gates of Jerusalem the Sheep Gate had special importance, since under Nehemiah it was the high priest himself who had it repaired (Neh. 3:1). While all this does not necessarily demand that the translation "at the sheep pool" is incorrect, a number of sound reasons can be given for the alternate translation, which for a long time has been considered original. The analysis that follows is therefore based on the reading "sheep gate."

For the present essay, it is important to ask what this understanding of the text says about the relationship between the author of this tradition and the situation in Jerusalem. Two answers are possible: 1) the author knows of a sheep gate in Jerusalem from references in the LXX, or 2) the author knows Jerusalem and the situation there himself. As no connection between the Sheep Gate and a pool installation is established in the LXX, the latter assumption seems more likely, if we have here a correct description of a Jerusalem site. At the same time, the author considers the Sheep Gate so well known that he does not have to mention it specifically and can say "at the sheep" without completing the reference. As we cannot take it for granted that any Diaspora Jew knew the LXX so well as to connect the word "sheep" at once with the gate mentioned in Nehemiah 3 and 12, we might be justified to conclude that the story (not necessarily in the context of a written gospel) was originally addressed to a Jerusalem audience.

The Porticoes of Bethesda

The question whether and how far the author of the tradition underlying John 5 really knows Jerusalem cannot be answered with certainty merely from the mention of the Sheep Gate. As we have seen, the evidence thus far leads only to the conclusion that the author and the anticipated audience seem to know of

a sheep gate from personal knowledge of Jerusalem rather than from a deduc-
tion based on the LXX. To move to a decisive conclusion, the further mention
of the pool's columned porticoes may be critical. The importance of this question not only concerns the reliability of the geographic information in the Johannine tradition, but it goes far beyond this. The modern claim that the ancient
Bethesda installation stands on the current grounds of the White Fathers' complex in Jerusalem is based on the fact that the modern site includes remains of
two pools, one of which may have been the site of FG's five-columned porticoes.
For this reason, those who defend the identification of the modern site with
ancient Bethesda often put forward the argument that other potential sites do
not evidence porticoes, or at least not five. FE's reference to the five porticoes
of Bethesda is thus of both exegetical and archaeological interest.

The nineteenth and twentieth centuries' understanding of the excavations
on the property of the White Fathers was at first very enthusiastic, so that
people—especially Jeremias—spoke of a "rediscovery" of John's Bethesda. In
the rubble of the modern pools some remains of columns (bases and parts of
capitals) were found, and these were attributed to an installation erected in
Herodian times. Jeremias, referring to Vincent, writes that

> the columns were seven meters high while the overall height of the por-
> ticoes must have been 8.47 meters. Taken together with the pieces of
> the stone balustrades also found, the resulting picture is one of five mag-
> nificent galleries, four of which surrounded the [double] pool while the
> fifth, being 6.5 meters wide, cut across the pools. . . . Since the work-
> manship is Roman and since I found a graffito in Hebrew characters
> inscribed on the wall of the southern side of the southern pool . . . , which
> indicates that Bethesda is pre-Hadrianic [117–138 C.E.], it may be con-
> cluded that the porticoes were built by Herod the Great in connection
> with the enlargement of the Temple and the extension of the Temple
> area [before 4 B.C.E.]. They were not constructed primarily with a view
> toward practicality, but rather as an ornate show place, a fine specimen
> of Herod's fondness for building (Jeremias 1966, 31).

Jeremias's conclusion shows how far the information from the excavations in the
1860s was considered to be exact and to correlate with John 5.

This euphoria, however, has more recently given way to deep skepticism. A
more precise study of the remains found in the rubble has shown that the earlier dating of the site is not correct, that in fact all the archaeological evidence
points to a later, Christian time. Duprez comes to the following conclusion:
"Since the study of the large pools, we see that archaeology does not confirm
the classical interpretation of the two pools as the place of the gospel miracle.
The five porticoes are uncertain, the baths for the sick in these huge pools (are)
not very likely, and the disturbing of this amount of water remains problematic." And of the alleged porticoes in particular he says definitively, "Archaeology does not support the existence of the porticoes" (1970, 38). These

conclusions are taken over in Küchler's recent study, where he very clearly points out how much the existence of the five porticoes presupposed by Cyril's interpretation of John 5 is ruled out by the lack of archaeological evidence from the first centuries B.C.E. and C.E. Such an installation would have left traces after its destruction, whether by friends or by enemies. After the destruction of such an installation in the course of the siege of Jerusalem during the Jewish War (70 C.E.), when the Romans had a rampart erected in this area of the new town, some remains of porticoes would have been preserved in the rubble. But such is not the case. Küchler therefore concludes, "From the standpoint of archaeology five Stoas, in the sense of five porticoes along the sides of the two huge pools, never existed" (1999, 150). Hengel has said that this judgment is not beyond all doubt (1999, 311ff.), but for the moment, because of the complete lack of archaeological evidence, we will have to assume that before the destruction in the Jewish War there did not exist any columned porticoes.

In light of these data, where did FE get the idea of the five porticoes? Did he mistake Bethesda for the Pool of Siloam (John 9:7) because of the disturbance of the water mentioned in 5:7? Or should we consider these porticoes an element of narrative decoration rather than a description of historical fact? According to his understanding of the text's mention of a sheep pool and an installation called Bethesda with five porticoes, Küchler goes a different way and asks if the installation that is located east of the two pools on the White Fathers' property, where there are several elaborate wells, might show archaeological traces of five porticoes. But there turns out to be no evidence of the kind. The Greek term for portico (*stoa*) occurs again in John 10:23 and also twice in the Acts of the Apostles (3:1; 5:12), each time in reference to the magnificent portico attributed to Solomon that closes the Temple area to the east. The LXX also uses the term in 2 Chronicles 6:33 for a fourfold divided portico, and in Ezekiel 40 and 42 for porticoes in the Temple area. Therefore we can probably assume that the five porticoes in John 5:2 are to be understood as massive columned porticoes, which to our actual knowledge were neither directly around the White Fathers' pool nor in the area that adjoins it to the east.

The Installation at Bethesda—A Place of Healing?

So far our results are contradictory. Whereas the vague reference to the Sheep Gate suggests a knowledge of Jerusalem, maybe even an original Jerusalem audience for our story, FG's five porticoes do not appear to have existed and therefore weigh against a historical reference to a Jerusalem site. Perhaps the porticoes are only a narrative decoration. One thinks here of the angels in the

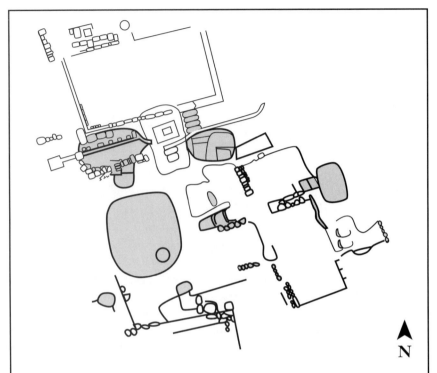

The Site of Ancient Bethesda, now on the grounds of the complex of the White Fathers' monastery. Areas in gray represent pools of water or grottoes with stairs leading to underground washbasins, some of which may date to the Jewish period. The bold lines indicate the buildings of the later Asklepios Temple.

FIGURE 7.1

empty tomb in Luke 24, of Pilate's wife's dream in Matthew 27, of the water jugs for the purification of "the Jews" in John 2, and of the removal of the tomb of Jesus into a garden so that the risen Christ can at first be taken for the gardener in John 19. Is all of this story only, an invention of poetic fantasy? Whether our criteria of historical investigation are adequate to confirm or deny Jesus' miracle at Bethesda does not have to be discussed here. But as to the question of possible local knowledge behind the story, a positive answer seems more obvious.

To this point we have been dealing with a miracle story, located at the Sheep Gate near a pool. Clearly the area of the White Fathers' complex near Stephen's or the Lion's Gate could be meant, in view of the fact that the Sheep Gate was situated farther north in the Temple area. If that is the case, and if at the same time we cannot solve the problem of the historicity of FG's miracle story, we have to answer the question, Why is it that FE or the tradition he used located the miracle at this location? Good reasons for FE's choice of setting can be given, and the identification of the sites mentioned in John 5 with a pool found in this area may be correct.

The excavations on the grounds of the White Fathers' complex in Jerusalem have brought to light not only the double pool and the many Christian buildings in, on, and around it, but also Roman items from Aelia Capitolina (after 70 C.E.). These Roman artifacts, however, are concentrated in an area east of the pool, that is, on the modern site of St. Anne's Crusader Church and the area northwest of it, where the Byzantines erected a three-nave basilica, the Church of the Sheep Pool. After the second Jewish rebellion (132–135 C.E.) there was most probably a sanctuary of Asclepius or Serapis at that location. The wells, underground rooms, and bathing installations, going back to Hellenistic-Jewish times, were partly enlarged and used for this cult.

Some votive items have been discovered that suggest that from the second century until the erection of the first Christian basilica in the fifth century there was a sanitarium together with a temple in this area, like many others known from antiquity. The best-documented have been discovered at Epidaurus, Pergamum, and Kos. On the other hand, such votive offerings from Jewish times have not been found. It seems improbable that there was a pagan temple and religious sanitarium on the Temple mount before 70 C.E. We must therefore ask why the Romans built a pagan temple and sanitarium at this location sometime in the second century C.E. It is reasonable to assume that not only in Roman times but already in the preceding Jewish era this site was known as a place of healing. This Jewish tradition probably persisted into the Roman period, explaining the later construction of the pagan sanctuary.

John 5:2, with its exceptional emphasis on the location of the following miracle, may be the earliest reference to this healing place, possibly quite well known in Jerusalem in the days of Jesus and therefore a strong indication of a reliable local tradition—without, however, the five-columned porticoes.

Notes

1. This manuscript was translated from the German original by Marianne Broer and Robert Fortna, with the English text adapted by Tom Thatcher under the author's scrutiny.

2. An electronic search of the *Thesaurus Linguae Graecae* reveals this adjective in a scholion on Homer's *Iliad* 16.353b, in which Eupolis (fifth century B.C.E.) is cited: "And Eupolis calls the chorus of goats a *probatikon coron*." In this case, the adjective *probatikon* refers to a goat, not a sheep (see also Liddell and Scott 1996).

8

The Legend
of the Beloved Disciple

TOM THATCHER

Most North Americans are acquainted with folk heroes such as Paul Bunyan, John Henry, Pecos Bill, and Johnny Appleseed. At some point in their lives, children are taught, usually indirectly, that Paul Bunyan was the superlative lumberjack, a giant of a man who traveled the Northwest with his huge blue ox, Babe, felling trees with a single stroke of his enormous ax. John Henry, the "steel-drivin' man," could lay railroad track faster than a steam engine. The theme song from a 1960s television program about the early American frontiersman Davy Crockett dubbed its protagonist "King of the Wild Frontier" and touted that Crockett had "killed him a bear when he was only three." The exploits of Robin Hood are recounted in hundreds of books and movies, a corpus that even includes parodies of the legendary bandit. In the modern Western world, these heroes exist as fictional characters who function to amuse or inspire.

But despite their current cultural status, such traditional heroes are generally born out of social contexts in which they play a much more serious role. All of the characters mentioned above are trade legends, personifying and epitomizing the values of their respective vocations. Each is the ultimate worker, who does everything that the average worker would love to be able to do superlatively, even hyperbolically. As the ultimate frontiersman, Davy Crockett could kill a bear at age three; John Henry could lay track faster than a pile driver; Robin Hood was the consummate honorable thief. Legendary stories about these heroes transmit the values held by practitioners of their trades

91

and legitimize these trades by showing the ultimate potential and worth of the worker.

Legendary Storytellers:
The Anthropological Evidence

Legendary figures also sometimes develop within the guild of those who use and transmit oral traditions. This point has been highlighted in a recent article by John Miles Foley, a legend himself in the field of folkloristics. Foley's conclusions are based on data collected by Milman Parry and Albert Lord, the founders of the "oral-formulaic theory" to explain the production of traditional texts. From 1933–1935, Parry and Lord spent two years observing the performance and transmission of oral stories in central Herzegovina (Yugoslavia), which was then largely illiterate. Parry was seeking field evidence to support his thesis that Homer's *Iliad* and *Odyssey* were oral, rather than literary, compositions. To do this, he interviewed and recorded as many *guslari* as he could find. A *guslar* is a Slavic folksinger who performs traditional oral epics to the accompaniment of a one-stringed instrument called the *gusle*. In Parry's view, the social function of the *guslari* and their compositional techniques closely corresponded to those of ancient oral bards like Homer and Hesiod (for detailed description of this research, see the Introduction to Lord 1979, vol. 1).

In the course of these interviews, Parry would generally inquire about the source of a particular epic. On many occasions he was told that the story originated with a famous oral bard, whose name and biographical details varied from one informant to the next but who always possessed almost superhuman abilities. For example, the great *guslar* had lived to a very advanced age, dying some two generations before the informant. He was so good at telling stories that he had no other occupation, a social phenomenon entirely unknown among the singers Parry interviewed, all of whom supported themselves primarily through other trades. The great singer often performed for pay in the homes of wealthy aristocrats. He was, in fact, so popular that he rarely appeared in his home village, which the informants located in various places. Aside from all this, the great singer's physical feats were almost as legendary as those of the heroes he described: one informant said he could jump twelve paces at age 101; another said he could sing for six straight hours whereas the average *guslar* could rarely perform longer than thirty minutes; another said he had a unique song for every day of the year. But the great singer was still understood to be a real human being; therefore his legendary attributes could not save him from a mysterious death (all refs. Foley 1998, 154–165, 175).

More significant to the development of oral-performance traditions, Parry's informants asserted that the great singer of the past had an enormous repertoire of stories, all of which were regarded as the very finest. Hence, whatever his name or origin, this person was always "the ultimate source for the best songs they [the *guslar* informants] knew," even when the individual *guslar* would cite another mentor or relative as the immediate source for the tale (Foley 1998, 156). For example, when asked by Parry where he had learned a particular story, the Slavic *guslar* might say that he heard it from an uncle or another singer, but that that person had previously learned it from the great singer. This sort of attribution is a typical feature of oral traditions in other cultures as well. Foley collected similar data from Mongolia in 1997 and observed that the legendary poet at the source of the Mongolian oral-perfor-mance tradition was so highly regarded that even several generations after his death a number of popular expressions, proverbs, and stories were said to have originated with him, being introduced with the formula "these are Choibang's words" (Foley 1998, 174).

From these data, Foley makes three related observations about the leg-endary progenitors of oral-performance traditions (1998, 149–150):

1. Just as oral stories and sayings vary from one presentation to the next, the specific biographical details of the great singer at the source of the tradi-tion will vary from one informant to the next. It appears that the source of the stories, like the stories themselves, is adapted to meet the needs and interests of the particular local context.
2. The legendary singer is represented as a real-life historical individual but at the same time serves the broader function of designating the entire oral tradition. In other words, the names of the sources also become code names for the traditions with which they are associated, just as the name Paul Bunyan is now synonymous with the lumber trade.
3. Biographical details about the legendary singers are important primarily for what they reveal about the principles that are valued within the oral traditions with which they are associated. This point is the logical corol-lary of the first two. If details about the life of the legendary source of an oral tradition are inconsistent and sometimes contradictory, and if the leg-endary source has come to symbolize the tradition itself, then the bio-graphical profile of the source person will most likely reflect the interests of the oral performers who continue to preserve the tradition and connect themselves with the source person. Therefore, by identifying trends in the presentation of the great singer's biography, it is possible to identify those qualities that are valued within the oral-performance guild.

Foley, who is interested in every species of oral tradition but ultimately in the classics and specifically the Homeric corpus, proceeds to argue from these conclusions that "[Homer] may be more an eponym than a name," designating not a gifted historical individual but the entire tradition of Greek epic poetry (Foley 1998, 153). The most ancient extant sources say that Homer was a real person who was the tangible source for the best Greek epics, but the specific details of his life are presented differently. There is even conflicting evidence from the sources about the extent of Homer's actual corpus, a situation that has arisen because "each [ancient] poet or commentator appropriates 'Homer' as the source of all that is valuable in the poetic tradition and derives his [own] authority and position from that legendary attribution" (Foley 1998, 168). Foley therefore warns against attempts to create definitive biographies for persons who, as the source of legends and traditions, exist mainly as legends and traditions themselves.

Tales, Tellers, and Retrojection

Gregory Nagy (1996, 76) refers to the process by which the source of an oral tradition becomes a legendary figure and then a representation of the values of the tradition itself as "retrojection." The illustration of this phenomenon in Table 8.1 is drawn from Parry's research in Herzegovina, where informants frequently associated themselves and their stories with a legendary oral singer whom some called "Hasan Coso." Note that the model employed in this study is based on the conclusions of Foley and Nagy but does not necessarily represent their own method of analysis.

Table 8.1

Tradition Development of the Name "Hasan Coso"

Stage 1	Stage 2	Stage 3
The source or "author," a historical or fictional person or group of people to whom a traditional story is ascribed. Represents the real person(s) who first performed the story, although the name used in the tradition may not be this person's actual name.	The source or "author," a legendary figure to whom a traditional story is ascribed. This individual possesses remarkable attributes and is capable of legendary feats.	The performance tradition, embodying the values encoded in the presentation of the legendary storyteller. The "author" is now effaced by the tradition.

At the first stage of this model, the name of the supposed author of an oral story refers to the person (or group of people) who actually developed that story, the "source" of the tradition. Of course, this may or may not be the actual name of that person or group, or even the name of any real person, and later ideas about the source person's identity may be inaccurate. Nevertheless, at Stage 1 the supposed author's name serves the semiotic function of representing the human source of the tradition. At Stage 2, the name of the supposed source comes to refer to a legendary figure who has extraordinary abilities and who represents in various ways the ultimate storyteller. This legendary figure is an extension of the identity of the original supposed source at Stage 1, possessing qualities that normal storytellers wish they possessed. At Stage 3, the name of the supposed source comes to refer to the entire oral-performance tradition, as that tradition embodies the qualities and values epitomized in the legendary storyteller from Stage 2.

"Retrojection" occurs between Stages 1 and 2 and Stages 2 and 3 as *the later referents of the name of the source are shifted backwards onto the earlier stages.* In other words, as the meaning of the name "Hasan Coso" changes, the earlier meanings of that name are erased or forgotten. Once legendary abilities have been attributed to the great singer, these will be retrojected to efface the actual biographical details of the supposed source. Then, once the legendary singer has come to epitomize the tradition, the values of contemporary oral performance (Stage 3) will be retrojected onto the legendary figure at Stage 2, possibly leading to a revision of his portrait that will leave him even more distant from the actual source person at Stage 1.[1] In Nagy's words, the "tradition of oral poetry appropriates the poet, potentially transforming even historical figures [Stage 1] into generic ones [Stage 2] who represent the traditional functions of their poetry [Stage 3]. The wider the diffusion and the longer the chain of recomposition [of the oral material], the more remote the identity of the [source] composer becomes" (1990, 79).

The Legend of the Beloved Disciple

It is possible that the mysterious "Beloved Disciple" (BD) of the Fourth Gospel (FG) was developed through a process of retrojection, as a sort of trade hero for the bearers of the Johannine tradition. In this process, BD became a symbol for the Johannine Jesus tradition itself, embodying everything that Johannine storytellers judged to be most important about their craft, just as Paul Bunyan has become a metaphor for what is important to the logging industry. As such, BD epitomizes the goals and values of this select guild of Johannine storytellers.

Following the retrojection model, there are at least three ways to explain the origin of the Beloved Disciple in the Johannine tradition. Note that these are not mutually exclusive, and also that any could apply whether the sources of FG were primarily written or oral.

1. The Beloved Disciple may be a purely legendary or "ideal" figure. If this is the case, BD is a fictional character who was invented to add validity to the Johannine tradition. Here BD is a personification of the "we who have seen" in the plural verbs of 1 John 1:1–3, a collective symbol for the group of people who preserved the Johannine witness. By appeal to this figure, later Johannine preachers could associate themselves and their stories more closely with the historical Jesus.

2. As a second possibility, BD may have been generated to complement another character already known in the Johannine tradition. Legendary figures often travel in pairs: Paul Bunyan and his blue ox, Babe; the Lone Ranger and Tonto; Sherlock Holmes and Watson; Robin Hood and his Merry Men. Since BD functions primarily as a witness to Jesus, it may be that his profile was developed by contrast to some other character's witness to Jesus, with a view to balancing that witness and supplying anything that might have been lacking in it.

While any speculation along these lines is inherently subjective, one might suggest that the Beloved Disciple was crafted from traditional stories involving Peter. BD always appears with Peter in FG (John 1:35–39; 13:23–26; 18:15–16; 19:26–27; 20:2–10; 21:7; 21:20–24),[2] a fact that is readily explained if BD was simply added to preexisting episodes that involved Peter in order to complete Peter's witness to Jesus. Peter was a well-known character in many early Jesus traditions, but the Johannine Beloved Disciple is always one step beyond him, always a bit closer to Jesus and always coming to key insights before Peter does. BD, then, may have developed in the Johannine tradition as a reflection of Peter, of course polished up a bit. This would be especially interesting if there was, as some have suggested, a tension between the Petrine and Johannine branches of the church at this time.

3. Third, it may be that the Beloved Disciple in the current FG is a legendary expansion of a real person who was a key player early in the Johannine tradition. By way of analogy, Davy Crockett was a real historical person, even though he did not kill or tame a bear at age three. John Chapman was a real person, even if he did not do everything now ascribed to Johnny Appleseed. Edward Kelly was a real person, even though he certainly did not do everything that Australian legends currently associate with "Ned Kelly" as a representative of the wild west and a free spirit. Following this third model, the final stage in the evolution of the legend of the Beloved Disciple would be the association of BD with John the Apostle in the second century, an attempt to rehistoricize a historical figure who had become mythical.

The third model enjoys the advantage of being able to encompass all the possibilities presented by the other two. Combining these three scenarios, one may suggest that a key person early in the Johannine tradition, who possibly had some contact with Jesus, was gradually developed into a legendary figure by setting him against Peter: whatever Peter did, this source person did better. As a consequence, this person became the ultimate witness to those events in Jesus' life that were critical to Johannine Christology, so that the very mention of his name would symbolize and re-enforce the veracity of the entire Johannine tradition. In the course of this semiotic shift, the actual identity of the original source person was entirely swallowed up in the archetypal figure that BD had become. By the time FG and 1–2–3 John took their current form, the Beloved Disciple had come to function in the Johannine tradition in three different ways at once: as a character in the story about Jesus, as the narrator of the story about Jesus (John 21:24; but see 19:35), and as the foundation for the community's claims for the historical credibility of their story about Jesus.

The retrojection process that turned the person, or group of people, at the foundation of the Johannine tradition into the Beloved Disciple of the current FG is particularly complicated. As the source was transformed into a symbol for the veracity of the tradition, the proper name of the actual source person was erased by the moniker "Beloved Disciple." This fact makes it especially difficult to reconstruct the biographical details of the source (assuming such a person or group did in fact exist). Further, the current text of FG treats this person both as the source of the tradition and as a character in the tradition. As a result, it is impossible to tell at what stage the actual name of the source was replaced by the name of the legend. Despite these problems, however, the retrojection process implied by the model adopted here may be diagrammed as seen in Table 8.2.

In any case, any of the three models of legendary retrojection described here would explain the following notable features of the presentation of the Beloved Disciple in FG:

1. BD appears only at key points in the narrative where eyewitness testimony would be crucial for historical or theological reasons: Jesus' relationship with the Baptist (John 1:35–39); the Farewell Address (13–17); the Annas trial (18:15); the crucifixion (19:25–26); the water and blood that flowed from Jesus' dead body (19:34–35); the empty tomb (20:2–9); and the resurrection appearances (21:7, 20–23). These are events that all later Johannine preachers would wish they could have witnessed.

2. BD is presented as superior to other witnesses by way of his special intimacy with Jesus, a position that seems to have been enjoyed by Peter in the synoptic tradition and possibly also at an earlier stage of the Johannine tradition. Consistent with this intimacy, the Beloved Disciple is the first person to believe in Jesus' resurrection (John 20:8).

3. BD's relationship with Jesus is presented in terms analogous to Jesus'

Table 8.2

The Name: ???? (the actual name of the source person at Stage 1, now lost)		The Name: "Beloved Disciple" (a character in the Johannine story and the narrator of FG)
Stage 1	Stage 2	Stage 3
The source or "author," the historical or fictional person who was the primary original source of the Johannine tradition. Ultimately, this is the real person who first performed the materials underlying the current FG. This person's name and identity have been effaced by the tradition and may have been unknown to the final redactor of John 21.	The "Beloved Disciple," a character in the Johannine tradition who witnesses events that are critical to the Johannine understanding of Jesus. At this stage, the source is integrated into the narrative as a legendary figure, functioning as both character and narrator.	The Johannine performance tradition, embodying the values encoded in the presentation of the Beloved Disciple. Reference to BD supports the validity and authority of the continuing witness. Includes the final redactor of John 21 and people like Demetrius and the "brothers" in 3 John.

relationship with the Father. The Prologue says that Jesus was "in the bosom of the Father" (John 1:18), and likewise BD "leaned on Jesus' bosom" during the Farewell (13:23–25). Jesus "narrates" (*exēgēsato*; NRSV: "made known") about God (1:18), and BD witnesses and writes about Jesus (21:24).

4. Biographical details about the Beloved Disciple are remarkably vague, despite the fact that the characters in FG are generally much more developed than those that appear in other ancient gospels. FE knows that Simon, Andrew, and Philip are from Bethsaida (John 1:43); that Nicodemus was a Pharisee and a ruler of the Jews (3:1); that John was baptizing near Aenon in Salim because there was a lot of water there (3:23); that the lame man had been at Bethesda for thirty-eight years before Jesus met him (5:5); that Jesus' brothers did not believe in him (7:5); that Lazarus, Martha, and Mary were siblings and lived in Bethany, which is two miles away from Jerusalem (11:18); that the slave whose ear was cut off by Peter during the arrest was named Malchus (18:10); that Peter stood at a charcoal fire outside Annas's house during Jesus' trial (18:18); and that Pilate had to leave his headquarters to talk to the Jews because they did not want to defile themselves before the Passover (18:28). Whether or not any of these details are historical, FE tends to provide incidental infor-

mation about people and places in the story. One is therefore struck by the paucity of information about the Beloved Disciple in FG. FE does not relate a single biographical fact about BD, not even his name, except possibly that he was somehow associated with John the Baptist before he met Jesus (1:34–35) and that he was known to the high priest (18:15). Remarkably, FE knows that Judas the betrayer was from Iscariot (14:22) but does not seem to know where BD is from. Perhaps the author of FG no longer knew about the actual identity of the person at the foundation of his tradition, or even whether such a person had ever really existed.

5. Despite the lack of biographical information, FE relates that the Beloved Disciple, like the legendary oral poets described by Parry, Lord, and Foley, died a mysterious death (John 21:18–23). Notably, Peter also dies a mysterious death in FG (see John 21:18–19), a fact that would be especially significant if BD has been constructed as a foil to Peter.

6. As a further point from outside FG, the author of 1–2–3 John frequently insists that his information about Jesus comes "from the beginning" (*ap archē*), and he highlights the motifs of "witness" and physical contact with Jesus without naming the specific source of this information (see 1 John 1:1–3). It may be that the terms "from the beginning" and "witness" characterize the Johannine tradition itself as synonymous with the Beloved Disciple, a person who, according to legend, enjoyed a privileged intimacy with the historical Jesus.

Notes

1. I stress that the model presented here implies a logical progression, not necessarily a chronological one. Particularly, the interplay between Stages 2 and 3 would be a continual process that, as Parry's research indicates, might vary from one storyteller to the next depending on the needs of the local situation. It would be fruitless to speculate about how long it might take to move from one stage to another in a specific instance without clear external evidence.
2. For purposes of this essay, I have included references to the term "other disciple," which some scholars take to be another moniker for the "Beloved Disciple" in FG. Whether or not the terms "other disciple" and "Beloved Disciple" are truly synonymous will not affect my conclusions.

9

The Audience
of the Fourth Gospel

RICHARD BAUCKHAM

During the last three decades, many important studies of the Fourth Gospel
(FG) have focused attention on the so-called "Johannine Community." Such
studies use this term to refer to a particular church or small group of churches
in a specific locality (in some versions, the community moved from one place
to another in the course of its history). FG is understood to be a product of
this community, taking shape during the course of the community's history and
reflecting its experiences. Most who write about the Johannine Community
also assume that FG was written for this community *alone* and not with the
wider Christian movement in view. Indeed, it is generally assumed that the
Johannine Community had little or no contact with the wider Christian movement until perhaps the final stage of FG's redaction, the period when chapter
21 was added to the earlier work. The proposed close relationship between FG
and the isolated and distinctive Johannine Community functions as an explanation for the striking differences between FG and the Synoptic Gospels. As
a result, the theological distinctiveness of the Fourth Gospel, which was once
attributed to the creative thought of a single Johannine author or a "Johannine School" of Christian leaders and writers, has come to be attributed to the
life experience and sociological setting of the isolated Christian community
within which the author of FG lived and worked.

Of course, all conclusions about this Johannine Community and its history
must be deduced from the Fourth Gospel and 1–2–3 John, for there is no relevant external evidence. There are second-century traditions that attribute FG

to "John," the Beloved Disciple. Other traditions suggest that FG's original audience was the Christian community in Ephesus, one of the most prominent churches in the early Christian movement, and also suggest that FG was written for *all* churches, not just its community of origin. But modern theories about the Johannine Community are rarely able to allow more than a tiny grain of truth to these traditions about FG's original audience and usually dismiss them as incompatible with information that can be derived from the text itself. This deduced information then takes priority over the early traditions in discussions of FG's character, origins, and intended audience.

The prominence of the Johannine Community in Johannine scholarship corresponds to the increasing focus on the Matthean, Markan, and Lukan communities in the study of the Synoptics. Like the Johannine Community, these groups are understood as the particular communities within which and for which those Gospels were written. Elsewhere I have argued against this approach to the gospels in general (Bauckham 1998). Yet the assumption that each gospel was written for a specific church or group of churches has come to be widely taken for granted, despite the fact that it has never been established by serious argument. Most scholars treat this principle as virtually self-evident and have not hesitated to use it as a foundation on which to build increasingly sophisticated edifices of scholarly reconstruction. It remains, however, an unproven assumption that needs to be tested against the other, most plausible possibility that *all* the gospels were written with the intention that they should be widely circulated around *all* the churches.

In favor of the hypothesis that the early gospels were written for a broad, general Christian audience, I have elsewhere argued that the early Christian movement was not a scattering of relatively isolated, introverted communities, but rather a network of communities in constant close communication with one another. Moreover, all the evidence we have about early Christian leaders (the potential authors of a gospel) suggests that such people typically traveled widely and worked in more than one community at different times. Thus, neither the early communities nor their teachers would have been locally minded; both would have had a strong, lively, and informed sense of participation in a worldwide movement. Even rivalry and conflict between early Christian communities took place across the general network of Christian communication: it did not produce exclusive enclaves of churches which were out of communication with others. In addition, the evidence we have shows that early Christian literature circulated around the churches very rapidly, and in some cases that literature produced in one major church was deliberately launched into general circulation.

For this reason, in my view it is implausible that someone would write a gospel simply for members of the specific community in which he was then living, with its specific, local issues determining the scope and nature of his presentation. Knowing that his work was bound to reach many other churches very quickly, the author would instead address the Christians in any and every church to which his gospel might circulate. His intended readership would not be a specific community or even a defined group of communities, however large, but rather an open and indefinite category: any and every Christian community of his time in which Greek was understood. But if the early gospels were not addressed to particular communities, we cannot expect to learn much from them about their author's own communities, even if those communities did, indeed, influence the authors' thinking and writing. On this view of the intended audience of the gospels, the Matthean, Markan, Lukan, and Johannine Communities can no longer play the hermeneutically significant role to which they have been elevated in the scholarship of the last three decades.

In the past, my discussion of this issue has been general, with examples drawn from, and conclusions applied to, the Fourth Gospel as well as the Synoptics. But there are respects in which FG is a special case. Even if my general portrait of the early Christian movement is accurate, might there not have been a Christian group in some remote spot, out of contact with other churches, in which the Fourth Gospel originated? Because Johannine scholars have increasingly tended to set the Johannine Community in just such splendid isolation, it may not be easy to persuade them that arguments about the Christian movement in general should apply to FG as a particular case. Does not this Gospel bear all the marks of a "sectarian" (i.e., an ideologically and sociologically closed) group? Does not its very special character demand an origin apart from the rest of the Christian movement? Further, the presence of 1–2–3 John to complement the evidence of FG has allowed reconstructions of the Johannine Community, including the distinct stages of its history, to be bolder and fuller than most attempts to reconstruct the communities behind the Synoptics. In any case, there are significant arguments in play in the case of FG that do not have the same importance in the case of the Synoptics. If my general argument about the intended audiences of all the gospels is to be sustained in the case of FG, it will be necessary to address specific questions of Johannine scholarship. What follows is a brief account of the way I should wish to do this.

A Two-Level Reading?

Most attempts to reconstruct the Johannine Community and its history depend on the type of two-level reading strategy pioneered by J. Louis Martyn (1979). This approach treats FG not only as the story of Jesus but also as the story of the Johannine Community. The community, it is suggested, would have seen its own story encoded in FG's narratives about the past history of Jesus. Martyn's paradigm is based on the story of the blind man in John 9, which, in his view, represents the community's own experience of exclusion from the local synagogue, an experience that is attributed a high level of historical certainty by most scholars who have attempted to reconstruct the Johannine Community's history. From such a view of the narrative, the conclusion inevitably follows that much of FG's story about Jesus has been decisively shaped by the Johannine Community's experiences. Of course, FG is rooted in the traditions about Jesus preserved in the community, but these traditions have been reshaped and developed to reflect the community's history. Martyn's approach, and that of those who have followed his precedent, is therefore the most recent way to explain the peculiarities of the Johannine narrative that are considered not to reflect early Jesus traditions. Ironically, scholars who take this approach generally lack confidence in FG's historical value as a narrative about Jesus but display remarkable confidence in its evidence for the history of the Johannine Community.

Martyn's argument is built on the fact that the blind man in John 9 is expelled from the synagogue (9:22; cf. 12:42; 16:2). In Martyn's view, such an event is historically inconceivable during the ministry of Jesus but appears to correspond to what happened to Jewish Christians in the late first century when the *Birkhat ha-Minim* (a liturgical curse against heretics) was introduced into the synagogue liturgy. Against this argument, we should first note that the historical issue of the status of Jewish Christians in the late first century has been much debated, and it is not at all clear that what happened to Diaspora-Jewish Christians resembles what happens to the blind man in John 9. The trend of scholarly opinion is certainly against such a resemblance. Second, if it is the case that expulsion from the synagogue is anachronistic in John 9, Martyn's two-level reading of the passage is not the most obvious explanation for the problem. Anachronisms in historical writing are not uncommon, but they are not usually explained through the sort of two-level reading Martyn supposes.

More generally, the most damaging criticism of Martyn's two-level reading strategy is the fact that it has no basis in the literary genre of the Fourth Gospel. The genre of a particular text generally guides readers to the appropriate strategy of interpretation. But what genre gives its readers to understand that they should approach the story of a historical individual (here Jesus) as an encoded version of the history of their own community? Recent discussion of the gospel genre strongly favors the view that first-century readers would have recognized all four canonical gospels as a special form of Greco-Roman biography. While FG's original readers would certainly expect such a work to be relevant to their own community and situation, they would not expect it to address the very specific circumstances of one particular community, and much less would they suspect that it required the kind of two-level reading strategy Martyn proposes. Moreover, the Fourth Gospel itself displays a strong sense of the "pastness" of the story of Jesus, temporally and geographically located in its own time and space, and not infrequently draws explicit attention to the difference between the periods before and after the resurrection of Jesus (e.g., John 2:22; 7:39; 12:16; 13:7). Insofar as FG says anything explicit about its own content and purpose, that purpose is described in terms of the history of Jesus (20:30–31; 21:24–25), not the history of the Johannine Community.

We should also note that the two-level reading strategy is not easy to practice, for those who take this position generally do not believe that the current version of FG's narrative can be read sequentially as a story about the Johannine Community. Rather, the sequence of events and theological developments in the history of the community can only be perceived when the various parts of FG are restored to the actual chronological order of their composition. Moreover, the two-level strategy cannot be applied to every part of the narrative and is generally applied inconsistently to the parts of the narrative to which it is applied. Not every character in FG can plausibly represent some group in the community's history, as is evident from the absence of Judas and Pilate in most reconstructions of this sort. For these reasons, every reconstruction of the Johannine Community's history based on the two-level reading strategy is riddled with arbitrariness and uncertainty. The more one realizes how complex and selective the use of this reading strategy must be, the less plausible it becomes.

A Two-Level Text?

Closely associated with the two-level reading strategy is the view that FG is a multilayered work, in which texts from various stages of the community's history have been preserved alongside one another. This perspective posits a complex history of literary redaction as the key to the Johannine Community's social and theological history. The ability to distinguish these various sources and levels of redaction depends primarily on the identification of aporias and ideological tensions between different parts of FG.

But this approach to FG's composition has not yet adequately addressed or resolved two major issues. The first concerns the relationship between interpretive approaches that appeal to discontinuities of all kinds as indications of sources and redactional layers and the newer literary-critical approaches that treat the final form of the text as a literary and rhetorical whole. In light of literary criticism's sensitivity to the strategies of the text, many of the apparent aporias on which source critics depend are seen to be much less problematic. A passage that seems awkward to the source critic, whose judgment often amounts merely to observing that he or she "would not have written it like that," can appear quite reasonable to a critic who is attentive to the literary dynamics of the text. Thus, the conclusions of literary criticism cannot just be added to the concerns of source and redaction criticism, leaving their results intact, as most Johannine scholars seem to suppose. Instead, these conclusions must pose serious questions about the interpretation of the evidence on which the older source-oriented approaches were based.

The second issue concerns assumptions about the Fourth Evangelist's (FE) theology. If diachronic stratification of the text too often lacks literary sensitivity, it also often displays a rather wooden and overly modern reaction to the ideological tensions and seeming conceptual contradictions between the different parts of FG. We need to be much more open to the possibility that these tensions belong to the character and method of FE's theology. After all, the redactors who are generally believed to have put the various parts of FG together were evidently content with these contradictions, which they could have edited out. It is no more difficult to view these tensions as the deliberate theological strategies of a single author, and this direction of thought may lead us back to an older view about the distinctiveness of the Fourth Gospel. Perhaps we are dealing not with the product of an idiosyncratic community and its history, but rather with the work of a creative theologian who, in his long experience of teaching and on the basis of his special access to traditions about Jesus, developed his own distinctive interpretation of the history of Jesus.

In-group Language?

With this topic we reach the point where it will be possible to decisively turn the tables on those who argue that an isolated Johannine Community was the intended audience of the Fourth Gospel. The evidence to be considered in fact points to the opposite conclusion.

An influential strain of Johannine scholarship has identified the distinctive terminology and symbolism in FG as the language of a sectarian community. The Fourth Gospel, it is claimed, could only have been understood by members of the community in which this special in-group language had developed. In fact, FE even uses everyday language in a novel sense to confuse outsiders and to confirm insiders in their sense of belonging and superiority. This literary strategy is especially evident when characters in FG, notably the Jews, are depicted as misunderstanding Jesus' enigmatic sayings. At such points in the narrative, members of the Johannine Community (and only they) find themselves "in the know," aligned with Jesus in radical distinction from the culpable incomprehension of outsiders, whom the community would identify with the non-Christian Jews of the synagogue from which they had separated.

It should be said that this line of argument is not *primarily* concerned with the relationship between the Johannine Community and other Christian groups or the Christian movement in general, but rather with its relationship to the non-Christian world (especially Jewish, but also pagan) with which it was in daily contact. The Johannine Community is usually classified as "sectarian" in sociological terms specifically in relation to society at large. But the argument does bear on the relationship between the Johannine Community and the rest of the Christian movement, in that the in-group language of FG is not treated as the common language of all Christians but rather as the special language of the Johannine Community. Perhaps non-Johannine Christians would have some advantage over non-Christians in understanding the Fourth Gospel, but the impression one gains from scholars who take this approach is that the advantage would not be very great.

Those who are not already familiar with this line of argument may well find it surprising. In the modern church's experience, the Fourth Gospel has been seen as the most accessible of the New Testament books both to Christians with little education in the faith and to complete outsiders who have minimal knowledge of the Christian tradition. How can this be the case, given that the characters in FG so often misunderstand or are puzzled by the sayings of the Johannine Jesus? There are at least three reasons within the literary strategy of this Gospel that demonstrate that FG's special language and symbolism would be accessible to noninitiates. Against the line of argument previously cited, these three reasons also show that FG is designed precisely to introduce this in-group language to readers not already familiar with it.

First, FE sometimes explicitly explains the meaning of figurative or enigmatic sayings of Jesus (John 2:21; 6:71; 7:39; 11:13; 12:33; 13:11; cf. 11:51–52). Of these, the first example is particularly instructive. The saying at John 2:19 is the first case in FG where Jesus uses figurative language: "Jesus answered them, 'Destroy this temple, and in three days I will raise it up.'" As in many later instances, Jesus' words have both an obvious, literal meaning, referring to a physical reality, and also a metaphorical meaning that turns the physical image into a symbol of his salvific activity or the salvation he brings. The Jews (i.e., the Jewish leaders), however, understand only the literal sense and therefore misunderstand (2:20); indeed, not even the disciples understood Jesus' words at the time (2:22). But FE explains the meaning of the puzzling saying directly to the readers: "But he was speaking of the temple of his body. After he was raised from the dead, his disciples remembered that he had said this; and they believed the scripture and the word that Jesus had spoken" (2:21–22). FE surely intends this to be an illustrative example: he will not always help his readers on later occasions, but he has shown them how to figure out what Jesus means.

Second, the misunderstandings by Jesus' hearers (disciples, Jewish leaders, individuals such as the Samaritan woman) frequently have the literary function of leading Jesus to explain the image he has used or to develop it in ways that clarify its meaning (John 3:3–8; 4:10–15, 31–34; 6:32–35; 8:31–36, 56–58; 10:6; 11:23–26; 14:4–6). Sometimes the characters in the narrative come to understand as a result of these explanations by Jesus, and sometimes they do not (e.g., 4:15; 10:6, 19). But in either case, the reader of FG always comes to understand. The dialogues teach the reader the Johannine language and symbolism. Hence, the symbols are often introduced and developed in Jesus' dialogues, like those with Nicodemus (John 3) and the Samaritan woman (chap. 4). Even if a symbol, at its first occurrence, is as puzzling to readers as it is to the characters in the Gospel, this is not because readers must already be familiar with it in order to understand it. Rather, it is because FE wishes to stir readers into a desire to understand, a desire that the continuing development of the dialogue then helps them to fulfill.

When read sequentially, FG progressively leads its audience into a greater understanding of its themes by initiating them step-by-step into its symbolic world. For example, at John 4:13–14 the reader learns that, in Jesus' usage, the everyday language of "water" refers to the source of eternal life that Jesus will give. Jewish or Christian readers might naturally detect such symbolism in Jesus' words to the Samaritan woman from their knowledge of the broad use of water as a symbol of the Holy Spirit. But readers who do not detect this nevertheless learn enough to follow the story, and later in the narrative they will gain the further insight that "water" symbolizes the Spirit that Jesus will give to those who believe in him (7:37–39). Of course, FE's explanations of the symbolism are never adequate, because the symbolism is not just a code that can be translated into an adequate literal description, as the sociological reduction of these symbols to an in-group language tends to suggest. The realities to which the symbols refer are transcendent realities that escape linguistic capture. This is why symbols proliferate through FG without redundancy: each new symbol moves the reader closer to what they symbolize. But FE gives sufficient explanation of the symbols to point readers in the direction of their meaning.

The third point which demonstrates that the language of FG would be accessible to noninitiates relates to the specific point that confuses the characters in the story. Specifically, the misunderstandings that occur before Jesus' resurrection involve his many enigmatic references to his coming death. FE makes it clear, especially in his paradigmatic explanation of the first of Jesus' figurative sayings (John 2:21–22), that not even the disciples could have understood these references to Jesus' "glorification" (cf. 13:7; 12:16; 20:9). However, by pointing this out in 2:21–22, FE puts his readers in a better position than any of the characters in the story to understand this major theme in the words of Jesus. But the knowledge the readers have to bring to the text is not some esoteric information known only to members of the Johannine Community, but the fact that Jesus is going to be crucified and then rise from the dead. Even non-Christian readers interested enough to read FG would surely know that Christians believed this about Jesus.

None of this should be taken to suggest that readers of FG would find the text uniformly easy to understand. Jesus sometimes seems to speak in unexplained riddles (as he does also in the Synoptics). These would be more puzzling for some readers than for others but would probably be somewhat puzzling to most first-time readers. But such riddles are part of a larger literary strategy that drives readers both to think about their meaning and to read on in hope of learning their answers. A good example is the "lifted up sayings" (John 3:14–15; 8:28; 12:32–34), an instance of Johannine double entendre that combines a literal use of the verb (referring to the manner of Jesus' death: "lifted up" on the cross) with a figurative use (referring to his resurrection/ exaltation). FE in fact explains the literal meaning, leaving the paradox of its concurrence with the figurative meaning to be inferred, but it is only on the last occasion when Jesus uses the figure that he provides this explanation (12:33). Such a procedure is inexplicable under the theory that this is in-group language that Johannine Christians would already know but which other readers would find impenetrably opaque. It makes sense, however, if these Johannine enigmas are meant to tease initially uncomprehending readers into theological enlightenment. To those who have not managed to penetrate the meaning through the first two occurrences of the figure "lifted up," FE gives substantial help on its third occurrence but avoids depotentiating the riddle by giving too much help too soon.

Why have scholars who read FE's language as the in-group talk of a sectarian community missed the fact that FG seems designed, on the contrary, to introduce readers to its special language and symbolism? Perhaps a focus on the stratification of FG into sources and redactional layers has distracted such scholars from the literary strategies of the narrative as a text designed to be read sequentially and as a whole. This literary approach to FG's figurative language has, in fact, inclined me to change my mind about the book's intended audience. Not only do I still think that FG was written for the church at large, I am also now inclined to think that its intended readership included interested non-Christians. The latter is not an alternative to the supposition that FG would reach its readers through circulation among the churches, since it is unlikely that Christian literature would interest or even come into the hands of outsiders other than through the mediation of Christians. Such non-Christian readers would already have been acquainted with the Christian message by Christian friends and would have to be seriously interested. But it appears to me that FG is designed in such a way that it could be sufficiently understood by interested outsiders. These people would doubtless miss the deeper levels of meaning that would be accessible to more informed readers, but they would have been puzzled only enough to keep them reading.

It is noteworthy that most of FG's major symbolic images come from the common experience of all people of that time period: light and darkness, water, bread, vines and wine, shepherds and sheep, judgment and witness, birth and death. Many of these symbols have a background in the Hebrew Bible and Jewish tradition that would enhance their meaning for some readers, but it is rarely the case that this kind of background knowledge is required to such an extent that non-Jewish readers would be simply baffled. Such language would mean *something* to them, even if it might mean more to those who were better informed. For example, FG's account of Jesus at the Feast of Tabernacles (John 7–8) is considerably informed by the way this festival was celebrated in the first-century Jerusalem Temple (which could not be known from the Hebrew Bible). Readers with this knowledge would certainly benefit from it in their reading of these chapters, but the chapters are nevertheless quite intelligible to readers who lack this knowledge.

It is also true that most of the major Johannine images have some place in the synoptic teaching of Jesus and would therefore not be wholly unfamiliar to non-Johannine Christians. What is distinctive in FG is the extensive development of these images. Every Christian familiar with the traditional words of Jesus at the Last Supper would recognize the bread-of-life discourse in John 6 as a further development of the same images that he or she knew in a much more concise form in the Last Supper tradition. It becomes clear that FG is designed to "work" for readers from a variety of backgrounds and to continue to work for those who read it again and again it with increasing understanding. It contains riches that only a scripturally informed reader could unearth, but it also speaks accessibly to a reader with only minimal prior knowledge of Christian belief. In any case, FG is certainly not a gospel directed only to those who already understand everything it has to say.

Universal References

Our necessarily brief study of the way the language and imagery of FG function has taken us in precisely the opposite direction from the view that sees the Fourth

Gospel as a text written for an isolated Johannine Community. In fact, FG may envisage a wider readership than perhaps any other New Testament text.

A final indication that the Fourth Gospel does not reflect an introverted and isolated group of Christians, uninterested in or even alienated from the rest of the Christian movement, can be found in its use of universal language. FE's multivalent use of the word "world" includes a neutral usage in which the sense is "humanity in general." In this sense, it is the world that God loved and Jesus came to save (John 3:16–17; 4:42; 6:33, 51; 17:21; and cf. 12:32). It is hard to reconcile this repeated and quite emphatic universal perspective with the outlook of a community that deliberately set itself apart from the worldwide Christian movement.

Most commentators recognize that John 21 is also irreconcilable with such an outlook. Here the flock that Jesus commissions Peter to tend is the universal church, not the Johannine Community, a fact confirmed by the allusion to Peter's martyrdom in Rome (21:18). The chapter acknowledges Peter's generally recognized apostolic authority in the whole church, while also asserting the Beloved Disciple's less generally recognized role in the whole church. BD's special role as a witness to Jesus, which FE has already highlighted (see esp. 19:15), now becomes a role of witness to the whole church as BD writes his testimony for the whole church to read (21:24). Thus, the Beloved Disciple's witness, as well as Peter's apostolic pastorate, is given a role in the universal mission of the church, of which the miraculous catch of every kind of fish (21:5–11) functions as an acted parable.

The evidence from John 21 can, of course, be dismissed with the claim that the chapter is a later addition to a book that originally ended at 20:31, part of the last redaction of the text by a writer attempting to integrate the Johannine Community into the wider church. The alternate view, that chapter 21 is an epilogue and an integral feature of the design of FG, cannot be argued here, but it is at least suggestive that this epilogue forms so appropriate a conclusion to the reading of the rest of FG that we have explored in this essay. Once again, the issue concerns the difference between a vertical reading of the text as accumulated layers of evidence for the Johannine Community's history and a horizontal reading of the text as a literary whole. From the latter perspective, the Johannine Community (the community in which the Beloved Disciple lived at the end of his life) finally makes its one and only appearance at John 21:23: "So the rumor spread in the community that this disciple would not die. Yet Jesus did not say to him that he would not die, but, 'If it is my will that he remain until I come, what is that to you?'" This where the Johannine Community belongs, leaving the rest of FG free to be the narrative about Jesus that it patently claims to be.

Part 2

The Fourth Evangelist's Sources

The last one hundred years have seen a vast number of studies on the sources of the Fourth Gospel (FG). The shifting trends in the consensus view have made this issue one of the more interesting features of Johannine scholarship. Early in the twentieth century, most scholars believed that the Fourth Evangelist (FE) had drawn much of his material from the Synoptic Gospels. This view was successfully challenged by Gardner-Smith, Bultmann, and others, so that by mid-century the consensus had moved toward the notion that FE either did not know about the Synoptics or did not care to use them if he did. Many of the great commentaries on John and studies of the Johannine Community from the 1950s, '60s, and '70s reflect this perspective. This period also saw renewed interest in alternate sources for FG, both oral and written. Robert Fortna's "Signs Gospel" was the zenith of these efforts, a complete reconstruction of the hypothetical written source that Fortna and others believe underlies the narrative portions of John. But by the mid-1970s the tide began to turn once again under the influence of scholars such as C. K. Barrett and Franz Neirynck, who argued that certain parallels between FG and the Synoptics can only be explained under the theory that FE borrowed material from those works. Today, there is no solid consensus on the sources FE used to compose his gospel.

The essays in Part 2 address three sets of concerns related to the complex question of FG's sources. The first group compare and contrast the use of Jesus tradition in John and the Synoptics. Unlike most studies of this issue, the authors of these essays neither assume nor deny that FE actually used the Synoptics as sources. Instead, they take a synchronic approach, analyzing ways in which key issues are treated in both John and the Synoptics. The conclusions of each analysis are then used to make observations about the way FE uses traditional material, regardless of its origin. The second group of essays reconsider the possibility that FE borrowed much of his material from a written "Signs Gospel" such as that proposed by Fortna. The third group consider the possibility that FE may have incorporated oral traditions into FG and discuss how such material may have been used.

The authors in Part 2 have been asked to focus their discussion not only on specific sources that FE may have used, but on the ways he may have used them and how this has shaped the presentation of Jesus in FG.

John and the Synoptic Gospels

10

"The Son of the Man" in the Gospel of John

WALTER WINK

The following facts make the use of the title "Son of Man" in the Fourth Gospel (FG) puzzling. First, just as in the Synoptic Gospels, the expression appears in FG only on the lips of Jesus, as a form of third-person self-reference. But *none* of John's "Son of Man" sayings finds a parallel in the Synoptics. Second, with a single exception (5:27), the Fourth Evangelist (FE) preserves the unrefined Greek version of the title with the double article (*ho huios tou anthrōpou*; "the son of the man"), despite what must have been strong pressures to translate the expression into good idiomatic Greek. And third, John's "Son of Man" sayings show no trace of the apocalyptic motifs associated with that title in the Synoptics. For FE, Jesus' exaltation to the Father completes the work he came to do. In all these points, then, FE shows no knowledge of the synoptic usage yet employs exactly the same odd construction. The expression must have been invested with deep meaning for both Jesus and the early church for it to be consistently repeated in the same mysterious form.

In this essay, I will use a variety of expressions to translate FG's phrase "the son of the man." The Semitic idiom on which it is based means simply "human being." But as early as Ezekiel and Daniel, "son of man" was invested with profound meaning and archetypal force. In the New Testament, in eighty-three of its eighty-four occurrences it takes the awkward form "the son of the man," evidently as a way of signaling to the reader that something extraordinary is indicated. English translations not only mask the awkwardness of the expression but also beg the question by deleting the articles and supplying capital letters without justification to produce the familiar "Son of Man." In order to preserve the deliberate oddness of the title, I have used "HumanBeing" (as one word) most frequently here, but also, occasionally, "Wisdom's Child." Other reasonable translations, based on the ancient milieu in which the term was used, include "mortal," "Motherchild," "truly human being," "child of the Source," "the New Being," "Humanchild," "Sophia's Child," or, following the Ethiopic version of *1 Enoch*, "son of the offspring of the Mother of the Living."

Jesus the Ladder

John 1:51 provides a window into FE's understanding of the HumanBeing. Jesus has just astonished Nathaniel with his extrasensory prowess, to which Nathaniel responds (with the kind of acclamation the gospels usually reserve until people know Jesus better): "Rabbi, you are the Son of God! You are the King of Israel!" But Jesus shatters this messianic projection, telling Nathaniel, in effect, to forget about psychic powers: "Do you [singular] believe because I told you that I saw you under the fig tree? You [singular] will see greater things than these." He clarifies the last statement by adding, "Very truly, I tell you [plural], you [plural] will see heaven opened and the angels of God ascending and descending upon the HumanBeing." In other words, "you too, and others like you" (note the plural), will be able to see visions of angels; you too will be open to the transcendent, which so astonishes you when you see it manifested in others. In the words of William Blake, it is Jesus' task as HumanBeing to unite heaven and earth, to cause the disciples to "see" with the eye of the imagination, to transform them by cleansing their sight so that they can see the world as it is, infinite.

The imagery here is from Jacob's dream of a ladder extending from earth to heaven, with angels ascending and descending on it (Gen. 28:10–17). In the Hebrew text, *bo* is ambiguous: it could mean either "on it" or "on him." The ancient rabbis were divided on the proper way to translate the phrase. An early Jewish commentary on Genesis includes the following discussion between Rabbi Hiyya and Rabbi Jannai (early third century C.E.):

> R. Hiyya the Elder and R. Jannai disagreed. One maintained: They [the angels] were ascending and descending the ladder; while the other said: they were ascending and descending on Jacob. The statement that they were ascending and descending the ladder presents no difficulty. The statement that they were ascending and descending on Jacob we must take to mean that some were exalting him and others degrading him, dancing, leaping, and maligning him. Thus it says, Israel [=Jacob] in whom I will be glorified [Isa. 49:3]; it is thou, [said the angels,] whose features are engraved on high; they ascended on

high and saw his [Jacob's] features and they descended below and found him sleeping. (*Genesis Rabba* 68:12)

Elsewhere in the rabbinic literature we read that the mystic is like a person "who has a ladder in his home which he ascends and descends, and nobody can interfere with what he does" (*Hekhalot Rabbati* 13:2; 20:3). Again, mention is made of a "heavenly ladder which stands on earth and reaches up to the right leg of the Throne of Glory" (14:1). These ideas reflect the popular Platonism of the period: as the father of the Jewish nation, Jacob summarizes in his person the ideal, archetypal Israel.

John 1 has taken over this platonic mode of thought in its depiction of Jesus as the HumanBeing. "He is archetypal," says C. H. Dodd, "at least in the sense that His relation to the Father is the archetype of the true and ultimate relation" of human beings to God (1968, 243–244). Moreover, the HumanBeing is represented symbolically in FG's "I am" sayings by light, bread, and the vine, in relation to which he is *alêthinos*, the "true" or ultimate reality lying behind material existence, or that to which these symbols ultimately point. It is not a long step from this to say that FE sees the HumanBeing as the *alêthinos anthrôpos*, the real or archetypal HumanBeing. The HumanBeing is the inclusive representative of ideal or redeemed humanity, just as Jacob was the representative of the ideal nation of Israel. The HumanBeing is the vine; the disciples are the branches (John 15:1–11). As the incarnate Humanchild, Jesus dies and ascends to God, that where he is they may be also (14:3). In his death "the son of the man" thus draws all people everywhere into union with himself, and so affirms his character as inclusive representative of the redeemed race. The revelation of Jesus therefore becomes critical in FG: you are saved by what you see.

Commenting on John 3:14–15, Dodd continues, "As the 'looking' at the serpent caused Israel to 'live,' so the 'contemplation' of the Son of Man in His exaltation brings life eternal." As the ladder to an open heaven, the Human-Being is not simply the revealer, then, but "the inclusive representative of true humanity," who "incorporates in Himself the people of God, or humanity in its ideal aspect." But what had previously been merely an abstraction has now become flesh, actual and incarnate. He is, Dodd contends, "the true self of the human race, standing in that perfect union with God to which others can attain only as they are incorporate in Him." Hence, the HumanBeing is both corporate and individual: the truly human being who gathers into itself those who aspire to true humanity. That is why Nathaniel is overwhelmed by his presence. In Bultmann's words, Jesus is the Revealer who knows his "own" (10:14), "and in his word reveals to them what they are and what they will be. . . . Thus faith in him is grounded in the fact that in the encounter with him the believer's own existence is uncovered" (1971, 107).

Faith in the Earthly
Archetypal HumanBeing

"The son of the man" in FG is not the apocalyptic figure we find in the Synoptics who will come on the clouds of heaven at the end of time. Yet the Fourth Gospel's HumanBeing is invested with all the archetypal significance with which faith could imbue it. When the blind man whom Jesus healed shows himself ignorant of who the HumanBeing might be, Jesus lets him know in a manner that prompts instantaneous faith and even worship (John 9:35–38). The word "believe" (*pisteuō*) appears ninety-eight times in John. But believe what? Sometimes FE asks the reader to "believe" Jesus' words, yet he elsewhere uses the word to mean "believe in" something. Thus, at John 3:14–15, Jesus says, "And just as Moses lifted up the serpent in the wilderness, so must the Son of Man be lifted up, that whoever *believes in him* may have eternal life" (italics added). The idea seems to be that one must commit oneself to Jesus, placing one's trust, hope, or salvation in him. For John, then, "the son of the man" has become a christological confession, equivalent to "the Son of God" and "the Son." These metaphors are all fundamentally filial and relational: they express Jesus' sonship, his relation to the Father. "This filial relationship to God is the central aspect of Jesus' identity in the Fourth Gospel. All other facets of his identity are subordinate to this central feature" (Burkett 1991, 171). But while "Son of God" expresses Jesus' Sonship explicitly, "the son of the man" does so cryptically. According to John, Jesus understood this riddle, but apparently no one else did until he explained it to them. Hence, the term is used only by Jesus.

Clearly, then, "the son of the man" is not, as Hare thought, simply "a name for the earthly Jesus" (1990, 99) in FG. In Margaret Pamment's words, "the son of the man" in FG, "while referring to Jesus, draws particular attention to his representative humanity, that is, Jesus is pictured as representing not what every [one] is, but what [one] could and should be" (1985, 58). Pilate's declaration in the heart of the passion narrative—"Behold the Man" (John 19:5)—may well highlight the HumanBeing as the epitome of humanity. The end that Jesus' hearers expect in the future is already present in Jesus. So Bultmann can conclude, "Thus everything that he [Jesus] is, can be referred to by the mysterious title 'Son of Man'" (1971, 349).

The absence of the apocalyptic scenario in FG means that there is no split between "earthly," "suffering," and "archetypal" Son-of-Man sayings. The historical Jesus has, so to speak, been swallowed by the archetypal "son of the man." Jesus is not so much related to the HumanBeing as identical with it. But the Johannine Jesus is not the son of the man seated at the right hand of God and coming with the clouds of heaven, as in the Synoptics. Instead, John's Jesus is identified with the HumanBeing from all eternity. He is the past, present, and future of humanity in its destiny before God. Jesus, as the incarnate

HumanBeing, reveals God's ultimate statement about the goal of the human enterprise. Yet his followers are not excluded from the reality that the Human-Being represents. In ways that go far beyond the Synoptic Gospels, Jesus the HumanBeing incorporates his disciples into union with himself in God. He gives them "power to become children of God," as he is (John 1:12). They are not just born of earthly parents, but of God, as he is (1:13). Jesus ascends to heaven (3:13) and so will his disciples (14:2). Jesus testifies to what he has seen and heard from God (3:32) and the disciples do likewise (12:17). Jesus judges and forgives (3:17–21) and the disciples will also (20:23). Jesus does the works of God and his followers do so as well (6:28–29; 9:4) and they will do even greater works (14:12). Jesus is God's son, and his followers are "gods" and "children of the Most High" (John 10:34–35). Where Jesus is, his disciples will be also (14:3). Jesus alone sees and knows the Father but, despite the apparent inconsistency, the disciples do also (14:6–7, 9). He is the vine, they are the branches, and the Father is the vinedresser (15:1–11). Nothing could express more completely the collective, corporate nature of the Johannine Human-Being than 14:20—"you will know that I am in my Father, and you in me, and I in you." FE has, in short, not only preserved the collective aspect of the HumanBeing but brings this aspect to the forefront.

The supreme revelation provided by the HumanBeing, then, is not a trip into the heavenly spheres, as we see in so many first- and second-century doc-uments. For FE, the Gospel is not the disclosure of heavenly secrets or mys-tical visions, but rather the unveiling of "this world" (*kosmos*) and the inauguration of an alternative reality, the reign of God. John refers to this other reality as "eternal life"—life in a new dimension that begins the moment one throws one's entire life onto the side of the HumanBeing. To "believe in" the HumanBeing (John 9:35) is to affirm that this new reality that Jesus incar-nates and reveals is truly from God. To believe in him is to join in the strug-gle against the authorities and powers that seek to extinguish this new revelation (like the religious leaders in the healing of the blind man, 9:13–41). That the powers will crush him is certain; that their victory will prove empty is God's great secret: "No one has ascended into heaven except the one who descended from heaven, the [HumanBeing]. And just as Moses lifted up the serpent in the wilderness, so must the [HumanBeing] be lifted up, that who-ever believes in him may have eternal life" (3:14–15). The comparison here seems to be between a death-dealing power (the serpent, possibly suggesting Satan) that is neutralized by being "lifted up" on a pole, and a death-dealing pole (the cross) on which the crucified HumanBeing neutralizes death. His "lifting up" is not to the divine throne room in heaven, but onto the cross: "When you have lifted up [=crucified] the HumanBeing, then you will realize that I am, and that I do nothing on my own, but I speak these things as the Father instructed me" (8:28).

The HumanBeing
and the Historical Jesus

The Johannine HumanBeing is "glorified" in his crucifixion (John 12:23, 32; 13:31) precisely because it is his death that exposes the world and liberates those who were hostage to it (in Hebrew, "lifting up" can refer both to hanging and honoring—Gen. 40:13, 19). And here is the pathos of the Fourth Gospel: the promise of visions of angels ascending and descending upon the son of the man is not fulfilled (Abbott 1910, 561). After the hopeful pronouncement at 1:51, the Gospel of John is the story of a succession of disappointing misunderstandings that culminate in a voice from heaven that no one can comprehend (12:27–29). Even at the close of his public ministry, people still ask, with no perception, "How can you say that the Son of Man must be lifted up? Who is this Son of Man?" (12:34). And well they might. For the only "son of the man" they might have had any knowledge of was that described in Daniel 7, and there the "one like a son of man" appears in heaven, coming to the throne of God and receiving dominion and great glory. But Jesus is only a little-known charismatic healer and preacher, a nobody among the nobodies of Palestine.

Who then is this HumanBeing in the Fourth Gospel? In John 5:26–27, Jesus declares, "For just as the Father has life in himself, so he has granted the Son also to have life in himself; and he has given him authority to execute judgment, because he is the Son of Man." John 5:27 is the only case (out of more than eighty instances in the New Testament) where "son of man" in Greek appears without the definite articles (as in "the son of the man"). Why do we not find more examples of this usage? If John can do without the articles here, why not elsewhere, especially since, as noted earlier, the presence of the articles is awkward in Greek?

It is possible that the definite articles emphasize that "the son of the man" is neither "the son of the Adam" nor humanity generally ("the son of humanity"), but "the son of the Human One" whom Ezekiel encountered at the fountainhead of Jewish mysticism (Ezekiel 1). In Ezekiel, "son of man" is consistently used in the vocative case as a direct address ("O mortal," *ben adam*); hence the absence of the articles there. In Jesus' use of the phrase, now in Aramaic (*bar enosh*), however, the expression is no longer vocative, and some way was needed, when the tradition was translated into Greek, to make clear that it was not a way of referring to all of humanity or to Adam, but in an utterly unique way to Jesus and his followers. If Jesus himself did indeed develop the term in this way, it accounts for the remarkable consistency in early Christian sources—Matthew, Mark, Luke, John, Q, L, M, Thomas, and the Nag Hammadi texts generally—in reproducing the expression with both articles when they could so easily have been dropped.

In FG, however, Jesus' expression has been developed in service of an exaltation Christology. At John 8:28–29, Jesus again takes on the role of exalted HumanBeing: "When you have lifted up the Son of Man, then you will realize that I am he, and that I do nothing on my own, but I speak these things as the Father instructed me. And the one who sent me is with me; he has not left me alone, for I always do what is pleasing to [God]." "The son of the man" here is a transcendent heavenly reality that Jesus has become as a result of his incarnation and glorification through suffering. The double meaning of "lifted up" refers to not just his crucifixion but the crucifixion as the means by which he is exalted to heaven.

In order to communicate this exaltation-through-crucifixion, John has developed a new way of using the tradition, in which the exalted HumanBeing shines through the earthly Jesus. This creates a portrait of Jesus that has seemed "docetic" to many, making Jesus only "appear" to be a real human being. But John's intention is to thereby guide the reader into the "eternal" dimension of life lived in the "now." Consequently, "seeing" Jesus becomes an act of spiritual vision and not mere sight: it involves recognizing that Jesus is an archetypal image capable of spurring unlived life. "Exalted" or "elevated" to the right hand of God can also be seen as an inward movement, however. John's repeated use of the verb "to believe" has usually been taken in the sense of a creed: *believing that* Jesus is the Son of God. In light of our discussion, we might interpret "to believe" as something more akin to the "birth from above," or "rebirth," that Jesus discusses with Nicodemus (John 3:1–21). To believe is not just to weigh, consider, think about, ponder, reflect on, or entertain the idea of following Jesus. It is to throw one's whole life on the side of Jesus. It is to die, to enter the womb for a second time, and to be reborn to the other world.

We spoke earlier of John's statement "no one has ascended into heaven except the one who descended from heaven, the [HumanBeing]" (John 3:13). One does not have to scale the ramparts of heaven to find God. Spirituality is not the confine of a few religious athletes who have mastered their bodies and tethered their souls. God has found people where they are. If the Johannine Jesus sometimes appears more divine than human, it is because John is intent on showing him in his eternal, archetypal form. Now all can know God through Jesus, can know God as well as any mystic. What the Johannine Jesus does is to establish a democracy of mystics: people who have experienced, in their own selves, the reality of the presence of God.

11

The Kingdom of God

Common and Distinct Elements Between John and the Synoptics

Chrys C. Caragounis

The commonness of the Jesus tradition between the Fourth Gospel (FG) and the Synoptics, as well as the variation of the Johannine outworking, can be clearly demonstrated in the case of the Kingdom of God (KOG). This sharing of traditions is especially obvious concerning the following points:

1. One of the most obvious points of shared traditions is the Johannine language of "seeing" or "entering" the KOG in John 3:3, 5. Several synoptic texts also speak of "entering" the Kingdom (see Matt. 5:20; 7:21; 18:13; Mark 10:23–25). Even in John 3:3, "seeing" the KOG might be compared with Mark 9:1 and 13:28 ("seeing Abraham in the Kingdom of God").

2. FG, more often than any of the Synoptics, presents Jesus as King (John 1:49; 6:15; 12:13, 15; 18:33, 37 [twice], 39; 19:3, 14, 15a, 19, 21 [twice]), as against Matthew (eight times), Mark (six times), and Luke (four times).

3. FG's presentation of Jesus as the Son of Man, for all its difference from the Synoptics in conception and presentation, has certain points of contact. In particular, the ideas that the Son of Man is followed by a retinue of servants, has authority to execute royal judgment (John 5:19–27), and is vindicated and exalted by God (12:23–26; 13:31–32) find close parallel in Matthew 25:31–46.

4. But the shared tradition about the KOG goes still deeper. The infrequent synoptic phrase "eternal life" (Matt. 19:16, 29; 25:46; Luke 10:25; 18:18, 30) has in FG assumed the place that the Synoptics give to the idea of the KOG. "Eternal life" occurs in FG no less than seventeen times while the simple "life"

occurs nineteen times (though not always in reference to eternal life; see
Caragounis 1992a, 476).

5. The Johannine concept of the Eschaton, which at a deeper level is inextricably interwoven with the idea of the KOG, recalls the Synoptics' association of the Kingdom with the end time (e.g., Matthew 24–25 pars.).

These points of contact show in a general way that FG and the Synoptics
share a common slate of traditions. This essay will seek to discover the particular treatment of these issues in FG, and show how this treatment fits within
the Fourth Evangelist's (FE) general ideology.

The Johannine Logia
on the Kingdom of God

FG has two direct Kingdom sayings, and both occur in Jesus' conversation
with Nicodemus (John 3:1–15). The verbs used in that passage refer to "seeing" and "entering" the KOG. Thus, the very rich variation in the synoptic
presentation of the KOG (see Ladd 1966, 101–300; Beasley-Murray 1986,
71–337) is absent from FG, and parallels can only be established with those
synoptic texts that speak of "seeing" or "entering" the Kingdom.

Several synoptic texts speak of "seeing the Kingdom." Assuming the priority of Mark, I translate Mark 9:1 to read, "There are some of those who are
standing here who will not taste of death till they see that the Kingdom of God
has come in power." Mark's statement proved too much for Luke, who
changed it to the simple "till they see the Kingdom of God" (9:27; my translation throughout). Mark's saying addresses the eschatological question, the
"when" of the KOG. But despite of the omission of the phrase "has come in
power," Luke, too, must be referring to the coming of the KOG. The difficulty of discovering the exact meaning of the "power" phrase is therefore not
entirely removed. This difficulty probably explains why Matthew turned it
into a Son of Man saying: "till they see the Son of Man coming in his Kingdom (or royal rule)" (16:28).

Of the Markan and Lukan versions of the saying, the Lukan one appears
nearer to that of FG. However, this is so only on the surface. The context in
which "seeing" the KOG takes place in the Synoptics and FG respectively are
entirely different. In the Synoptics, it is a question of the imminence of the
Kingdom, so that the emphasis is eschatological; but in John 3 the question of
eschatology is not raised. FE's "seeing" is not conditioned by a temporal factor, the *when* of the KOG, but by the basic prerequisites for catching a glimpse
of it, that is, the *conditions* for seeing the Kingdom at all (John 3:3–8). In FG,
"seeing" is experiential: those "born of God" "have beheld" (*etheasamatha*) his

glory (John 1:13–14); no one has ever "seen" (*heōraken*) God, but God's only Son has divulged (or "explained," "interpreted"; *exēgēsato*) him; unless a person be born again, she cannot "see" (*idein*) the Kingdom. Thus, although both FG and the Synoptics speak of "seeing" the KOG, there is hardly anything common in the ideology connected with their respective sayings.

Both FG and the Synoptics also speak of "entering" the Kingdom. The second Johannine KOG saying, "no one can enter the kingdom of God without being born of water and Spirit" (John 3:5; NRSV), initially has a broader connection with the synoptic tradition than the previous one. The verb "to enter," with KOG as the object, occurs four times in Mark, five times in Matthew, and three times in Luke, representing a total of seven distinct sayings. Matthew 5:20, with its demand that a person's righteousness exceed that of the scribes and Pharisees to qualify for entering the Kingdom, and 7:21, which speaks of doing God's will as a basis for entering the KOG, are not relevant to the FG saying. The three occurrences of the expression at Mark 10:23–25 and parallels about the impossibility of entering the KOG for the servants of mammon also have nothing in common with the Johannine saying. There remain, then, Mark 10:15 and Matthew 18:3 as possible parallels.

The saying at Mark 10:15 is uttered on the occasion of the bringing of children to Jesus, whom the disciples sought to turn away. This provokes Jesus to say, "Whoever does not receive the Kingdom of God as a child, will never enter it." The Matthean parallel to this statement (19:14) also mentions the Kingdom, but not as being "entered." Matthew 18:3 gives a second Kingdom saying, "If you do not let yourselves be converted and become like children, you will never enter the kingdom of Heaven." The Markan (9:37) and Lukan (9:48) parallels to this pericope do not include the idea of "entering" the KOG. These two sayings (Mark 10:15 and Matt. 18:3), then, which bring together the ideas of conversion and receiving the KOG as a child, are the closest ideological parallels to John 3:5, which speaks of "being born again" ("from above"; *anothen*) as a condition for entering the Kingdom. The synoptic sayings are constructed around the motif of the child as a natural representative of the qualities necessary for inheriting the KOG (openness, simple trust and acceptance). In a radical oxymoron, FE uses the motif of an old man and demands not merely that he should return to his childhood outlook but that he should be "born again." In FG, entering the Kingdom is not a question of assuming something or putting on something, but of starting all over again, of coming into a new existence, of becoming something entirely new. It could not have been expressed more radically.

This connection between the KOG and the concept of regeneration is indicative of FE's theological concerns (cf. the frequency of *gennaō* in FG and 1 John). Indeed, the theme of "being born of God" is adumbrated already in

the Prologue (John 1:12–13). It appears to have its ultimate ground in the
Johannine concept of the Logos becoming "flesh" (1:14). Just as the eternal
Logos comes to the world through the medium of incarnation, that is, by participating in human nature, so too human beings can come into the KOG by
being born of water (= the Word; cf. 13:5–10; 15:3) and the Spirit of God (3:6),
that is, by participating in the divine nature (the thought is implicitly present
at John 1:13 and 1 John 3:9).

The Exploitation
of the Grammatical Idiom

If there are differences between FG and the Synoptics in their respective
understandings of the KOG, there is at least one area in which a deeper underlying agreement exists. This pertains to the handling of the time perspective
as this is conditioned by a specialized use of aorist tense verbs. Perhaps the
most important synoptic saying about the imminence of the KOG appears in
Matthew 12:28 and Luke 11:20: "But if I drive out the demons through the
Spirit/finger of God, then the kingdom of God is about to break in upon you
[*ephthasen eph' hymas*]." C. H. Dodd understood the aorist indicative *ephthasen*
to signify a past or completed action and, accordingly, translated it "has
come/arrived" (1935, 36; 1936, 91–94). The verse thus became a mainstay for
his doctrine of "realized eschatology," in which he has been followed by count-
less other scholars. Dodd's understanding has also influenced many of the
modern translations. Yet this conclusion is based on a misunderstanding of the
meaning and function of the aorist indicative verb in this context.

One of the peculiar uses of the aorist (and perfect) tense is that it can be
used to describe both past *and future* actions. In other words, the aorist indicative may be used instead of the future. But this happens only under certain conditions and in order to emphasize a particular aspect of the action described.
When the aorist (or perfect) indicative is used where the future indicative
might have been used, *it underlines either the certainty or the imminence of a future
action, or both*. The use of the aorist for future events gives a far more vivid perspective than the future tense, and the imminence of the impending action is
highlighted. This peculiar use of the aorist and perfect is no replacement for
the future indicative in ordinary usage, so one must assume that there is always
a special reason for using the aorist or perfect indicative rather than the future
indicative.

This specialized use of the aorist tense is evidenced in all periods of the
Greek language from Euripides to the present day (where it occurs extremely
frequently). I will illustrate with one or two examples. In Euripides, *Alkestis*

386, King Admetos, unable to bear the prospect of losing his beloved wife, cries in desperation: *apolomen ara ei de me leipseis* ("I am/have been lost if you leave me"), meaning "I shall be lost if you leave me." The certainty of his wretched state subsequent to the death of his wife makes Admetos express the bitter truth as if it were already a fact, and hence he uses the aorist *apolomen* rather than the future tense. In the LXX of Daniel 4:24, the coming judgment of God on Nebuchadnezzar is spoken of not in the future indicative (as would be expected), but in the aorist indicative, as though it were an already accomplished event: *syncrima Hypsistou estin ho ephthasen epi ton kyrion mou ton basilea kai se ekdioxousin* ("it is the judgment of the Most High, which has come [*ephthasen*, aorist] over my lord the king, and they will drive you away [*ekdioxousin*, future]"; see Caragounis 1989, 12–32). In such cases, the aorist tense is used to emphasize the certainty of an upcoming event.

This idiomatic usage of the aorist has escaped the attention of biblical scholarship, leading to many ill-informed arguments and conclusions. As a case in point, the saying in Matthew 18:3 does not mean that "the Kingdom of God has come upon you." Rather, its force may be paraphrased as follows: "If I drive out the demons [i.e., prepare for the coming of the KOG by defeating the forces of evil] by the Spirit/finger of God [rather than by Beelzebul, as you claim], then the Kingdom of God *is about to break in* upon you [and overtake you in your obstinate and unrepentant state]" (Caragounis 1992b, 423). While this statement is certainly an advance on the *eggiken* type of logia ("the Kingdom of God is *near*"), it does not quite imply the actual presence of the KOG, only its imminence. Moreover, the statement is not strictly informative; its function is one of warning, almost a threat (this is the force of *eph' hymas*), and the objective is to prevail upon the hearers to repent. This understanding is corroborated by the following verses that lead up to the equally pertinent climactic warning about blasphemy against the Holy Spirit.

The imminence and urgency about the KOG that the Synoptics express by the idiomatic use of the aorist *ephthasen* is similarly advanced in FG by the use of other aorist verbs. But this fact has been lost in Schweitzer's century-old position of "*Konsequente Eschatologie*," which became the standard German position, and in Dodd's "realized eschatology," which became the mainline English viewpoint. Neither of these theories has done justice to the dynamics of the biblical terminology. The German viewpoint is too flat while the British viewpoint is too simplistic. The plethora of middle-of-the-line interpretations that have been generated in reaction to these two extreme positions are to be understood as a damaging criticism of them. At the same time, they have contributed to a more nuanced and relatively more correct understanding of what is involved in the Kingdom sayings. Thus, Kümmel's mediating position (1961, 2), Jeremias's awkward expression "*sich realiserende Eschatologie*" (1960,

194), Hunter's "inaugurated eschatology" (1972, 94), Fuller's "proleptic eschatology" (1954, 20–34), and Ladd's rather obscure description "eschatology of
biblical realism" (1966, xiii), to the extent to which they have avoided polar-
ization, are welcome correctives. But to the extent that these views remain
caught in the maelstrom of *Konsequente* and "realized" eschatology, trying to
hold both present and future aspects together in tension, they must be deemed
failures. Consequently, even these attempts have missed the main point of the
KOG sayings: *the Kingdom is potentially present in the teaching and acts of Jesus.*
If we wish to define this reality in terms of eschatology, we must speak of a
"potentially present eschatology." This is quite different from the previously
described positions, including Fuller's proleptic eschatology, which all suggest
that the Kingdom is somehow present already in Jesus' teaching and works,
though its full manifestation lies in the future.

A position of "potential presence" faces its first serious problem in the definition of the KOG itself. It is symptomatic of both *"Konsequente Eschatologie"*
and "realized eschatology" that they have evaded the issue of definition. Does
the KOG consist simply of Jesus' miracles, as Dodd seems to imply? Moreover, is the KOG something that can be entered already during Jesus' ministry
(as the advocates of the mediating positions suppose)? And what does it mean
for the believer on earth to be "already" in the Kingdom? Further, if the KOG
has already arrived in and through Jesus' proclamation and mighty works, how
is the rest of Jesus' public ministry to be understood? Again, it is clear from
the biblical statements that the Kingdom is inextricably interwoven with the
fate of the Son of Man (Caragounis 1986, 145–243). But if the KOG has
already arrived during Jesus' public ministry, how is it related to his death? And
how can the KOG have already arrived during Jesus' earthly life when at the
very end of that life it is said to be still future (Luke 22:16–18 pars.)? It is easy
to posit a partial fulfillment now with a full consummation of the Kingdom at
the Eschaton, but this does not solve the above difficulties. These difficulties
are so serious that they render problematic every interpretation of the KOG
as wholly present, as wholly future, or as partially present from the standpoint
of Jesus' utterances.

A Potentially Present Eschatology

Against the previously described views, I will now set forth the case for a potentially present eschatology in understanding Jesus' Kingdom of God sayings.
The use of the term "potentially" here is susceptible to misunderstanding.
Because the English word technically refers to "something that exists in a state
of potency or possibility for changing or developing into a state of actuality"

(*Webster's Third New International Dictionary*, 1986), it may be supposed that the objective existence of the KOG is in doubt. As used here, the term "potentially" does not qualify the term "Kingdom of God," but rather the term "present." What is "potential" is not the KOG itself, but its presence in Jesus during his earthly ministry. Similarly, the neater term "potential eschatology" does not imply any doubt as to the Eschaton but is merely an abbreviation for "potentially present eschatology." The potential presence of the KOG in Jesus is evident in the following three areas of the Fourth Gospel: the "eternal life" sayings, the references to Jesus' "hour," and FE's understanding of the Eschaton and faith.

The *Aiōnios Zōē* Logia

There are four sayings in FG that use the expression "has eternal life": John 3:36 ("He who believes in the Son has eternal life"); 5:24 ("He who hears my word and believes in him who sent me, has eternal life"); 6:47 ("He who believes has eternal life"); and 6:54 ("He who eats my flesh and drinks my blood has eternal life"). The use of the verb "to have" in the present tense with *aiōnios zōē* ("eternal life") as its object has led some to conclude that these texts teach a realized eschatology, which implies that the believer enters the sphere of eternal life or begins an everlasting existence at the moment the act of faith takes place (de Jonge 1992, 482ff.; Frey 1998). A careful scrutiny of these texts, however, reveals that the emphasis is not on the present "has" but on the fact that faith is the *condition* for receiving eternal life. None of these texts supports the notion of a realized eschatology. Instead, they explain the *means* by which eternal life is acquired (by believing in Jesus and consuming his flesh). Eternal life is, therefore, still future from the standpoint of these sayings (Caragounis 1992a, 477–478).

Futurity, albeit in a very vivid way, is expressed also by those Johannine texts that use the aorist or perfect indicative: John 12:23 ("the hour has come [*elelythen*] for the Son of Man to be glorified"); 13:31 ("Now is the Son of Man glorified" [*edoxasthe*]); 17:4 ("I have glorified [*edoxasa*] you on earth"). All of these sayings use the idiomatic aorist, which transports an event from the future to the present in order to enhance its reality and force by underlying its certainty and especially its imminence (Caragounis 1992a, 478–479).

The "Hour" of Jesus

Twelve texts in FG speak of the time or "hour" (*hē hōra*) of Jesus. Jesus' hour is portrayed as "coming" (John 4:21, 23; 5:25, 28; 12:27; 16:32), as "having come" (12:23; 17:1), and as "not having yet come" (2:4; 7:30; 8:20), while 13:1

uses the aorist "came." The third group of verses, which describe Jesus' hour
as not yet having come, are significant here. At 2:4, Jesus refuses Mary's request
to supply wine for the wedding feast by explaining, "My time has not yet come"
(*hekei*), a covert reference to the coming revelation of his true identity. At 7:30,
the narrator explains that, although the Jewish leaders wanted to arrest Jesus,
no one laid hands on him because his time (i.e., the time of his death) had not
yet come (*elelythei*). The same thought occurs at 8:20, while at 12:27 the
"hour" refers to the death awaiting Jesus. In all these texts, the hour of Jesus
is, from the perspective of the speaker, something future.

Four other texts in FG refer to a future time when God will be worshiped
in a new way (4:21, 23) and when the resurrection of Jesus will cause the dead
to rise (5:25, 28). One of these texts, 5:25 (*erchetai hōra kai nyn estin*), has been
seized upon by Frey and made the key to realized eschatology in FG. Frey
emphasizes the present tense *erchetai* in proximity to the present *estin* and the
temporal particle *nyn*: "the time is coming and is now [here] when the dead
will hear the voice of the Son of God and those who hear it will live." But a
number of Greek verbs, such as *erchomai* and *hypagō*, naturally denote an
imperfective or ongoing action and consequently suggest the future completion of an event. The present tense form *erchetai* in John 4:21 must have a
future reference, as is clear from the accompanying future indicative *proskyne-
sete* ("will worship"). In 5:25, where the intention is to emphasize the imminence of Jesus' hour, the present tense *erchetai* is made more definite by the
addition of *kai nyn estin* ("and now is [here]"). But despite this phrase, the saying has not acquired the status of realization, as Frey suggests (1998, 2ff.); *nyn
estin* ("now is") only emphasizes the imminence of the "coming" (*erchetai*).
That the thought is still future is shown also by the fact that Jesus is speaking
of the time following his death, an event that has not yet taken place. In other
words, the aorist tense refers to actions that are, from the speaker's standpoint,
future. This is further confirmed by 4:23, which, using an identical expression,
refers to a future time when God will be worshiped (*proskynēsousin*) in Spirit
and in truth (cf. 7:39, *oupō gar ēn pneuma hoti Iēsous oudepō edoxasthē*, a clearly
future condition). Likewise, 12:23 (*elelythen*), 13:1 (*elthen*), and 17:1 (*elēlythen*)
are all cases of the idiomatic use of the aorist and perfect indicatives to present
future events in a vivid way as if they had already transpired.

The Eschaton and Faith

The word *eschatos* is used six times in FG in reference to the last day (*eschate
hemera*). In five of these instances (John 6:39, 40, 44, 54; 11:24), Jesus promises
to raise up those who believe in him, while the sixth occurrence speaks of the
final judgment (12:48). Bultmann and his followers see in this a redactor's

attempt to bring the eschatology of FG in line with his own futuristic eschatology (Bultmann 1971, 194; Haenchen 1980; Becker 1979–1981). Barrett and Beasley-Murray argue that the compositional unity of the passage cannot be impugned, yet both remain trapped in the misplaced emphasis on the present element in the KOG sayings that still bedevils New Testament scholarship. Thus, Barrett states that "it seems that it was John's intention to retain just enough futuristic eschatology" (1978, 283, 294), while Beasley-Murray concludes that "the duality of present and future participation in the kingdom of God is fundamental to the proclamation of Jesus in all four [canonical] Gospels" (1987, 92).

It is important here to observe that "the last day" does not refer to a particular day at the end of the world, but to the new age in which the KOG, that is, the rule of God, will be revealed. This places the Kingdom at the Eschaton, showing it to be of an other-worldly order. But in Jesus' ministry the Eschaton is brought into contact with the present, because both the KOG and the Eschaton are bound up with Jesus' person. In his person, ministry, and death Jesus gathers all those strands that emanate from God: God's eternal counsel, salvation, eternal life, dynamic rule over his creation—everything finds in him the key for its fulfillment. And everything is made contingent on the attitude that one adopts toward him. It is this nexus between present faith—the decisive factor for one's eschatological destiny—and the future character of the Eschaton that brings future and present together in Jesus. This does not mean that the Eschaton has ceased to be future, but that the decisive act that will determine the believer's place at the Eschaton is occurring already in the present. Thus, although the KOG is a wholly eschatological concept, entrance into it is determined *now* by the act of faith in Jesus as the Christ. As Moloney expresses it, "Jesus makes God known, and the judgment flows from an acceptance or refusal of that revelation" (1998, 366).

Conclusions

The present discussion has indicated that FG and the Synoptics share several common aspects in their presentation of the Kingdom of God. These aspects, although indicating the very limited diversity in FE's presentation, nevertheless form a sufficient basis for the postulation of common traditions between them. There are, however, two significant differences in FE's appropriation of this tradition. First, in FG the theme of the believer's eschatological existence is set forth not so much in terms of the Kingdom motif but in terms of something that is more characteristic of Johannine thought—eternal life. Second, whether it is a question of the KOG or of eternal life, FE has interpreted the common tradition in an emphatically realized manner, in which the dividing line between present and future has been greatly effaced, almost obliterated. A careful study of the texts supposed to support a "realized eschatology" in FG, as well as a critical scrutiny of the arguments put forth to defend this interpretation, shows that this view is based on a misunderstanding. Central to this misunderstanding is the failure to perceive the idiomatic use of the Greek aorist tense previously described.

According to my analysis, the eschatology of FG, as also that of the Synoptics, has a future orientation. However, the future is decided in the present. This decision rests wholly on the attitude of faith or unbelief toward Jesus. The Fourth Gospel presents the Eschaton in a way that was commensurable with the early church's experience of salvation as based on faith and decided here and now. Hence, faith is transmuted into eternal life while unbelief is transmuted into condemnation. It is this dynamic transmutation that has been wrongly interpreted in terms of a realized eschatology, forgetting that nothing other than faith itself is transmuted. However, faith would not have been faith if the thing believed and hoped for were already present (cf. Rom. 8:24; Heb. 11:1).

12

Exorcisms in the Fourth Gospel and the Synoptics

GRAHAM H. TWELFTREE

The prominence of Jesus as an exorcist in the synoptics, yet the silence of the Fourth Gospel on the matter is a puzzle this essay attempts to explain. A survey of the synoptic traditions as well as evidence from outside the New Testament leaves little doubt that Jesus was a successful and widely known exorcist (Twelftree 1993, 136–42). In view of the messianic function of the exorcism stories in the synoptics (e.g., Matt. 12:28; Luke 11:20) and the stated agenda of the Fourth Gospel (FG) that readers "may come to believe that Jesus is the Messiah" (John 20:31), exorcisms would have served such an agenda well. Further, if the signs of FG anticipate the great sign of the cross (e.g., 2:4; 6:11), would not exorcism stories aptly prefigure the casting down of Satan in the cross (12:31)? But FG has not followed these paths. Why?

Inadequate Solutions

Let us first consider a number of answers given to this question and the reasons why they are unacceptable.

First, an early explanation relied on the speculative view that the Fourth Evangelist (FE) belonged to the Sadducean party, which rejected belief in angels and demons (Acts 23:8). On this view there are no exorcism stories in FG because the author found them uncongenial. But this will not do. The positive association of ascending and descending angels of God with the Son of

135

Man (John 1:51), the key role of angels in witnessing to the resurrection (20:12), and the ease with which FE reports accusations that Jesus was being accused of demon possession (7:20; 8:48–52; 10:20–21) would all be inimical to this explanation.

A second answer, and the simplest, is that FE did not know of Jesus as an exorcist. This is highly unlikely. Jesus had a widespread reputation as a powerful and popular exorcist. Further, if one accepts the emerging view that ancient gospels were not written for isolated communities but rather for a broad Christian readership, it is hard to imagine that the Christians involved in the development of the Johannine tradition had never heard that Jesus was known as an exorcist. And there *may be* hints at John 6:66–71 that FE was aware of exorcism traditions reflected in synoptic tradition (Broadhead 1995). It is only reasonable to conclude that FE has deliberately excluded reference to exorcism from his gospel.

Third, could it be that in eliminating reference to Jesus as exorcist FG avoided facing the synoptic charge that Jesus performed his exorcisms by the power of Satan (cf. Mark 3:22)? Probably not. FG does not avoid the equally damaging charge of Jesus' having a demon (7:20; 8:48–52; 10:20–21).

Fourth, might the absence of exorcism stories in FG be linked to its origins in Judea, the supposed home of the Beloved Disciple, upon whom FG may depend (Plumer 1997, 350–351), while the synoptic exorcisms take place in Galilee (Mark 1:21–28; 5:1–20)? But this too is unlikely. Four of the seven signs or miracles in FG have a Galilean setting (2:1–12; 4:46–54; 6:1–14, 16–21). And it is probably unreasonable to suppose that FE knew nothing of synoptic traditions.

A fifth solution postulates that FE was using a signs source, which did not contain exorcism stories. But if FG was dependent on such a source, the question remains, Why did the source not contain allusions to exorcism? Or why did FE not supplement the supposed signs source with either a story or at least an allusion to Jesus' ministry of exorcism, alongside the other miracles or signs of Jesus that he repeatedly mentions (cf. 2:23; 3:2; 4:45; 6:2, 26; 7:31; 10:32; 11:47; 12:37; 20:30)?

Sixth, it cannot be that FE was embarrassed about portraying Jesus' healing techniques, which might expose him to a charge of magic (so Plumer 1995, 356–358). FG depicts Jesus healing from a distance (4:46–54), a feat familiar in the ancient world (Twelftree 1993, 145–146), and elsewhere Jesus uses spittle (9:1–7), also a common feature of cures (Twelftree 1993, 158).

Seventh, it cannot be that exorcism is lost to the Johannine traditions simply because of a particular aversion to the notion of the Kingdom of God itself— which is tied to exorcism in the synoptic traditions. Even though the phrase "Kingdom of God" is rare in FG, it does occur (3:3, 5; cf. 18:26). On the contrary, it is more likely that a concern to leave aside exorcism has led to the Kingdom of God's disappearance—to be replaced with a focus on Jesus' kingship.

Having set aside these inadequate explanations for the absence of exorcism in FG we must look elsewhere. We shall see that a number of interwoven aspects of FE's intentions and theology have probably contributed to the deliberate suppression of Jesus' association with exorcism.

The Johannine Purpose and Audience

Bauckham (1998, 147–171) has recently argued again for the older view that FG was written to supplement Mark's Gospel. Even if we reject this thesis as a whole, we can take up the more specific view that FG was aware of traditions reflected in the Synoptics and attempted to supplement them. This may clarify FE's selection of miracle stories. Not only are there no exorcisms but also no healing of people with withered limbs; no cleansing of lepers; no fevers cured; no hemorrhages stopped; no deaf made to hear; no dropsy mentioned; no stilling of a storm; nor is there a story of the withering of a fig tree.

It cannot be that FE wished to avoid repeating any of the stories his readers may already have known. FG parallels the synoptic stories of Jesus' feeding a multitude and walking on the sea, and has stories of the blind receiving their sight, the dead raised, a paralytic healed, an official's servant or son healed, and the disciples catching many fish. The only entirely unique story in FG is the changing of water into wine. Nor can it be that FE wanted to downplay Jesus as healer, even though most of the miracle stories not found in FG are healings; three (four if raising Lazarus is included) of the seven miracle stories in the body of FG deal with healing. In part, the absence of exorcism in FG is probably FE's attempt to supplement the *perspective* on the miracles in the synoptic traditions. Indeed, this may be at least part of the reason other kinds of miracle stories are also missing from FG. A close examination of the miracles in FG and the exorcisms in the Synoptics confirms this and shows that FE intended to qualify the traditions perhaps already known to his readers.

Exorcism and the Johannine Miracles

The most obvious feature of the miracle stories in FG is that they are few and take up little space. Yet they dominate FG because they are spectacular and relatively uncommon. The Cana story of water into wine is a miracle of immense proportions: six jars of twenty or thirty gallons of water each are turned into wine (John 2:6). The paralytic at Bethesda had been paralyzed for thirty-eight years but was immediately made well merely by Jesus' word (5:5,

9). The story of Lazarus is self-evidently stupendous, not least because he had been in the tomb four days (11:39). (It was held that a person's soul hovered in the vicinity of the body for three days after death, after which time a resurrection was impossible. Indeed, John 11:39 implies the body is rotting already.) The story of the large catch of fish (21:4–14) was probably appended to an earlier edition of FG. It is not particularly spectacular, and it simply highlights the magnitude of the seven stories in the body of the Gospel.

Some synoptic miracles are also stupendous: the feeding of a multitude and the widow's son are certainly stories that would have been considered spectacular. Exorcisms, however, are not spectacular. The Greek magical papyri preserve numerous incantations and recipes for exorcists (e.g., *PGM* 5:99–171) that show how widespread and common exorcism was, most often performed by healers whose identity mattered little in the success of their art (Twelftree 1993, 38–39). And the literature of the period, including the New Testament, witnesses to a number of historical figures who performed exorcisms, such as the sons of Sceva, Rabbi Simeon ben Yose, and Apollonius of Tyana. The unspectacular nature of exorcisms can also be seen in Tobit 6:17, the unadorned method of the pupils of the Pharisees (Matt. 12:24), rabbinic material (e.g., *Numbers Rabbah* 19:8), and the Dead Sea Scrolls (e.g., *1QapGen* 20). Even in the synoptic traditions, apart from the Gerasene demoniac (Mark 5:1–20), exorcisms are portrayed as relatively unspectacular and commonplace events in Jesus' ministry (Twelftree 1993, 22–47; cf. Mark 1:32–34, 39; 3:11–12).

In contrast to the relatively commonplace nature of the synoptic exorcism stories, it is the consistently astounding, extraordinary, or uncommon nature of the Johannine miracles that would have stood out to the readers. Moreover, that FE intends the miracles to be considered unique can be seen from Jesus' claim that he had done "the works that no one else did" (John 15:24).

Further, FE chose miracles not only because they were unique but because they could be understood both as divine in origin and as a revelation of the divine. For example, it was widely held that gods and heroes could walk on seas and across rivers (e.g., *Iliad* 13.27–30; Dio Chrysostom, *Third Discourse on Kingship* 30–31; cf. Job 9:8). However, none of these stories is as clear and as graphic as the one in FG (6:16–21); it can be supposed that Jesus' miracle would have been seen as astounding. In that story Jesus says—in the absolute— "I am!" (6:20), and the readers of FG are likely to recall God's saying to Moses, "I am who I am" (Exod. 3:14). In this way, FG gives the story a divine origin as well as the capacity to reveal Jesus' divine nature. The divine origin of the miracles in FG is summed up by the character Nicodemus—"No one can do these signs that you do unless God is with him" (John 3:2). It is also evident in FE's notion that the glory of God is seen in Jesus' miracles (e.g., 2:11; 11:40), so that there ought to be no doubt that Jesus was the Messiah (20:30–31a).

So FE's portrayal of the miracles as consistently astounding is in sharp contrast to the way exorcisms were viewed at the time, including those in the synoptic traditions. We can suppose, then, that the inclusion of exorcism among FE's other stories would have detracted from his consistent view that Jesus' miracles were grand in scale. So relatively common a healing as an exorcism fails as a programmatic act in the ministry of Jesus (as in Mark 1:21–28; 2:1–12). It could not carry the significance FE sought to invest in the miracle stories.

The Ambiguity of Exorcism

From what we know about ancient exorcisms, Jesus' success might have been understood to depend simply on what he himself said or did, or on any of a number of sources of power/authority outside himself. Combined with his social and religious deviance, such ambiguous healing methods afforded Jesus' opponents the opportunity to deem him mad and satanic (Matt. 12:24; Luke 11:15). But in eschewing exorcisms, FE avoided this obvious ambiguity. It is not that he was distancing Jesus from other healers in his methods, which were much like those of others. Any distancing that took place was a byproduct of FE's attempt to maintain the divine origin and revelatory character of Jesus' miracles.

A related view of exorcisms probably caused FE to omit all mention of them. It was rare for an exorcist to cast out demons entirely on his own authority. The synoptic traditions depict Jesus relying on his own power/authority by using the emphatic "I (*egō*) command you . . . ," but they also say that Jesus used the Spirit (Luke has "finger") of God as his power/ authority (Matt. 12:28; Luke 11:20). By contrast, in FG, even though given his tasks and authorized by the Father (5:36), Jesus is never portrayed as relying on a source of power/authority outside himself in performing miracles. Here we are taking up a more nuanced version of the view that FE avoided exorcism in order to distance Jesus from other healers—not because of their technique but because they depended on unspecified, unknown, or even outside sources of power/authority. Thus, in establishing the uniqueness of Jesus and his miracles, FE focuses on the close relationship, even identity, between the Father and the Son advertised in John 1:51 and repeated one way or another through the ensuing narrative (5:18).

FG's larger-than-life miracles, as well their divine origin and revelatory capacity, may also explain why FE has left aside so many other synoptic miracles: healings of cripples, the deaf, those with dropsy, lepers, and people with withered limbs, fevers, and hemorrhages; even stories of a storm calmed and a fig tree made to wither. Such miracles were comparatively minor and—in the case of exorcism—obviously ambiguous in their origin. Instead, the divine and unambiguous miracles of FG highlight the blindness and lack of faith of those who refuse to see in them clear signals of Jesus' identity.

Johannine Miracles as "Signs"

In contrast to the Synoptic Gospels, one of the distinctive features of the Johannine miracles is that they are called signs (*sēmeia*). FG's use of "sign" is best understood in light of the Septuagint, where the word is almost always used of God's showing himself to be the Almighty and Israel to be his chosen people through the miraculous events of the exodus (Deut. 26:8). Further, a sign could demonstrate the authenticity of the word of a prophet of God as well as the prophet himself (Exod. 4:1–9). And, just as an Old Testament sign could represent (Ezek. 4:1–3) or announce (Isa. 7:10–16) things to come, we are not surprised that in FG the miracles of Jesus are also a foretaste of a future time of even greater things by God (14:12). But there is no precedent in the Hebrew Bible for seeing exorcism as a "sign." Thus, while the miracles in FG may be portrayed as divine in origin and as innately revealing the divine, they also signify more than the immediately obvious, as is seen from the misunderstandings and ambiguities embedded in the stories.

What the Johannine miracles "signify" is easily determined. First, in light of the Septuagint, God himself is at work in these acts of Jesus, and through them his character is disclosed. In turn, the signs reveal the glory of Jesus; they point to his true identity or glory and his filial relationship—even unity—with the Father. And the appended story of the large catch of fish is consistent with this Johannine theology of miracles, at least in that it is used to reveal (*phanerō*) Jesus to the disciples (John 21:1, 14), encouraging them to trust in him. Second, in FG the signs point to the death and resurrection of Jesus where the glory of Jesus is also clearly seen. For example, the story of the official's son is not simply a healing of a sick boy. In twice repeating the phrase "your son will live" (4:50–53) FE probably intends an echo of the resurrection of Jesus (cf. 14:19). The story of the giving of sight to a blind man (9:1–7) can be seen to reflect the life of Jesus, so that, for example, both Jesus and the man born blind use the same self-identification, "I am," and both elicit hostile response. And, as if prefiguring the trial of Jesus, the man is not believed when he testifies before the authorities.

The synoptic miracle stories have a symbolic function (Mark 11:12–14, 20–25; Matt. 17:24–27; Luke 5:1–11). Exorcisms were a kind of sign; they signified the realization of the Kingdom of God, the new state of affairs attending the appearance of Jesus (Matt. 12:28; Luke 11:20). By contrast, the Johannine signs did not actualize the Kingdom; they revealed the glory of God's son.

Jesus' Ministry: A Battle with Satan

Perhaps undergirding all these various factors that may have caused FE to leave aside mention of exorcisms, there is a perspective on the ministry of Jesus in FG that is fundamentally at variance with the synoptic traditions. Although in the Synoptics Jesus battles against religious authorities and the natural elements, apart from the isolated exorcisms there is little to indicate that Jesus' *whole ministry*, as in FG, is to be understood as a battle with Satan. Concomitantly, other synoptic miracles are not distinguished from the exorcisms (Mark 1:34), nor are they consistently portrayed as battle zones with Satan. Moreover, that the battle with demons in exorcism is a battle with Satan can only generally be inferred in the Synoptics, for these demons with which Jesus contends are rarely tied explicitly to Satan. Further, the latter part of Jesus' synoptic ministry—including the passion narrative—reflects little of the battle with Satan.

In contrast, there are signals in FG that Jesus' *entire ministry* is to be understood as, or at least is pervaded by, a battle with Satan: one of Jesus' immediate companions is called a devil (John 6:70); a number of times Jesus is charged with being motivated by a demon (7:20; 8:48; 10:20); and, notably, the religious opponents with whom he contends throughout his ministry are said to have the devil as their father (8:44). Finally, the climax of FG is portrayed as a battle with Satan (12:31; 14:30; 16:11; cf. 13:27).

To put the matter sharply, on the one hand, in the synoptic traditions the battle with Satan is centered during the public ministry of Jesus, in his exorcisms. But then it is severely attenuated in the passion narrative. The reverse is the case for FG. The battle with Satan permeates the proleptic ministry of Jesus, reaching its climax and realization in the cross event—the grand cosmic exorcism. In this way FE is able to affirm that the lie of Satan's control of this world is far more pervasive than the possession of some sick individuals and that the defeat of Satan requires more than isolated exorcisms.

For all these reasons FE may have felt the need to leave aside the exorcism stories. They would distract from his view that Jesus' whole ministry was a battle with Satan and detract from the centrality of the cross as the locus of Jesus' defeat of Satan. In any case, from what we have seen of the stupendous and divine nature of the miracles in FG, it is unlikely that commonplace and ambiguous exorcisms could aptly prefigure the casting down of Satan to take place in the cross, let alone encapsulate it.

Not only does the whole of Jesus' Johannine ministry take on the character of a battle with Satan, but FE has radically reinterpreted the nature of that battle. As the battle is set up in FG, Jesus does not confront Satan in the form of demons or demoniacs but in the unbelief of those who, inspired by the father of lies (8:44), refuse to see the truth revealed in his teaching and his glory revealed in the miracles. Thus it is in response to his teaching that Jesus is accused of being mad (7:20). And, in response to the miracles there is not the awe or praise familiar in the Synoptic Gospels but rather either belief or unbelief (9:16; 10:21; cf. Twelftree 1999, 230–233). Therefore, every miracle in FG takes on the character of a battle with Satan. In turn, the Jesus of FG liberates people not from demons but from unbelief. Demons are not exorcised by the power of the Spirit; as the Son of God, Jesus confronts unbelievers with the truth. Notably, the scale or level of the battle in which Jesus is involved is heightened in that Jesus is not dealing with messengers of Satan but with the devil himself (6:71; 8:44). In short, in leaving aside the exorcism tradition, FE radically reinterprets Jesus' mission as one of liberating people from the demonic darkness of unbelief rather than freeing them from demonic sickness. This presentation is consistent with FE's emphasis on Jesus as teacher and revealer.

Finally, in the synoptic battles of exorcism Jesus is confronted, verbally abused, cursed, and—notably—disobeyed. He appears to fail. Such a portrait is so at variance with the decisively powerful, self-determining, and successful Jesus of FG that it may have been yet another contributing factor in FE's omission of exorcism stories.

Conclusions

In contrast to the synoptic focusing of Jesus' battle with Satan in the exorcisms, for FE the whole of Jesus' ministry is a battle with Satan that climaxes in the cross. However, that battle has been comprehensively reinterpreted so that Satan, who fathers the lie of unbelief, is confronted not through the expulsion of demons but directly through the confrontation of those he inspires with the truth. Table 12.1 contrasts the potential reasons for the absence of exorcisms in FG with those of the Synoptic Gospels.

In that those miracles in the synoptic tradition not found in FG resemble the exorcisms—unspectacular, commonplace, of more obviously ambiguous origins, and actualizing the Kingdom of God—in this set of solutions we have, at least in part, also explained their absence. More important, though, there is overlap with the synoptic traditions in the genre of stories. If FE saw his gospel as supplementing the synoptic traditions, we can see that he probably wanted to use miracle stories of a consistently different stamp to convey the uniqueness of Jesus in his divine nature and relationship to the Father: in FG, God himself is encountered and seen at work in Jesus' activities.

In short, an exorcism could not, without further and considerable explana-

Table 12.1

Synoptic Exorcisms vs. Miracles of Fourth Gospel

Synoptic Exorcism Traditions	Miracles of the Fourth Gospel
Exorcism is a commonplace occurrence, typical of Jesus' activity.	Signs are relatively rare occurrences.
Jesus' methods are unspectacular and typical of general techniques of exorcism in the ancient world.	Signs are always done on a grand scale and are therefore unique and astounding.
The source of Jesus' power over demons is ambiguous, even capable of being labeled "satanic."	God is the clear source of Jesus' miraculous power.
Exorcisms are the focal point of Jesus' battle with Satan.	Signs provide the arena in which Jesus' broader battle with Satan occurs.
Jesus' power over demons is given by the Spirit.	Jesus' miraculous power is an inherent aspect of his divine identity.
Exorcisms reveal the actualization and in-breaking of the Kingdom of God.	Miracles are signs of Jesus' glory and point to the ultimate revelation of God in the cross.
The place and implication of the exorcisms in Jesus' overall ministry are ambiguous.	The signs function specifically to reveal God at work through Jesus.

tion, be expected to reflect on the identity or origin of Jesus, nor on the divine dimension of a miracle. Nor could any number of exorcisms convey the grand cosmic scale and other-worldly setting of the battle that FE wished to convey was taking place. This battle was won in the cross event, yet it was adumbrated throughout the life and ministry of Jesus. For that, FE was able to take over from his (signs?) source astounding stories that could be portrayed as divine in origin and having a revelatory capacity. To allay any remaining misunderstandings, he called them "signs."

13

The Temple Incident

An Integral Element in the Fourth Gospel's Narrative

Mark A. Matson

An analysis of the Temple Incident (a term preferable to "cleansing" since that implies a prior judgment of the meaning of the event) in the Fourth Gospel (FG) shows that it is an integral part of John's narrative, and thus originates from the earliest strata of the Gospel's construction. The Temple Incident in FG marks the beginning of Jesus' public messianic ministry, as well as the beginning of opposition by "the Jews," a fundamental Johannine theme. FG's Temple Incident also anticipates the Passion, thus providing an initial frame with which to interpret the entire gospel story. Moreover, the way the incident is developed shows that it is best understood as an independent interpretation of a core Jesus tradition rather than a secondary adaptation of the synoptic story.

FG's presentation of the Temple Incident is, in broad terms, very similar to that found in the Synoptics. In each case Jesus enters the Temple in Jerusalem during the Passover festival and creates a disturbance, driving out those who are providing sacrificial animals. Moreover, Jesus is depicted in similar terms in Matthew, Mark, and FG as interfering with the exchange of money for the Temple offering. In support of these actions, Jesus quotes or paraphrases texts from the Hebrew Bible that allude to the Temple as God's house: Isaiah 56:7 in the Synoptics; in FG, Zechariah 14:21 and Psalm 69:9.

But while the Johannine Temple Incident has strong similarities with the synoptic account, it also has striking differences. The most obvious is the placement of the narrative, with FG's account located near the beginning of Jesus' ministry, shortly after his first sign. In contrast, the Synoptics relate the story near the close of the public ministry, at the beginning of the passion week shortly after Jesus' entry into Jerusalem. This difference is crucial and has prompted a number of explanations. The most common explanation is that the Fourth Evangelist (FE) has transferred the account from its proper place in the passion story to the beginning of the narrative for a theological purpose (Brown 1966, 1.118; Fortna 1970, 104). A second explanation suggests that FE's placement is more historically accurate but that the synoptic evangelists were forced to relocate the episode to the passion narrative because they do not represent Jesus traveling to Jerusalem before that time (Robinson 1985, 185). It is difficult to assess the historicity of either placement, but the fact that the placement in FG supports its theology does not necessarily imply a secondary transferral from the passion story. Each of the canonical gospels has a systematic and coherent theological conception that has guided the selection and ordering of events.

The synoptic and Johannine presentations of the Temple Incident also differ in details, although not strikingly so. In FG, Jesus drives out not only the sellers of animals but also the sheep and oxen themselves. To highlight this act, FE has Jesus making a whip of cords to help drive out the animals, thus underscoring their presence in the Temple court and emphasizing the dramatic nature of the action. In similar fashion, FE's account has Jesus actually pouring out the coins of the money changers—again a dramatic emphasis of an action only implied in the other accounts.

A Starting Point for Comparison: The Use of Scripture

Perhaps the most significant difference between the accounts of the Temple Incident in the Synoptics and FG relates to the citation of texts from the Hebrew Bible in each. In both the Synoptics and FG, the scripture citations are specifically used to refer to the Temple. All three synoptic accounts cite two texts, Isaiah 56:7 and Jeremiah 7:11, strung together as a composite quote. FG's first citation does share an affinity with Isaiah 56:7 in that it seems to refer to the Temple as the house of God. FG's actual quotation, though, appears to be a loose adaptation of Zechariah 14:21, following the LXX translation of "Canaanites" as "traders" and switching the phrase "house of the Lord of hosts" to "my Father's house." FG's second citation, from Psalm 69, bears no relationship to the Synoptics' use of Jeremiah 7:11. Instead, it places a future orientation on Jesus' activity; the LXX verb "consumed me" has been transformed from the aorist to the future tense: "zeal for your house *will consume me*" (italics added). These citations in FG and the Synoptics support, but do not clearly explain, the theological focus of the action in the Temple. The difference in the citations suggests a different tradition history and also gives some indication of how these traditions were interpreted by each evangelist.

In none of these cases should the Temple Incident be understood as a critique of Temple practices, but rather as a prophetic symbolic act pointing to God's eschatological intervention, which would involve the Temple in some way. In the Synoptics, the Isaiah quote seems to emphasize a coming time when the Temple would be open to all peoples: "it shall be a house of prayer for *all nations*." And the use of "brigand" (*lēstēs*) from Jeremiah for the traders probably does not imply economic chicanery so much as political resistance or interference in the Temple, thus preventing or discouraging Gentiles from access to the Temple. By tipping over the tables and driving people out, Jesus was enacting, for Mark, the coming destruction of the Temple as a precursor to God's restoration of it. His subsequent teaching about the destruction (Mark 13:1) confirms this. Jesus' actions seem to have been understood by the Jewish hierarchy as predicting this destruction, hence the charge of threatening to tear down the Temple at his trial (Mark 14:58; cf. John 2:19). Although many of these eschatological implications have been lost in the transmission of this account and its retelling by the synoptic evangelists, the Temple Incident in the Synoptics is best understood in terms of expectations for a restored Temple in God's coming Kingdom (Sanders 1985, 61ff., 78ff.).

I suggest that FG's version of the Temple Incident supports the same understanding: Jesus' action in the Temple was primarily prophetic, referring to God's coming eschatological activity on behalf of his people. FE's presentation is, once again, somewhat cryptic but does not necessarily indicate opposition to the Temple practices. "The Jews" ask, almost benignly, why Jesus does what he does, and his answer is based on an anticipated destruction of the Temple (John 2:18–20). It coheres, in other words, with a prophetic act about the coming new Temple. This explains Jesus' allusion to Zechariah 14:21, which comes from the apocalyptic conclusion to the prophetic work. There Zechariah is referring to God's intervention on behalf of his people, a final victory with eschatological significance. The result of God's final intervention is the sanctification of all Israel, so that all will turn to the Lord (Jews and Gentiles) and worship in Jerusalem year after year (Zech. 14:16). At that time, there will no longer be any need for traders in the Temple since everything will be holy to God. This is, then, an eschatological prediction that FE's Jesus uses as a basis for his activity. Of course, FE understands the prophecy to refer to Jesus himself, as the rest of the narrative makes clear. In the same way, Psalm 69 is transformed into a future reference and thus becomes in FG an even more poignant prophetic prediction ("zeal for your house has consumed me" [John 2:17]), since the Passion does indeed consume the physical life of Jesus.

But while the Johannine and synoptic versions of the story have a similar focus on an eschatological action by God, FE understands the restoration of the Temple to be metaphorical in and through the body of Jesus, not a building in Jerusalem (John 2:21). By indicating that the "temple" is a metaphor for Jesus himself, FE makes Jesus' resurrection the fulfillment of the Temple's restoration (John 2:21–22). But the eschatological expectation, as reflected in the use of scriptures that draw on this expectation, still remains central to FE's understanding of the event. Moreover, the eschatological expectation in FG is more directly associated with the rejection of Jesus and his death than in the Synoptics. The Synoptics link the Temple Incident with the rejection and death of Jesus temporally by placing the event at the beginning of the passion week. FG, however, links the two events at a deeper level by stating directly that Jesus' actions in the Temple somehow symbolize the destruction of his own body (2:21–22).

The Temple Incident's Function in the Developing Narrative

Does FE's direct association of the Temple Incident with the death of Jesus reveal an earlier placement within the passion narrative? Is the current placement simply a dislocation of the event from its proper place in the sequence of events that take place in the final week of Jesus' life? A close examination of John 2 suggests, to the contrary, that this event is an integral part of the developing narrative as it currently stands in FG. Reading FE's account as a coherent narrative shows the integral function of the Temple Incident in the construction of FE's story of Jesus.

First, FG's Temple Incident is linked in several ways to the story of the wedding in Cana that immediately precedes it (John 2:1–11). As has been noted (Moloney 1993, 94), there are structural similarities between the two episodes. The Temple scene opens with a setting of the account (v. 13), followed by an action (vv. 14–17), then a verbal exchange (vv. 18–20); the action then slows down so the narrator can interpret the words of Jesus (vv. 21–22); and finally there is a concluding statement that rounds out the event (vv. 23–25). This is essentially the same structure as the Cana story, although there Jesus' words precede his action whereas in the Temple Incident the action leads to the question by "the Jews" and the response by Jesus. More important than the structural similarities, though, is the fact that both events foreshadow the rejection and death of Jesus and develop the distinctive difference in the reception of Jesus by disciples and opponents. Note that the initial reaction of Jesus to his mother's request at Cana is "My hour has not yet come" (John 2:4), a pregnant remark that has no meaning except to anticipate the coming Passion. The editorial comment at the conclusion of the Temple Incident, interpreting

Jesus' "sign" to "the Jews," is an even clearer forecast of the Passion (2:21–22). The dialogue at Cana thus anticipates the stronger passion statement to come in the Temple Incident, linking the two passages together.[1]

As a further parallel, the Cana miracle concludes with the important editorial comment that this was the first of Jesus' "signs," and that this sign functioned as a revelation of his glory and a basis for the disciples' belief (John 2:11). Similarly, "the Jews" request a sign following the Temple action (2:18), and Jesus' prophetic explanation—the destruction and rebuilding of the sanctuary—provides a significant and telling counterpoint to the Cana event. Contrary to arguments that Jesus fails to give the Jews a sign (Brown 1966, 1.115), he does in fact offer the most compelling of signs, his own death and resurrection (2:19). The sign offered in the Temple Incident, however, generates a very different reaction than the wine miracle. The Jews react with astonishment and consternation, not faith (2:20). In contrast, the disciples are again characterized as faithful; in view of the sign of the resurrection they believed the scripture and Jesus' word, albeit later on (v. 22). Both Cana and the Temple Incident, then, allow FE to develop the importance of Jesus as the giver of signs, signs that are apprehended and believed by some but disbelieved by others.

The linkage of the Cana event and the Temple Incident can perhaps be most clearly seen in the conclusion to the sequence, John 2:23–25. Here FE makes a generalization that suggests Jesus was performing many signs of his glory. These signs are the basis for faith by many ("many believed in his name because of the signs"), but also fail to produce genuine faith in others ("but he would not entrust himself to them, because he knew all people"). For FE, then, the Cana miracle and the Temple Incident provide a two-sided perspective on signs that anticipates and frames the entire gospel story.

Just as the Cana story anticipates certain themes that FE fleshes out and develops in the Temple story, so also the Temple Incident anticipates the exchange that follows with Nicodemus in John 3. The Temple Incident establishes the geographical and temporal setting for the Nicodemus exchange, since it is the Passover celebration that brings Jesus to Jerusalem where he meets Nicodemus. And the Nicodemus incident begins with an inquiry about the signs. But more than simply providing the geographical framework for the Nicodemus exchange, the Temple Incident gives the first indication of a major motif in FG: the failure of the Jews to believe in Jesus, a failure that drives them to oppose and ultimately persecute and kill him. The entrance of the Jews as opponents to Jesus is found in the Temple Incident with the request for a sign, a request that reflects a lack of understanding. This disjuncture between Jesus' revelatory words and his reception by "the Jews" provides the conceptual backdrop for the Nicodemus exchange.

The exchange with Nicodemus in John 3 is a further commentary on the reaction of the Jews at the Temple Incident and the summary statement in

2:23–25. Nicodemus, a leader of "the Jews," ultimately shows a lack of understanding that is indicative of disbelief and an inability to accept metaphorical or spiritual language (3:10–12). Nicodemus is clearly not one of the believers from 2:23 (contra Brown 1966, 1.135). More important, FE has interpreted Nicodemus's lack of understanding in terms of "the Jews'" lack of faith; the plural forms of the verbs in verse 12 appear to be rhetorical expansions from Nicodemus alone to the Jews as a group (notice the shift from "I say to you [sing.]" in verse 11 to "you [pl.] have not received . . . you [pl.] don't believe . . . how will you [pl.] believe?" in verse 12). The Nicodemus dialogue, then, expands on and carries further the initial reaction of the Jews to Jesus' prophetic action in the Temple. While some do believe in Jesus, overall the Jews fail to apprehend the prophetic nature of his actions and sayings, and in doing so they are increasingly portrayed as opponents of Jesus.

The Temple Incident, then, as the beginning of Jesus' public ministry, is also the beginning of opposition by "the Jews," a motif that dominates the structure of FG. Note the following crucial developments in the narrative:

> Jesus comes to Jerusalem for the Passover (John 2:13–25) and while there finds a failed understanding of the nature of the Temple Incident, and then a failed understanding of being "born again," a failure characterized as lack of faith (3:11–12).
>
> Jesus returns to Jerusalem for a "festival of the Jews" (5:1), and at the conclusion of a healing "the Jews" seek to kill him because he had broken the Sabbath and called God his own Father.
>
> Once again Jesus comes to Jerusalem to celebrate Tabernacles and goes to the Temple, despite the fact that "the Jews" are looking for him (7:10). He is almost arrested for his teaching in the Temple precincts (7:30).
>
> At the Festival of Dedication in Jerusalem (10:22) "the Jews" attempt first to stone Jesus, and then to arrest him. Jesus narrowly escapes, and then goes out to the desert regions.
>
> Following the raising of Lazarus at Bethany, near Jerusalem, "the Jews" form a council to deal with Jesus. The result is a plot to put him to death. This is followed immediately by the Passover, in which Jesus enters Jerusalem for the last time.

What is apparent is a steady increase in misunderstanding and opposition by the Jews throughout FG. It begins, however, with the Temple Incident. The Temple Incident, then, seems to anticipate and provide the initial narrative basis for this major theme that runs through the entire Gospel like a backbone.

What is particularly interesting about the pattern of developing opposition by the Jews is the way FE locates them almost entirely around Jerusalem and the Temple, where they appear mostly on feast days. Since the feast days are centered in the Temple, even when it is not explicitly mentioned, it serves as a conceptual backdrop to their encounters with Jesus. FE sees the opposition to Jesus focused on those days that exemplify Temple worship and the Jewish festival calendar. With good reason, one can say that John's Jesus is depicted as the replacement for the Temple (M. Davies 1992, 230–233). Especially in the Tabernacles discourses, Jesus uses imagery that pertains to the eschatological temple: "I am the light of the world" (8:12); "Let anyone who is thirsty come to me . . . out of [them] shall flow rivers of living water" (7:38). These statements are especially important given the passages in Zechariah 14 about the eschatological temple: the whole of Jerusalem will be lighted by God, presumably from the Temple (Zech. 14:7); living waters will flow from Jerusalem (Zech 14:8; cf. Ezek 47:1–9). And this identification of Jesus with the eschatological temple is exactly what the Temple Incident makes clear, again drawing on Zechariah 14 for much of its basis. FE's theological orientation toward Jerusalem and the Temple, which is closely linked to the growing opposition from the Jews, runs throughout FG and is anticipated in the Temple Incident in such a way that it serves as an interpretive grid for the subsequent incidents.

Dislocation or Reliance on Synoptics?

What I have argued in the preceding sections can be summarized under two major heads:

1. The Temple Incident in FG has an underlying theme of eschatological expectation. Jesus' action in the Temple is related to an expectation of God's coming to Israel and restoring the Temple in such a way that all people will know God and worship him. But FE has interpreted this eschatological expectation as present in Jesus himself in light of the resurrection.
2. The Temple Incident is an integral part of FG's narrative. It picks up smoothly from the Cana story and anticipates major themes and structures that dominate the rest of the Gospel.

The question can be raised, however, whether this is a derivative understanding of the Temple Incident, adapted and developed from another source by FE. Specifically, it has been proposed that the Fourth Evangelist has transposed the Temple Incident from a previous source in which it was located in the passion narrative. This could have been a noncanonical source or the Synoptic Gospels. It is to these possibilities that we now turn.

It is certainly possible, and even probable, that the author of FG based his gospel on a previous narrative that consisted of a number of signs (Fortna 1970; von Wahlde 1989; Heekerens 1984). But our study suggests that any earlier narrative has been systematically and effectively reworked, so that the Temple

Incident is crucially located in the new narrative structure. *It is difficult to imagine the Fourth Gospel in even an approximate reflection of its current form without the Temple Incident being located near the beginning of the story.* The narrative structure of developing opposition to Jesus, of repeated trips to Jerusalem and the Temple, of Jesus revealing himself as uniquely related to God and bringing glory to the Father in his life and death—all this is anticipated in the Temple Incident. Even if we stripped FG of the revelatory discourses, the remaining narrative structure that carries the plot of the Gospel has, as a central motif, the developing opposition from the Jews. The Temple Incident is a key to this developing opposition. If, then, FG was based on a previous Signs Gospel, the Fourth Evangelist has reworked the source so thoroughly that any reconstruction would be tentative and conjectural. The narrative analysis of the Temple Incident, then, supports the literary analyses of Ruckstuhl and Schweizer, who have demonstrated a consistency of language and style throughout FG, a consistency that resists easy attempts to locate displacements or seams in the narrative.

In a similar fashion, it is very difficult to see reliance on the Synoptic Gospels in FG's Temple Incident (Matson 1992, 495–499). There are simply too few points of literary contact to suggest a relationship, despite the overall similarity. But more importantly, the role the scripture citations play in the formation and meaning of the various narratives seems to resist any derivation of FG's account from the Synoptics. Both accounts record memories of scripture that have an eschatological reference to the Temple. But the respective evangelists (Mark and John) have not extensively developed this idea—the scriptures cited remain somewhat as ciphers in the current texts. For Mark the Temple does not yet become a house of prayer for all nations—the destruction of the Temple and its rebuilding remain still a future and unfulfilled expectation (Mark 13:1–2, 14–27). In FG, the expectation is viewed as having been fulfilled, but in the risen Jesus rather than in a literal, restored Temple. But if FG were derivative of Mark, then we must imagine that FE has chosen to replace Mark's Isaiah 56 and Jeremiah 7 citations with those from Psalm 69 and Zechariah 14. And if so, one would expect a far clearer use of the citations to support FE's central understanding.

While one might understand FE's use of Psalm 69 as an anticipation of the Passion, the Zechariah 14 passage is vague and only tangentially tied to FE's interpretation of the event by means of the reference to traders. In this case, FE appears to have retained a biblical citation from his independent tradition. He realized, however, that Zechariah's view of a future restoration of the Temple was incompatible with his own view that Jesus was the new Temple. He therefore modified the application of Zechariah 14 to fit Jesus' action of disrupting activity in the Temple courts. In the process, the underlying eschatological nature of the Temple Incident, which coheres with Jesus' response to the Jews' request for a sign, has been lost in FG. This disjuncture between the eschatological meaning of Zechariah 14 and its application in FG hardly suggests FE's adaptation of synoptic texts, but rather reveals FE's struggle with his own independent tradition.

Note

1. It has also been suggested that the Cana miracle and the Temple Incident are parallel in that both deal with purification issues. The water turned to wine was stored in stone jars used for rites of purification (John 2:6), suggesting an interest in purity that anticipates the subsequent cleansing of the Temple (cf. Witherington 1995, 86). This connection is, however, unlikely. The Cana miracle makes nothing of the purification aspect except to explain why such a large volume of water was on hand. Nor is there inherently an interest in purification in the Temple Incident.

14

The Sacramental Tradition in the Fourth Gospel and the Synoptics

There are both fundamental similarities and striking differences in the way that baptism and the Lord's Supper are spoken of (or alluded to) in the Fourth Gospel (FG) and the Synoptics. The similarities probably arise from common sacramental traditions, while the differences result from the differing theological perspectives of the respective authors. This essay will examine several of these similarities and differences. The discussion will begin with the Lord's Supper, proceed to baptism, and then consider how the two are metaphorically linked in Johannine thought through a detailed analysis of John 2:1–11, the wedding at Cana.

The Lord's Supper: Joy or Sorrow?

The evidence from the New Testament suggests that the early history of the Lord's Supper was complex. At least two very distinct strands of thought are evident: some texts point to what may be called an "eschatological" understanding of the Eucharist; other texts point to a "passion" understanding of the Eucharist. The eschatological understanding would interpret the Supper as a joyous anticipation of the eternal union between Christ and the church, while the passion position would see the Supper as a memorial of Jesus' death. It is clear from both FG and the Synoptics that these two themes were gradually intertwined in a variety of ways in early Jesus traditions.

Joy and Sorrow

The very early church remembered that the risen Jesus had appeared to the disciples while they were sharing a meal of broiled fish (Luke 24:42; see John 21:9–13). The fact that he had come to them at table and eaten with them was taken as Jesus' own encouragement to celebrate the Eucharist as an experience that anticipated his coming Kingdom (Cullmann 1958, 10–12). Accordingly, the Lord's Supper was, at first, a purely eschatological celebration. Jesus' disciples therefore assembled for this sacrament on the first day of the week (see Acts 20:7), the day on which Jesus' empty tomb had been discovered. At this sacred assembly, the disciples recalled Jesus' appearances with joy and thanksgiving, and they anticipated and prayed for his speedy return (1 Cor. 16:22; Rev. 22:20; *Didache* 10:6). As an example, the ancient eucharistic liturgy described at *Didache* 9–10 includes resurrection themes and eagerly awaits Jesus' second coming, with no reference whatsoever to his death—the bread and cup sayings are notably absent. The early eschatological emphasis of the weekly Lord's Supper also explains why the apostolic church later chose (Easter) Sunday rather than (Good) Friday as the day when the Supper was to be universally celebrated.

At some point, however, it appears that the weekly celebration of the eschatological Supper was joined with themes from the passion memorial recalled annually at Passover by Jewish Christians. Traces of this Jewish passion memorial are reflected in the Synoptics' presentation of the "Last Supper." Because God's "servant" Jesus was "led like a lamb to the slaughter" just before Passover (Isaiah 53; see John 19:14), Christians quickly identified him with the Passover lamb whose blood had saved Israel from death in Egypt (Exod. 12:21–23; see 1 Cor. 5:7–8; John 1:29). Jewish Christians would therefore emphasize the suffering and death of Jesus in their annual Passover ritual. At some point, the weekly eucharistic bread and wine, which had previously symbolized eschatological life and joy in the risen Lord's Kingdom, began to be associated with the bread and cup sayings from the "Last Supper" traditions, sayings that reflected the sorrowful tone of the annual passion memorial. Perhaps this reinterpretation of the weekly rite was initiated to curtail abuses of the Supper resulting from the influx of Gentiles into the church by connecting the rite more explicitly to the example of the historical Jesus (see 1 Cor. 11:17–29). In any case, once this connection had been made in the liturgy, it seemed fitting to suggest that Jesus had, in fact, inaugurated the Christian observance of the weekly "Lord's Supper" at the "Last Supper" (see 1 Cor. 11:20, 23–25), a decision that naturally connected the Eucharist with the death of Jesus. It is evident that Matthew, Mark, and Luke all accepted the expanded version of the Lord's Supper that included Jesus' passion memorial, for the Synoptics, which were composed after this Pauline union of joy and sorrow had been accomplished, reflect this perspective (see Mark 14:22–24 pars).

Traces of Joy in the Synoptics

Despite the fact that Matthew, Mark, and Luke accepted and promoted the connection between the weekly Lord's Supper and the Passion of Jesus, we nevertheless find in the Synoptics traces of a tradition that reflects the earlier understanding of a purely eschatological Eucharist. This earlier perspective is evident in their presentation of the traditional miracle story popularly known as the feeding of the five thousand (Mark 6:30–44), a version of which appears at John 6:1–14. In all four canonical gospels, the narrative of the feeding miracle clearly alludes to elements from the church's eucharistic traditions but also clearly *lacks* any allusion to Jesus' passion. All of its Eucharistic symbols signify the life-giving Spirit mediated by Jesus through the bread of his word at his Kingdom-anticipating supper. The primitive nature of this feeding tradition is further evident from the fact that none of the canonical accounts makes even a veiled allusion to the eucharistic wine. After the passion memorial, which included traditional statements about "the cup," was joined to the eschatological Supper, wine had to be mentioned or alluded to in a manner that recalled Jesus' death ("my blood"). Because the feeding story under consideration makes no direct allusion to Jesus' passion, it was probably created by the very early church at a time when the Lord's Supper was still celebrated in a purely eschatological form.

The synoptic feeding of the five thousand presents Jesus as the new Moses (Deut. 18:15, 18) who feeds God's flock with true manna as he leads them through the desert (note *erēmos* at Mark 6:35 pars) of this life to the promised land of eternal life. The true manna is the eucharistic bread, which signifies God's life-giving word mediated through Jesus (cf. Matt. 4:4 pars). To strengthen this symbolism, the Synoptics follow the feeding story with another account that further alludes to Jesus as the new Moses. After miraculously feeding the multitude, Jesus goes up onto a mountain to commune alone with God (cf. Exod. 19:20; 34:28); he then descends and joins his disciples by walking across the water, an event that reveals his power over wind and sea (cf. Exod. 14:21–29). It appears, then, that the eucharistic midrash on the Exodus story that influenced the traditions behind this complex of passages also depicted Jesus as one who is able to mediate the saving power of God's Spirit through the water of baptism (see below). The implied connection between the Lord's Supper (the feeding) and baptism (walking on water) appears to be very early, arising from the period when the Eucharist was still understood primarily in eschatological terms.

The Johannine Passion Memorial

It appears that the Johannine church joined the annual passion memorial to its weekly celebration of the Lord's Supper later than the churches for whom the

Synoptics were written. It is also uncertain whether the Johannine Christians combined these two understandings of the celebration for the same reasons as the Pauline churches, that is, in order to connect Gentile converts more closely to the example of Jesus. Rather, in the Johannine context it appears more likely that the revision of the Eucharist occurred at some point after the crisis caused by the community's expulsion from the synagogue (John 9:22; 12:42; 16:2). The introduction of the passion memorial to the weekly celebration of the Eucharist would encourage the community to imitate Jesus' endurance during this new period of suffering. It also, however, necessarily affected the Johannine Community's Jesus tradition.

The effects of this revision in the Johannine understanding of the Eucharist appear to be reflected in the long dialogue between Jesus and the Jews that follows FG's version of the feeding miracle, John 6:22ff. The earlier, eschatological understanding of the Lord's Supper underlies Jesus' remarks at 6:35–51a, which, like the synoptic accounts, focus on the Moses/manna symbolism. The new reading of the Supper as a symbol for Jesus' crucified flesh and blood underlies 6:51b–56, a passage that many scholars have viewed as an interpolation into the earlier dialogue. But the verses that close the section reveal that not all Johannine Christians accepted this modification of their joyful Supper tradition. While all could tolerate the Johannine version of the bread and cup sayings in the context of the somber ambiance of their annual Passover observance, the weekly recital of these sayings at the joyful Lord's Supper proved unbearable to some. Regular talk about "eating flesh" and "drinking blood" violated the customary spirit of their Supper tradition and was profoundly repugnant to them (6:60–61). A group of dissenters, therefore, left the community (6:66), and their departure was remembered with pain and regret (10:16).

Surprisingly, the lengthy Farewell Address in FG (John 13–17), which takes the place of the synoptic Upper Room, makes no mention of the bread and cup sayings from Jesus' passion memorial. In light of John 6:51b–56, it is almost certain that the community possessed such sayings in their Jesus tradition. Perhaps the sayings are missing because the Johannine church had long persisted in restricting the ritual recitation of these sayings to the annual Passover observance. But their absence may also have resulted from the inner-community conflict previously mentioned: recalling the graphic bread and cup sayings during the Passover meal was quite possibly offensive to one sector of the community from early on. This opposition to the weekly recital of the traditional bread and cup sayings from the annual passion memorial may have been a factor in FE's decision to omit them from his account of the Upper Room. If he intended the Farewell to be read and reflected on regularly by his community, he may have judged that the presence of the controversial sayings would exacerbate an already volatile situation and cloud the repeated calls for love and unity (13:34–35; 14:21–24; 15:9–10, 12–14, 17). In fact, this dispute over the Supper may be one reason the call to love is stressed so urgently in FG.

Baptism

The disciples of Jesus experienced his resurrection appearances as revelatory confirmations of his Kingdom message. They assumed that these appearances heralded his imminent return as God's eschatological King and Judge. Accordingly, very soon after they began to proclaim the risen Jesus, they also began to reinterpret the eschatological cleansing with water that Jesus had received earlier from John the Baptizer. The canonical gospels and Acts treat Jesus' baptism by John as the inauguration of his public ministry. And because Jesus' eschatological message essentially agreed with that of the Baptizer, Jesus' disciples began to assign new and conclusive meaning to the baptism that Jesus had received from John and to confer it on their own converts "in Jesus' name" (Acts 2:38). This procedure distinguished Christian baptism (which was believed to confer the Holy Spirit) from that of John, and baptism in (or into) the name of Jesus became the earliest rite of entry into the Christian assembly. It seems likely that Christian baptism originally signified an inner experience of spiritual cleansing (perhaps via the convert's experience of God's Spirit) for those who had turned to God from sin and unbelief. The washing of the physical body gave concrete assurance to believers that they had been accepted and forgiven by God and were therefore able to enter God's approaching Kingdom.

But with the passage of time and the spread of the Jesus movement, it was inevitable that additional shades of meaning would accrue to local interpretations of baptism. Paul, for example, describes baptism as a participation in the saving death and resurrection of Jesus (Rom. 6:1–11). While Mark never speaks directly of Christian baptism, he alludes to this sacrament as preparation for eating the Lord's Supper (8:2). Matthew views baptism as the first step in "making disciples" and believes it should be conferred "in the name of the Father and of the Son and of the Holy Spirit" (28:19). For Luke, baptism "in the name of Jesus" is the sign of faith and repentance that forgives sins by bestowing God's Holy Spirit (Acts 2:38–39). FG presents baptism as a second birth from above that empowers believers to enter the Kingdom of God (John 3:3–8). While the Synoptics never mention baptism as a feature of Jesus' ministry, the Fourth Evangelist (FE) also claims that Jesus' followers baptized people (4:1–2). Perhaps here FE has combined the practice of his later community with a memory of the mission of Jesus, but this at least suggests that the Johannine Christians practiced water baptism.

A careful reading of FG suggests that Johannine theology used marriage symbolism to illustrate the relationship between God and Jesus' disciples (see John 3:29). Within this symbolic world, Jesus is the bridegroom who weds his disciples to himself, a union that begins in baptism. Jesus thereby empowers the disciples to follow him through death (11:23–26; 14:2–3) to the marriage feast of eternal life in the bridal chamber of God's bosom (1:18). There they will be privileged to participate forever in the great marriage between heaven and earth to which God has called them through Jesus (17:22–24). Water baptism seems to have functioned in Johannine thought as the initial step toward the believer's, and the community's, union with Christ.

The Three-Day Journey
to the Marriage Feast at Cana

FE's presentation of the Cana wedding (John 2:1–11), which seems to have been adapted from the Signs Source, reveals the underlying connection between baptism and Eucharist in the Johannine Jesus tradition. FE has created the narrative motif of a three-day journey to a wedding in order to teach that Jesus prepares his disciples to partake of his Supper through baptism, experiences that prefigure the marriage feast of eternal life in God's Kingdom. Notably, the Cana story is "the first of his [Jesus'] signs" in FG and seems to have been the first episode in the Signs Source as well (see John 2:11; cf. 4:54). Its position in the narratives of the source and the current text of FG indicates the importance of its nuptial symbolism for the Johannine church.[1]

The Narrative Cues

FE prepares the reader for a sacramental reading of the Cana story by beginning with John the Baptizer four days prior to the arrival of Jesus and his disciples at the wedding. At John 1:29, the Baptizer announces that Jesus has been revealed to him as the Spirit-anointed "Son of God" who is empowered to baptize "with the Holy Spirit" (1:33b–34). On "the next day" (1:35) the Baptizer again bears witness to him, and two of the Baptizer's disciples begin to follow Jesus on a journey that will eventually take them to a wedding feast (3:1). On yet "the next day" (1:43), Jesus leads his disciples to Galilee, and while on the way invites Philip also to "follow" him. Philip, in turn, finds and testifies to Nathaniel (1:45), who eventually concurs that Jesus is, indeed, "the Son of God . . . the King of Israel" (1:49). Finally, "on the third day" (2:1) Jesus and the disciples who have followed him are invited to a wedding feast: "On the third day there was a wedding in Cana of Galilee . . . Jesus and his disciples had also been invited to the wedding."

Members of the Johannine Community would have perceived a number of allusions that connect the marriage feast at Cana to the Lord's Supper. First, the Cana story opens with a time marker that recalls Jesus' resurrection: "*On the third day* there was a marriage at Cana in Galilee" (2:1a; italics added). The introductory words of this statement reappear verbatim in the early Christian creed quoted by Paul at 1 Corinthians 15:4, which refers to Jesus being raised by God "on the third day according to the Scriptures." It appears that FE added these well-known words to the older account from the Signs Source as a sort of theological introduction to his own version of the story. In the current text of FG, reference to "the third day" signals that the story which follows will reveal some aspect of the resurrection mystery in which Johannine Christians are privileged to participate through baptism and the Lord's Supper.

Second, the latter part of the introduction to the Cana story stages the episode at "a wedding in Cana of Galilee" (2:1a), which clues the reader to see the events to follow as a symbolic preview of the marriage feast of eternal life. Isaiah uses the joy occasioned by marriage as a symbol of the future blessings that God will bestow on the righteous (61:10; 62:4–5), and this prophetic theme was taken up by Jesus and developed further by his disciples after the resurrection (Mark 2:20; Matt. 25:11–13). At their weekly celebrations of the Lord's Supper, the Johannine Christians joyfully anticipated the return of the risen Jesus to take them to the great marriage between heaven and earth. This sacramental practice led the author of the Cana story to create a eucharistic midrash about the joyful occasion of a "marriage feast" to which Jesus and his disciples were invited. Of course, it is quite possible that Jesus and his disciples were actually invited to a wedding at Cana, and that the midrash is based on that memory. But it is also possible that a Johannine Christian created the story in Cana to historicize this midrash, and in either case the current presentation of the episode in FG reflects the community's experience of Jesus at their celebrations of his Supper.

The sacramental development of the wedding motif may also explain the sudden indication at John 2:1b that "the mother of Jesus" was also invited to the wedding. Within the Johannine symbolic world, the mother of Jesus appears to represent the church in its role as the new Eve, the mother of Christians. FE alludes to Jesus as the new Adam (20:15b) and to the church as the new Eve (19:26–27; 20:15a), and both are presented as God's instruments in conferring new birth through baptism. Only by receiving the new life of the Spirit through baptism (3:5) are God's children (1:13) able to enter the new creation. Further, the actions of Jesus' mother in the Cana story may also reflect this broader

Eucharistic motif: until her bridegroom returns for her in glory (6:40; 21:22–23), the church has been assigned the task of teaching Jesus' disciples what they must "do" (cf. "Do whatever he tells you" at 2:5) to receive the reassuring foretaste of the Spirit that God mediates through Jesus (7:39; 19:22). It is therefore possible that the very presence of Jesus' mother would prepare the Johannine reader to understand the Cana story as an allusion to the Eucharist.

A fourth allusion to the Eucharist may be found in the references to wine in the Cana story. Wine is a common symbol of divine blessing in the Hebrew Bible (see Amos 9:13–14; Jer. 31:12). Accordingly, the apocalyptic addition to Isaiah that describes God's eschatological banquet (25:6–8) uses wine as a symbol of the joy to be experienced in the new creation. Furthermore, because the Johannine Community believed that Jesus is God's Wisdom incarnate, the wine that he provides in the Cana story would also have reminded them of the sacred wine offered to God's servants by personified Wisdom (Prov. 9:2–5; Sir. 24:17, 21). For the author of the Signs Source, then, the "wine" provided by Jesus at the marriage feast signified the "intoxicating" Spirit mediated by the risen Jesus (John 15:11) at his eschatological Supper. This suggests that the eucharistic wine alluded to by the miraculous wine at the Cana wedding was still a purely joyful experience for the author of the Signs Source. It was not meant to evoke the death of Jesus by suggesting the blood of his passion memorial.

FE's Development

While the Signs Source appears to reflect a purely eschatological understanding of the Lord's Supper, the version in the present text of FG indicates that FE has made certain theological adjustments to the source. When the Johannine Community began to interpret the eucharistic bread and wine as the crucified body and blood of Jesus, the presentation of the Cana miracle in the Signs Source became inadequate. FE therefore added 2:3b–4 to the source's version in order to incorporate the new "passion" interpretation of the wine into the Cana story: "The mother of Jesus said to him, 'They have no wine.' And Jesus said to her, 'Woman, what concern is that to you and to me? My hour has not yet come.'" This move parallels FE's addition of 6:51b–56 to the purely eschatological midrash on the eucharistic bread in 6:26–51a.

In the Signs Source version of the story, the mother of Jesus goes directly to the servants without informing Jesus of the shortage of wine (see John 2:5). FE's addition of her comment to Jesus and Jesus' reply allowed a link between the wine miracle and Jesus' "hour," a code word for his passion and death in FG and the major emphasis of the passion memorial. Notably, when Jesus' climactic "hour" has fully arrived at John 19:23–37, his mother again appears and is again addressed by him as "woman." This connects the Cana story to the death episode and would again remind the Johannine reader that Jesus' mother functions as a symbol of the new Eve, for whom the archetypal "woman" in Genesis 2:23 is the midrashic prototype. The new Eve (the church) is "the helper" (Gen. 3:18) of the new Adam (Christ), for the church sacramentally confers the new birth of baptism and then spreads the table of the Lord's Supper for those who are "born again" (John 3:3–5). The church's maternal role as the new Eve ("the mother of all the living"; Gen. 3:20) is specifically alluded to when the dying Jesus recommends his mother to the Beloved Disciple: "When Jesus saw his mother and the disciple whom he loved standing beside her, he said to his mother, 'Woman, here is your son.' Then he said to the disciple, 'Here is your mother'" (John 19:26–27a). It is evident that the church, construed as the new Eve, plays a major role in FE's sacramental theology.

Further clues to FE's development of the Signs Source version of the Cana story become evident when we turn our attention more fully to the cross episode. From the pierced side of Jesus (John 19:34), God is beginning to pour out the Spirit that Jesus shares with his church, the new Eve, signified by the mother of Jesus standing below. Indeed, the blood and water that flow from the side of the Johannine Jesus (John 19:34) likely represent the two Johannine sacraments: the "water" symbolizes the new birth of baptism bestowed on believers by God through Jesus and his church; the "blood" symbolizes the Eucharist, which by FE's time had absorbed the overtones of the passion memorial. The fact that these symbols, and their respective sacraments, flow from Jesus indicates FE's belief that Jesus the bridegroom-savior and his bride-church spiritually nourish those born again while they are on the way to the "marriage feast of the Lamb." It is significant that Jesus, while at the marriage feast at Cana, looks forward to the "hour" when the new Eve will receive the Spirit through the signs of "blood" and "water." The theological connection thus established between these two events by FE is evidence that he understands the wine of the Cana story to be eucharistic.

Against this larger backdrop, Jesus' enigmatic reply to his mother, which FE has added to the Cana story, becomes intelligible: "Woman, what concern is that [lack of wine] to you and to me? My hour has not yet come." Here, FE portrays Jesus as reassuring the new Eve (the church) that the hour has not yet arrived when he, the new Adam, will "hand over" (see 19:30b) the Spirit to her through the wine that signifies his passion memorial.

The almost baroque complexity of the sacramental teaching in John 1:29–2:11 stands in sharp contrast with its far simpler parallel in Mark 8:1–9. Both accounts, however, are manifestly intent on presenting the three-day baptismal journey as a preamble to the Lord's Supper.

Note

1. It is relevant to note that the Cana story bears a family resemblance to the miraculous feeding at John 6:1–14 with its eucharistic overtones. Both stories reflect on eucharistic food, and both were created to arouse wonder at the way in which Jesus mediates God's Spirit at his Supper. In the feeding story, eucharistic bread is miraculously multiplied to feed a multitude, whereas in the Cana story eucharistic wine is marvelously supplied for a wedding celebration. Further, both stories are devoid of passion symbolism, which means they developed in the Johannine tradition at a point when the community still celebrated a purely eschatological form of the Supper; both were probably drawn from the Signs Source.

15

Synoptic Jesus Tradition in the Johannine Farewell Discourse

JOHANNES BEUTLER, S.J.

Most scholars would agree that the discourses of Jesus in John 13:31–16:33, along with his final prayer in chapter 17, are largely Johannine compositions, not previously connected with known narrative material. The more commonly debated question is how the different parts of the Fourth Gospel (FG) are related to each other and whether there was some process of growth that led to the present text. In the case of John 13:31–17:26, the "Farewell Discourse," it seems highly probable that such a process of growth has occurred. In the first place, the text of the Farewell shows various inexplicable repetitions. For example, the theme of the disciples' mutual love appears first at 13:34ff., then reemerges at 15:9–17, and finally echoes through 17:20–23. Similarly, the theme of effective prayer at 14:13ff. recurs at 15:7 and again at 16:23ff. Such repetitions suggest that new materials were added to existing texts that already discussed similar topics. Second, the interests of the Fourth Evangelist (FE) seem to shift from christological concerns in 13:31–38 and chapter 14 to subjects more closely related to the disciples and ecclesial matters in chapters 15–17 (see Becker 1981, 572–573). This shift in subject matter may reflect a series of additions that made the text more relevant to the developing needs of the Johannine Community. Evidence of this kind suggests that the current text of the Farewell was developed over time in a series of stages.

Structure, Development, and Tradition

Regardless of its composition history, the outline of the present Farewell is clearly concentric. After a narrative prelude (John 13:1–30), Jesus' remarks may be broken into five distinct sections: 13:31–38 (Introduction); chapter 14 (first discourse); 15:1–16:4a (second discourse); 16:4b–33 (third discourse); and chapter 17 (Final Prayer of Jesus). There are strong parallels between the first and third discourses (14 and 16:4b–33): the theme of Jesus' departure and return to the disciples, either in person or in the form of the Paraclete, is prominent (14:16–17, 26; 16:7–15); and the announcement of peace and joy also repeats. At the center of the Farewell stands 15:1–16:4a, which evidences a symmetric structure within itself: the theme of relationship with Jesus and mutual love (15:1–17) contrasts with the experience of the world's hatred (15:18–16:4a). Finally, there seems to be some correspondence between the Introduction (13:31–38) and the Final Prayer of Jesus in chapter 17. Especially notable here is the concept of "glorification," a term that appears five times in 13:31–32 and that is taken up again at length in the prayer. Hence, the outline of the Farewell forms a sort of "bull's-eye," with 15:1–16:4a in the center, chapter 14 and 16:4b–33 bracketing this central section, and the Introduction (13:31–38) and the Final Prayer (chapter 17) as the larger frame:

13:31–38—Introduction: glorification
    14:1ff.—First discourse: Jesus' departure and return; disciples' peace and joy
        15:1–16:4a—Second discourse: Jesus' love and the world's hatred
    16:4b–33—Third discourse: Jesus' departure and return; disciples' peace and joy
17:1ff.—Final Prayer: glorification

Of course, the fact that the Farewell evidences a tight concentric structure does not prove the compositional unity of these chapters. It could well be that they were developed through a process of growth, with new material being added gradually over time. Fernando Segovia popularized this hypothesis through a series of source-critical studies in the early 1980s and retains it even in his more recent work on the Farewell, which explicitly attempts to highlight the literary unity of the current text (Segovia 1991). It may well be that John 13–17 was written over a period of a decade or more, moving from christological concerns to ecclesial issues as the Johannine Community faced new experiences of persecution and internal doctrinal strife. The author(s) of the final version of the text may have used the older sections as models for successive ones, thereby creating the impression of a unified and well-structured whole in the final product.

But regardless of its compositional history, Jesus tradition is obviously present in all sections of the Farewell. If one studies the margin of Nestle-Aland's *GNT4*, one finds ample parallels between the Synoptics and FG's expressions and statements, suggesting some relationship at the level of tradition. It would perhaps be profitable to examine each of these parallels individually in order to identify potential Jesus tradition in John 13–17 and to see whether FE has used the Synoptics as a source, but such an enterprise would go beyond the limits of this essay. I will therefore concentrate here on "semantic fields," that is, groups of words that appear in both the Synoptics and the Johannine Farewell. This method simplifies our investigation while still allowing us to identify material common to FG and the synoptic Jesus traditions. My analysis does not presuppose any particular theory concerning the relationship between FG and the Synoptics, but will simply focus on synoptic-type materials that appear in FG and that may have influenced the composition of FG. As will be seen, every section of the present Farewell address shows some contact with broader Christian traditions.

The Introduction (John 13:31–38)

In the Introduction to the Farewell, four units can be distinguished: a hymn fragment (vv. 31–32); a logion about the short time Jesus will be with his own (v. 33); the "new commandment" (vv. 34–35); and the announcement of Peter's betrayal (vv. 36–38).

The Introduction opens with five lines apparently drawn from an ancient Christian hymn (vv. 31–32). The first two of these lines ("Now the Son of Man has been glorified, and God has been glorified in him") sound like a liturgical formula. Several close parallels appear in what may be hymn fragments in the book of Revelation. A formula similar to that in the first line appears at Revelation 12:10: "Now have come the salvation and the power and the kingdom of our God and the authority of his Messiah." Also like FG, Revelation 1:7, 13 refer to Jesus as the "Son of Man," and the theme of glory/glorification, prominent in the Farewell, appears also in hymnic contexts in Revelation 5:13; 7:12; 15:3ff.; 19:1, 7. The two lines of the hymn fragment in John 13 were perhaps reinterpreted and historicized when they were inserted into their present context: the hour of the glorification of Jesus is still at hand, but it is soon to come. While the present composition is thoroughly Johannine, it seems to contain elements older than FG and common to early Christian tradition.

The Johannine theme of the "glorification of the Son of Man" has apparently been developed through a combination of two different motifs from the Hebrew Bible: the coming of the Son of Man (Dan. 7:14), and the "Suffering Servant of God" who "will be exalted and glorified" (Isa. 52:13 LXX; see Beutler 1998, 175–189). FG and the Synoptics both connect sayings about Jesus' passion, death, and resurrection with the title Son of Man (see Mark 8:31–32 pars; 9:31 pars; 10:32–34 pars). But unlike the Synoptics, FE reinterprets this title by superimposing on it the theological implications of the Suffering Servant motif, a procedure that is paralleled in Peter's speech in Acts 3, where the glorification of the Servant is developed in the context of Jesus' resurrection: "The God of Abraham and of Isaac and of Jacob, the God of our fathers, *glorified* his servant Jesus *whom you delivered up* and denied in the presence of Pilate, when he had decided to release him" (Acts 3:13; italics added). Further, the noun "glory" (*doxa*) is used repeatedly in the Synoptics in connection with the title Son of Man, although in these cases the context is the coming of this eschatological figure at the end of time (Mark 8:38 pars; 13:26f. pars; Matt. 19:28; 25:31). It appears, then, that the allegedly "Johannine" formula at John 13:31–32 in fact resonates with a number of features in the broader Jesus tradition.

The hymn fragment is followed by a saying about the short time Jesus will be with his disciples (v. 33). This statement echoes the three synoptic announcements of the Passion, death, and resurrection of the Son of Man that have already been discussed above.

The "new commandment of Jesus" (vv. 34–35) is closely related to the love command in the synoptic tradition: "Jesus answered, 'The first [commandment] is, "Hear, O Israel: the Lord our God, the Lord is one; you shall love the Lord your God with all your heart, and with all your soul, and with all your mind, and with all your strength." The second is this, "You shall love your neighbor as yourself." There is no other commandment greater than these'" (Mark 12:29–31). The most striking difference between the Johannine and Markan sayings is FE's restricted focus on love *among believers*: "I give you a new commandment, that you love one another. Just as I have loved you, you also should love one another. By this everyone will know that you are my disciples, if you have love for one another." FE's omission of the Markan command to love God may represent an earlier stage of a common tradition. Weiss has concluded that the synoptic love command represents a developed form of an older tradition that originally spoke only of love for one's neighbor. In Weiss's view, it was only in a later, Diaspora context that love for God, in the sense of his exclusive worship, became a necessary part of Christian preaching (1989, 249–266). This thesis is supported by the fact that the earliest NT summary of the Mosaic Law, Romans 13:9, also speaks only of love for one's neighbor: "The commandments, 'You shall not commit adultery; You shall not murder; You shall not steal; You shall not covet'; and any other commandment, are summed up in this word, 'Love your neighbor as yourself.'" Even closer to the Johannine "new commandment" is the exhortation of Paul in Galatians 6:2, which also highlights mutual love among Christians: "Bear one another's burdens, and so fulfill the law of Christ." Here the command to love concerns love for fellow human beings, not for God, and Paul calls the exhortation "the law of Christ." Finally, 1 Peter 1:22 explicitly requires mutual love in the community but does not mention love for God. FG's version of the love command is therefore not far from other early Christian traditions.

Finally, the fourth movement of the Introduction to the Johannine Farewell, the prediction of Peter's denial, finds its synoptic counterpart in Mark 14:29–31. Of course, there are some differences between the synoptic and Johannine versions. In Mark, the dialogue between Jesus and Peter opens with Jesus' announcement that the disciples will stumble because of him, while in FG the dialogue opens with a discussion of Jesus' coming departure and Peter's inability to follow him. FG's version of Jesus' prediction that Peter will deny him comes closest in wording to Luke's account (22:34), which is shorter than that of Mark (14:30) and Matthew (26:34). According to FG, Peter declares himself ready to "give his life for" Jesus, a formula that FE also uses in other contexts (John 10:15, 17ff.; 15:13). FE's formulation seems to make Peter's words a parody of the Suffering Servant's giving of his life for the multitude (Isa. 53:4ff.; cf. Mark 10:45), although Peter's desire to follow Jesus wherever he goes is eventually ironically fulfilled (John 21:18ff.).

It seems clear from even this brief survey that the Introduction to the Johannine Farewell borrows and adapts a number of themes from the broader Jesus tradition. In some cases, FG's version of this tradition appears more primitive than that which appears in the Synoptics.

The First Farewell Discourse (John 14)

The first discourse of the Farewell falls into three sections: the departure of Jesus and the disciples' ongoing union with him (vv. 1–14), the return of Christ and the disciples' reunion with him (vv. 15–24), and final promises and announcements (vv. 25–31).

At John 14:1–3, Jesus reassures his disciples about his imminent departure with the announcement that he will come and take them to an eternal dwelling place with his Father. This theme strongly recalls a very early Christian tradition attested in the earliest letter of Paul, perhaps the oldest document of the New Testament, 1 Thessalonians 4:17: "[w]e will be caught up in the clouds . . . to meet the Lord in the air; and so *we will be with the Lord forever.*" FE seems to know this tradition but drastically reinterprets it at John 14:4–14: now the eternal vision of God takes place through faith in Christ, not in a grandiose eschatological event. In fact, the one who sees Jesus sees the Father *now* (v. 8), with no need for a more intense future vision. As I have tried to show elsewhere (Beutler 1984, 25–36), Psalms 42 and 43 appear to stand behind John 14:1–8. Note particularly the antiphon, "Why so downcast, my soul, why do you sigh within me? Put your hope in God: I shall praise him yet, my saviour, my God" (Ps. 42:5, 11; 43:5). These same two psalms seem to underlie the synoptic Gethsemane tradition (Mark 14:34 pars), and may have come to the Johannine passion account through this synoptic tradition (see John 12:27; 13:21; 14:1, 27). Further, the announcement in John 14:13–14 that the prayers of the disciples will be heard also finds a parallel in synoptic tradition (Mark 11:24; Matt. 21:22). In both FG and Mark this promise is linked to faith (John 14:10–12; Mark 11:22ff.).

In the central section of John 14, verses 15–24, one notes the influences of covenant and Trinitarian theologies. The notions of loving God and keeping his commandments are key elements of the Deuteronomic theology of covenant union with God (Beutler 1984, 55–86). In Johannine thought, the love of God shows itself in the love of Christ, which in turn becomes concrete in love among fellow Christians (John 15:9–10; 1 John 2:3–11; 3:11–24; 5:1–4; 2 John 5–6). The Johannine combination of love with obedience thus seems to be rooted in the Pentateuch. FE introduces his first reference to the Spirit-Paraclete in the context of this covenant theology (14:16–17). Like the Paraclete, the Markan Holy Spirit is bestowed by the Messiah (1:8) and comes to assist the disciples in the moment of trial (Mark 13:11; Matt. 24:20), an idea quite similar to the Johannine description of the Spirit as an "Advocate" (NRSV) who will remain with the disciples (14:16). Jesus' reference to the Paraclete introduces a series of sayings about his future coming (John 14:16–24). We see in these verses a Trinitarian sequence: *Jesus* leaves his own, but he is coming again by the *Spirit-Paraclete* (vv. 16ff.) together with the *Father* (vv. 23ff.; see Beutler 1984, 53, 62–77). Apparently, FE has taken an early Christian tradition about a future coming of Christ or the Son of Man (cf. Mark 13:26) and used it in a very creative and personal way to develop his doctrine of the Paraclete, thus preparing the way for later Christian thought about the Trinity.

In both the Synoptics and FG, the Coming One will "be seen" or will "manifest" himself, another point of contact between the two traditions. It seems reasonable to connect the expectation of the future gift of the Spirit with the idea of the "new covenant" as expressed in Ezekiel 36:26ff. and Jeremiah 31:34 (Beutler 1984, 62–69). The immanence formulas of John 14:20 would fit well with this perspective, as well as the covenant terminology of verse 15 and the announcement of the disciples' future knowledge of Christ and the Father.

The last section of John 14, verses 25–31, seems to have been influenced by the postexilic prophetic tradition, a train of thought with roots in very ancient oriental concepts that were taken up by Jesus in the announcement of the coming Kingdom of God (Beutler 1984, 90–104). The Johannine Jesus promises the disciples joy and peace (vv. 27–28), royal gifts that, along with justice, are associated in Jewish thought with the messianic hope and the gift of the spirit that would be bestowed upon the Anointed One. A key text for the interconnection of these gifts with the idea of the Kingdom is Romans 14:17: "For the kingdom of God is not food and drink but righteousness [Greek *dikaiosunē*, "justice"] and peace and joy in the Holy Spirit." In a well-known parallel passage, Paul opens his description of the fruits of the Spirit with "love, joy, peace" (Gal. 5:22). By analogy with Romans 14:17, it may be said that the Spirit's gifts of peace and joy in John 14 are eschatological gifts from Jesus and expressions of the Kingdom of God. This reading is supported by the fact that the risen Jesus offers the disciples the Spirit, peace, and joy during one of the Johannine resurrection stories (John 20:19–23; cf. Luke 24:36–49).

In the last two verses of John 14 (vv. 30–31), the synoptic Gethsemane tradition is again taken up. The problematic 14:31, "Rise, let us go," comes almost verbatim from Mark 14:32. Further, the mention of the traitor in the same Markan verse is transformed in John 14:30 into the announcement of the coming of the "ruler of this world." In this way, FE gives Judas's arrival in the garden an eschatological dimension (cf. John 6:70f.; 13:2, 27).

In all these cases, then, it is clear that the second major section of the Farewell, John 14, has been heavily influenced by a variety of motifs from the Hebrew Bible and synoptic tradition.

The Second Discourse (John 15:1–16:4a)

As noted earlier, this central discourse of the Farewell evidences its own internal antithetic parallelism, with the love of the disciples toward Christ and each other (John 15:1–17) being countered by the world's hatred (15:18–16:4a). In the first half of this section there is little independent Jesus tradition. The image of the vine (vv. 1–8) is FE's version of the synoptic parable of the vineyard (Mark 12:1–12 pars). But whereas the synoptic parable is based on Isaiah 5:1ff., the Johannine version seems to find its antecedent in Psalm 80:9–20 (Borig 1967, 98ff.), suggesting an independent development. The closest candidate is the motif of election at John 15:16 (also 13:18; 15:19), which seems to recall Mark 3:13ff., the listing of the Twelve. A direct connection between Mark and FG at this point is suggested by the fact that in 6:70 the Johannine Jesus also speaks of the "election" of the Twelve.

FE seems to rely strongly on synoptic tradition in the second half of this central section, John 15:18–16:4a. Specifically, several announcements from Jesus' eschatological discourse at Mark 13:9–13 seem to stand behind the Johannine text. The key concept in the Johannine passage is the disciples' experience of hatred, which is clearly paralleled in the saying of Mark 13:13: "[Y]ou will be hated by all because of my name." Notably, FE has reinterpreted and narrowed the Markan concept "hated by *all*" so that it now refers specifically to "the world's" hatred of the disciples, a hatred that they in fact experience by association, because the true object of the world's hatred is Jesus: "If the world hates you, be aware that it hated me before it hated you." The rationale for this hatred is given in terms of the relationship between Jesus and his disciples at John 15:20, "Servants are not greater than their master," a saying that finds a close parallel at Matthew 10:24. Two other elements central to Mark 13:9–13 are the assistance of the Holy Spirit in the moment of the disciples' trial (13:11) and the term "witness" (13:9). Whereas Mark treats these themes separately, FE combines them in a characteristic way: the Spirit-Paraclete is in fact the one who bears witness in favor of the disciples or, more precisely, in favor of Christ as the disciples bear witness to him (John 15:26ff.). In this way, FE adapts the synoptic tradition to his own definition of "witness" as confession of Christ in a forensic context (Beutler 1972, 273–275, 303). The forensic application of the tradition comes out most clearly at John 16:1–4a, the concluding verses of the central section of the Farewell. Legal action will be taken against the disciples: they will be expelled from the synagogue, and possibly even killed, for their belief in Jesus (cf. 9:22, 34; 12:42). Again, Mark 13:9–13 stands behind this passage text: verse 9 predicts that "they will hand you over to councils; and you will be beaten in synagogues," while verse 12 warns that "brother will betray brother to death." By comparison, the Johannine version sets the persecution of the disciples in the larger theological context of the world's ignorance of Jesus and the Father (16:3). FG emphasizes in verse 1 that Jesus is announcing the coming destiny of the disciples before it happens "to keep you from stumbling," language that echoes Matthew 11:6.

    In this pivotal section of the Farewell, it is clear that FE has borrowed and adapted a number of themes from the broader Jesus tradition. In some cases he has appropriated traditions similar to those that underlie the Synoptic Gospels, or perhaps has even used the Synoptics themselves.

The Third Discourse (John 16:4b–33)

As noted earlier, in the overall structure of the Farewell the third discourse strongly resembles the first. The main subject is again Christ's imminent departure and his subsequent return to his own. The point that characterized John 14:26–28—the eschatological gifts of the Spirit, peace, and joy—is now taken up as the dominant theme of the third discourse: the announcement of the Spirit's mission is developed at 16:7–15; the theme of joy is treated in verses 20–22; and the discourse concludes with an announcement of the coming of Christ's peace in verse 33. As we saw earlier, Paul connects peace and joy with justice under the broader rubric of the Kingdom of God; remarkably, FE now also develops the concept of justice (NRSV: "righteousness") along with joy and peace at 16:4b–33. According to the Johannine Jesus, the Spirit-Paraclete "will prove the world wrong [KJV: "convict"] about sin and righteousness and judgment" (v. 8). Righteousness or justice will be established when Jesus returns to his Father and the disciples do not see him any longer (v. 10). But it is probable that FE has in mind the vindication of Christ's own claims about himself after his return to the Father, whereas Paul develops the theme in terms of the justification of the unjust: the Pauline Christ, returned to his Father, works justification for others, not himself.

At the end of the third discourse, John 15:32, Jesus speaks of the imminent scattering of the disciples: "The hour is coming, indeed it has come, when you will be scattered, each one to his own home, and you will leave me alone." This seems to echo the citation of Zechariah 13:7 at Mark 14:27 and Matthew 26:31. If so, this is yet another link between the Johannine Farewell and the Synoptics, showing the ongoing connection between the two traditions.

The Final Prayer of Jesus (John 17)

In the Final Prayer the connections between FG and other early Christian traditions are relatively loose. From the beginning of the prayer, there are some parallels with the Gethsemane tradition: Jesus addresses God as his "Father" and speaks of the "hour" that has "come" (John 17:1; cf. Mark 14:35ff., where Jesus asks that the "hour" may pass). For the Farewell, this reference to Jesus' "hour" is an unusually direct reference back to the narrative of FG, for John 13:1 stages the footwashing by saying that "Jesus knew that his hour had come to depart from the world." The subject of Jesus' glorification, which dominates the prayer, has already appeared in the Introduction to the Farewell. As noted above, this concept is connected with the destiny of the Son of Man, as that destiny is reinterpreted through the Suffering Servant of Isaiah 53. Echoes of a variety of synoptic themes resonate throughout John 17: Jesus' "power over all flesh" (17:2; cf. Matt. 28:18); the mutual knowledge between Father and Son (17:3, 25; cf. Matt. 11:27); eschatological joy in the face of the world's hatred; the disciples' mission (17:18; cf. Mark 8:14; Matt. 10:5); and Christ's consecration of his own mission (v. 19, with the same formula "acting for" another as used by Peter in John 13:37ff.).

Summing up our results, we can say that John 13–17 is pervaded by early Jesus tradition, mostly tradition of a synoptic character and perhaps even derived from the Synoptics themselves. But while FE seems to have relied on synoptic tradition in written or oral form, no single coherent discourse source can be uncovered. Rather, there has been a creative use of the traditional material, forging it into a new form that expresses FE's peculiar view of Jesus as the Son of Man and Son of God who returns to his Father but does not leave his own alone in this hostile world.

16

John and Mark

The Bi-Optic Gospels

PAUL N. ANDERSON

The relationship between the Fourth Gospel (FG) and the Synoptics is often treated as "three against one," evoking distorted perceptions of John and the Synoptics alike. Differences between the presentations and contents of these four books contribute to the flawed assumption that the Synoptics are "historical" while John is "spiritual." However, if Matthew and Luke indeed used Mark in constructing their gospels, differences in perspective between the Synoptics and FG may be rooted primarily in differences between the Markan and Johannine traditions. There may even have been contacts between these two traditions, and perhaps some of their similarities *and differences* originated within this contact. Because the Johannine tradition developed in its own autonomous way, parallel to Mark, these two gospels should be considered the "Bi-Optic Gospels." Evidence for such a thesis presents itself in considering the development and origin of the Johannine material and the relationship between FG and the Synoptics.

Flawed Assumptions

Several sorts of fallacious assumptions enjoy the status of uncritical acceptance among many New Testament scholars today. One example is the popular maxim that gospel traditions are either factual (=historical) or spiritual (= ahistorical), by which Mark is described as "historical" and FG as "not historical."

But the pre-Markan traditional material was itself formulated to address the theological interests of the early church, and Mark's ordering and crafting of his material had its own "spiritual" concerns. Conversely, the Johannine witness appears to be concerned with preserving earlier material for later audiences, and FG poses more claims to eyewitness derivation than all three Synoptics combined (John 1:14; 19:35; 21:24). Historical and spiritual concerns were operative within *all four gospel's traditions*—at times in distinctive ways. Hence, attempts to explain Johannine-synoptic differences in terms of "spiritual" vs. "historical" gospels are based on a flawed foundation.

A second fallacy is the assumption that Johannine-synoptic similarities must have arisen because the Fourth Evangelist (FE) used one or more of the Synoptics as sources. One cannot assume that all contacts between early gospel traditions were derivative in nature rather than dialectical. There probably never was a time when all gospel traditions were entirely united in their presentations of Jesus' ministry; even the four NT gospels portray the disciples debating the meaning of Jesus' actions and teaching from the very beginning. Such reports suggest differences between earlier and later perceptions within individual gospel traditions, as well as lateral dialogues between gospel traditions. One or more of the synoptic traditions may have been influenced by the developing Johannine tradition, and there may have been an ongoing set of dialogues between several traditions at several periods of their development. Simple approaches to such complex issues are almost always wrong.

A third fallacy frequently encountered in Johannine-synoptic studies is the assumption that conclusions from the source-critical analysis of the Synoptics provide the best pattern for reconstructing the composition history of FG. While some clues from the synoptic situation may be helpful, others may have no relevance to the case of FG. For example, Matthew and Luke appear to have used a narrative source (Mark) and a sayings source (Q), and they also introduced other traditional material as well as their own distinctive theological and editorial perspectives. But does this prove that FE also made use of alien (non-Johannine) traditions, or that signs and discourses developed separately within the Johannine tradition? Such issues must be sorted out on the basis of evidence rather than by simply assuming that FE followed a synoptic pattern.

Recent Theories
of John's Origins

Recent theories of FG's origins deserve analytical consideration. Here I will briefly discuss the relative merits of several proposals, focusing on John 6 as a test case. While other texts are relevant to some theories, John 6 provides the most extensive backbone for launching into matters of FG's composition, development, and relation to the Synoptics (Anderson 1996, 33–69).

FE's Use of Alien Sources

The first theory to consider is the supposed use of alien sources by the Fourth Evangelist. Varying in range and character, source theories reflect an ambitious set of approaches to account for FG's distinctive material. The most impressive proposal along these lines is that of Rudolf Bultmann (1971), who develops an intricate theory inferring three underlying sources (a *sēmeia* source, a revelation-sayings source, and a passion source). Bultmann's claim that these sources can be distinguished from FE's later work is founded on three types of evidence: stylistic, contextual, and theological. His approach set an important precedent for Johannine source criticism: when studies by scholars such as Schweizer, Ruckstuhl, and Van Belle seem to demonstrate the stylistic unity of FG, one may still appeal to contextual and theological evidence to support source-critical theories. But when all of Bultmann's evidence for sources is gathered and plied out within John 6, the results are not only nonconvincing, they are entirely nonindicative (Anderson 1996, 72–136). It appears that Bultmann has correctly inferred the style of the narrator and observed that there are more verbs in the narrative and more abstract nouns in the discourse sections. But these observations do not prove that FE used non-Johannine material with which he disagreed.

More recently, Robert Fortna has reproduced the hypothetical Greek text of what he calls the "Signs Gospel," a narrative source underlying FG's miracle accounts and passion story (Fortna 1970). Fortna's approach is preferable to Bultmann's in that it is less extended in its inferences, yet it still does not adequately account for alternate explanations of the data. For example, Fortna analyzes the use of *kai* and *oun* and other stylistic features supposedly characteristic of the Signs Gospel but does not consider the possibility that the linguistic patterns he observes may simply reflect features of FE's own narrative style. More important is the way Fortna casts into sharp relief the tension between the thaumaturgic character of FG's miracle stories and the existentializing comments of the evangelist. Such tension is indeed present, but this does not prove that FE was "correcting" the theological tendency of an alien source as opposed to simply commenting on his own tradition. While FE may have employed various traditions, none of the so-called evidence for a non-Johannine source is strong enough to support the highly speculative schemes of composition that have been constructed upon it. All the material in John (except 7:53–8:11) hangs together in its own Johannine sort of way, and this being the case, other ways forward must be explored.

Synoptic Dependence

A second theory on the origins of FG suggests that the Fourth Evangelist employed one or more of the Synoptics as sources, and the most convincing argument along these lines infers FE's spiritualized use of Mark. C. K. Barrett, for instance, develops the implications of connections between the broad outlines of, and particular Greek phrases within, Mark and John (Barrett 1978, 5–15). While FG differs greatly from Mark, Barrett nonetheless infers that FE has borrowed from Mark's overall structure and has spiritualized some of Mark's content. But a closer analysis reveals the following facts. First, the general similarities between the Markan and Johannine passion narratives do not necessarily imply derivative influence in *either* direction. Important events and details are missing or present between each of these gospels, and this implies separate traditions and individual developments. Some contact may have existed between Mark's and John's traditions, but the relationship does not appear to have been a derivative one, at least not in the way that Matthew and Luke were derivative from Mark.

This conclusion is confirmed when one compares the feeding story in John 6 with its parallels in Mark 6 and 8. Barrett proposes six linguistic similarities and three points of contact in the outlines of these chapters, but in fact one may infer twenty-four points of contact between John 6 and Mark 6 and twenty-one contacts between John 6 and Mark 8. On close scrutiny, however, the number of *identical* contacts among these forty-five potential similarities is zero (Anderson 1996, 97–104). This fact makes it impossible to conceive that FE used Mark in a derivative way, at least not in the ways Matthew and Luke did. In that sense, Gardener-Smith's (1938) judgment that FG was independent of Mark remains essentially correct.

FG as Historicized Drama

A converse proposal, which often accompanies source theories, suggests that FG is a historicized drama to which names and details have been added in order to make the story more lucid. According to Bultmann and others, this phenomenon is characteristic of similar ancient narratives. A major problem with this third view is that when the three narratives most similar to FG, the Synoptic Gospels, are considered, the opposite inference must be drawn. When one considers the sort of things Luke and Matthew have left out in their use of Mark, the list includes primarily nonsymbolic, illustrative detail and theological asides (Anderson 1997). These materials are sometimes replaced by generalizations or common-sense conjecture, and Matthew and Luke also at times add units of their own traditional material. Such moves, however, are very different from the adding of detail for sake of dramatic effect.

In general, "historicized drama" theories, which infer that some of FG's material was invented for rhetorical reasons, confuse function for origin. If FG's nonsymbolic, illustrative narrative details had an origin similar to those in its closest parallel writings, one must conclude that John is closer to Mark than to Matthew and Luke. In other words, the literary character of FG's material appears closer to the material underlying Mark than the co-opted uses of Mark by Matthew and Luke. A critical analysis of the evidence suggests that John and Mark both reflect proximity to the oral stages of their respective traditions, and this likelihood accounts for many of FG's features and many of the Johannine/Markan parallels as well.

The Developmental Approach

The approach that addresses most plausibly the composition history and presentation of the Fourth Gospel involves multiple stages of FG's development. I propose a *two-edition theory of John's composition*, wherein the first edition was probably finalized around 80 C.E., before Matthew and Luke were written. This first edition included Jesus' intense debates with the Jewish religious leaders and sought to persuade readers to believe that Jesus was the Jewish Messiah sent from God as the Prophet-like-Moses (Deut. 18:15–22), who speaks not on his own behalf, but only as he has been instructed by God. FG's Father-Son relationship must be seen as a factor of the prophetic agency schema. In the supplementary material to this first edition of FG, however, new interests emerged. The first is an emphasis on Jesus' suffering and death, his incarnation and willingness to go to the cross. Thus, the Word became flesh (John 1:14), water and blood flowed out of Jesus' side (19:34–35), persecutions and martyrdoms are predicted (16:1–4; 21:18–22), and Jesus' followers are called to ingest his "flesh and blood" (6:51–58) in their willingness to participate in Jesus' passion if they wish to share in his resurrection (Anderson 1996, 194–220; 1997, 41–50).

A second set of themes emerging from FG's later material relates to *Christocracy*, the means by which the risen Lord continues to lead the church. Christ leads through the Paraclete, the Holy Spirit and Spirit of Truth who guides, comforts, convicts, and instructs believers faithfully. One can also infer the extension of the apostolic commission to a plurality of believers (John 20:21–23) over and against the more hierarchical and exclusive model suggested in Matthew 16:17–19. FE's juxtaposition of Peter with the Beloved Disciple presents itself as a corrective to the rising institutionalism in the late first-century church. Does this imply that the final edition of FG is Christocratically corrective in egalitarian, pneumatic, and familial ways? Quite possibly (Anderson 1996, 221–251; 1997, 50–57). The targets of FE's critique, however, were more probably such local irritants as Diotrephes (3 John 9–10) rather than Matthean Christianity proper. After the death of the Beloved Disciple (John 21:23–24), the editor appears to have compiled and finalized the current version of FG around 100 C.E., sending it out among the churches as the testimony of the Beloved Disciple, who by now exemplified authentic discipleship for later generations.

In summary, the evidence does not support reconstructions that suggest that FE used Mark or other unknown documents as sources. Much of FG's material appears to represent an independent tradition reflecting on many of the events in Jesus' ministry described in the Synoptics from a pervasively different perspective. Rather than being a historicized drama, John appears to be more of a "dramatized history." The first edition of FG was designed to convince a largely Jewish audience that Jesus was indeed the Messiah. The second-edition material reflects a move from evangelistic concerns to "abiding" with Jesus and the maintenance of group solidarity. At some point, Luke appears to have had access to the Johannine oral tradition (providing the best explanation for why Luke sides with FG against Mark at least three dozen times), and Johannine and Matthean sectors of the late first-century church often addressed the same sets of Jewish-Christian issues. They also probably engaged each other's traditions on matters of ecclesiology, and this resulted in the finalization and circulation of FG by the editor.

But what about Mark? In what sense were the Johannine and Markan traditions engaged or independent? This important question is the topic of the next section.

John's Relationship to Mark: Interfluential, Augmentive, and Corrective

When the points of contact between FG and Mark are analyzed, three major patterns emerge. The first pattern involves the similarity of detail typified by the sorts of linguistic contacts inferred by Barrett and others. Such similarities indeed suggest contact, but rather than implying the use of written sources they imply contacts during the *oral* stages of the Markan and Johannine traditions. These details resemble the sorts of material employed by storytellers and preachers, and they appear to reflect traces of early oral traditions. Both Mark and John offer translations of Aramaic terms into Greek and the explanations of Jewish customs for Gentile audiences. Such features are missing from Matthew and Luke, and the best inference is to consider these as bridges between earlier (Palestinian) oral traditions and later, more cosmopolitan written ones. Parallels also exist among other features of the narratives, such as references to the time of day, distances walked, topographical details, and mentions of ironic turns of events. These similarities lend credence to Papias's claim that at least some of Mark was drawn from Peter's preaching. FG contains even more of this sort of material than Mark does, and it is likely that such features are traces of orality in the Johannine written narrative. If FE or an earlier Johannine preacher preached alongside someone like Peter, this may account for many of the verbal and linguistic similarities between John and Mark.

If Johannine/Markan contacts can be traced, however, to oral stages of their respective traditions, it is impossible to infer which direction the influence may have gone. Indeed, "influence" may be the wrong term; the relationship may better be described as "interfluential" rather than influential. If both traditions appear primitive at times, and if the contacts were between preachers telling their own versions of Jesus stories, the Markan tradition may have picked up on early Johannine renderings of accounts rather than vice versa. Contacts between FG and Mark can clearly be seen at the beginning of Jesus' ministry, in the role of John the Baptist, in the feeding and sea-crossing miracles, in several teachings of Jesus, and in events surrounding the Passion, death, and resurrection of Jesus. If pre-Markan and early Johannine preachers picked up and reinforced details from one another, this hypothesis also may account for some of the differences in perspective between the two traditions. Indeed, gospel traditions were not simply disembodied sets of ideas floating from one religious setting to another. Rather, they represent living, feeling, thinking human beings, who perceived and reflected on events distinctively and creatively.

A second impression emerges when the first edition of FG is compared with Mark. It appears that John's material was crafted as an augmentive complement to Mark. In other words, while FG does not depend on Mark for material, it appears that FE engages Mark in a supplemental sort of way. If FE were aware of written Mark (probably finalized around 70 C.E.), several aspects of FG's first-edition material become interesting to consider. The fact that much of Mark's outline is similar to John's suggests that Mark may have provided something of a pattern for the first edition of FG. Jesus' healing and teaching ministries come across in their own distinctive ways in FG, but when the five signs included in the first edition of FG (the water into wine, the healings of the official's son, the paralytic, the blind man, and the raising of Lazarus) are considered in relation to Mark, it becomes apparent that *these are all absent from Mark*. Likewise, the explicit emphasis that the first two miracles are the first two signs done in Cana of Galilee (John 2:11; 4:54) may be FE's attempt to fill out the earlier part of Jesus' ministry. The contents of John 1–4 may reflect an opinion that the launching of Jesus' ministry was a bit more public, extensive, and festive than the Markan healing in the household of Simon Peter's mother-in-law (see Eusebius, *Ecclesiastical History* 24). FG's extended postresurrection material may have served to rectify the abrupt ending of Mark. Even the original ending of John

("Now Jesus did many other signs in the presence of his disciples, which *are not written in this book*, but these are written. . . . [20:30–31; italics added]) may be understood as an assumption that the reader is familiar with Mark, while at the same time explaining Mark's relative absence from FG's augmentation of it.

A third feature emerging from comparisons and contrasts between FG and Mark involves material in FG that appears dissonant with, and corrective to, Mark. Neither Matthew nor Luke was satisfied with Mark as it stood, let alone the contributor of Mark's "long ending." But Matthew and Luke simply built on Mark and added their own material and material from Q to produce "new and improved" versions of the earlier gospel. If FE, however, built *around* Mark and added distinctively Johannine material, this might account for a good deal of FG's independence from Mark without entirely rejecting FE's familiarity with Mark. FG's independence from Mark may be considered non-derivative and autonomous, but it also appears FE was engaged dialogically with Mark's tradition. Familiarity and dissonance together, however, imply a corrective to Mark.

In many ways, the Johannine presentation of Jesus' ministry is more realistic than Mark's rendering. In Mark, Jesus ministers for less than one year, goes to Jerusalem only once, and is then killed. FG, on the other hand, mentions three Passovers and portrays Jesus more realistically going to and from Jerusalem and Galilee. Mark suggests an abrupt transition between the ministries of John the Baptist and Jesus, whereas FG presents a more interwoven connection. FE's emphasis that Jesus did not baptize, though his disciples did (John 4:2), also seems to be a corrective clarification in the interest of realism,

Table 16.1

Augments to Mark in the First Edition of FG

—Parallel beginnings and endings: both Mark and FG begin with John the Baptist and conclude with the resurrection appearances of Jesus.
—Emphases upon the works and teachings of Jesus, including reactions from Jewish leaders, the world, and the disciples.
—Filling out the early miracles section, including the first two signs performed in Cana of Galilee, as well as a fuller set of appearance narratives.
—Filling out the Judean ministry of Jesus, including visits to Jerusalem and conflicts with Judean authorities.
—Adding five miracles not covered by Mark.
—Providing a Johannine rendering of Jesus' teachings heightening his sense of mission as the prophetic agency of God and the embodiment of the ideal Israel.
—Adding scripture-fulfillment passages not included in Mark.
—Contributing a spiritual reflection upon Jesus' ministry as a complement to Mark's more pedantic rendering.

and the absence of institutionalizing Eucharistic instructions at the Johannine Last Supper seems more authentic than the more formalized synoptic accounts, which had come to legitimate the evolving Christian sacramental practice. And, rather than presenting Jesus calling and designating twelve male apostles, the Johannine witness includes an inaugural christological confession by Nathaniel (not one of the Twelve) and a climactic one by Martha (a woman). Rather than considering FE's deemphasis of the Twelve and the juxtaposition of Peter and the Beloved Disciple a factor of FG's nonapostolicity, the converse may be implied. Some of FG's differences with Mark (and thus Matthew and Luke) may reflect an alternate opinion regarding at least some aspects of Jesus' ministry.

One intriguing difference between Mark and John is FE's placement of the Temple Incident at the beginning of Jesus' ministry rather than at the end. The standard explanation states that FE has shifted the event from its original location in the story for theological reasons, but this assumption has several problems. First, such theological motives must be assumed; they are not stated explicitly by the evangelist. Second, the Temple Incident appears to be one of Jesus' early demonstrations that the Galilean crowd had witnessed when they too were in Jerusalem (John 4:45). It also seems odd that the Jerusalem authorities should be ready to kill Jesus after so commendable a deed as the healing of the paralytic at John 5. Why would they have been so upset, unless Jesus had already caused a threatening disturbance such as the Temple Incident? As a third consideration, since Mark places all of his Jerusalem-related material at the end of Jesus' ministry, the Temple Incident may appear at the end of Mark less as a factor of historicity and more as a factor of common-sense conjecture. The fact that the Temple Incident offers a plausible reason for Jesus' arrest is precisely the reason that Matthew and Luke have accepted the Markan rendering as historical. However, if the criterion of dissimilarity is here applied, the very unlikelihood that the Jewish leaders would wish to kill Jesus because he raised Lazarus from the tomb (John 11:45–52; 12:9–11) argues in favor of the Johannine rendering. It is extremely unlikely that the Lazarus sign would have been concocted to function as the fictive straw that broke the camel's back between Jesus and the Jerusalem authorities. One wonders whether FG's dissonance with Mark in this particular instance may have been the issue that evoked the opinion of John the Elder that Mark wrote down the testimony of Peter accurately, but in the wrong order (see Eusebius's *Ecclesiastical History* 39). Perhaps the Johannine leadership held the same opinion.

While the above considerations are themselves somewhat conjectural, the inference that FE has written in dialogue with several aspects of Mark's theological content is quite compelling. For example, FG's descriptions of the Kingdom of God emphasize the transcendence and spiritual character of

God's active reign. The Kingdom can only be apprehended by being "born from above" (John 3:1–8), and Jesus' disciples do not fight because his reign is one of truth (18:36–38). A second corrective challenges the evaluation of the feeding miracle in Mark, where it is reported that the crowd "ate and were satisfied." At John 6:26, Jesus declares, "You seek me not because you saw the signs, but because you ate of the loaves and were satisfied." Again, it need not be inferred that the Fourth Evangelist intended to correct a particular synoptic text; rather, the rhetorical target was more likely to have been the prevalent view of Jesus' miraculous ministry within the larger Christian movement.

A third theological matter that is apparently corrected by the Johannine Jesus is Mark's presentation of the promise that the Son of Man would come again before those who were standing in his audience died (Mark 9:1). FE accounts for the apparent delay of Jesus' return by clarifying what Jesus did and did not say. In John 21, after the prediction of Peter's martyrdom and Peter's inquiry about the fate of the Beloved Disciple, the narrator intervenes to make two clarifications in verse 23. A rumor had spread that the Beloved Disciple would not die, but this unfortunate event has apparently transpired. Thus, the intention of Jesus' remarks about BD must be clarified: Jesus did not say to Peter (or to anyone else who might be considered the root of synoptic tradition) that the Beloved Disciple (or anyone else "standing here" at the Markan Mount of Transfiguration) would not die; rather, Jesus said to Peter, "What is it to you if he [BD] lives until I come again?" This Johannine correction to Mark explains the delay of Jesus' return not as a factor of the need to wait for the Lord's timing, but as a clarification of what Jesus did and did not say. False rumors had been spread, and perhaps even Peter got it wrong—let alone gospel narratives constructed upon a Petrine memory.

From these sample observations regarding FG's similarities and differences with Mark (a survey that could be greatly extended), it is arguable that theories about the relationship between these two books cannot be adequately constructed on only a narrow definition. Given the complexity of the evidence, any theory that attempts to summarize this relationship in one word ("dependent," "independent," "derivative," "theologizing," "novelistic," etc.) is certain to be wrong. John's relationship to Mark appears to have begun with contacts during the oral stages of both traditions, and the first edition of FG appears to have been crafted around Mark in an augmentive and supplemental way. On the other hand, dialogical and corrective interests can also be inferred, both in the early Johannine material, as well as in the material added to the first edition later on. While FG has been crafted with theological interests in mind, this does not mean that its material has no root in the historical ministry of Jesus or an independent Jesus tradition.

Table 16.2

Corrections to Mark in FG

—Locating the Temple Incident at the beginning of Jesus' ministry.
—Reserving associations with Moses and Elijah for Jesus rather than John the Baptist and their appearance at the Mount of Transfiguration.
—Special emphases upon the spiritual and transcendent character of God's reign.
—Challenging thaumaturgic valuations of Jesus' signs versus Mark's wonder attestations.
—Declaring openly the identity of the Son versus Mark's Messianic Secret.
—Challenging Mark's developed sacramental theology with a more primitive emphasis on suffering and service.
—Diminishing of the calling of "the Twelve" and broadening the concept of "apostolicity" to include women and others.
—A "clarification" of Jesus' original words and intentions regarding the second coming.

John and Mark: The Bi-Optic Gospels

The word "synoptic" implies not only that the first three gospels look alike, but that they perceive the ministry of Jesus through a similar lens. To posit a "bi-optic" relationship between the Markan and Johannine traditions is not only to acknowledge the different ways these gospels appear to the reader, but also to account for the epistemological origin of their similarities and differences on the basis of the fact that they appear to present differing yet parallel interpretations of the ministry of Jesus. Because Matthew and Luke constructed their gospel's narratives around the outline of Mark, and because Mark's project was as much a collecting and organizing of traditional material as a reconstructed itinerary of Jesus' ministry, attempts to marginalize FG's presentation of Jesus on the basis of a "three against one" contrast deserve reconsideration. Indeed, FG is a spiritual and theological presentation of Jesus, but this does not mean that the Johannine reflection was ever truncated from an independent Jesus tradition, nor does it imply a derivative relationship to Mark or alien sources. Rather, Mark and John reflect two parallel perspectives on Jesus' ministry that may have been dialogically engaged during the oral and written stages of their respective developments. From early preachers hearing the ways other preachers narrated stories about Jesus to the point when the first edition of FG was crafted around Mark in an augmentive sort of way, their relationship appears to have been a dialectic one. Such a dialectic extended to FE's reluctance to duplicate most of Mark's material, and it included a willingness to set the record straight in terms of the presentation of some events and the emphasizing of particular theological perspectives. John and Mark, then, reflect parallel-and-yet-distinctive traditions that were engaged with each other along the way. They are the Bi-Optic Gospels, and whereas Luke and Matthew built *on* Mark, the Fourth Evangelist built *around* it.

These assertions will be opposed by those scholars who question the authenticity of the Johannine tradition, and there are many reasons for doing so. Two of the most significant reasons will be considered here. First, FE's apparent attempt to minimize the authority of the Twelve and offer a more modest presentation of Peter appears to counter the idea that FG reflects an "apostolic" tradition. But the assumption that FE's critical view of ecclesial hierarchy excludes the Johannine witness from the apostolic core of Christianity is misguided. Did *all* early Christian leaders agree with the move toward a centralized, monarchical form of leadership, or did some see such developments as departures from the more egalitarian and charismatic way of Jesus? It may be that some leaders within apostolic Christianity felt that the appeal to Peter in support of the emerging hierarchical structure misrepresented Jesus' original intention for the church. Hence, this factor alone cannot imply that the Fourth Evangelist could not have been one of the Twelve, or at least a close associate of one of them. It is also possible that the Johannine tradition may represent the memory of more than one individual, and there were certainly more firsthand sources of Jesus tradition than would have come from the twelve apostles alone. Without claiming to know whom the Beloved Disciple may have been, or who in particular may have been the personal source of the Johannine witness—or the Markan witness, for that matter—the least to be inferred is that we have two individuated perspectives at the root of the Gospels of Mark and John.

This bi-optic relationship between Mark and FG is evident in the presentation of several aspects of Jesus' ministry, especially the feeding narratives and their associated materials. It is possible that Jesus may have performed more than one feeding, but other than differences in the size of the crowd, the numbers of baskets used to pick up the leftovers, and surrounding material (sea-crossings, debates over meanings, and Peter's confession) one may infer seventeen commonalities—in the same sequence—between the accounts reported in Mark 6 and 8 (Anderson 1997, 8–11, 28–32). It may therefore be that here we have three traditional renderings of the same set of events: Mark 6, Mark 8, and John 6. If this is the case, it is remarkable that FG gives the fullest treatment of the story and includes aspects from both Markan accounts. Like Mark 6, FG includes the feeding of the five thousand and the sea-crossing, and like Mark 8, FG includes a feeding, a discussion of the meaning of the feeding, and Peter's confession. FE's rendering is not only longer than both Markan narratives combined (John 6:1–71 versus Mark 6:32–52 and 8:1–38), but it is also fuller in its narrative presentation.

The point here is to illustrate the likelihood that here we have at least two independent, and yet engaged, traditions represented between John and Mark. On the feeding miracles, the Markan narratives both point out that the crowd "ate and were satisfied" (6:42; 8:37), and this same result is mentioned in the three feeding narratives in Matthew and Luke (Matt. 14:20; 15:37; Luke 9:17). In John, however, Jesus rebukes the crowd for seeking him because they had not "seen the sign" but instead had only eaten the loaves and were satisfied (6:26). The Johannine perspective may be seen as a challenge to other Christian evaluations of Jesus' miracles that failed to emphasize their revelatory significance. Likewise, the Markan and Johannine traditions offer contrasting reflections on the relative dearth of miracles (Anderson 1995, 4–12; 1996, 142–148). The Markan Jesus emphasizes that miracles follow faith and refers to a lack of faith to explain why miracles did not occur. This may reflect pre-Markan preaching to the effect that "it's not God's fault . . . it is your [the church's] lack of faith . . ." that causes miracles not to occur. The Johannine preaching, however, appears to have emphasized the revelatory significance of the miracles as an independent theological reflection upon their meaning: "It's not that one dies or is born blind . . . it is for the glorification of God, and that you might believe that Jesus is the Resurrection and the Life and the Light of the world." Likewise, according to Mark, even Jesus could do no miracles because of the Nazarenes' unbelief (Mark 6:5–6), while the Johannine Jesus declares, "Blessed are *those who have not seen*, and yet believe" (John 20:29; emphasis added).

As well as differing valuations of Jesus' miracles—reflecting later developments in the Markan and Johannine traditions—there appear to have been different sets of first impressions regarding at least the sea-crossing (Anderson 1995, 13–16; 1996, 148–151, 179–183). The source of the Markan rendering appears to have perceived the event as an epiphany (with Jesus' self-identification clarifying that it was he, not a ghost), while in FG the event has been interpreted as a theophany. No "ghost" is mentioned in John; Jesus simply declares, "I am! Fear not!" similar to the words of Yahweh in the LXX version of the burning bush incident (John 6:20; cf. Exod. 3:14). Other similar-yet-different reports are common to the Johannine and Markan versions of the Temple Incident, the Last Supper, the trials of Jesus, and the resurrection appearances, to name a few. These differing interpretations may have been early as well as late, making it valuable to see them as representative of distinctive larger sets of perspectives regarding the ministry of Jesus.

A second objection to a bi-optic approach to Mark and FG will be raised by those scholars who argue that the Gospel of John was divorced from eyewitness tradition. Until recently it was thought that the earliest clear attempt to connect the Fourth Gospel to John the Apostle was that of Irenaeus (ca. 180 C.E.). An impressive connection exists, however, in Acts 4:19–20, which moves this association a full century earlier (see Appendix 8 in Anderson 1996, 274–277). Here we have an unmistakable association of the disciple John with a Johannine cliché ("we cannot help speaking about *what we have seen and heard*"), a statement that finds its closest grammatical parallel in 1 John 1:3 (see also John 3:32, where the one from above testifies to what he has "seen and heard"). Given the fact that Luke borrows extensively from the Johannine tradition in his departures from Mark, this first-century connection of a Johannine phrase with an apostolic association approximates a fact. While much of the Markan account is still historically preferable to FG, it cannot be said that John's witness is late-and-only-late.

The Signs Gospel

17

The Signs Gospel in Context

TOM THATCHER

At the 1957 "Conference on the Four Gospels" in Oxford, John A. T. Robinson announced that Johannine studies were taking on a "New Look." Whereas earlier scholars had assumed that the Fourth Gospel (FG) was dependent on the Synoptics, the New Look asserted that John's tradition was independent, possibly even developing alongside the synoptic tradition. This being the case, scholars were forced to reconsider the age and origin of the Johannine Jesus tradition, even the possibility that this tradition developed before the fall of Jerusalem (70 C.E.). And if John's tradition was, in fact, older than was previously supposed, it would also be necessary to reconsider the assumption that FG represents a late stage in the evolution of the early church's theology. Robinson closed his remarks by noting that the New Look was "new" in its openness to the possibility that FG evidences "a real continuity . . . in the life of an ongoing community, with the earliest days of Christianity" (Robinson 1962, 96–103, 106).

The trend Robinson observed in the 1950s rose to a swell in the 1960s with a renewed interest in the Johannine Jesus tradition and the conditions under which FG was produced. C. H. Dodd's *Historical Tradition in the Fourth Gospel* (1963) sought to distill traditional, and perhaps authentic, sayings of Jesus from the Johannine speeches. Raymond Brown's exhaustive Anchor Bible commentary (1966) explained that the present text of FG is the result of five stages of development and revision. Rudolf Schnackenburg's three-volume commentary on John (1968) suggested that FG's narratives were based on an earlier written predecessor. A milestone of the New Look era appeared in J. Louis Martyn's *History and Theology in the Fourth Gospel* (1968). Martyn argued that John 9 can be read at two levels: as a story of Jesus' conflict with the Jews but at the same time as a reflection of John's own conflict with synagogue authorities after 85 C.E. (Martyn 1979, 30, 37–41). Martyn's thesis generated a new interest in the history of the Johannine Community and the relationship between this community's experience and the composition of FG. Today, most commentaries on FG and 1–2–3 John base their exegesis on an explicit theory about the experiences of the Fourth Evangelist (FE) and the effect this experience had on the Johannine Jesus tradition.

In 1960, early in the New Look period, Robert Fortna began doctoral studies at Union Theological Seminary under Martyn's direction. At that time, despite the renewed interest in the history of the Johannine Community, little effort was being made to identify possible written sources for FG. While many agreed that John was *not* dependent on the Synoptics, most scholars accepted the New Look principle that FG is a pastiche of oral traditions, Johannine compositions, and possibly a few narrative sources that can no longer be distinguished, all filtered through a series of revisions and expansions. Earlier in the twentieth century, scholars such as Schwartz, Wendt, Wellhausen, Bacon, and Faure had attempted to identify written sources in the current text of FG, but the search for such documents was all but ended by the work of Eduard Schweizer (1939) and Ernst Ruckstuhl (1958). Both scholars demonstrated that the Greek text of FG evidences a uniform style, making it impossible to separate earlier sources from the present text on the basis of linguistic criteria. The studies of Schweizer and Ruckstuhl were so well received that the search for FG's written predecessors might have been abandoned altogether were it not for the vote of the dominant voice in the New Look era, Rudolf Bultmann.

Bultmann's monumental commentary on John (1st ed. 1941) utilized a notoriously complex source analysis, which was described and dissected for the English world in D. Moody Smith's *The Composition and Order of the Fourth Gospel* (1965). Fortna summarized the state of Johannine source criticism in the late 1960s by observing that Bultmann's theory was "so exhaustive . . . but at the same time so unacceptable in parts . . . that since the Second World War there has been on the whole only a discussion of the problems raised by his work" (Fortna 1970, 1 n. 1). It will therefore be helpful to review Bultmann's theory in order to set a backdrop for Fortna's investigation.

Bultmann's source theory seems to have developed in the course of his exegesis, with remarks on method generally relegated to the voluminous footnotes in his John commentary. In his own words, "It goes without saying that the exegesis must expound the complete text, and the critical analysis [of the sources] is the servant of this exposition" (Bultmann 1971, 17). Nevertheless,

Bultmann consistently applied specific criteria for identifying FG's sources. He believed, for example, that each source had a distinct style, and that FE's own personal style is distinct from the sources. "Style" here includes linguistic features such as vocabulary, grammar, and poetic rhythm, and also larger literary devices like dialogue and misunderstanding. Also, the various sources promoted distinct theological concepts, which FE did not bring into complete harmony when composing FG. As a result, apparent theological tensions in FG may be taken as evidence that sources have been brought together. Using such criteria, Bultmann posited a number of written sources, including a "Signs Source" that underlies the miracle stories of FG, a passion source that underlies most of John 18–20, and the *Offenbarungsreden*, a series of "revelation-discourses" that formed the basis of Jesus' speeches.

Bultmann's Signs Source, a collection of stories that FE used to compose portions of the narrative sections of FG, is particularly important to Fortna's work. This document opened with what is now John 1:35–50, closed with a combination of John 12:37–41 and 20:30–31, and included at least portions of John 2:1–12 (the Cana wedding), 4:5–42 (the Samaritan woman), 4:46–54 (the nobleman's son), 5:1–8 (the paralytic at Bethesda), 6:1–26 (the miraculous feeding), 7:1–13 (Jesus at the feast), chapter 9 (the man born blind), and chapter 11 (Lazarus). Bultmann referred to this document as a "signs" source on the basis of John 2:11, 4:54, and 20:30–31, where Jesus' miracles are referred to as "signs" of his true identity. The stories in the Signs Source portrayed Jesus as the sort of "divine man" figure popular in many Hellenistic religions (Bultmann 1971, 179–180). Bultmann believed that portions of the Signs Source were drawn from the same traditions that make up the Synoptic Gospels, and that in some cases the source's presentation of these events was more primitive than the synoptic version (Bultmann 1971, 115, 204, 210, 330). FE combined this source with his other sources, adding his own original compositions, to produce an early version of FG, which was later redacted by another person to produce the current Gospel of John.

Robert Fortna's 1965 doctoral dissertation, which was published in 1970 as *The Gospel of Signs: A Reconstruction of the Narrative Source Underlying the Fourth Gospel*, inaugurated a new era in Johannine source criticism. In this work, Fortna proposed that most of the narrative portions of FG were derived from an earlier document, the "Signs Gospel," which included miracle stories and a passion narrative. FE expanded and elaborated this text to create the present version of FG. Fortna's proposal was, in the main, consistent with Bultmann's but went far beyond Bultmann's conclusions by using a more precise method for source separation. To best illustrate the innovative features of Fortna's theory, it will be helpful to briefly compare his method and conclusions with Bultmann's hypothesis.

Fortna's source-critical method relied heavily on "aporias." This term, introduced by Eduard Schwartz in 1907, refers to "the conspicuous seams and style differences" that many detect in the surface texture of FG (Nichol 1972, 4). These include interruptions, doublets, "passages with dense or overloaded wording" (Fortna 1988, 4), "inconsistencies, disjunctures and hard connections" (Fortna 1970, 2), "repetitive resumptions," sequence problems, terminological shifts, and theological inconsistencies (von Wahlde 1973, 520). Less controversial examples include the correction of John 3:22 at 4:2, the apparent geographical discrepancy of chapters 5 and 6, the continuation of the Farewell Address after 14:31, and the presence of John 21 after the closing statement at 20:31. In Fortna's view, "the unevenness of the text of John is due . . . to redaction, so that the aporias are indications—direct or indirect—of editorial seams," places where documents with different styles or different ideologies were put together (1970, 3). The presence of aporias, then, is the key to source separation, allowing the researcher to distinguish layers of material within FG.

In *The Gospel of Signs*, Fortna discussed three types of aporia that might indicate the presence of FG's sources. "Stylistic" aporias occur when the language of a passage seems to be inconsistent with the language of "material assigned on other grounds to the evangelist." "Contextual" aporias are disruptions in the flow of the text or irregular narrative features. Finally, "ideological" aporias depend on the principle that "no two authors have precisely the same point of view, so that anyone who adapts an earlier work . . . will nevertheless at times exhibit disagreement with it." This being the case, when portions of FG seem to be in some way theologically inconsistent with FE's beliefs, "it will offer clues to the separation of the various conceptual elements." To support the clues given by the various aporias, Fortna suggested that "the synoptic gospels can sometimes provide us with external criteria." When possible, one could compare a Johannine story with its synoptic parallel in order to discover the scope and presentation of the material in FE's source (all refs. Fortna 1970, 16–22). By using these four criteria, Fortna was able to separate FE's own contributions from the earlier text of the Signs Gospel.

Early on, Fortna professed a preference for contextual aporias on the grounds that obvious literary problems provide more objective data. But the research that followed *The Gospel of Signs* reveals that his reconstruction of the Signs Gospel depended heavily on ideological criteria. This is most evident in his later remarks on the Johannine speeches. In the early stages of his research, Fortna seemed open to the possibility of a discourse source similar to Bultmann's *Offenbarungsreden*. In his own words, "An obvious literary distinction to be made in John is that between narrative and discourse, but it will be of no use here as a starting point [for source separation]. Such a crude differentiation can hardly be the basis for separating Johannine and non-Johannine parts of the gospel, for both classes of material [narrative and discourse] are probably composite" (Fortna 1970, 22). Why, then, was *The Gospel of Signs* dedicated entirely to a narrative source? Fortna explained in a footnote, "This limitation has been made arbitrarily in the sense that it recognizes that the source analysis of the discourses is an exceedingly difficult, not to say impossible, task. . . . [I]n any case, it is only a working limitation that is made" (Fortna 1970, 22 n. 3).

But by 1988, when his magnum opus *The Fourth Gospel and Its Predecessor* appeared, the distinction between narratives and speeches had risen to the forefront of Fortna's analysis. The book opens with an explicit warning that the exegetical challenge of FG "centers in this disarming combination of two very nearly contradictory modes of Jesus' activity—his narrated deeds and the words of his discourses" (3). FG's miracle stories are "vivid, brief, and earthy . . . the type of narrative about Jesus familiar from the Synoptic Gospels." The discourses, on the other hand, offer "the more familiar portrait of the [exalted] Jesus of universal Christianity" (Fortna 1988, 1–2). Obviously, "the narratives and discourses stem from radically different origins . . . and they reflect distinct periods in the development of [FG]." Of the two, "the narratives almost certainly represent the older, more traditional—clearly 'pre-Johannine'—layer. . . . [T]he discourses by analogy can be attributed to the later author [FE], amplifying the earlier document(s)" (Fortna 1988, 3, 7). It is fair to say, then, that Fortna's Signs Gospel represents those portions of the narrative of FG that do not betray the theological or literary tendencies of the Johannine speeches. By treating the discourses as FE's theological commentary on an older narrative, Fortna could analyze the speeches to identify peculiarities of FE's style and theology. Elements of the narratives that reflected these same peculiarities could then be "lifted off" as glosses, leaving the original, unadulterated Signs Gospel.

As noted earlier, the results of Fortna's analysis were in many ways consistent with those of Bultmann. Both, for example, believed that FG's narratives derive from a *written* source. Although Bultmann believed that both FE and the later redactor occasionally used oral tradition, some of which also made its way into the Synoptics (1971, 393 n. 2, 420–425), he associated the majority of the current text of FG with earlier written documents. Similarly, while Fortna conceded that a few sayings in the narrative sections of FG "very likely came to the evangelist directly from free oral tradition," he nevertheless insisted that most of FG's narratives are based on a written document (Fortna 1970, 200). Second, both Bultmann and Fortna believed that the written sources with which Johannine Source Critics are concerned preceded the work of the Fourth Evangelist. Many earlier studies of FG's sources had assumed that FE was responsible for the *first* version of FG, with additions and expansions (such as John 21) made by *later* disciples to produce the current text. The goal of such research was therefore to recover and analyze the "original" Gospel of John. Bultmann, however, believed that FE actually based his composition on a number of earlier manuscripts; the goal of Bultmann's research was therefore to identify these sources in order to observe the evangelist's redactional tendencies. Similarly, Fortna posited two primary stages in the development of FG, "basic document and redaction," suggesting that the Signs Gospel was an earlier composition while the current text of FG belongs to FE (Fortna 1970, 4). In other words, while some scholars were primarily concerned with identifying materials added *after* John's work was finished, Bultmann and Fortna were primarily interested in material which existed *before* John's work began. Third, like Bultmann, Fortna believed the Johannine speeches were added to the narratives by FE. In Bultmann's case, these speeches came from another written source, the *Offenbarungsreden*, while in Fortna's case the speeches were treated largely as FE's own theological reflections.

The durability of Fortna's proposal has not, however, resulted from its similarities with that of Bultmann, but rather from the fact that his conclusions go far beyond those of Bultmann. Several of the most significant differences will be highlighted here to indicate the more innovative features of Fortna's research. First, Fortna, unlike Bultmann, believed that the Signs Gospel has been carefully preserved, so that it can be recovered from the present text of FG. While Bultmann posited a number of different sources, he did not offer a complete reconstruction of any, apparently because such was not essential to his exegesis. His remarks on John 15:18–16:11, which he believed to be derived from the discourse source, are typical of his approach: "The text of the source, which the Evangelist has frequently expanded with his own comments, cannot always be recognized with certainty, but is clearly visible in outline" (Bultmann 1971, 548). The Signs Source in particular cannot be reconstructed from the current text of FG because FE revised it freely to suit his own purposes. This included minor additions and rewordings, but also more significant alterations: John 6 preceded John 5 in the source, and 7:1–13 introduced 5:1–8; dialogues were occasionally eliminated or replaced; new endings were added to some episodes so as to "subserve his [FE's] purpose" (Bultmann 1971, 114, 206, 289 n. 1, 395). Fortna, on the other hand, insisted that FE's "redaction has been carried out so carefully that the text of the source survives on the whole intact within the present Gospel and can therefore be reconstructed with some facility and confidence, often simply by lifting off the patently redactional material" (Fortna 1988, 7). Indeed, an appendix to *The Gospel of Signs* offers a complete Greek text of the source, and Robert Miller's more recent compilation *The Complete Gospels* includes Fortna's English translation (Fortna 1970, 235–245; Miller 1994, 175–193).

A second major difference between Bultmann and Fortna relates to the nature of the narrative source. As noted earlier, Bultmann believed that the Signs Source consisted of eight embellished miracle stories with a brief introduction and conclusion. Fortna's source, on the other hand, is a rudimentary "gospel" in the sense that it combines a narrative of Jesus' signs with a passion and resurrection and interprets all three as evidence of Jesus' messianic identity (Fortna 1988, 205–207). At an earlier stage in the tradition, the Signs Gospel's narratives and passion story were distinct, originating in two separate documents, "SQ" (the signs source) and "PQ" (the passion source), which were combined by FE's predecessor, the author of the Signs Gospel. As such, "the only way to characterize the combined source's genre is to call it . . . a *Gospel of signs*" (Fortna 1988, 212).

Finally, because Fortna was able to delineate the scope and content of the Signs Gospel, he was also able to discuss the provenance of this source in much more detail than Bultmann had attempted. Following Martyn's reconstruction of the experiences of the Johannine Community, Fortna's Signs Gospel emerged from "an early and pure Christian Judaism" as "a missionary tract with a single end, to show . . . that Jesus is the Messiah" of Jewish expectation (Fortna 1988, 214–215). As such, the Signs Gospel did not promote the incarnational Christology espoused in the current FG and did not address concerns related to the Gentile mission. This being the case, "we can thus imagine a dating in the 40s or possibly the 50s of the first century" (Fortna 1988, 214–220), meaning that SG appeared alongside, or perhaps before, Q.

18

Jesus Tradition in the Signs Gospel

ROBERT T. FORTNA

The Hypothesis

Do you still believe—I'm sometimes asked—in your Signs Gospel?

Well, yes. For me, the hypothesis is, and no less clearly than before, the best way to understand a major stage in the development of the Fourth Gospel (FG). It is true that since my first book (1970) I have made several revisions in the reconstruction (I prefer, of course, to think of it as "recovery," however inexact). I no longer think that a source behind the stories of the Samaritan woman in John 4 or of Jesus' supper with his disciples (chap. 12) can be recovered. And following D. Moody Smith (1984, 90–93), I now include John 12:37–40 in the Signs Gospel (SG) as both explanation for the officials' plot against Jesus and transition to the passion account. Many of these revisions appear in the slightly revised text of SG that provided the basis for my redaction-critical investigation *The Fourth Gospel and Its Predecessor* (1988), sequel to the earlier, purely source-critical study. The most recent version of SG is to be found in *The Complete Gospels* (Miller 1994, 175–193).

But, yes, I still believe in a Signs Gospel.

Three issues are typically raised when people ask whether my mind has changed: a) FG's stylistic unity, b) its dependence on the Synoptic Gospels, and c) the application of folkloristics to NT studies. Let me briefly explain why none of these issues has radically altered my thinking.

FG's Stylistic Unity

The *stylistic unity* of FG is a chimera. In the words of Tom Stoppard, "It can't prove to be true, it can only not prove to be false yet" (1993, 74). That is, FG's stylistic unity can be asserted only so long as no reconstructed source uses a style distinguishable from the rest of FG. I believe SG does have such a distinct style. The early stylistic tests by Schweizer (1939) and Ruckstuhl (1958) of several alleged sources showed that none was stylistically different from the rest of FG, making those theories presumably invalid. Instead the Fourth Evangelist (FE)—author of the more or less finished gospel—must have been responsible for the supposed source material. As a consequence the stylistic unity of FG was asserted, especially by Ruckstuhl. At least it had not proved to be false. A subsequent investigation, by Ruckstuhl and Dschulnigg (1991), sought to show in great detail that my proposed SG has a style not distinct from that of the Fourth Gospel as a whole. And so the stylistic unity of FG was again claimed. But in the meantime, stylometry—a far more sophisticated procedure for the measuring of style—had been refined. Not merely lexical stylistic traits (such as vocabulary) but wholly unconscious and unintentional ones could be examined and the results statistically evaluated. Such is the work of Felton, now published in this volume and applied to SG. The results, he holds, demonstrate that SG, or something like it, has a style distinct from the rest of FG. If that is true, the unity of FG seems to me to have proved false and the possibility of a sort of signs gospel shown to be likely.

Synoptic Dependence?

The older consensus—based on Gardner-Smith's attempt (1938) to show that FE did not know any of the Synoptics, or at least make use of them—has fallen apart, no doubt permanently. So the question is, How did the very clearly synoptic-like material find its way into FG? I hold that such material stemmed from an earlier document, a rudimentary gospel. That seems to me more likely than the theory that it came to FE directly from the Synoptics. FG's narratives are not unique in the New Testament the way that the Johannine discourses are. But in FG the narratives are like a huge "bolt from a synoptic blue," just the reverse of the famous Johannine-like saying at Matthew 11:27 (= Luke 10:22). We are used to finding them in FG, but they don't smoothly fit with the entirely distinctive discourses. They have not been selectively chosen by FE from here and there in the Synoptics and remolded to become Johannine. Rather, they remain in the broad sense synoptic-like. And because FG's narratives are synoptic-like but different too from their synoptic parallels—sometimes appearing in a cruder, and so perhaps earlier, form—they can scarcely have been taken directly from the Synoptic Gospels; rather, they reflect presynoptic tradition.

There is another consideration here, a utilitarian one. If the Fourth Evangelist (FE) made use of the Synoptics, that use was intricate and untraceable except by the most ingenious imagining. And it tells us nothing about FG that we didn't already know. Redaction criticism is almost useless, indeed impossible, on such a basis. On the other hand, if FE made use of an earlier protogospel (like SG), and if that source can be to some degree recovered, it frequently becomes clear how it was used (i.e., what FE had in mind in the way the source was altered) and often for what reasons it was used. It is, then, the redaction-critical value of the source analysis of FG that suggests (it does not prove) the existence of a narrative source as the vehicle by which the synoptic-like material came to FE. It came via an early, rather primitive gospel, that was reshaped and amplified by the evangelist—but not obliterated, since it retains its pre-Johannine character.

Folkloristics

The third point on which I am sometimes challenged involves folkloristics, a discipline that includes, among other things, the study of how oral stories function and change in tradition. Has the application of this approach to FG called into question the hypothesis of a written signs source? Does not the persistence of relatively free oral tradition about Jesus suggest that such a hypothetical source is not needed to explain the composition of FG, and doesn't it further suggest that such a source did not exist? I don't believe so. As a method, folkloristics tells us a very great deal about oral tradition; in fact, I'd wager that it fundamentally supplements form criticism. It is therefore invaluable for understanding the extensive period when all traditions about Jesus were circulating and growing orally. But it does not, and cannot, account for the critical point when the oral became the written. The extensive material in Q also had a long oral background, but at some point it was written down in a form that can be identified with some precision. The differences between the Matthean and the Lukan versions of the Q sayings are partly accountable to varying "performances" of oral tradition but also, and perhaps to a larger degree, to editorial redaction at the written stage by Matthew and Luke themselves. Analogously, both the similarities to and differences from the synoptic tradition that are evident in the stories of FG must be accounted for. A fluid oral tradition at some point became more or less fixed Greek prose. That implies a written source behind FG.

The Historical Value of the Signs Gospel

The following discussion of the historical value of my reconstructed SG will focus on the two major types of material that I identify in the Signs Gospel: narratives about Jesus' miracles, or "signs," and the story of Jesus' passion.

The Signs of Jesus

Bultmann held, and I have concurred, that some of the stories in the Johannine Signs Source have a simpler form than parallel stories in the Synoptics. Do we have, then, a hypothetical document that takes us back closer to the deeds, especially the reported miracles, of the historical Jesus? No and Yes.

There is considerable doubt, I believe, that Jesus performed healings and other miracles *in order* to demonstrate any messianic status on his part—in other words, doubt that he performed what SG calls "signs." The saying (Mark 8:12; cf. John 4:48) that shows Jesus refusing to give any such signs may not be authentic to Jesus, but I believe that it reflects an early understanding of Jesus' purpose. In any case, I can scarcely believe that his intent in accomplishing healings was to say anything christological about himself. Instead, the healings were done in response to human need, and even the so-called "nature miracles" are most often depicted in the Synoptics as performed with the same motive. So I conclude that SG's presentation of the miracles as "signs" of Jesus' messianic identity is not historical.

But what of the deeds themselves, without the christological interpretation? Jesus' *healings* in SG—an official's son restored from apparent death (4:46–53), a lame man made whole (5:2–9), a blind man given sight (9:1–7), Lazarus raised from the dead (11:1–44)—are part and parcel of the synoptic tradition of Jesus' healings. So far as they can be attributed to the historical Jesus, and I believe that some of them can, the stories have factual basis. How do these stories add to the synoptic evidence about Jesus? Often they have been heightened in their miraculous character: at 4:51–53 we read that the boy was healed at the very moment of Jesus' pronouncing him alive; at 5:5 that the man at Bethesda had been lame for thirty-eight years, while the man in John 9 was blind from birth; Lazarus was dead four days in the tomb before Jesus came to him (11:39). That sort of dramatic heightening of detail is to be found also in some of the synoptic healing stories but usually to lesser degree. One can imagine how the oral tradition added to the miracle stories in this way, especially to show that Jesus was the messiah. So it seems to me that the extent of the miraculous in SG's healings is not to be taken at face value. With the exception of Lazarus, the healings in SG are parallel to episodes in the Synoptics. I have difficulty with the Lazarus story: it obviously prefigures Jesus' own resurrection—shown in SG to have been accomplished by Jesus himself (2:19); and its several contacts with the parable of the rich man and Lazarus (Luke 16:19–31) for me cast doubt on its independent historicity. So the element of extensive miraculous power attributed to Jesus in these healing stories, as messianic proofs, appears to me not to be factual.

Similarly, the exaggerated details of the Johannine *nature miracles* are the result of such enhancement: 120 or more gallons of water turned to wine (2:6); the boat at shore once Jesus, having walked on the water, boards it (6:21b); the net is not torn from the enormous catch of fish (21:11). But can we find any details in these nature-miracle stories that may go behind their obvious oral development? I think that some of the topographical data may belong to this category. That seems more likely than that such notices, which are mostly innocent of theological meaning, have been invented merely for verisimilitude: Cana (whatever actually took place there); Capernaum, more than once; the Sheep Gate and Bethesda (see Broer in this volume); the Sea of Tiberias twice; the pool at Siloam; Bethany "about two miles" from Jerusalem; and so on.

Finally, some of the incidental data having to do with SG's dramatis personae and even the timing of events may go back to very early memory: "the mother of Jesus" (never named); Tuesday (if the original meaning of "on the third day" at 2:1); "at one o'clock" (4:52); Andrew (6:8); Lazarus, Mary, and Martha (11:1, also 12:2–3); Peter, Thomas, Nathaniel, and Zebedee's sons (21:2).

So we seem to have a certain amount of original, if sometimes only incidental, information about Jesus' deeds in SG. And the same may be true of matters in the passion narrative.

The Passion Story

FG's passion narrative was once a separate tradition, written or oral, that the author of SG (not FE) combined with the signs tradition. This combining made SG into a primitive "gospel" of the same type that the author of Mark would (possibly somewhat later) produce—that is, the miraculous deeds of Jesus culminating in the account of his death.

SG's passion account is fundamentally apologetic. It was constructed, no doubt, from traditional materials but was written to counter widespread criticism to the effect that no one could be messiah whose life had ended ignominiously in failure, crucified by Rome. Such criticism was an attack on one of the most basic tenets of Christianity and the passion account was produced to demonstrate, from the Hebrew Bible, that the Christ had been destined to die in just such a way according to a series of "prophecies." These OT passages had been collected and were known as *testimonia*, witnesses to the necessary death of God's chosen one. It is widely held that the passion accounts that appear in the four canonical gospels were constructed, possibly at first in oral form, as much on the basis of these OT proof texts as on historical memory.

The Gospel of Mark uses an apologetic passion account remarkably similar to that found in SG. But in Mark the account has been fundamentally reinterpreted, so that the death of Jesus is no longer something to be explained away but rather the central focus of the Gospel's message, its *kerygma*. The account in SG was not so reinterpreted. It can hardly have been dependent on Mark itself, since there is no trace of any affirmation of Jesus' death. It must be the material *behind* Mark that SG's passion account resembles. We have, then, in the passion account of SG, or in something not unlike it, an earlier account than that in the present version of Mark and a rough idea what Mark's passion source might have looked like.

What, then, of the historicity of SG's passion story? The answer, at least the basic answer, is that it is so driven by apologetic impulses that its overall accuracy cannot readily be determined. SG's presentation of Jesus as a predestined victim is more naturally explained as an early Christian creation, justifying the messiah's death, than based on historical fact. Such an impulse is not to be judged altogether counterfeit on the basis of modern criteria of authentic historical accounting, but is to be understood as story fulfilling scripture rather than necessarily reporting facts. It is prophecy historicized, not history remembered, in Crossan's highly serviceable phrase; prophecy here is constitutive, not merely confirmative. Despite this, can some historical facts be gleaned from the passion account in SG—facts not available in the tradition lying behind the synoptic passion stories? In the case of SG's miracle stories we can only with difficulty make judgments about on-going plot, since each episode is a brief pericope, originally unattached to any other. But with SG's passion we have an ongoing connected story, whatever its components in the tradition. So I find that more can be said of the passion than the signs in SG. The remarks that follow touch only on those elements of the various passion stories as I think they existed in SG (see Miller 1994).

First, the narratives that lead up to the passion story, what I call the "culmination" of the signs and the "prelude" to the passion. I cannot believe that Jesus' shocking and drastic *action in the Temple* (2:14–19) originally belonged among the signs following the Cana story, as we have in the current text of FG. So we deal with it here. We are told that there were oxen and sheep in the Temple, that Jesus used a whip, and that he "poured out" the money changers' coins. These specific and graphic details are either very skilled fiction or, more likely, memories of a real event. Jesus' actions are justified by quoting a quite different OT passage (Psalm 69:9) from that in the synoptic version of the story. Nevertheless there are many parallels. Hence, it is unlikely that the whole event was created on the basis of two separate OT texts; rather, SG and the Synoptics represent two later and separate attempts to justify the same event.

Was there a *conspiracy* among the Jewish leaders to have Jesus done away with, "to kill him" (11:53)? That phrase, taken at face value, is in conflict with the fact that it was the Roman governor, not the Jewish leaders, who killed Jesus. So the Jewish plot may be a later Christian invention, and the notion that any Jewish hearing involved the entire Sanhedrin is anti-Jewish Christian elaboration. The conspiracy is depicted as a deliberate, formal decision on the part of those responsible for Jewish affairs in Palestine, more deliberate than in the Synoptics. It is explained as fulfilling OT prophecy (12:37–40), but only in general. So is it factual, or was the conspiracy story created simply from an anti-Jewish motive? It's hard to say.

The act by which Mary honored Jesus *in her home at Bethany* as a special guest (12:1–8) is usually understood as a messianic anointing. But it is not so understood by SG's Jesus, who interprets it rather as a foreshadowing of his burial (12:7–8). Can such a premonition on his part—whether or not it implies any unique self-understanding—be historical? I would think so. Even verse 8 ("The poor you always have with you [Deut. 15:11]; but you don't always have me") might be a remembered detail, unless it figures solely as an answer to the later demonized Judas. That such a dinner took place "six days before Passover" seems a gratuitous, and therefore possibly factual, memory.

SG's story of the *entry into Jerusalem* (12:12ff.) lacks Jesus' detailed instructions to the disciples found in Mark 14:12–16. But the historical Jesus may have chosen to identify himself and his message with a nonpolitical, nonviolent image of leadership and so deliberately acted out something like the prophecy in Zechariah 9:9, without any messianic implication. If so, the original kernel of the story was simply 12:14a ("Jesus found a donkey and sat on it"), and that is surely too slight a statement to carry us back to a historical event; how would such a fragment have been remembered and passed on? The story is so thoroughly christological that I cannot confidently find any historical kernel within it.

What about Jesus' final *meal with his followers?* As I've said, it seems impossible to retrieve a source from the present account in John 13. That may or may not argue against its historicity. It has no hint of the Lord's Supper that later commemorates it, but the foot washing is consonant with the lack of self-aggrandizement to be found in much of the Jesus tradition, so perhaps some authentic memories are present. It shows no hint of being a Passover meal. Beyond this I think nothing can be said.

Now to the body of the passion story. That Jesus was officially *arrested* "across the Wadi Kidron . . . in a garden" (18:1) seems likely, but the identity of those who made the arrest is not entirely clear. If the role played by (Annas and) Caiaphas in the hearing that follows (18:12ff.) is somehow authentic, then any Roman presence, as in the current text of 18:3, now seems unlikely to me. But it's also not likely that a sizable armed party "from the high priests" was used for the arrest. Judas is somehow elusive in FG, and so presumably in SG as well. He is always named the one who "turned Jesus in." Why was it necessary for him to bring a posse with him? There is no scene showing him arranging this with any authorities. The vivid picture of Peter's impetuous attack on one of the arresting party (18:10) and the giving of his name ("Malchus"—only in FG) is either skillful enhancement of the tradition or a gratuitous memory. Jesus' reply ("I am") seems a later invention.

Rudiments of Jesus' *interrogation by the high priest* (or priests; 18:12ff.) are either based on the eyewitness of a disciple of Jesus "who was known to the high priest" or have been created to enhance the Jews' part in Jesus' death. The historicity of Annas, as of comparable rank to Caiaphas, is known to the author of Luke-Acts. His appearance in this story is inessential and so possibly authentic; or is it a fiction, since it's but a shadow of the hearing before Caiaphas? Caiaphas is missing in Mark, but appears in both Matthew and Luke. He isn't likely, I judge, to be altogether an invention. What transpired during such interrogation as there actually was is probably unknowable; what we have in FG is clearly christological and so probably not historical. But what of Peter's denying all connection with Jesus? It seems to me highly unlikely that stories showing such a prominent disciple and later leader in the church failing Jesus could be fictions. That Jesus predicted any of this is doubtful, but the detail of the rooster's crowing is likely to be a remembered detail.

Was there a formal *trial by Pilate* as depicted in 18:28ff.? It depends on how significant Jesus was in Pilate's eyes, and of that we cannot be sure. There was certainly no right to a fair trial under Roman occupation, and evidently no observer who might have recounted to Jesus' followers what had happened. So perhaps the Pilate scene has been largely imagined, produced at a point in the tradition when Jesus' status as Christ was established in Christian eyes. Certainly, the portrayal in FG is an extravagant expansion of whatever SG told. The outcome is clear enough, of course, and the detail that Jesus' crime was attached to his cross in the next scene may have basis in fact, given the gratuitous detail that it was trilingual. But some would say that the charge ("Jesus of Nazareth, the King of the Jews"; 19:19) was only a Christological device added later. The role of the crowd, together with the Barabbas episode, could have been something remembered, but later anti-Jewish tendency can't be ruled out.

It is surely simple fact that Roman soldiers *executed* Jesus. Their mistreatment of him beforehand may have been sadistic horseplay or even ritual abuse of a pretender to a Jewish throne; or it implicitly reflects the mistreatment of God's servant, as in Isaiah 40–54, and so is portrayed theology.

The simple *crucifying* of Jesus is clear enough. Memory of a locale—Golgotha—would be likely. But the soldiers' gambling for Jesus' clothing, his thirst, spearing his side, and failing to break his legs—all this was created from biblical prophecy; it "happened so that scripture would come true" (19:23–24). And that he was crucified with two others fulfills the prediction that the messiah would be "numbered with transgressors" (Isa. 53:12). What Jesus may have said from the cross is possibly unretrievable. Who of Jesus' followers were present? The reports differ, not surprisingly. Jesus was probably killed on the eve of Passover, or near to it.

How was Jesus *buried?* Some scholars doubt that he was given a burial of his own; like most executed criminals he may have been thrown into a common grave. No doubt the stories have been amplified—certainly in the amount of spices used (seventy-five pounds) and by reintroducing Nicodemus. But if tradition says that there was a tomb, in a garden, and it was new (as in both Matt. 27:60 and Luke 23:53 independently) and that a Joseph of Arimathea played a role in the burial, perhaps some memory survived.

Finally, the tortured question of Jesus' *resurrection.* The accounts vary notoriously. I hold that resurrection is by definition transhistorical and so not subject to the historian's investigation. The empty tomb (20:1) is a created legend, but the belief that Jesus appeared to various disciples is certainly a fact.

Sayings of Jesus

My reconstruction of SG includes relatively few sayings. In the miracle stories Jesus gives terse directives (for example, "Fill the jars"; "Go, your son will live"; "Cast the net on the right side of the boat") or asks simple questions ("Where can we buy bread?"; "Where have they laid him?"; "Do you want to get better?"). The passion story is much the same: "Take these things out of here"; "Leave her alone"; "Put up your sword." Even if historically factual, these utterances tell us almost nothing about the historical Jesus. There are a few sayings in SG that are not so tied to the plots where they occur: "It's me, don't be afraid"; "Lazarus is not sleeping but dead"; "Destroy this temple and I'll raise it up in three days"; and so forth. But how is one to evaluate such remarks historically?

What of the possibility that other teachings of Jesus in FG, not deriving from SG, might take us back to, or toward, the historical Jesus? In other words, what about the discourses? My views on this question have perhaps not been clear. In the beginning (1970) I simply left open the question whether FE had used pre-Johannine sayings material. I did not intend to find a purely narrative source, but the more a narrative source seemed to emerge, the less I could believe that pre-Johannine sayings would yield to the same kind of analysis. And simply on the face of it, narrative and discourse in FG appear to stem from different origins; the one is very synoptic-like, the other not at all. So in time I came to speak of a rather fundamental distinction between story and saying in FG. It is only FE who has put the two genres alongside one another, for example using some of the stories as springboards for discourse. But I do not hold that all the discourse material is the creation of FE; on the contrary. And such a possibility is one of the motives for assembling this book.

19

Stylometry and the Signs Gospel

Tom Felton & Tom Thatcher

The proper place of style criteria in source-critical research has been heavily debated in the last one hundred years. Ideally, source-critical studies proceed by comparing multiple texts that presumably drew material from a common original. By observing the unique ideological and stylistic tendencies of each text, a process of elimination allows the researcher to speculate on what the earlier source may have included or not included. The early sayings gospel Q, for example, has been reconstructed through careful comparison and analysis of the sayings materials in Matthew and Luke. After defining the unique theological concerns and literary styles of Matthew and Luke through comparative study, it is possible to subtract these factors from the present texts of those works and speculate about the form of a particular saying in the Q document. But the sayings and deeds of Jesus in the Fourth Gospel (FG) find few parallels in other ancient gospels, making it difficult to determine which portions of FG may have been drawn from earlier sources. If two or more documents recount similar events in very similar ways, one may reasonably conclude that both have used a common source. But when no such parallels exist, any attempt to identify the source of specific material in a written gospel must appeal to other criteria. In the case of FG, style of writing has been a key criterion in source reconstruction.

"Style" is an inherently subjective topic. Different readers will come to different conclusions about the key characteristics of a particular author's style of writing. For this reason, source-critical studies must highlight those aspects of style that are more objective and that can be tested statistically. The careful application of a well-defined statistical model may reveal that certain segments of a document evidence a style of writing that is atypical of the rest of the document. If, for example, one scene of a Shakespeare play were found to include a large number of words and grammatical structures that Shakespeare does not typically use, one might speculate that this scene was added or edited by an author other than Shakespeare. Johannine source criticism has relied heavily on the notion that some sections of FG evidence a style inconsistent with the characteristic style of the Fourth Evangelist (FE). Once these sections have been identified, it remains to determine whether they represent earlier source materials that FE recopied into his gospel or later insertions into the evangelist's finished work.

Previous Efforts

While source-critical considerations are obviously significant to the exegesis of FG, studies of Johannine style have nevertheless been plagued by imprecise models of statistical analysis and by a general misunderstanding of the role style criteria can play in source reconstruction. As an example of the former set of difficulties, the earliest studies of Johannine style in the nineteenth century were skewed by the inclusion of 1–2–3 John in the database of style characteristics. This procedure obviously begs the question, for the relationship between these four documents is not certain enough to support a mathematical analysis. The first extensive, and still one of the most important, statistical treatments of the style of FG alone was published by Eduard Schweizer in 1939. Schweizer noted thirty-three stylistic idiosyncrasies that are, in his view, frequent in FG but infrequent in non-Johannine writings. These idiosyncracies are, he claimed, distributed randomly throughout the text of FG, making it impossible to identify distinct sections of the document that may have been copied or adapted from earlier sources. Schweizer's conclusions were reaffirmed in 1958 by the work of Ernst Ruckstuhl. Ruckstuhl extended Schweizer's list of stylistic criteria from thirty-three to fifty, and observed once again that these peculiarities appear randomly throughout the entire text of FG. From this he concluded that the style of FG is uniform, suggesting a unified composition and making the detection of earlier sources impossible.

The studies of Schweizer and Ruckstuhl have played a key role in all subsequent discussion of the possibility of isolating distinct sources for FG on the basis of style criteria. Ruckstuhl's efforts were, in fact, aimed specifically at the conclusions of Rudolf Bultmann (1971), who suggested that at least three major sources could be detected in the current text of FG. In 1987, Ruckstuhl addressed his efforts to the "Signs Gospel," a potential source for the miracle narratives in FG proposed by Robert Fortna. This study concluded that Fortna's reconstruction is invalid because the characteristically "Johannine" style elements are spread evenly throughout the proposed text of the Signs Gospel, suggesting that these passages were FE's own compositions. In a more detailed study in 1991, Ruckstuhl expanded his survey to include a remarkable 153 uniquely Johannine style characteristics. Again, he concluded that these characteristics are distributed randomly throughout FG, demonstrating the unity of FG and hence invalidating any attempt to reconstruct FE's sources.

The fact that an investigation fails to distinguish between the styles of two texts, or to identify a distinct alien style in a portion of a single text, may indeed indicate that the texts in question were produced by the same author. Such failure may also, however, indicate that inadequate criteria have been used to identify "style characteristics," or that the statistical models employed are not sophisticated enough to result in a significant conclusion. None of Ruckstuhl's studies of FG, for example, included sophisticated statistical modeling or formal testing for randomness, making his conclusions unacceptably imprecise by current canons of statistical analysis. The present study, by contrast, will appeal to the most recent developments in statistical modeling and stylometry.

While Ruckstuhl's statistical techniques were suspect, the overall object of his research was consistent with a legitimate application of style criteria. A number of source-critical studies on FG have attempted to *identify and demarcate* specific sources primarily on the basis of style. In these cases, the distribution of certain stylistic features is taken as evidence that various sources have been, or have not been, absorbed into FG. But this procedure, in light of the fact that statistics are notoriously vulnerable to subjective interpretations, is likely to produce inconclusive results. A more reasoned approach will use stylo-statistical research to evaluate potential sources that have *already been identified on other grounds*. In the present essay, a sophisticated stylometric model will be applied to Fortna's Signs Gospel, a document that has been identified on the grounds of theological anomalies and narrative aporias. Style criteria, then, will either add weight to Fortna's proposal or raise potential questions about its legitimacy, but will not be used here to demarcate any specific source behind FG.

Contemporary Stylometry and the Challenges of FG

"Stylometry" is the application of statistical techniques to the study of quantifiable features of style in a written or spoken text. In recent years it has been applied to a number of problems relating to the authorship of documents in a variety of fields. Statistical measures of style may consider the text at a variety of levels, depending on the specific issues being addressed: phonemes (meaningful sound units), syllables, words, syntactic structures, sentences, or even larger units. Early applications, including those in biblical studies related to the authorship of the Pauline epistles and the sources of Mark, tended to focus on lexical features, "word counts." The data were analyzed via measures based on totals, percentages, and means. More recent studies have included standard deviations. But word counts and percentages inherently ignore the order in which units of text are used and the rhetorical function of those units, as well as the relationship between different units in the text. The earlier methods, in fact, assumed an "urn model" of text production, in which any unit of text has an equal chance of being used anywhere, like beans shaken from a jar. More recent stylometric studies have recognized the need to consider word pairs, idioms, parts of speech, and the function of lexical units in the specific contexts in which they appear. These considerations have produced more objective analyses of the "quantifiable features" of oral and written texts.

But even the most sophisticated stylometric method faces a special challenge in the analysis of ancient texts such as FG. This is the case for several reasons. First, a number of studies have demonstrated that a single author's style may change over time or with respect to the genre of literature being written. But in the case of ancient authors, it is impossible to know how accurately their extant literary works represent the entire corpus of their text production. Second, in ancient times "authorship" was a much more flexible notion than it is in the modern world. A particular text evidencing a variety of styles may have been produced by an amanuensis or a disciple of the named "author" whose own style was influenced by that of the teacher. Also, modern authors discriminate between their own words and the words of their sources much more carefully than the author of FG could be expected to do. It will therefore be necessary to describe a statistical model that accounts for the peculiar problems inherent in the reconstruction of FG's sources.

First, the classic stylometric approach assumes that an exhaustive list of potential authors is available, along with samples of the works of each. When authorship is in doubt, one simply determines which author from the list evidences a style most similar to the text in question. But in the case of ancient texts such as FG, it is unwarranted to assume that a complete list of prospective authors is available, much less that sufficient samples of their works exist. In other words, it is impossible to determine with certainty which historical figures might have been the Fourth Evangelist, and then to identify a writing sample from each of these potential authors. These problems are magnified one-hundred-fold in considerations of the Signs Gospel. The present study must therefore adopt a method that uses the style variation internal to a text to estimate boundaries for the author's variation in style. If the disputed section does not fall within these boundaries, it should not be allocated to the author of the larger document. In other words, our method must be able to compare one text to another without depending on a specific knowledge of the authorship of either.

Second, the standard stylometric approach assumes simple random sampling. In biblical studies, this has generally meant random sampling of the occurrence of particular words or particles of language in the Greek text. This method is inadequate, however, because it does not compensate for features of an author's rhetorical style that are not evident at the level of individual words. These larger features are, in fact, more likely to be significant in determining what makes an individual's use of language unique. Further, it is necessary to consider factors that may affect the way an author uses a particular unit of language in a specific context. These factors may include genre, subject matter, and grammatical context.

Closely related to the problem of random sampling is the need to account adequately for serial correlation in stylometric analysis. A fundamental assumption of the statistical techniques used in stylo-statistical analysis is that the data are random with respect to the units of text. In other words, the words and other linguistic units under consideration are treated as if "they just happen to be there," appearing almost accidentally in a particular context as if the text were generated randomly by a computer. The inherent danger of such an approach is obvious. In connected prose texts, the language units are not random but rather a sequentially ordered series of observations. Very often, when data of this sort are considered over time (in this case, through the progress of the narrative), it becomes evident that the units under consideration are serially correlated, meaning that certain features tend to appear together. In other words, FE may tend to connect particular adjectives to certain names or to follow one grammatical structure with another even when the words and subject matter are different, or, on the other hand, to avoid using certain particles in proximity to other features of the text. The current stylo-statistical literature gives little attention to the fact that a variable calculated from a continuous block of text may, in fact, be serially correlated to other variables in the same block. An adequate method must therefore allow for serial correlation between quantifiable stylistic features within larger blocks of text.

Finally, it goes without saying that any stylo-statistical model, and especially any model applied to a problem so complex as the sources of FG, must use statistical concepts and procedures that have a well-developed theoretical basis. Also, the procedure should be theoretically independent of the variables being measured, not derived from them. In other words, the method cannot be derived from the specific data under analysis if objectivity is to be achieved. It must also be noted that standard statistical procedures frequently indicate multiple authorship in cases where few specialists in the literature under consideration would agree. Thus, a methodology is required that makes it more difficult for a disputed text to be rejected. If many sophisticated style variables are measured and used in a powerful statistical routine, then style and authorship should become almost indistinguishable concepts, with the result that a difference in style would almost certainly mean a difference in authorship.

A methodology that compensates for the above considerations is the univariate linear model. "Univariate" means that each variable under consideration is tested individually to produce a cumulative profile of statistical data. "Linear" here indicates that each of the underlying factors for which the statistical model can compensate will be entered as mathematical values that are *added* to the equation, rather than multiplied, divided, or otherwise weighted. A "univariate linear model" thus assumes that the result of the statistical inquiry is a summary of the specific variables and factors.

A Stylometric Analysis of FG

The following statistical method was applied to determine whether there are significant differences between the style of the Fourth Evangelist and the style of Fortna's reconstructed Signs Gospel.

The Database

To create the necessary samples for analysis, the text of FG was divided into three sections: those passages included in the Signs Gospel, as outlined in Fortna's 1970 *The Gospel of Signs*; other narrative material not in Fortna's Signs Gospel; and sayings and discourses (note that Fortna's reconstruction of the Signs Gospel does not include sayings material). In order to balance the samples, the narrative and discourse sections of FG were shortened to be of a similar length to Fortna's proposed source. Each sample was then divided into thirty blocks of one hundred words each. Each block began at the beginning of a modified complete sentence (a sentence ending in a period or question mark). Modified complete sentences that contain quotations from the Hebrew Bible (as indicated in the United Bible Society's Greek New Testament) were omitted, as these would theoretically evidence a distinct style in themselves. The specific breakdown of the text of FG for purposes of this study is indicated in Table 19.1. Note that the blocks of text under consideration are separated by semicolons. "John 1:22–24, 25, 28–31," for example, represents one text block of one hundred words.

Three points about this database should be stressed. First, the versification

Table 19.1

Stylometric Analysis of FG

Sample	Text Blocks (Verses from FG)
Fortna's Signs Gospel	John 1:6–33; 1:32–39; 1:40–46; 1:47–2:3; 2:5–12; 4:47–21:2; 21:3–8; 21:10–6:7; 6:8–15; 6:16–22; 6:25–4:5; 4:6–19; 4:19–11:18; 11:19–38; 11:39–9:3; 9:6–5:5; 5:6–14, 2:14–15; 2:16–12:3; 12:3–14; 18:1–10; 18:11–19; 18:20–18; 18:18–38; 18:38–19:12; 19:12–18; 19:19–30; 19:25–37; 19:38–20:1; 20:2–12; 20:14–30
Other Narrative	John 1:22–24, 25, 28–31; 2:4, 13, 20–25; 3:22, 25–30; 4:1–3, 8, 10–15, 27, 31–33, 39, 41, 43–46, 48; 5:1, 9–13, 15–17; 6:4, 6, 23, 24; 7:1–13; 9:4, 5, 9–41; 10:6, 19–33, 35–40; 11:5, 8–10, 12–14, 16, 21–27, 29–31, 35–37, 40, 42, 46, 48–51, 54–57; 12:6, 9–11, 16–18, 20–23, 27–36, 41–43; 13:1–2, 5–11, 21–27
Sayings/Discourse	John 3:2–13; 5:19–42; 8:12–56; 10:7–12; 14:1–31; 15:1–24, 26–27; 16:1–32

noted in Table 19.1 is for the reader's convenience only. The actual analysis was based on the number of linguistic features in each block of one hundred words, not the number of features in a particular set of verses. Some verses may therefore overlap two text blocks. Because the sayings material in FG generally appears in long speeches of Jesus, all thirty of the sayings blocks were derived from the seven passages indicated in the table. Second, the verse numbers for the Signs Gospel indicate the outside limits of the proposed signs material in a given block. Words and phrases within each span of verses that Fortna does not attribute to the Signs Gospel were removed. Third, the unusual versification of the Signs Gospel in the table reflects Fortna's own rearrangement of the current text of FG. In Fortna's view, some dislocation occurred when the Fourth Evangelist appropriated the signs material. Text blocks such as "John 4:19–11:18" and "6:25–4:5" therefore represent Fortna's reconstruction and relocation of material. It is beyond the scope of this essay to comment on the validity of this rearrangement, and in any case such issues would not have a significant impact on the conclusions offered here.

The Test Variables

Each of the ninety blocks of one hundred words indicated previously was measured in terms of the following twenty-four variables. These variables are simple to measure and have been found to be generally useful in stylometric studies. They were chosen independently of specific literary features in FG, thereby enhancing the objectivity of the study. Note that the term "other" refers to linguistic units that are not nouns or verbs (articles, prepositions, particles, etc.).

> Variables 1–10—number of words in the block containing "I" number of letters, where I = 1–10. This variable measures the typical length of words used in each block, up to ten letters per word.
> Variable 11—number of definite articles beginning with the Greek letter *t* (tau)
> Variable 12—number of other words beginning with the Greek letter *t* (tau)
> Variable 13—total number of definite articles in the block
> Variable 14—number of indefinite and relative pronouns
> Variable 15—the average word position of the first noun in a modified complete sentence
> Variable 16—number of modified complete sentences
> Variable 17—number of verb-verb combination sequences
> Variable 18—number of verb-noun combination sequences
> Variable 19—number of verb-other combination sequences
> Variable 20—number of noun-verb combination sequences
> Variable 21—number of noun-noun combination sequences
> Variable 22—number of noun-other combination sequences
> Variable 23—number of other-verb combination sequences
> Variable 24—number of other-noun combination sequences

The occurrence of each stylistic variable within each individual text block was assigned a numeric value. The difference between the overall statistical mean for the occurrence of each feature in the disputed text and for the occurrence of the feature in the undisputed text was calculated. In other words, once a particular linguistic feature was assigned a numerical value, the occurrence of that feature in both Fortna's Signs Gospel and the remainder of FG was analyzed. This produced a statistical mean for the appearance of the variable in the Signs Gospel and in the remainder of FG, and these two statistical means were compared. To correct and standardize the statistical means, each was divided by an estimated standard deviation.

The Problem of Text Effect

Many of the variables previously listed involve the correlation of multiple factors in each block of text. A verb-verb combination sequence, for example (number 17), involves a larger and more complex unit of text than the number of letters in a particular word (variables 1–10). The use of variables that measure *relationships* between individual words and parts of speech in the texts sets this investigation apart from many previous studies. Such a procedure compensates for factors that might affect the correlation of linguistic elements within the text, factors such as genre, subject matter, and language.

As used here, "text effect" represents the possibility that context, genre, and subject matter may influence, perhaps subconsciously, the way a particular author uses words and word combinations. For example, regarding variable 18 (the number of verb-noun combination sequences in a block), it may be that FE would naturally tend to use a higher number of these combinations in a narrative passage than in a discourse passage. Or perhaps, for variable 13, FE tends to use more definite articles when discussing certain topics. This problem is magnified when one attempts to account for such phenomena in two or more texts, in this case FG and the Signs Gospel, before comparing them. The fact that stylistic variations can occur systematically in a text may produce false results by disrupting the randomness of the distribution of certain features across the blocks under consideration.

To compensate for this phenomenon, the present study introduced a term into the linear model to allow for possible systematic differences between and within the texts under consideration. This variable term, representing the text effect, increases the amount of randomness allowed in the mathematical model, thereby accounting for differences in context, genre, and subject.

Results

Using the model described here, Fortna's Signs Gospel and the remaining text of FG were compared mathematically on the basis of the twenty-four variables previously indicated. Variables 7, 14, 16, and 23 were significant at the 5 percent level, with variable 10 being borderline. For all five of these variables, the estimate of the text effect was 0, meaning that no genre distinction was evident. "Significant at the 5 percent level" means that the same results would be expected in at least 95 percent of any future tests of the data. The fact that the text effect was 0 does not mean that there was no text effect, but that the statistical procedure was unable to significantly distinguish a systematic difference between texts of varying subject and genre and mere random fluctuations. This level of significance (5 percent) in the case of five distinct variables suggests that Fortna's Signs Gospel does, in fact, evidence a "distinct style."

The conclusion of this investigation, that there are significant and meaningful differences in style between Fortna's proposed source and the rest of FG, is to be recognized as only as good as the data. The tests were limited to the respective scopes of Fortna's Signs Gospel and the remainder of FG, both of which represent small data pools. The method used, however, is not sensitive to small perturbations in the data, so that similar results would presumably be obtained even with moderate changes to Fortna's proposed reconstruction of the source. It must be emphasized that this investigation was based on the minimum number of uncontested texts of short length in FG. Results could well be different if there were more uncontested longer texts available, but limitations in the corpus make such data impossible to obtain. However, the results of this investigation shift the balance of probabilities in the direction of the existence of a signs source. The further application of more linguistically complex style characteristics may result in a more decisive conclusion.

The results of a study such as this are inherently limited by the scope and nature of the data. Hence, as previously noted, they, like all other stylo-statistical results, will be used most convincingly as secondary support for theories developed on the basis of other criteria. In the case of the Signs Gospel, stylometric analysis adds further support to a theory that was developed on the basis of theological and narrative considerations.

20

Little Flags

The Scope and Reconstruction of the Signs Gospel

SARA C. WINTER

Robert Fortna's careful reconstruction of the Signs Gospel (SG) has given us a source document for the Fourth Gospel (FG). Up to this point, however, Fortna has confined his reconstruction to narrative materials, noting that "the question whether our source contained sayings that found their way into other parts of the [fourth] gospel is outside our scope, for the canons governing the source analysis of the narrative material can hardly apply to the discourses" (1970, 200).

But one suspects that the Signs Gospel must have contained as-yet-unidentified sayings, perhaps even protodiscourses, because of the way discourse functions in FG. Direct discourse is central to FG's narrative even where events pivot around dialogue (e.g., Jesus and the Samaritan woman in John 4) and recognition of Jesus (e.g., John 1:19–51). In this respect, FG's narrative style contrasts with that of Mark. FG discusses Jesus' identity through the dialogue of characters, and then integrates this dialogue into the narrative. But when Mark integrates direct discourse into the narrative, the narrative still pivots around what Jesus *does*. Mark's direct discourse may set the scene (Mark 8:2–3), advance or substitute for action (e.g., Mark 8:4–5; 5:23, 41), or duplicate or reinforce action (e.g., Mark 5:28, 38–39, 41). The unique role of dialogue in FG hints at the presence of discourse material in the Signs Gospel as well. This article proposes a technique for identifying Signs Gospel sayings material and takes John 17, the prayer of Jesus, as a preliminary test case.

A Technique for Identifying
Signs Gospel Sayings

Comparing the reconstructed SG with the Fourth Evangelist's (FE) additions
shows that both FE and the author of the Signs Gospel employ characteristic
patterns of syntax and an identifiable, limited vocabulary (Fortna 1970,
203–218; von Wahlde 1989, 30–46). In SG, verbs usually precede their subject, and often they come first in the sentence. Sentences are usually simple.
When sentences are compound, their clauses are paratactic, that is, joined by
"and" (*kai*) instead of by subordination. Two tenses, the historical present and
the aorist, predominate. The imperfect tense is rare in FG, and possibly never
occurs in the source. On the other hand, FE's additions have more complex
sentence structure and standard Greek word order (subject preceding verb).
The aorist tense predominates, with the historical present occurring rarely or
never. Subjunctive verbs are frequent because of the complex sentence structure. In light of these stylistic differences, word order and tense may assist in
the assignment of material to FE or the source. If a verb precedes its subject,
for example, chances are good that the clause derives from SG, especially if
the verb is in the (historical) present tense.

Although participles, participial clauses, and occasionally sentences using
the perfect tense are scattered throughout FG, neither SG nor FE's additions
employ the perfect tense with any consistency. The Greek perfect, like the
present and aorist, is not actually a tense but a tense stem from which several
tenses, participles, and infinitives may be constructed. These tense stems
denote aspect, the *kind* of action implied in the verb. The perfect stem expresses
"action completed with a permanent result"; the present stem, "action continued or repeated (in process of development)"; and the aorist stem, "action simply brought to pass (simple occurrence)" (Smyth 1984, 412). Perfect forms
occur in some 173 of FG's 878 verses. Both the pattern of usage and the distribution of occurrences of the perfect in FG is irregular. There are no occurrences in John 21; one in John 10 (counting each verse containing a perfect as
one occurrence); three each in John 2 and John 13; thirteen in John 17 (of
twenty-six verses); and fifteen in John 3 (of thrity-six verses). *Consideration of FG
as a whole shows that phrases and clauses in which the perfect tense occurs belong to a
stage of composition between the Signs Gospel and the current text of John.*

The perfect appears to be used inconsistently in FG. Jesus refers to his
being "sent" both in the aorist ("he sent me" [7:29]; all translations mine) and
the perfect ("the father sent me" [5:36]). The usage in John 15:15 is striking.
The verse may be literally translated "no longer do I say you are 'slaves,'
because the slave does not know what his lord does; but I have said you are
'friends' because everything that I heard from my father I made known to you."
In this verse, Jesus describes communication with the disciples with a present

tense "I say" (*legō*), a perfect tense "I have said" (*eirēka*), and an aorist tense "I made known" (*egnorisa*). The perfect, "I have said you are friends," might be construed as theological, that is, the perfect implies that Jesus called the disciples "friends" in the past and this designation continues to apply to the later community. But if this is the case, "I made known" should also be in the perfect tense rather than the aorist, for something Jesus made known to the disciples in the past should continue to have effect in the present. A similar unpredictability can be observed in the use of the perfect tense in FG's testimonials. Mary Magdalene's "I have seen the Lord" (20:18) in the perfect implies that she saw Jesus and that the effects of her seeing continue into the present. The disciples' "we have found" (1:41, 45) is also perfect tense. But in 4:42 the Samaritan woman acclaims Jesus with "I know," a form of *oida* that functions as a present tense, used also for John the Baptist's acclamation in 1:29. In 11:22, Martha acclaims Jesus first with a form of *oida* but then in 11:27 with a perfect of *pisteuo* ("I believe").

Despite the seeming inconsistency in usage and distribution of perfect verbs in FG, collecting and examining all occurrences reveals a pattern: all perfects in FG function to introduce additions to a preexisting text. Perfects, which occur as participles, as participial phrases, in genitive absolutes, or in entire clauses, either 1) introduce scripture citations, 2) fill out narrative details, or 3) add to discourse. From category 1, perfect forms of *graphō* ("write") introduce references to scripture at John 2:17; 6:31, 45; 8:17; 10:34; 12:14; and 15:25. In other instances, biblical citations are introduced by "say" (*legō* or *phēmi*) in the present or aorist tense (1:23; 12:39; 19:37); "cried" in the aorist (12:13); "be fulfilled" in the aorist subjunctive (13:18; 19:36); or combinations of these (12:38; 19:24). As an example of category 2 above, in John 11:44 the perfect participles ("the dead man, wrapped in . . .") make explicit the subject of "he [Lazarus] came out" of the tomb. In the account of Jesus and the Samaritan woman, a perfect tense phrase explains why Jesus' disciples are not present—they *had gone* into the city to buy food (4:8). In John 2:9 a participial phrase makes the miracle explicit: "[it] had become wine" (*oinon gegenemenon*; see Fortna 1970, 33). In 19:41 a relative clause defines a "new" grave as one in which no one has ever been placed. In 3:24 a clause with verbs in the perfect explains that John the Baptist had not yet been thrown in prison. Phrases in the perfect elsewhere introduce references to the Pharisees (e.g., 1:24; 7:47; 11:57) and affirm John the Baptist's witness to Jesus (e.g., 1:6, 32, 34). The perfect participle of *histēmi* ("stand") serves to introduce named figures, notably Peter and Judas in the passion narrative. In many cases, then, perfect tense verbs in FG introduce citations of scripture or add clarifying details to the narrative.

More significant to the present study are the occurrences of the perfect tense in category 3: additions to discourse. In FG's discourses the perfect occurs in independent clauses and in relative clauses, often with indefinite antecedents. In some cases Jesus asserts that he has come (*elēlytha*; perfect form of *erchomai*) from God or has been sent (*apestalkē*; perfect form of *apostellō*) by God. Other perfect tense verbs in this category refer to "seeing" ("What I *have seen* from the father," John 8:38), judgment (*krisis*, esp. John 5), Moses and the Law (5:45; 6:32; 7:19, 22), the Baptist's testimony to Jesus (3:24, 26–28; 5:33), Jesus' "hour" (16:32; 17:1), and the disciples' authority to forgive sins (20:23).

The phrases and clauses of all three types that use the perfect tense constitute a class of additions to SG distinct from FE's later additions. They evidently function to signal insertions into a coherent work, and, when removed, leave a self-contained account. When the perfect tense occurs in a clause, the entire clause often has the word order found in the Signs Gospel—verb preceding its subject and often coming first in the clause. Unlike FE's additions, some of which significantly recast the theology of SG, many of the perfect insertions conform to SG's theology. The clauses that close Fortna's reconstruction of SG use the perfect (John 20:30–31), and the retrospective scripture citations in 2:17 and 12:16, for example, assume the existence of SG yet clearly predate FE's recasting of it. Fortna classifies some of the perfect tense material with SG. Indeed, it is difficult to classify, because most of it is so close to SG stylistically and theologically.

To summarize, the use of the perfect tense is inconsistent in FG, but the occurrences show a pattern: 1) they function to mark the insertion of new material; 2) the phrases in which they appear are close to SG theologically and predate FE's work. In light of this trend, the perfect tense insertions may be classified as *glosses on the Signs Gospel*. These glosses derive from a stage in the composition history of FG intermediate between SG and FG. As such, they shed light on issues vital to this intermediate stage of the Johannine Community. And because they gloss the Signs Gospel, they function as little flags marking SG material. Granted, it may be difficult to excavate SG sayings from FG's discourses; problems include determining whether clauses with present indicative verbs and *hina* clauses with subjunctive verbs are part of the gloss, and determining when a gloss has been repeated by FE surrounding an insertion. Nevertheless, the little flags give us starting points.

The Glosses of the Signs Gospel

Table 20.1 indicates the location of each gloss of the Signs Gospel in the present text of the Gospel of John, along with the Greek text and the NRSV translation (except for 5:42 and 17:23, which are my translation). Note that the chart gives only the minimal extent of each gloss; some glosses may well have included more than what is given here—for example, a nearby clause in the

Table 20.1

Glosses of the Signs Gospel

Text	Greek Text of Gloss	Translation
1:6	*apestalmenos para theou*	sent from God
1:15	*kai kekragen . . . gegonen*	and cried out
1:18	*theon . . . pōpote*	no one has ever seen God
1:24	*kai apestalmenoi . . . Pharisaion*	Now they had been sent from the Pharisees
1:26	*mesos . . . hestēken*	among you stands
1:30	*hos emprosthen mou gegonen*	[who] was before me
1:32	*tetheamai [to pneuma]*	I saw the spirit descending
1:34	*k'ago heōraka kai memartyrēka*	and I myself have seen and have testified
1:51	*ton ouranon aneōgota*	the heaven opened
2:9	*oinon gegenēmenon*	that had become wine
2:10	*sy tetērēkas . . . arti*	but you have kept the good wine until now
2:17	*hoti gegrammenon estin*	that it was written
3:2	*apo theou elēlythas*	who has come from God
3:6	*to gegennēmenon ek tēs sarkos . . . pneuma estin*	what is born of the flesh is flesh, and what is born of the Spirit is spirit
3:8	*gegennēmenos*	who is born of the spirit
3:11	*ho heōrakamen*	what we have seen
3:13	*oudeis anabebēken eis ton ouranon*	no one has ascended into heaven
3:18	*ho de mē . . . huiou tou theou*	but those who do not believe are condemned already, because they have not believed in the name of the only Son of God
3:19	*elēlythen*	that the light has come into the world
3:21	*ta erga . . . eirgasmena*	[deeds] have been done in God
3:24	*oupō gar ēn beblēmenos eis tēn phylakēn ho Iōannēs*	John, of course, had not yet been thrown into prison
3:26	*hō su memartyrēkas*	to whom you testified

Table 20.1 (*continued*)

3:27	*[ean] mē [ē] dedomenon autō ek tou ourano*	except what has been given [to him] from heaven
3:28	*all' hoti apestalmenos eimi emprosthen ekeinou*	but I have been sent ahead of him
3:29	*ho hestēkōs kai akouōn autou*	The friend of the bridegroom, who stands and hears him
3:35	*kai panta dedōken en tē cheiri autou*	and has placed all things in his hands
4:6	*kekopiakōs ek tēs hodoiporias*	tired out by his journey
4:8	*hoi gar mathētai autou apelēlytheisan eis tēn polin hina trophas agorasōsin*	his disciples had gone to the city to buy food
4:18	*touto alēthes eirēkas*	what you have said is true
4:38	*ho ouch hymeis kekopiakate . . . eiselēlythate*	that for which you did not labor
4:42	*autoi gar akēkoamen*	for we have heard for ourselves
4:45	*heōrakotes*	since they had seen
5:22	*tēn krisin pasan dedōken tō huiō*	but [he] has given all judgment to the Son
5:24	*metabebēken ek tou thanatou eis tēn zōēn*	but has passed from death to life
5:33	*hymeis apestalkate pros Iōannēn, kai memartyrēken tē alētheia*	you sent messengers to John, and he testified to the truth
5:36	*ha dedōken moi ho patēr;*	that the father has given me;
	ho patēr me apestalken	that the Father has sent me
5:37	*ekeinos emartyrēken peri emou . . . . heōrakate*	And the Father who sent me has himself testified on my behalf. You have never heard his voice or seen his form
5:42	*alla egnōka hymas hoti*	But I know you
5:43	*elēlytha en tō onomati tou patros mou*	I have come in my Father's name
5:45	*eis hon hymeis ēlpikate*	on whom you have set your hope
6:13	*tois bebrōkosin*	by those who had eaten
6:17	*kai skotia . . . Iēsous*	It was now dark and Jesus had not yet come to them

Table 20.1 (*continued*)

6:19	*elēlakotes . . . triakonta*	When they had rowed about three or four miles
6:22	*ho hestēkōs peran tēs thalassēs*	that had stayed on the other side of the sea
6:25	*gegonas*	did you come?
6:32	*ou Mōusēs dedōken . . . ouranou*	It was not Moses who gave you the bread from heaven
6:36	*heōrakate kai mē*	you had seen me and
6:39	*pan ho dedōken moi*	of all that he has given me
6:42	*ek tou ouranou katabebēka*	I have come down from heaven
6:45	*estin gegrammenon . . . didaktoi theou*	It is written in the prophets
6:46	*ton patera heōraken tis;*	Not that anyone has seen the Father;
	houtos heōraken ton patera	he has seen the Father
6:63	*ha egō lelalēka*	that I have spoken to you
6:65	*dia touto eirēka hymin . . . dedomenon*	For this reason I have told you that
6:69	*kai hēmeis pepisteukamen kai egnōkamen*	We have come to believe and know that you are the Holy One of God.
7:8	*oupō peplērōtai*	for my time has not yet fully come
7:15	*mē memathēkōs*	when he has never been taught
7:19	*ou Mōusēs dedōken hymin ton nomon*	Did not Moses give you the law?
7:22	*Mōusēs dedōken hymin tēn peritomēn*	Moses gave you circumcision
7:28	*ap' emautou ouk elēlytha*	I have not come on my own
7:30	*oupō elēlythei hē hōra autou*	because his hour had not yet come
7:37	*heistēkei ho Iēsous kai*	while Jesus was standing there
7:47	*mē kai hymeis peplanēsthe*	surely you have not been deceived too, have you?
8:3	*epi moicheia kateilēmmenēn*	who had been caught in adultery
8:4	*hautē hē gynē kateilēptai*	this woman was caught in the very act of committing adultery
8:17	*en tō . . . gegraptai*	in your law it is written

Table 20.1 (*continued*)

8:20	*oupō elēlythei hē hōra autou*	because his hour had not yet come
8:33	*kai oudeni dedouleukamen pōpote*	and have never been slaves to anyone
8:38	*ha egō heōraka para tō patri*	what I have seen in the Father's presence
8:40	*hos tēn alētheian hymin lelalēka*	a man who has told you the truth
8:41	*hēmeis ek porneias ou gegennēmetha*	we are not illegitimate children
8:42	*oude gar ap' emautou elēlytha*	I did not come on my own
8:44	*en tē alētheia ouch hestēken*	and does not stand in the truth
8:52	*nun egnōkamen hoti*	now we know that
8:55	*kai ouk egnōkate auton*	though you do not know him
9:29	*[hēmeis oidamen] hoti Mōusei lelalēken ho theos*	that God has spoken to Moses
9:32	*typhlou gegennēmenou*	of a person born blind
9:37	*kai heōrakas auton*	you have seen him
10:29	*ho dedōken moi pantōn*	what my father has given me
11:11	*Lazaros ho philos hēmōn kekoimētai*	our friend Lazarus has fallen asleep
11:12	*ei kekoimētai*	if he has fallen asleep
11:13	*eirēkei de ho Iēsous peri tou thanatou autou*	Jesus, however, had been speaking about his death
11:19	*polloi . . . elēlytheisan pros tēn Marthan kai Mariam*	and many of the Jews had come to Martha and Mary
11:27	*egō pepisteuka hoti*	I believe that
11:30	*oupō de elēlythei ho Iēsous eis tēn kōmēn*	now Jesus had not yet come to the village
11:34	*pou tetheikate auton*	where have you laid him?
11:39	*hē adelphē tou teteleutēkotos*	the sister of the dead man
11:44	*ho tethnēkōs dedemenos; . . . soudariō periededeto*	the dead man; his hands and feet bound with strips of cloth, and his face wrapped in a cloth
11:56	*en tō hierō hestēkotes*	as they stood in the temple

Table 20.1 (*continued*)

11:57	*dedōkeisan de hoi archiereis . . . hopōs piasōsin auton*	now the chief priests and the Pharisees had given orders
12:14	*kathōs estin gegrammenon*	as it is written
12:16	*tauta ēn . . . gegrammena*	these things had been written of him and
12:18	*auton pepoiēkenai to sēmeion*	that he had performed this sign
12:23	*elēlythen hē hōra*	the hour has come
12:27	*nyn hē psychē mou tetaraktai*	now my soul is troubled
12:29	*ho hestōs . . . brontēn genonenai*	standing there
12:37	*tosauta de autou sēmeia pepoiēkotos*	although he had performed so many signs
12:46	*egō [phōs] eis ton kosmon elēlytha*	I have come into the world
12:49	*ho pempsas . . . dedōken*	the Father [who sent me] has himself given me a commandment
12:50	*kathōs eirēken moi ho patēr*	just as the Father has told me
13:2	*tou diabolou ēdē beblēkotos eis tēn kardian . . . Ioudas Simōnos Iskariōtou*	the devil had already put . . . Iscariot
13:10	*ho leloumenos ouk echei chreian . . . nipsasthai*	one who has bathed does not need to wash
13:12	*ginōskete ti pepoiēka hymin*	Do you know what I have done to you?
14:7	*ei egnōkate me; kai heōrakate auton*	if you know me; and [you] have seen him
14:9	*kai ouk egnōkas me; ho heōrakōs eme heōraken ton patera*	and you still do not know me; whoever has seen me has seen the Father
14:22	*ti gegonen*	how is it?
14:25	*tauta lelalēka hymin*	I have said these things to you
14:29	*kai nyn eirēka hymin*	and now I have told you this
15:3	*hon lelalēka hymin*	that I have spoken to you
15:10	*kathōs egō . . . tetērēka kai*	just as I have kept my Father's commandments

Table 20.1 (*continued*)

15:11	*tauta lelalēka hymin*	I have said these things to you
15:15	*hymas de eirēka philous*	I have called you friends
15:18	*memisēken*	it hated me before it hated you
15:24	*nyn de kai heōrakasin kai memisēkasin . . . mou*	but now they have seen and hated both me and my Father
15:25	*gegrammenos . . . dōrean*	it is written
16:1	*tauta lelalēka hymin*	I have said these things to you
16:4	*tauta lelalēka hymin*	I have said these things to you
16:6	*tauta . . . tēn kardian*	but because I have said these things to you, sorrow has filled your hearts
16:11	*kekritai*	has been condemned
16:24	*hina hē chara hymōn ē peplērōmenē*	so that your joy may be complete
16:25	*tauta en paroimiais lelalēka hymin*	I have said these things to you in figures of speech
16:27	*hoti hymeis eme pephilēkate kai pepisteukate*	because you have loved me and have believed
16:28	*kai elēlythen eis ton kosmon*	and [I] have come into the world
16:32	*kai elēlythen*	indeed it has come
16:33	*tauta lelalēka hymin;* *egō nenikēka ton kosmon*	I have said this to you; I have conquered the world
17:1	*elēlythen hē hōra*	the hour has come
17:2	*ho dedōkas autō*	whom you have given him
17:4	*ho dedōkas moi hina poiēsō*	that you gave me to do
17:6	*kai ton logon sou tetērēkan*	and they have kept your word
17:7	*nyn egnōkan hoti panta hosa dedōkas moi para sou eisin*	Now they know that everything you have given me is from you
17:9	*peri hōn dedōkas moi*	on behalf of those whom you gave me
17:10	*kai dedoxasmai en autois*	and I have been glorified in them
17:11	*hō dedōkas moi*	that you have given me
17:12	*hō dedōkas moi*	that you have given me

Table 20.1 (*continued*)

17:13	*hina echōsin tēn charan . . . peplērōmenēn en heautois*	so that they might have joy made complete in themselves
17:14	*egō dedōka autois ton logon sou*	I have given them your word
17:19	*hina ōsin kai autoi hēgiasmenoi en alētheia*	so that they also may be sanctified in truth
17:22	*tēn doxan hēn dedōkas moi dedōka autois*	the glory that you have given me I have given them
17:23	*hina ōsin teteleiōmenoi*	so that they might be perfected
17:24	*ho dedōkas moi;* *hēn dedōkas moi*	whom you have given me; which you have given me
18:5	*heistēkei . . . met' autōn*	Judas, who betrayed him, was standing with them
18:9	*hous dedōkas moi*	of those whom you gave me
18:11	*ho dedōken . . . patēr*	that the Father has given me
18:16	*ho de . . . exō*	but Peter was standing outside at the gate
18:18	*heistēkeisan . . . pepoiēkotes; ēn de kai ho Petros . . . hestōs*	now the slaves and the police had made a charcoal fire . . . and they were standing around it; Peter also was standing with them
18:20	*egō [parrēsia] lelalēka*	I have spoken openly to the world
18:21	*tous akēkootas*	those who heard
18:22	*parestēkōs*	standing nearby
18:24	*dedemenon*	bound
18:37	*egō eis . . . kosmon*	for this I was born, and for this I came into the world
19:11	*ei mē ēn dedomenon soi anōthen*	unless it had been given you from above
19:19	*ēn de gegrammenon*	it read
19:25	*heistēkeisan de . . . Magdalēnē*	meanwhile standing near the cross of Jesus were his mother, and his mother's sister, Mary the wife of Clopas, and Mary Magdalene
19:26	*kai ton mathētēn parestōta*	and the disciple [standing]

Table 20.1 (*continued*)

19:28	*hoti ēdē panta tetelestai*	that all was now finished
19:30	*tetelestia*	it is finished
19:33	*ēdē auton tethnēkota*	that he was already dead
19:35	*kai ho heōrakōs memartyrēken*	he who saw this testified
19:38	*kekrymmenos*	though a secret one
19:41	*en hō oudepō oudeis ēn tetheimenos*	in which no one had ever been laid
20:7	*alla chōris entetyligmenon eis hena topon*	but rolled up in a place by itself
20:11	*Maria de heistēkei . . . klaiousa*	but Mary stood weeping outside the tomb
20:14	*hestōta*	standing there
20:17	*oupō gar anabebēka . . . patera*	because I have not yet ascended to the Father
20:18	*heōraka ton kyrion*	I have seen the Lord
20:19	*kai tōn thyrōn kekleismenōn*	the doors . . . were locked
20:21	*kathōs apestalken me . . . hymas*	As the Father has sent me, so I send you
20:23	*an tinōn aphēte . . . kekratēntai*	If you forgive the sins of any, they are forgiven them; if you retain the sins of any, they are retained
20:25	*eōrakamen ton kyrion*	We have seen the Lord
20:26	*tōn thyrōn keklesimenōn*	Although the doors were shut
20:29	*hoti heōrakas me pepisteukas*	Have you believed because you have seen?
20:30	*ha ouk estin gegrammena . . . toutō*	which are not written in this book
20:31	*tauta de gegraptai*	But these things are written

present tense. Further study of each instance is required. In the Greek text of each gloss, an ellipsis (. . .) means that all words between the terms given belong within the gloss. For example, at John 1:15 all words between *kekragen* and *gegonen* are part of the gloss. When two or more glosses appear in a single verse, they are separated by a semicolon (;) in both the Greek text and the translation. As the table indicates, the method used in this study reveals the presence of 180 glosses to the Signs Gospel in the current text of FG.[1]

Surveying the instances of the perfect tense provides information on word usage in the glosses, which in turn can be further applied to analysis both of the Signs Gospel and FE's redaction. For example, the many acclamations in the perfect, especially Mary Magdalene's "I have seen" (20:18) and the other glosses on "seeing," suggest a specific christological emphasis vital to this intermediate stage. John 20:30b asserts that there were more signs than are written. Both in the use of the perfect and in the emphasis on "the name," 3 John 5–12 offers intriguing parallels for further study. The perfect glosses emphasize Jesus' connection with God, perhaps to reinforce the authority of his teachings, perhaps to reinforce his subordination to God. Glosses pertaining to Moses suggest ambivalence with respect to Judaism: they take Moses' authority as a starting point (7:19, 22) but reflect distance ("Moses gave *you* the law," not *us*, 7:19). John 12:18 reinforces Jesus' signs. A gloss expresses Jesus' distress at Lazarus's death (12:27). Many glosses harmonize Jesus' authority with that of John the Baptist, perhaps to retain, perhaps to attract, the Baptist's followers.

Words and themes recurring in the glosses include "truth" (*alētheia*), "the name" (*onoma*), "joy" (*chara*), "friend" (*philos*), and "the word" (*ho logos*) used for sayings of Jesus. The glosses employ *hōs* to introduce clauses and adverbs, and use "not yet" (*oupō*) with "already" (*ēdē*). Intriguing glosses add Peter to the passion narrative. Did the promotion of Peter coincide with the death of the Beloved Disciple?

Why do the glosses employ the perfect instead of matching the tenses of the Signs Gospel in their respective contexts? If SG already enjoyed the status of scripture in FE's community, perhaps the shift in tense was intended to mark the glosses as additions. Certainly testimonials in the perfect (and note the perfect in 3 John 11: "the evildoer has not seen God") would have been appropriate christologically and also consistent with the Johannine doctrine of the Paraclete, whose witness to the past continues to be effective in the present.

A Test Case: John 17

John 17, the Final Prayer of Jesus, provides a useful test case in using the glosses to flag SG discourse. Indeed, almost half the verses of John 17 include perfect tense verbs. For the reconstruction of the SG version, each verse must be analyzed individually for word usage, vocabulary, Christology, and literary correspondence with similar phrases elsewhere in FG. My procedure, which is necessarily somewhat circular, follows six assumptions:

1. Because SG already had the status of scripture, FE edited by addition and revision and almost never deleted material from the source.

2. Reconstruction should begin with the elimination of later material. Some material deriving from FE is readily recognizable and may be easily eliminated. Characteristic vocabulary and syntax distinguish FE's additions, which include all of verses 3, 16, and 20. In verse 3, "Jesus Christ" is intrusive, as is "eternal life" with the article and the adjective form of "true" instead of the noun (Schnackenburg 1987, 3.172–173). The reference to second generation believers, as well as word order, identifies verse 20 as FE's. For FE "the world" (*kosmos*) is distinct from Jesus, even personified as something antithetical to him (e.g., most of vv. 9a, 14, 16, and the middle of 25). By contrast, in the Signs Gospel and the glosses *kosmos* is a neutral term meaning "this world," "this life" (vv. 5, 11, 15, 21, 23). In verse 24, FE's *agapaō* accompanies a Christology of preexistence, contrasting with the reference to the preexistence of God's glory in verse 5 and suggesting that the latter verse derives from SG.

3. Constructions in which the verb precedes its subject are a strong indication that a clause derives from SG or the glosses, although SG's use of symmetry (see #5) may affect word order.

4. FE may repeat a phrase from SG or the glosses to bracket his own insertions. This Johannine redactional technique is known as reprise or *Wiederaufnahme* (Boismard 1975) and occurs here in verses 11–12.

5. SG prefers symmetrical constructions. The symmetry of the prayer combined with careful examination of word usage elsewhere in FG give guidelines about more subtle recasting of the SG prayer. Here in verse 1 FE has Jesus speak of himself in the third person, "glorify your son," contrasting with the use of first person throughout the rest of the prayer. John 17:1 has "your son," not "the son" or "son of man," suggesting that the SG version opened with "glorify your name" like 12:28. John 12:23, 27, 38 introduce "glorifying" in connection with Jesus' death, also mentioning both "the name" and "the hour."

6. FE's Christology sometimes motivates omissions and alterations as well as additions. As noted above, guideline 6 works together with #5. The SG prayer very likely did not ask "glorify me" (v. 5). The petitions in the body of the prayer are to "keep" and "sanctify" the disciples. Symmetry in SG argues that the petition was also to "glorify them," the disciples, something that FE would have found problematic and recast. Conversely, FE would have had no problem with "glorify me" (v. 5).

The following is a preliminary reconstruction of the SG core of John 17 in my translation. The version of the prayer that existed in SG is printed in normal type and the glosses which were added later are italicized. Where the SG version was revised by FE rather than the gloss editor, my emendation appears in brackets—{ }—and is explained in the commentary that follows. Phrases and verses not printed were presumably added by FE.

[1] Jesus said, Father, *the hour is come*; glorify your {name}. [2] Just as you gave your name authority over all flesh, it will give to all flesh *whom you have given to it* eternal life [4] {through} the work *that you gave me to do*. [5] Now glorify {them}, Father, with the glory you had before the world existed. [6] I made known your name to people *and they kept your word*. [7] *Now they know that all that you gave me is from you* [8] *because* the words *I gave them* they received and knew truthfully that they came from you. [9] I ask about them—*those whom you gave me*—because [10] *I have been glorified among them*. [11] I am no longer in the world. Holy Father, keep them in your name *which you gave me*. [13] I say these things now in the world *so that they might have joy fulfilled in them*. [14] *I gave them your word*. [15] I do not ask that you remove them from the world, but that you keep them from evil. [17] Consecrate them in the truth. [18] Just as you sent me into the world, so I have sent them into the world [19] and on their behalf I consecrate myself *so that they might also be consecrated in truth*. [21] Just as you, father, are in me, so I am in {them}. [22] *I have given them the glory that you gave me* [23] *so that they might be perfected*. [24] Father, I wish {those} *that you have given me*, that where I am also they might be with me, so that they might see the glory *that you gave me*. [25] Righteous father, [26] they knew that you sent me and I made known to them your name so that it might be among them as I am among them.

The Signs Gospel core of John 17 is clearly a prayer. Its symmetries and repetitions are reminiscent of SG's narrative, which is structured around enumerated signs and repetitive parallelism. The prayer has six vocatives: "father" (vv. 1, 5, 21, 24); "holy father" (v. 11); and "righteous father" (v. 25). The body of the prayer comprises three requests, all aorist imperatives: "glorify" (v. 5); "keep in your name" (v. 11); and "sanctify in truth" (v. 17). The phrases "I am no longer in the world" (v. 11), "when I was with them" (v. 12), and "I have sent them into the world" (v. 18) suggest that the prayer is a postresurrection discourse, consistent with 14:31 terminating the SG dinner scene.

Specific comments on several problem verses are in order. Verse 2 is particularly problematic. The verb *dōsē* (here translated "it will give") is usually read as an aorist subjunctive. But *dōsē* has a future, not an aorist, stem, suggesting that in SG it was future; FE's addition of the *hina* clause ("in order that") led it to be read as a subjunctive. Also in verse 2, the referent of "to it" (which I take to be "the name") is unclear.

In verse 5 the SG prayer asks that the disciples be glorified, although FE has successfully recast the prayer to focus on Jesus himself (e.g., Haenchen 1984, 2.158). The emphasis on "glory" prompts the question, How close was FE to the glosses theologically (Fortna 1988, 233)? Further, did the glosses intersect with other trajectories of early Christian thought (cf. 2 Cor. 3:7)?

Verse 10 has been productively studied in connection with Hellenistic Greek thought (Bultmann 1971, 490–492). But the passive verb, here translated "be glorified," more likely has a Jewish context, alluding to Moses' face via the perfect passive in the LXX version of Exodus 34:29. Also in verse 10, "your word" (*ho logos ho sos*) must be FE's term, for SG and the glosses prefer genitives, "your name" (*onoma sou*).

Verses 11–12 and 15 illustrate FE's technique of reprise. "In your name which you gave me" in verse 12 is a reprise of its occurrence in verse 11, and the intervening material is FE's addition. In verse 12 FE has *ephylaxa* ("guard"), whereas SG (v. 11) and the gloss (v. 6) employ *tēreō* ; but in verse 12 FE imitates the style of SG with *egō eteroun autous*. Also in verse 12 the reference to Judas is FE's and the apparent perfect tense gloss, "which you gave me," is FE's repetition of the gloss of verse 11, a form of redaction by repetitive "bracketing" of material that FE often employs. In verse 6 the past tense ("they were yours") is problematic, and "you gave them to me" lacks the balance of the Signs Gospel, indicating FE's bracketing here as well. Bracketing is also to be found in verse 21, "that the world might believe," which evidently replaces the Signs Gospel's "know" in verses 23 and 8 ("which you gave me"). In verse 22, in the phrase "that they might be" (*hina ōsin*) the reprise comes first, taken from verse 23 ("that they might be perfected," *hina ōsin teteleiōmenoi*).

Verse 18 paradigmatically gives the reciprocity formula, stating a relationship between Jesus and the Father in the first clause, and the reciprocal relationship between Jesus and the disciples in the second. SG's formula has "just as (*kathōs*) you . . . me, so I (*k'agō*) . . . them." FE's additions also have a reciprocity formula, but there *kathōs* introduces the second clause (vv. 16, 23b). Generally, whereas SG's prayer has Jesus make a request to the Father for the disciples, FE has Jesus arrogate authority for himself. Because FE added to an already existing discourse, sometimes the clauses are not completely balanced and may even change person.

In verse 26, the future tense, "I shall make known," contradicts the theme throughout the prayer that Jesus hands the disciples over to God, and therefore must be FE's. The prayer culminates in Jesus' statement that he has left "his name" with the disciples (v. 26). The glosses throughout FG flag the centrality of "the name" for SG.

Although this reconstruction is preliminary, it illustrates the potential of using the perfect tense glosses to flag SG sayings, offers insights into early Jesus traditions, and opens up directions for further study. Recovering the various strata of the Final Prayer reopens many questions scholars have posed about John 17, allowing us to situate them in a historical context, presumably the 40s through 50s, and to explore them anew in connection with early Jesus traditions. Many of FE's additions concern "being one" and are therefore consistent with other evidence of conflict in the later stages of the Johannine Community. Possible links between SG's concept of "the name" and, for example, Philippians 2:9 also show promise for further study.

Note

1. Several entries on the table warrant further explanation. At John 9:7, the phrase *ho hermēneuetai apestalmenos* ("which means 'Sent'") uses the perfect tense but probably represents FE's translation of an Aramaic phrase rather than a gloss. The SG version of the saying at 10:29 was "my father is greater than all," which the gloss revised to "what my Father has given me is greater than all else." At 11:57, the *hopōs* clause is from the gloss, with the *hina* clause added later by FE. At 12:49, the gloss probably referred to the Father's sending of Jesus with the term *apostellō*, which FE seems to have changed to *pempō*. The SG version of John 13:12 was "just as I have done for you, also you do for each other," which the gloss converted to a question: "Do you know what I have done for you?"

Oral Tradition

21

The Gospel of John in Its Oral-Written Media World

JOANNA DEWEY

Contrary to our implicit belief, written texts were peripheral in antiquity. The first-century C.E. world was primarily an oral world, with some influence and control exerted by writing. Of course, it was not a purely oral world: writing had been around for millennia, and alphabetic writing for several hundred years. Yet the overwhelming majority of people—perhaps 95 percent—were not literate at all, and those few who were literate used writing to serve the larger functions of orality. Unless we are self-conscious about first-century orality, we are likely to bring our own print-based Western understandings to the texts still extant from antiquity. This article describes some of the characteristics of the highly oral first-century world, of oral texts, and of the process of oral composition, so that we may better grasp the assumptions first-century people would bring to hearing, composing, performing, and (very occasionally) writing texts. I will begin by describing the first-century media world, and then conclude with a few implications for understanding the Fourth Gospel (FG) within that context.

Literacy in Antiquity

The very term "literacy" is problematic: it can mean anything from the ability to write one's name, to the ability to slowly decipher a simple text, to the ability to read and write fluently. However, using even the most basic definition of "literate" (possession of *any* ability to read or write), agrarian and advanced agrarian societies generally show an overall literacy rate of only 2 to 4 percent (Rohrbaugh 1993, 115; Bar-Ilan 1992, 56; J. Dewey 1995, 39–47). Among those ancients who could read, a disproportionate majority were urban males of high social status, although the ruling elite retained a few literate slaves to do most of the reading and writing for them. But even in that case, William Harris has concluded, on the basis of an exhaustive study of Greek and Latin literacy, that the literacy rate for urban males in the Greco-Roman world may have been no higher than 15 percent (Harris 1989, 267).

Within this largely nonliterate setting, writing was a utilitarian tool used mainly to communicate over distance and time, contexts in which the spoken word was less reliable. The administrative letter was absolutely essential to the maintenance of the Roman Empire because it enabled those in power to communicate with each other. For the general populace, however, information was conveyed orally by public criers, who were attached to all levels of government. The ruling elite used writing for cultural, philosophical, and literary pursuits, but again in a way that reinforced orality. For the overwhelming majority of people, apprenticeship agreements and letters to family and friends living at a distance would be the only instances in which writing was usually employed. Even in those cases, the letters and agreements were generally written by someone else, most likely a professional scribe. For this 95 percent of the population, illiteracy was neither a shame nor an inconvenience. They would know the traditions of their cultures well, primarily through oral storytelling. Yet writing did have an important influence on their lives. It maintained the empire under which they lived and the debt records that often mandated their fate. Artisans and peasants both esteemed writing as almost magical in its power and at the same time were suspicious of its power over them.

The limited spread and uses of literacy detailed above suggest that people could and did become Christian without any dependence on reading or writing. While the documents of the early church are central to our modern understanding of early Christianity, they were much more peripheral to the early Christians, who relied instead on the spoken word.

Oral, Manuscript, and Print Cultures:
Transitions and Divides

Christianity began as an oral movement. Jesus himself was an oral teacher, and as a village artisan he would not have been literate. Jesus would have known the Jewish scriptures primarily through oral stories from popular tradition and through occasionally hearing them read aloud by some scribe or official. Likewise, most first-century Christians would only know the Gospel as an oral story; only very rarely, if at all, would they have had the Hebrew Bible or the Christian writings read to them. While a few Christians began to write texts early—Paul in the middle of the first century; most of the remainder of the New Testament authors by the end of the century—these texts first functioned as aids to orality and probably were not widely known. The shift towards a wider use of writing and the attribution of greater authority to written texts began in the early second century, when the first references to the reading of scripture in Christian worship and the first exact quotations from the gospels (rather than paraphrases from memory) appear. Even at this point, however, the written texts were used only by the few who could read or write to augment oral speech, and increasingly—with the gradual formation of the canon—to control the oral tradition. Documents were not yet an integral part of day-to-day Christian experience.

Through most of the twentieth century, biblical scholars assumed that the medium of communication does not make much difference, so that early Christian oral material could slide effortlessly into written documents with little change. Werner Kelber challenged this assumption in 1983. Using the seminal work of Eric Havelock and Walter Ong, he argued forcefully that a great divide separated early Christian oral tradition from the written text of Mark (Kelber 1983, 95). Since then, scholars have recognized that oral and written media were more blended in the first-century world than today. Vernon Robbins, for example, has indicated the need to develop a more precise taxonomy to describe a society's level of dependence on writing. He proposes the following categories: oral culture, scribal culture, rhetorical culture, reading culture, literary culture, print culture, and hypertext culture (Robbins 1995, 77–82). In a rhetorical culture, "oral operations (presentation and hearing) and literary operations (reading and writing) were (1) inescapably interlocked, and (2) . . . communal activities" (Cartlidge 1990, 14). This means that "writing in a rhetorical culture imitates both speech and writing, and speech in a rhetorical culture imitates both speech and writing" (Robbins 1995, 80). Following Robbins's model, first-century Palestine would represent a scribal culture while the Greco-Roman world would represent a rhetorical culture. This suggests that the early Christians, unlike modern writers, would not sharply distinguish the style and purposes of oral and written speech. For them, both written and spoken texts were communal in nature, evidenced similar styles, and served similar purposes; neither would be necessarily preferred.

For this reason, the New Testament documents are indebted to both orality and writing. All were composed for the ear, not the eye, and thus use many of the practices of oral composition to facilitate comprehension and memory for speaker and hearer. Further, all found their way into writing, whether they were composed in writing, dictated by an individual or group, or transcribed from oral memory. At the same time, however, it is possible, for sake of comparison, to situate the New Testament documents along a continuum from "more literate" to "more oral." Of the New Testament authors, Hebrews was written by a person who was able to write eloquently according to the educated rhetorical standards of his day. Luke clearly had considerable skills in writing, although not at the level demonstrated in Hebrews. Paul had considerable rhetorical ability but not the educated standards of either the author of Hebrews or Luke. In all probability, Paul dictated his letters, and part of the style we see in his writings today may be attributed to the scribes who wrote them down. The Gospels of Mark and John are at the oral end of the continuum, showing abundant evidence of oral compositional techniques and little if any evidence of the incorporation of writing conventions. It is possible that Mark and the Fourth Evangelist (FE) were not literate.

Once written texts came into existence, they would have continued to interact with orality in the life of Christian communities. In modern print culture, we expect written documents to be read silently, read aloud word-for-word, or memorized and recited verbatim (as in the performance of a play). But these practices were not customary in the first century. Oral performers would have been very familiar with the general story and would have recreated it each time they performed it, much as we retell cherished family stories freely rather than reciting them word-for-word from a memorized text. In contexts where written texts are performed orally in this fashion, there is a great deal of feedback or cross-influence between oral and literate versions of particular stories. A written version of a story would have been recycled orally through performance from memory and in interaction with new audiences, naturally changing in the process. It would then be written down again, with or without changes added by the transcriber or author, and again recycled into oral performance. Such a process was the norm, not the exception, for texts that were performed orally in the first century.

The continuing interaction of oral and written texts is important for our understanding of early Christianity. First, we have no idea how close our current texts of the Fourth Gospel (which are based mostly on fourth- and fifth-century manuscripts) are to first-century renditions of the story, but we can be sure that there has been considerable change. Second, the large majority of Christians in the first several centuries were probably familiar only with oral versions of the gospels, and these certainly deviated a good bit from the written versions and from other oral recitations of the stories. While literate bishops and scholars argued theological niceties in written letters and treatises, most Christians continued to experience the Gospel as an oral text.

In summary, then, there was no great divide between the oral and the written word in the first century, no great gulf between those who could read and those who could not. Overall, the communications system of antiquity for both literate and nonliterate persons was thoroughly imbued with orality. Conventions of orality undergirded all composition, performance, and reception of texts, whether a particular performance was based entirely on oral traditions or dependent in some ways on written documents. On the other hand, there is a great gulf of sorts between the people of the first century and those of us accustomed to modern, silent print. In his seminal study of the interaction of oral and written traditions in scripture-based religions, William Graham writes, "In the West at least, the really major displacement of oral modes of thought and communication came only as a postprint phenomenon. . . . In terms of changes in modes of consciousness as well as sheer material change, the great chasm in forms of communication turns out to be not that between literate societies and nonliterate societies but . . . the gulf between our own modern Western, post-Enlightenment world of the printed page and *all* past cultures . . . as well as most contemporary ones" (1987, 17, 29). Thus, if we wish to understand the New Testament texts in terms of their own media environment, we must self-consciously turn from the instinctive assumptions we have derived from our print culture and learn about oral and oral-written cultures.

Characteristics of Orality

When we think of written texts, we think of exact wording and of multiple copies of the same document, identical both in content and even in spacing on the page. This was not so with written texts, much less oral stories, in antiquity. Oral stories are never fixed. Although some oral storytellers insist that they repeat their stories verbatim, comparisons of electronic recordings easily demonstrate that this is not the case. Oral tradition is multiform. Furthermore, the audience always affects the content of an oral performance. Changes are inevitably made, some minor and some major, depending on the storyteller, the context, and the audience. It is true that people in oral cultures can remember some material with extreme accuracy. As late as the 1960s, the Ibadan cattle market in Nigeria handled some 75,000 animals per year with all sales on credit (total debt of 100,000 pounds at any one time) without the aid of writing, banks, or courts (Finnegan 1988, 149). A small and carefully trained group among the South Sea Islanders learned chants with detailed, accurate navigational information (Couch 1989, 595–597). This sort of accuracy, however, is atypical and only occurs where something critical is at stake—the navigator who got the chant wrong might well never return! And even in these cases, the aim of verbatim memory is usefulness, not accuracy or fidelity for its own sake.

Usefulness strongly affects the transmission of oral tradition, which is continually adapting to changed conditions. This is true even (perhaps especially) of traditions that are important for the constitution of groups, as the gospels were for early Christian communities. In such cases, traditions expand, omit, and adapt to fit the needs of the storyteller's current situation. The classic example of this phenomenon is the Gonja oral tradition in Ghana (Goody and Watt 1968, 33). When the oral legends about the origins of the Gonja state were first recorded around 1900, the founder of the state had seven sons, each a ruler of one of seven territorial divisions. But when the legends were recorded again some sixty years later, the story mentioned only five sons, because at that time the Gonja state had only five territorial divisions. Clearly, the content of the legend had been adapted to accommodate the new political reality. In oral settings, "historical facts in the remembered past are under constant pressure from the needs of the present. The memory adapts, transposes them, or eliminates them altogether, when they are no longer useful" (Clanchy 1970, 166). Oral tradition is not fixed but continues to adapt to present contexts.

Composition, reception, and transmission of texts exist as one event in oral culture: a story is told (composed) and people hear (receive) it, thus transmitting its content. An oral story that is not retold is rapidly forgotten. Oral storytellers generally compose their stories in the moment of performance: the storyteller does not repeat a memorized script but rather develops the material spontaneously on the basis of a tradition and a story line. In the case of FG, it is unlikely that John's story of Jesus would have been read aloud word-for-word with a scroll or codex in hand. Rather, a Christian oral performer would retell it on the basis of her own prior hearing or, less likely, prior reading of the text. A good storyteller could hear the story of FG told once and then be able to retell it in entirety. FG, as we have it, is short enough to be told in one storytelling session, so it was probably often heard in its entirety in one-and-a-half- to two-and-a-half-hour sittings. In addition, length is one of the most variable elements in oral narration: a storyteller will shrink or expand a story from as little as ten minutes to several hours depending on the receptivity of the audience. Therefore, audiences undoubtedly heard both expanded and contracted versions of FG.

The performance context is relevant to the composition of an oral story in three ways. First, the oral story builds on traditions known to both the performer and the audience. As John Miles Foley has shown, references in oral literature are generally metonymic, recalling the larger tradition rather than some specific objective reality. The part stands for the whole and reminds the hearers of a whole complex of traditions with which they are already familiar (Foley 1995, 53–59). For example, Homer's references to "swift-footed Achilles" function not so much to tell the audience that Achilles was quick on his feet as to recall to the hearer the whole complex of ideas and motifs that they already know and associate with Achilles. Insofar as we no longer know the broader traditions that first-century Christians associated with various features of the gospel story, we are at a disadvantage in interpreting the written gospels. Second, in an oral performance much of the "meaning" comes not through the words but through other aspects of performance. As a result, oral performances lose much of their power when committed to written transcripts. Finnegan notes that when she heard Limba (West African) storytellers in live performance she was impressed "by their subtlety, imaginativeness, creativity, drama and human qualities," but when she studied written transcripts of their stories back in England they seemed lifeless and dull (Finnegan 1990, 134–135). Elements of characterization present in the oral performance are often completely lost in writing since they are not conveyed by the words alone, and unfortunately today we have only the words of the ancient Christian texts and not the performers who gave them life. Third, as mentioned earlier, oral stories always adapt to the particular audience and situation in which they are being told. Writing about North Turkic tribal singers, Wilhelm Radloff says, "If wealthy and noble Kirgiz are present, [a singer] knows how to skillfully weave in praises of their dynasties, and he sings about those episodes which he expects will stir the nobility's applause in particular. If only poor people are in his audience, he includes some bitter remarks about the arrogance of the noble and wealthy" (Radloff 1990, 85). This suggests that individual performances of a gospel would have been adapted to the social levels and cultural contexts of their immediate audiences and that what was written down represents only one particular oral rendition. We are again at a disadvantage in understanding the New Testament texts because we no longer share or understand their contexts and because we no longer have the full live experience.

The compositional characteristics of oral performance have been well described by Havelock and Ong. Several of these characteristics relate to the *form* of oral texts. First, oral stories are made up of *happenings*, that is, events in time, episodes, little stories, or situations. Teaching is embedded in these happenings, rather than being presented as general propositional truths organized topically. Second, oral literature consists of the *visible*: the happenings can easily be visualized in the mind's eye, so that the audience can picture them and thus more easily remember them. Third, oral literature consists of the *many*: happenings are placed side by side, not integrated with one another (Havelock 1963, 180). For this reason, the structure of oral stories tends to be additive rather than subordinating. The normal way of connecting clauses, sentences, and whole episodes is paratactic, stacking them together with simple formulas like "and," "and next," "and then." Material is not organized in cause/effect or chronological patterns but rather in symmetrical clusters that use simple parallelism (abc//abc), chiastic parallelism (abc//cba), and concentric structures (abcdcba). For this reason, oral styles often appear redundant or copious to our print sensibilities, focusing on repetition with variations.

The *content* and *subject matter* of oral texts are also distinct. Oral stories are close to human experience, told in a narrative about people who are usually gathered around a major hero or group of heroes. Stories tend to be agonistically toned, that is, so polemical and argumentative that they often strike people from print cultures as verbally abusive. Finally, oral performances are empathetic and participatory, seeking to arouse the audience's emotion rather than retain objective distance. Performer and audience alike identify with the characters, fighting, weeping, and rejoicing with them, experiencing what they experience (Havelock 1963, 20–34). Thus, the focus for both oral performer and audience is on the *experience* of the performance event, not on the specific information being learned or reinforced. By contrast, literate audiences tend to think of the printed word as a tool that provides us with information about something outside of the printed page. Modern literate Christians read the Bible in search of objective cognitive information about what to believe and how to act. We rarely approach the gospel narratives as "experiences" that may transform our relation to the world, yet this is how the gospels would have been experienced in the oral world of the first century.

The Solidification of Oral Tradition

As noted earlier, oral tradition is multiform and always changing. Such is also the nature of human memory. Modern studies of the brain show that memory is not exact. Similar memories overlay earlier memories and become conflated, so that what we believe are clear memories of one particular event can generally be shown to be composite memories of several related events. This is also true of the early Christians' memories about Jesus and his sayings. If Jesus had trained his disciples in verbatim memorization, exact memory would be more likely, but as a nonliterate oral teacher Jesus himself probably had no concept of either verbatim repetition or "memorization." On the other hand, studies of the brain have also shown that memory solidifies quickly. In a famous study of the way people remember where they were when the space shuttle Challenger exploded, a considerable difference was noted in what students reported the day after the event and what they remembered two-and-a-half years later. At the later time, none could remember exactly where they were and what they were doing when they heard news of the disaster, and 25 percent were positively wrong about every circumstance surrounding the occasion: where they were, what they were doing when they heard, and how they found out. Six months after the second interview the students were asked to recall the situation a third time, and on this occasion their memories were consistent with what they had reported the second time. Right or wrong, their memories had solidified into a clear and visually vivid picture (Lewis, Amini, and Lannon 2000, 134–135).

Though oral tradition is much more communal than the personal memories investigated in the Challenger study, it also has a tendency to solidify into inexact complexes of stories and sayings. Furthermore, traditional stories tend to coalesce into a single larger story centered around a hero. Havelock writes, "The tighter . . . the group structure . . . the more urgent is the need for the creation of a great story which shall compendiously gather up all the little stories into a coherent succession, grouped round several prominent agents who shall act and speak with some over-all consistency" (Havelock 1963, 175). Jan Vansina, an authority on oral history, argues that this process of solidification and coalescence may happen quickly. "When accounts of events have been told for a generation or so the messages then current may still represent the tenor of the original message, but in most cases the resulting story has been fused out of several accounts and has acquired a stabilized form. The plot and sequence of episodes changes only gradually after this" (Vansina 1985, 17). As largely oral subgroups with "tight group structures," early Christian communities in the Roman Empire would have needed such a "great" or all-inclusive story about Jesus. Contrary to most scholars' assumptions, it is extremely likely that connected narratives—or a single, flexible, connected narrative—about the life and death of Jesus began to be told by the forties or fifties C.E., as the oral tradition coalesced. Certainly there would be variations on this story by different storytellers in different communities with different nascent theologies. The social class and gender of the tellers and audiences would also affect the story. Nonetheless, trends in the use of oral tradition suggest that such a larger comprehensive narrative would have existed and been generally known in the early church.

The Fourth Gospel in Its Oral World

Recognition of the highly oral nature of the first-century world adds to our already great difficulty in reaching historical certainty. At the same time, though, an understanding of some of the ways that this oral/written media culture operated can aid us in interpreting the early Christian documents. In the remainder of this article, I shall briefly indicate some areas of Johannine studies in which knowledge of the oral context may help us understand the Fourth Gospel. I am not attempting to interpret FG and its prehistory in light of the first-century media world; rather, I am naming areas where orality studies may have a contribution to make. Specifically, an understanding of the oral world in which FG was produced may help us answer seven key questions about its composition history and the Johannine Jesus tradition.

1. Does knowledge of orality help us to determine which traditions go back to Jesus? As noted earlier, memory alters, conflates, and adapts to present situations. This is as true for the Synoptic Gospels as for FG. Both are far removed from the days of Jesus. The workings of memory and the process of solidification of oral tradition must make us question the historical reliability of *all* gospels. Furthermore, traces of oral style in a written text do not necessarily indicate that the text is "earlier" or closer to what actually happened than a written text with fewer oral characteristics. The degree of orality is not in itself a useful criterion for sifting historicity out of gospel texts.

2. Was there a larger oral narrative underlying the Fourth Gospel? I argued earlier that oral stories do not continue to circulate as isolated, independent units until they are drawn together in written texts, as form criticism has traditionally supposed. Rather, individual stories tend to aggregate into a larger, more or less coherent overall oral narrative focused on a hero or heroes, and such an oral narrative is likely to underlie the gospels. The substantial differences between FG and the Synoptics lead me to ask whether there were two different comprehensive oral narratives in existence, one that underlies Mark and another that underlies FG. Is FG evidence for a somewhat different traditional oral story? I doubt that this can be proved or disproved, but it seems quite probable. The two stories might originate from different geographical centers: Jerusalem for FG; Galilee for the Synoptics. Furthermore, marginalized groups normally know the traditions of the dominant group but also develop their own, often critical, versions of tradition (Scott 1990). The community that produced FG seems to have understood itself as a minority group among Christians, and as such it might well have developed its own alternate oral narrative.

3. Was there a written signs source behind the narratives of FG? Many scholars posit that there was a written source, containing many of the miracles or "signs" of John 1–12, which the Fourth Evangelist used in composing his gospel. Knowledge of first-century media culture suggests that such a written source is improbable. Unlike isolated sayings or discourse material, miracle stories are narrative and thus easy to remember. In a culture where very few people could read, where writing materials were expensive and cumbersome, and where memory was well developed, it seems unlikely that anyone would go to the trouble of writing a signs source. The inconsistencies and sudden shifts (aporias) in the Johannine narrative that the signs source theory resolves can also be explained as the result of oral composition or of the interaction between oral and written versions of the story. Listening audiences tolerate narrative inconsistencies and even theological tensions, much more easily than we with our print-formed minds do. Furthermore, the colloquial nature of the Greek of FG suggests that its author was not highly educated, and thus probably not a fluent reader. He would more likely have garnered his information from hearing than from working with a written source. Recognition of the first-century oral culture thus argues against the existence of a signs source.

4. Was there a pre-Johannine passion narrative? I think we have much too little evidence to posit a pre-Johannine written passion narrative, for the same reasons that I think a signs source is improbable. If a larger oral narrative does indeed underlie FG, then some of the peculiarities of FG's passion narrative could easily derive from it, and the possibility of associating certain parts of John 18–20 with a "pre-Johannine source" seems highly problematic. First, it assumes a fixity and reliability of both the written text of FG and of the proposed written passion source that are not characteristic of texts in antiquity. Second, our modern tools for separating source from redaction often rely on subtle analytic distinctions that are incompatible with the additive and aggregative nature of oral narrative and the style of most first-century writing.

5. What is the relationship between FG and the Synoptics? Scholars continue to debate different positions on FG's relation to the Synoptics. Some argue for literary dependence on Mark or Luke; others for complete independence; others for some mediating position that FE was acquainted with Mark and/or Luke but did not use them as sources. The conditions of first-century oral manuscript transmission make the last option seem most probable. There are occasional echoes of Mark in FG that are so specific and idiosyncratic that it seems most likely the Fourth Evangelist had heard Mark performed at some time. However, FE's limited use of Mark suggests that a written text of Mark was not used for composing FG. Furthermore, as noted above, the level of FG's Greek suggests reliance on oral memory rather than use of written source texts.

6. How oral or written is the style of the Fourth Gospel? As noted earlier, speech imitated writing and writing imitated speech in the first-century, oral-manuscript media world. We frequently cannot tell with any great degree of certainty whether a text we now have was composed orally and later transcribed, or whether a text was initially created in writing. As certain conventions of writing become the norm, they are often incorporated into oral performances. Speakers thoroughly familiar with the oral tradition can compose in an oral style as they write or dictate. All ancient writers wrote for the ear, and those with less formal education were likely to rely heavily on oral compositional techniques. Further, even if FG had been created entirely orally or entirely in writing, the ongoing interchange between written text and oral performance would likely have left residues in the manuscripts that have survived.

The current text of FG gives clear evidence that its author thought of himself as a writer. It concludes, "Now Jesus did many other signs in the presence of his disciples, which are not written in this book. But these are written so that you may come to believe that Jesus is the Messiah, the Son of God, and that through believing you may have life in his name" (John 20:30–31). The later appendix to FG, John 21, concludes, "This is the disciple who is testifying to these things and has written them, and we know that his testimony is true" (21:24). The question to raise here is whether FG was conceived as a "writing" from the beginning, or whether these statements were added in the process of oral and written transmission of the material. As they stand, these statements suggest (but do not prove) that FG was initially conceived as a written text.

At the same time, the style of FG is heavily oral. Its Greek contains mainly simple clauses and frequent instances of present-tense verbs where written convention would normally require a past tense. The style, however, is slightly less oral than Mark's (J. Dewey 1989). Mark connects almost all episodes simply with an "and" (*kai*). FE also uses a fair number of "ands," but he also regularly uses "the next day," "after this," and other similar connectors. However, they remain simple paratactic connectors: "and next," "and then," and so on. Further, using Havelock's terms, FG's narrative is made up of "happenings" that are "visible" and "many." In contrast to the Synoptics, the episodes are long, evolving into dialogue and often monologue; that is, the episodes conclude with relatively long sections of teaching or discourse material. As is characteristic of orality, teaching is embedded in or tagged onto the events; the discourses are not presented as freestanding teaching. This is true even of the last discourses of John 13–17. As in oral narrative, FG's dialogue is restricted to two characters at a time (e.g., the sequential dialogues of the Samaritan woman, Jesus, and the disciples [John 4:7–42], or the sequential dialogues around the blind man [John 9]). In addition, both the episodes in FG and the dialogues that follow them are "visualizable." The ensuing monologues are not easy to remember by visualizing them. The added cues, however, provided in live performance likely clarified issues such as the identity of the speaker/narrator in John 3:31–36. The Fourth Gospel is definitely made up of the "many"—many miracles, many dialogues and discourses—that could well be described as repetitions with variation. It involves not a tight linear plot but the unfolding of similar events and discourses.

Much more work needs to be done on FG's discourse material to understand better its relation to oral and written media. Did the discourses evolve only in writing with little or no prior existence orally? Or were they oral, perhaps the speech of Christian prophets speaking to the community? Is their apparent confusion and repetition due to the difficulty of remembering them orally and embedding them in a connected narrative? Or, as a third possibility, were they composed in writing perhaps more systematically than we now have them, but became confused and conflated as the Gospel was recycled orally? Or, perhaps most probable, did they begin orally in much shorter form and expand in succeeding written versions? All of these options are possible in light of the first-century media culture. Detailed analysis of the text may shed some light on the discourses' oral and/or written characteristics, but it is unlikely to provide proof.

Finally, one feature of FG that has puzzled scholars and readers is the tension between the present and future eschatologies contained in the narrative, between the idea that you are already saved if you believe (John 5:24) and the idea of a coming future judgment (5:29; 6:40). Knowledge of the ancient oral media world suggests two possible explanations. First, oral-type narrative can embrace material that seems contradictory to modern Western readers. It tends to create a "both/and" world, in which both present and future salvation are compatible. Second, this tension in eschatologies could be the result of the recycling sequence of oral performance/written text/oral performance that characterized the use of FG through the second and probably much of the third century. Updated or corrected material would naturally be added as the Gospel was continually readapted to new situations, without the old necessarily dropping out. In a totally oral world, the old would probably be lost altogether. In a manuscript world, the text maintains some stability, so the old is more likely to remain.

It would appear, then, that FG is a document that remains very close to the oral performance world but that is also indebted to writing. Its composer probably did not use any written sources but most likely did use a preexisting oral narrative. That person was certainly immersed in much of the early Christian oral tradition and had probably heard Mark.

7. *How does oral reception of the Fourth Gospel affect interpretation?* Again, what I present here is not a full exploration but rather some preliminary suggestions. First, as noted earlier, we need to take less seriously the aporias of FG, the inconsistencies and disjunctions of the text. We need to take more seriously the "both/and" nature of oral thought and see how we can integrate rather than analyze and separate the different strands of thought found in FG. Second, it helps to remember that oral cultures are heavily agonistic. First-century audiences probably took much less seriously than we the negative portrayal of "the Jews" and of other Christian groups in FG simply because they expected discourse to be polemical. Third, and most important, in order to assist memory, both the performer and the audience would identify with each character in turn. For the episode of the woman at the well (John 4), they would identify with Jesus *and* with the Samaritan woman, the disciples, and the villagers, thus experiencing each character sympathetically in turn. This process of identification would also extend to "the Jews" and thus ameliorate the negativity of their portrayal to some extent. More work is needed on how oral reception differs from the experience of reading silent print.

Conclusion

I have presented some of the major features of the first-century oral-written media world that contrast with the assumptions we bring from our training in Western print culture. I have also suggested some areas where recognition of the high degree of orality may impact our study of FG and its prehistory. Orality studies are still in their infancy, and much needs to be done to understand and apply them to the New Testament. Yet I think we understand enough to know that the communication medium does make a difference in interpretation. On the one hand, orality makes our reconstructions of early Christian history even more problematic and uncertain; on the other hand, it also gives us new ways of investigating and new insights into our texts.

22

The Origin of the "Amen, Amen" Sayings in the Gospel of John

R. ALAN CULPEPPER

There is no parallel outside the New Testament for the use of *amēn* as a particle at the beginning of a saying, and within the New Testament this usage is confined to the sayings of Jesus ("Amen/truly I say to you . . ."). Further, only in the Fourth Gospel (FG) do we find the double "amen," used to introduce Jesus' sayings ("Amen, amen, I say to you . . ."). FG includes twenty-five sayings that begin with the double-*amen* formula, twenty of which use a plural "you" and five of which are delivered to a single person. On the other hand, the single *amen* at the beginning of a saying, which occurs thirty-one times in Matthew, thirteen times in Mark, and six times in Luke, never appears in FG. Why are so many of Jesus' statements in FG marked off by this unutterably solemn formula of affirmation? Is it merely a Johannine stylistic device, or was it attached to these sayings earlier in the development of the tradition? And are there common features that set these sayings apart from the rest of the discourse material in FG? As will be seen, in some cases it appears that the Fourth Evangelist (FE) uses the double-*amen* formula to introduce sayings that have been drawn from earlier Jesus traditions.

The Origin of the "Amen, Amen" Sayings

It appears that the formula "amen, amen" was associated early in Christian history with prophetic, oracular pronouncements. Some of these announcements may have come from Jesus himself, while others originated with early prophets who spoke on behalf of the risen Lord. In support of the first possibility, Barnabas Lindars argues that the "amen, amen" formula is used in FG to identify primitive tradition or authentic words of Jesus: "the formula, 'Truly, truly I say to you' . . . is not merely a stylistic device; in nearly every case it points to . . . [a] very primitive, and for the most part certainly authentic, tradition of the words of Jesus" (Lindars 1972, 48). In support of the second possibility, J. N. Sanders and B. A. Mastin conclude that "amen, amen" is used in FG to introduce prophetic sayings composed by FE himself: "The double *Amēn, amēn* is characteristic of, peculiar to, the FG, and is used to introduce solemn, almost oracular, declarations . . . usually in passages of which the form and phraseology often suggest the prophetic activity of the evangelist himself or of his authority" (1968, 105).

In weighing these two options, one must conclude that the double-*amēn* formula is unlikely to be a distinctive feature of Jesus' idiom. If Jesus did use this phrase to introduce his own sayings, it is impossible to explain why the formula appears only in FG among all extant gospels. But at the same time, Lindars's contention that FE uses "amen, amen" to identify primitive or authentic tradition merits further consideration. Although the formula itself is certainly a later development, it is possible that FE attaches it to statements that he wishes to identify as primitive words of Jesus. Given the prevalence of skepticism about the historical value of the Johannine sayings tradition in modern scholarship, this possibility has important implications for our understanding of the compositional techniques of FE, the nature of the sayings tradition that lies behind FG, and the recovery of Jesus' authentic teaching.

How, then, is it possible to determine whether statements of Jesus in FG that are introduced by the formula "amen, amen" represent primitive Jesus tradition? Progress toward answering this question is admittedly difficult, but a consideration of the following four questions can provide a useful direction:

1) Are there any close parallels to particular "amen, amen" sayings in other sources?
2) How does each saying function in its present context in FG?
3) Are the "amen, amen" sayings marked off by a distinctive form or content?
4) How pronounced is Johannine style or idiom in these sayings? In other words, to what extent does their language compare to or contrast with FE's own typical style?

The first factor—parallels outside FG—provides an objective, external control. If a significant number of these sayings find parallels in the Synoptics, it would suggest that the double-*amen* formula does indeed identify sayings received by the Johannine Community from primitive Jesus traditions. Like-wise, close parallels in early Christian documents that do not otherwise quote FG may also serve as evidence that these sayings come from primitive tradition. The second factor—the function of the double-*amen* sayings in the context of the Johannine discourses—considers whether these sayings provide the central theme for specific speeches in FG. If one or several of these sayings seem to set the themes and tone for a longer discourse, it can be argued that FE borrowed these sayings from the tradition and developed the rest of the speech as a commentary on those sayings. The third factor—form and content—examines whether FG's twenty-five "amen, amen" sayings have common structural elements or address themes that are not typical of the rest of FG. Notable differences may suggest that FE has simply borrowed and adapted sayings that he received from an earlier tradition. Finally, the fourth factor—style and idiom—considers whether the double-*amen* sayings have been preserved within FG in pristine form, or whether they have been re-minted in Johannine language.

The Traditional "Amen, Amen" Sayings

The four factors described above may be used to analyze the twenty-five "amen, amen" sayings in FG to determine whether each is a primitive tradition of Jesus' sayings or FE's own composition. Such an analysis reveals that at least thirteen of these sayings appear to be citations of Jesus tradition that FE has borrowed and adapted: John 1:51; 3:3, 5; 6:47; 6:53; 8:51; 10:1–5, 11b–13; 12:24; 13:16; 13:20; 13:21; 13:38; 16:23; 21:18. The factors relevant to each of these sayings are discussed below. Note that, in order to highlight the unique language of the sayings under consideration, my own translations are used throughout the following discussion.

> Amen, amen, I say to you, you will see heaven opened and the angels
> of God ascending and descending upon the Son of man. (John 1:51)

This verse and John 6:53 (see following discussion) are the only "Son of Man" sayings introduced by the double-*amen* formula. While there are no close parallels to this saying outside FG, it clearly alludes to Genesis 28:12 ("And he [Jacob] dreamed that there was a ladder set up on the earth, the top of it reaching to heaven; and the angels of God were ascending and descending on it"). The saying is rooted in primitive gospel traditions, but the current version reflects Johannine thought forms and language and is closely tied to its literary context in FG. It appears to be the product of early Christian reflection on the significance of Jesus both as the Son of Man and as the one in whom the promises to Israel would be fulfilled. It is therefore rooted in both the traditions of the baptism of Jesus and in reflection on the figure of Jacob/Israel. John 1:51 reflects the formative influence of early Christian reflection on the relationship between Jesus and the scriptures of Israel.

> Amen, amen, I say to you, unless one is born anew, he cannot see the kingdom of God. . . . Amen, amen, I say to you, unless one is born of water and the Spirit, he cannot enter the kingdom of God. (John 3:3, 5)

These two verses are variations of the same saying. Both share the following four elements: 1) "Amen, amen"; 2) "I say to you"; 3) "unless one is . . ."; 4) "he cannot [enter] the kingdom of God." When viewed in terms of these four structural elements, the saying clearly parallels Matthew 18:3: 1) "Amen"; 2) "I say to you"; 3) "unless you turn and become like children"; (4) "you will never enter the kingdom of heaven." It appears, therefore, that John 3:3, 5 is a Johannine adaptation of a saying that appears independently, following Matthean redaction, in Matthew 18:3. Other parallels may be found in Mark 10:15, Justin Martyr's *Apology* 1.61.4, and the *Epistle of Diognetus* 9. FE adapts the traditional logion, rendering it with an ambiguous reference ("born anew") that can then be used to develop themes fundamental to Johannine theology: "new birth," "from above," through the Spirit, and baptism. John 3:3 is therefore a classic example of how FE can take a traditional logion and build a discourse around it.

> Amen, amen, I say to you, you seek me, not because you saw signs, but because you ate your fill of the loaves. . . . Amen, amen, I say to you, it was not Moses who gave you the bread from heaven; my Father gives you the true bread from heaven. . . . Amen, amen, I say to you, he who believes has eternal life. . . . Amen, amen, I say to you, unless you eat the flesh of the Son of man and drink his blood, you have no life in you; he who eats my flesh and drinks my blood has eternal life, and I will raise him up at the last day (John 6:26, 32, 47, 53)

The four "amen, amen" sayings in John 6 are all found in the long discourse on the bread from heaven. The sayings in verses 26, 32, and 53 are closely tied to this discourse by their content: all relate specifically to the theme of eating and drinking. John 6:47, however, is a general axiom that could hypothetically appear in a variety of contexts.

Lindars believes that John 6:26 is derived from the same tradition as Mark 8:11–12, which would add weight to the claim that the verse reflects a primitive tradition (1972, 254). But the version of the verse in the current text of FG is so tied to its narrative setting that it can hardly be regarded as a saying or Johannine maxim that circulated independently. The same can also be said of John 6:32; it does not have the character of a saying that circulated apart from its current narrative context. But if these sayings are not traditional, why did FE introduce them with the double-*amen*? The clue may be found in noting the significance of the previous verse. The crowd, speaking of the manna that Moses provided in the wilderness, reminds Jesus that "he gave them bread from heaven to eat" (6:31), a statement that echoes various verses from the Hebrew Bible but does not quote any passage verbatim (see Exod. 16:4, 15; Neh. 9:15; Ps. 78:24). Regardless of its origin, however, this "citation" becomes the text on which Jesus' subsequent remarks about "bread" are based. It seems likely, then, that FE introduces Jesus' remarks in verse 32 with "amen, amen" based on the important role this saying plays in its immediate context, as an introduction to the remarks that follow.

John 6:47 may be a Johannine maxim introduced here because it fits the context. If this is the case, the use of "amen, amen" functions to mark the saying as traditional. On the other hand, it may be that this verse, like 6:32, is introduced with the double-*amen* simply to draw the reader's attention because it serves as a basis for the statements that follow. But given the fact that John 6:31–32 has already established the general outline of Jesus' speech, it seems unnecessary for FE to use the double-*amen* formula for emphasis a second time so soon in the same context. We may therefore tentatively accept John 6:47 as a traditional maxim in the Johannine tradition.

Like several other "amen, amen" sayings, John 6:53 has a legislative character. It provides a norm for discriminating between those who have life and those who do not. Moreover, this norm appears to be tied to the eucharistic bread and wine, which are understood to be the flesh and blood of the Son of Man. In the context of debate with the Jewish synagogue, participation in the Lord's Supper would have been a clear test of whether one was willing to make a public declaration of one's faith in Jesus as the Christ. Further, in its immediate context the saying is the opening line of Jesus' response to a question. The confluence of these factors—the eucharistic use of the term "Son of Man," the legislative character of the saying, its possible function in reference to the debate with the synagogue, and its function as the core saying for John 6:52–59—provides sufficient grounds for viewing John 6:53 as a traditional maxim of the Johannine Community. The saying seems to have been formed on the basis of reflection on the Eucharist and possibly also the broader tradition of the words of institution (see Mark 14:23ff.).

> Amen, amen, I say to you, if any one keeps my word, he will never see death. (John 8:51)

Several commentators have argued that John 8:51 is a paraphrase of Mark 9:1 ("Amen, I say to you, there are some standing here who will not taste death before they see the kingdom of God come with power"). While the promise

of John 8:51 bears some resemblance to Mark 9:1, the parallel is not sufficiently close to posit more than a distant relationship between the two sayings.
Further, if John 8:51 is a variation of Mark 9:1, FE has changed the idiom "taste
death" to "see death," has added a condition ("if any one keeps my word"), and
has radically altered the temporal clause so that it reads "not . . . for ever" in
place of Mark's "until." On the other hand, parallels with Oxyrhynchus
Papyrus 654.1 and Gospel of Thomas 1 indicate that some form of this saying
circulated as an independent logion.

> Amen, amen, I say to you, he who does not enter the sheepfold by the
> door but climbs in by another way, that man is a thief and a robber;
> but he who enters by the door is the shepherd of the sheep. . . . (John
> 10:1–5, 11b–13)

John 10 is key to any study of the Johannine sayings tradition. Whether or
not FE has used traditional sayings in this section, the way one interprets this
passage will set the course for judgments on a number of other logia.

John 10:1–5, 11b–13 stand out from the other verses in 10:1–18. These sayings set up contrasts and define roles, while the rest of the verses are clearly interpretive and introduce explicitly christological language. Several issues must be
taken into account when analyzing this section. The first concerns the genre of
the material: Is John 10:1–5 a parable, an allegory, a christological discourse, or
something entirely unique? Second, how many sayings are under consideration:
Are we dealing with one extended logion, or two or three related sayings that FE
has combined? Finally, what is the source or origin of this material?

While space does not permit a detailed discussion of these issues, I am per-
suaded that John 10:1–5 presents one figurative discourse rather than a combination of two distinct parables. In my view, the argument that FE has
combined two traditional parables here appears to be driven by an effort to
identify parallels between this text and the Synoptics. Further, I believe that it
is best to regard verses 11b–13 as originally part of the figurative discourse
contained in verses 1–5. The fact that FE identifies verses 1–5 collectively as
a *paroimia* (v. 6; NRSV: "figure of speech") favors the conclusion that FE is
presenting traditional material drawn from early Christian oral tradition. This
tradition appears to ultimately reach back to Jesus' own metaphors, riddles,
and parables that made use of the imagery of the door, the doorkeeper, the
shepherd, and his sheep.

> Amen, amen, I say to you, unless a grain of wheat falls into the ground
> and dies, it remains alone; but if it dies, it bears much fruit. (John
> 12:24)

Although John 12:24 could fit nicely into a collection of the seed parables in
the Synoptics, it has no close verbal parallel among those texts. The most strik-

ing parallel appears in 1 Corinthians 15:36: "What you sow does not come to life unless it dies." Since it appears from 1 Thessalonians 5:2 that Paul knew the traditional parable of the thief in the night (see Matt. 24:43; Luke 12:39), it is quite possible that Paul also knew the parable of the seed falling into the ground. The only words in FG's version of the parable that have a Johannine ring are "it remains alone" and "it bears much fruit"; otherwise, the language of this parable is remarkably free of Johannine idioms. It appears, therefore, that FE has adapted a seed parable known to Paul but not found in the Synoptics. In its present context, this statement functions as a passion prediction, but that need not have been its original intent. Regardless of the original setting of the parable, the double-*amen* formula here introduces not just one but a collection of sayings that stem from a pre-Johannine tradition. John 12:24 preserves a gem from the teachings of Jesus that was passed over by the synoptic evangelists.

> Amen, amen, I say to you, a servant is not greater than his master; nor is he who is sent greater than he who sent him. . . . Amen, amen, I say to you, he who receives any one whom I send receives me; and he who receives me receives him who sent me. (John 13:16, 20)

Another cluster of synoptic-like sayings of Jesus emerges in the discourse following the footwashing. In this context, Jesus makes a number of statements that define the authority and role of the disciples. Luke and FG contain variant forms of the saying on the greater authority of the master (Luke 6:40; John 13:16), while Matthew combines the two forms (Matt. 10:24; see also Tertullian's *Prescription Against Heretics* 34). John 13:20 is also firmly rooted in the synoptic tradition (see Matt. 10:40; 18:5; Mark 9:37; Luke 10:16) and is only loosely related to its present context; it may have been introduced to the narrative by association with verse 16. In the current text of FG, these two sayings serve to justify FE's radical ethic: because Jesus laid down his life for the disciples, they should be prepared to die also (see John 15:18ff.; 16:2).

> Amen, amen, I say to you, one of you will betray me. . . . Amen, amen, I say to you, the cock will not crow till you have denied me three times. (John 13:21, 38)

FE is clearly dependent on a broad tradition for these sayings. This tradition was so widely used by the church, however, that direct dependence on one or more of the Synoptics cannot be established. The use of the double-*amen* formula in these sayings is significant, both because their synoptic character is beyond dispute and because the sayings are introduced by "Amen I say to you" in the Synoptics. FE's formula is therefore an adaptation of one that was already fixed in the tradition, apparently the same tradition that underlies the Synoptics at this point. Nevertheless, FE's freedom in adapting such traditional material is evident even in these sayings.

> Amen, amen, I say to you, if you ask anything of the Father, he will
> give it to you in my name. (John 16:23)

In this case, the core of the traditional saying introduced by the "amen,
amen" formula does not appear until the following verse ("ask, and you will
receive" [16:24]), which repeats one element of the synoptic triad, "*Ask, and it
will be given to you*; seek, and you will find; knock, and it will be opened to you"
(Matt. 7:7; Luke 11:9; italics added). There can be little doubt that FE knows
of and is alluding to the same logion that underlies the synoptic saying here.
Here again, FE uses a traditional saying as the basis for Jesus' discourse in the
following verses, which focuses on the theme of "asking in Jesus' name."

> Amen, amen, I say to you, when you were young, you girded yourself
> and walked where you would; but when you are old, you will stretch
> out your hands, and another will gird you and carry you where you do
> not wish to go. (John 21:18)

Although there is considerable debate over the form and interpretation of
the proverb in John 21:18, it appears that here the "amen, amen" formula
introduces a saying that was linked with martyrdom and perhaps a call to discipleship earlier in the tradition. The version of the saying in the present text
of FG seems to have gone through four stages of interpretation and revision,
the second of which is the most speculative: (1) a proverb contrasting the
strength of youth with the helplessness of old age, (2) an interpretation of the
proverb (perhaps by Jesus himself) as a call to use the strength of one's youth
as an opportunity for discipleship, (3) an interpretation of the proverb as an
allusion to one's death (or martyrdom), and (4) the addition of the phrase "you
will stretch out your hands" as a specific allusion to crucifixion.

Conclusion

As the preceding survey has indicated, Lindars's contention that FG's double-
amen formula introduces traditional or authentic sayings of Jesus appears accurate in some instances but cannot be accepted uncritically for all the sayings
under consideration. The strongest case for traditional/authentic words of
Jesus can be made for those "amen, amen" sayings that have clear parallels in
the Synoptics: John 3:3, 5 (// Matt. 18:3); John 6:53 (//Mark 14:22–25); John
8:51 (//Mark 9:1); John 13:16 (//Luke 6:40; Matt. 10:24); John 13:20 (//Matt.
10:40; 18:5; Mark 9:37; Luke 9:48a; 10:16); John 13:21 (//Mark 14:18; Matt.
26:21); John 13:38 (//Mark 14:30; Matt. 26:34; Luke 22:34); and John
16:23–24 (//Matt. 7:7; Luke 11:9). John 12:24 is supported by a possibly inde-

pendent attestation from the Pauline literature, 1 Corinthians 15:36. Two other "amen, amen" sayings, John 1:51 and 10:1–5, contain language or imagery that is clearly rooted in primitive gospel tradition, even though a specific synoptic parallel cannot be identified.

Several of the traditional "amen, amen" sayings are proverbs, metaphors, or parables (John 10:1–5; 12:24; 16:20–24; 21:18). Others contain ambiguous terms and images that are at times interpreted in the ensuing discourse. Several are closely related to references from the Hebrew Bible (John 1:51; 10:1–5; 16:20–24). Several of the traditional sayings function as predictions or prophecies (John 1:51; 13:21; 13:38; 21:18). Others have a legislative quality that makes them comparable to the "sentences of holy law" identified by Ernst Käsemann (John 3:3, 5; 6:47; 6:53; 8:51; 12:24; 13:16; 13:20; see Käsemann 1969, 21). These sayings generally define the conditions of discipleship: believing, entering the kingdom, or receiving eternal life.

As Dodd and Lindars contended, many of the "amen, amen" sayings function as core statements that generate the dialogue or discourse material that follows (John 3:3, 5; 6:53; 10:1–5; 12:24; 13:16; 16:24). In these cases, it appears that FE has cited a traditional saying and then developed a speech of Jesus that functions as a commentary on that saying or an extension of its implications. On the other hand, FE also sometimes presents a speech and then cites the traditional saying at the conclusion (John 1:51; 8:58; 21:18).

While it may be argued that many of FG's "amen, amen" sayings are "traditional" in the sense that FE borrowed them rather than composed them, it is more difficult to specify which of these sayings represent a) authentic words of Jesus, b) sayings traditionally attributed to Jesus, or c) maxims of the Johannine Community. The issue is further complicated by the fact that the categories overlap as obviously authentic sayings of Jesus could have been later accepted by the Johannine Community as maxims that guided community life. Among the sayings discussed in this essay, the following are most likely to have functioned as maxims of the Johannine Community (category "c"): John 3:3, 5; 6:47; 6:53; 8:51; 13:16; 13:20. Inevitably there must have been a close relationship between these maxims and the "sentences of holy law" previously listed, which the community used to identify key issues of ethics and discipleship. While sayings in category "a," authentic Jesus material, are the most difficult to identify, the odds are greater when a particular saying has synoptic or other independent attestation, contains non-Johannine terms, and is metaphorical or proverbial in character. The following "amen, amen" sayings in FG are the best candidates to merit serious consideration for inclusion among the words of Jesus: John 3:3; 10:1–5; 12:24; 13:16; 13:20; 13:38; 21:18.

Study of FG's "amen, amen" sayings exposes the fluidity of the early Christian sayings tradition and reveals some of the contacts between the Johannine

discourses and sayings drawn from earlier tradition. Further study of the trans-
formations of these traditional sayings, and FE's interpretation of them
through the discourses in FG, may eventually help us to understand more
clearly the role of traditional sayings in the life of the Johannine Community.
Are there other formulas or typical constructions that identify groups of sayings that were important in the development of the Johannine discourses?
Eventually a full analysis of the formation and function of the Johannine sayings material will need to be written.

23

The Riddles of Jesus
in the Johannine Dialogues

TOM THATCHER

Johannine source criticism has failed to reveal a substantial body of traditional material behind the discourses of the Fourth Gospel (FG). The most significant attempt appears in Rudolf Bultmann's 1941 commentary, which suggested that FG's discourses were adapted from the *Offenbarungsreden*, a collection of Gnostic speech materials. Despite Bultmann's influence, D. A. Carson's 1978 survey of "the most significant literary source theories" to that date revealed that the *Offenbarungsreden* had all but disappeared from Johannine source criticism (1978, 414–418). Today, Rudolf Schnackenburg's summary of the issue remains the consensus position: "a logia or discourse source [for FG] must be rejected" (1968, 1.167). Many Johannine scholars have concluded that little more can be done to delineate FG's narrative sources and that nothing can be done to identify FG's discourse sources. It is therefore unlikely that source-critical inquiry will expose the traditional base of FG's discourses in the immediate future. The search for a sayings tradition behind FG instead requires an alternate analytical method, and this essay will suggest that the findings of folkloristics can produce interesting results in this area. Traditional form criticism relies heavily on literary parallels as keys to textual history, and therefore focuses on those few Johannine passages that parallel the Synoptics. Folklore research, however, offers guidelines for identifying oral forms when clear literary parallels do not exist. Certain folk forms can be shown to be cross-cultural and ancient, and when such forms can be defined they offer entry points for exploring the traditions behind the discourses of FG.

One such oral form, the riddle, will be explored here. This essay will attempt to demonstrate that riddles were a significant component of the Johannine tradition, and that the riddles of Jesus in FG raise significant implications for the literary structure of that book and for our understanding of the ideological outlook of the Johannine Community. The reader should note that all translations in the analysis that follow are my own.

What Is a Riddle?

Most people have an inherent sense of "what a riddle is" based on their experience of language. More technical definitions, however, are difficult, because the riddle eludes strict definition on the basis of form or style. It is best understood as a language *function* or a rhetorical strategy that manifests itself in different ways in different cultures. Jack and Phyllis Glazier define the riddle succinctly as a verbal challenge that creates purposeful ambiguity between description (the words in the riddle) and referent (the thing to which the words refer) (1976, 211). A statement is "ambiguous" when it can reasonably refer to more than one thing at once and the listener cannot determine which is correct. For example, if a person is ordering food in a cafeteria and says, "Give me some of that," when there are several food items available, the server may not be able to identify the item to which the word "that" refers. The statement would therefore be ambiguous, requiring further clarification. Ambiguity alone, however, does not make a statement a riddle, for human language is imperfect and people often say or write things that are accidentally unclear. The example above would represent such accidental ambiguity, for the person placing the cafeteria order presumably intended to refer to one specific item but did not indicate the selection clearly enough. In order for an ambiguous statement to be classified as a "riddle," two further criteria must be met. First, the speaker must make the ambiguous statement *intentionally*, for the express purpose of confusing the listener. Second, the intentionally ambiguous statement must *seek an answer*. The speaker offers a challenge to her audience, asking that the listener figure out what she is describing. Riddles use common language to describe common things in an uncommon way. They are unique in that normal language avoids confusion, while riddles hide their referents through intentional confusion.

The principle of intentional ambiguity may be seen in the following riddles. These riddles also illustrate other relevant aspects of cross-cultural riddle performance, and all have been discussed in folklore studies of the subject.

    1. *Question:* What's black and white and red all over?
    Answer: A newspaper, or a sunburned zebra.

2. *Question:* What goes on four legs in the morning, two legs in the afternoon, three legs in the evening?
Answer: A human being. The four legs represent a baby crawling; the two legs an adult walking upright; the three legs represent an elderly person walking with a cane.
3. *Question:* What room can't be entered?
Answer: A mushroom.
4. *Question:* Would you rather have a lion kill you or a gorilla?
Answer: I would rather have the lion kill the gorilla than kill me.
5. *Question:* What grows without roots?
Answer: A woman.
6. *Question:* One pig, two snouts.
Answer: A double-bladed plough.
7. *Question:* There is something with a heart in its head.
Answer: A cherry or a peach.
8. *Question:* Humpty Dumpty sat on a wall, Humpty Dumpty had a great fall. All the king's horses and all the king's men, couldn't put Humpty together again.
Answer: Humpty Dumpty is an egg.
9. *Question:* Thirty white horses on a red hill. First they champ, then they stamp, then they stand still.
Answer: Your teeth.
10. *Question:* A box without hinges, key, or lid, yet golden treasure inside is hid.
Answer: An egg.

These sample riddles illustrate a number of important principles. First, contemporary Western riddles generally take the form of questions. But as examples 6–10 indicate, riddles can appear in many different forms in various cultures and eras, from short, formulaic statements to complex literary constructions. Many riddles do not take the form of questions even when they expect an answer (see Pepicello and Green 1979, 16–17; Maranda 1971, 54). Such is the case with almost all of the riddles that appear in FG. Second, modern Western riddles are used almost exclusively in jokes, nursery rhymes, the Sunday comics page, or other forms of entertainment. Most of the sample riddles listed fit this category. Many cultures use riddles, however, in more serious contexts, such as greetings, initiatory rituals, courtship, weddings, wakes, and educational settings in which students are expected to provide memorized answers to the teacher's obscure questions. Third, some riddles are embedded in a larger narrative, such as numbers 9 and 10. Both are taken from J. R. R. Tolkien's *The Hobbit*.

A fourth and final principle is especially relevant to this study. Most Western riddles observe the "criterion of solvability," the unstated rule that the answer to a riddle must be somehow logically deducible from the question itself. In many cases, however, the correct answer to a riddle can only be provided by those with special cultural or esoteric knowledge. Edgar Slotkin notes that

> we find comparatively few riddles that are solvable on any rational
> ground. That is, few so-called "true" riddles admit to logical solutions
> where one and only one answer satisfies the riddle topic [i.e., where
> only one answer is logically correct]. . . . Some riddles are solvable in
> that they depend on general or sometimes . . . arcane cultural knowl-
> edge. . . . [M]ost riddles depend for their solution either on inspired
> guessing or simply knowing the riddle—which is to say, knowing tra-
> ditions. (Slotkin 1990, 154).

Riddles 5 and 6, for example, derive from Finland. The first can be answered
only by those who know the riddle, as the statement "grows without roots" can
refer to millions of possible subjects, and the correct answer, "a woman," is
certainly not the most obvious. The second, riddle 6, can only be answered by
those who are familiar with pigs and the Finnish double-bladed plough. Riddle 2, the riddle of the Sphinx, depends on the motif that human life can be
represented metaphorically by the stages of the day or seasons of the year.
Obviously, those whose cultural experience has not provided such information
could not possibly hope to provide the correct answer. "Those who are outsiders to a particular society and do not partake in the common experiences
and do not form symbols from the same substance [as that society], would not
be able to relate to these riddles in any meaningful way" (Ben-Amos 1976,
253).

The fact that riddles require special knowledge for their resolution makes
them especially useful for establishing cultural boundaries. To resolve the
ambiguity posed by the riddle and offer the correct answer, the audience must
organize possible answers "based on the taxonomic principles the riddle
offers." "Taxonomy" here refers to the organization of information in a person's worldview. Riddles do not describe things in a way that supports conventional worldviews, and therefore require their audience to look at things,
or the relationships between them, in a different way (Ben-Amos 1976, p. 252).
Riddles require, in other words, a particular type of logic as well as special
information. Social groups often use riddles that seem to suggest blasphemous
or obscene answers in order to "explore ambiguous and disturbing aspects of
life which are potentially destructive of community values." To ensure that the
audience understands that the riddle is not intended to give offense, riddle performance is usually carefully regulated in specific social contexts. In these contexts, or game environments, both the riddler and the audience understand
from specific social cues that statements are intentionally ambiguous and that
an answer is expected. Such game environments range from complex rituals to
informal gatherings around the coffee machine at work and jokes and puzzles
in the Sunday newspaper. These "riddling sessions" function as group labora-
tories for testing and rejecting that which violates natural and cultural rules.

Incorrect answers will generally violate group norms, while "correct" answers to riddles will generally advocate the group's norms and beliefs. "Riddles play with boundaries, but ultimately to affirm them" (Maranda 1976, 131).

In summary, two points are critical to the present essay: 1) a "riddle" is any statement that is *intentionally ambiguous* and that *challenges the audience* to resolve this ambiguity, and 2) riddles can be answered only by those who possess *special group knowledge and systems of logic*.

Riddles in Written Texts

As noted, riddles sometimes appear embedded in larger texts, such as narratives. To identify riddles in a narrative such as FG, criteria must be established to determine which sayings are intentionally ambiguous. Four such criteria will be used here. First, *the narrator may directly inform the audience* in an aside that a particular character is using language that could be understood in more than one way. An obvious case occurs at John 10:6, where FE indicates that Jesus has just spoken a *paroimia* ("riddle," "proverb"—namely, in verses 1–5) that the crowd did not understand. Less explicitly, at John 2:19–21 Jesus urges the Jews to "destroy this temple," which he will raise in three days. Since Jesus is standing in the Temple courts, the Jews assume that his words refer to the buildings of the Temple complex. "But," the narrator tells us, "he spoke of the temple of his body." In these cases, the reader is simply told that riddles are in use.

Second, *a character may introduce discourse with the type of framing signal one might expect with a "real world" riddle*. In this case, the author situates the story in a setting that the reader would recognize as a context for riddle performance. To take an example from the Hebrew Bible, Samson's riddle about the "sweet eater" opens with a formula that explicitly informs the Philistines that he is about to propose a puzzle:

> Samson said to them [the wedding guests], "Let me now put a riddle to you. If you can explain it to me within the seven days of the feast, and find it out, then I will give you thirty linen garments and thirty festal garments. But if you cannot explain it to me, then you shall give me thirty linen garments and thirty festal garments." So they said to him, "Ask your riddle; let us hear it." He said to them, "Out of the eater came something to eat. Out of the strong came something sweet." But for three days they could not explain the riddle. (Judg. 14:12–14)

Because riddles are performed during wedding festivals in many cultures and because Samson explicitly says, "Let me now put a riddle to you," the reader of Judges can scarcely miss the fact that the statement he puts forward is a riddle.

In other cases, the riddle setting may be signaled less explicitly by the context of the remark. For an example from FG, when the disciples ask Jesus if a man has been born blind because of his own sin or the sin of his parents (John 9:2), the overall setting of the question is a theological discussion between a rabbi and his followers. The context and the wording of the question suggest that one of the proposed answers must be right and that it is difficult to determine which. In all these cases, the setting of the riddle in the story somehow corresponds to the type of setting in which the reader would experience riddles in the real world.

As a third criterion, *the characters in the story to whom a statement is made may respond in a way which indicates that the statement is ambiguous*. For example, at John 7:33 Jesus tells the Jews that he is going away to a place where they cannot come. Their response indicates that this statement could refer to several ideas, and so it creates confusion (7:35–36). When the same riddle is posed again at 8:21, the Jews speculate that Jesus may even be speaking of suicide. In these cases, the audience highlights the fact that the riddler's words can reasonably refer to more than one thing.

As a fourth criterion, *some statements are ambiguous because they seem to require answers that the listener would consider impossible*. Such riddles ask the audience to go beyond the bounds of normal logic. At John 6:51, for example, Jesus informs the Jews that the bread that has come down from heaven to provide life for the world is his flesh, which they must eat. The Jews respond with the obvious question, "How can this man give us his flesh to eat?" (v. 52). At 7:23, Jesus defends himself by asking, "If a man receives circumcision on the sabbath in order that the law of Moses may not be broken, are you angry with me because I healed a man's whole body on the sabbath?" This question challenges the Jews' normal way of thinking by suggesting that the laws of circumcision and the sabbath laws are somehow inconsistent, a problem they cannot resolve. This fourth criterion, apparent impossibility, requires some degree of investigation into the worldview of the intended original reader of the narrative, in this case the original audience of FG, in order to see what aspects of their worldview may be challenged by the riddle.

Riddles and Riddling Sessions in John

Applying these four criteria to the dialogue sections of FG, the sayings in Table 23.1 may be labeled "riddles." The "criteria" column indicates which of the above criteria four identifies the saying in question as a riddle. The "riddler" is the person who proposes the riddle, and the "riddlee" is the immediate audience of the riddle, the character who is challenged to answer it. Note that all citations in the "text" column are my translation.

Table 23.1

Riddles in FG

Verses	Text	Criteria	Riddler/Riddlee
1:15	"The one coming behind me became ahead of me because he was before me"	4	John the Baptist/?
2:4b	"My hour has not yet come"	3	Jesus/Mary
2:16	"Do not make my father's house a house of merchandise"	1, 3	Jesus/the Jews
2:19	"Destroy this temple and in three days I will raise it"	1, 3	Jesus/the Jews
3:3, 5	"Unless you are born [anōthen/of water and spirit] you cannot see the Kingdom of God"	2, 3	Jesus/Nicodemus
4:7, 10	"Give me a drink"	2, 3	Jesus/Samaritan
4:20	"Our fathers worshiped on this mountain, and you [Jews] say that in Jerusalem is the place where it is necessary to worship"	4	Samaritan/Jesus
4:32	"I have food to eat that you don't know about"	2, 3	Jesus/the Disciples
6:5	"Where will we buy bread?"	1, 3	Jesus/Philip
6:32	"Moses did not give you the bread from heaven; rather, my father gave you the true bread from heaven"	2, 3	Jesus/the Jews
6:51	"This bread I will give for the life of the world is my flesh"	2, 3, 4	Jesus/the Jews
7:23	"If a man receives circumcision on Sabbath so that the Law of Moses would not be broken, are you angry with me because I made a whole man healthy on the Sabbath?"	4	Jesus/the Jews
7:34; 8:21; 13:33	"Where I am going you cannot come"	3	Jesus/the Jews; Jesus/the Disciples
7:37–38	"If anyone is thirsty let her come to me, and let the one who believes in me drink"	1	Jesus/?
8:4–5	"We caught this woman in adultery, in the very act. In the Law of Moses it says to stone such a woman. What do you say?"	2	Pharisees/Jesus
8:18	"I witness on behalf of myself and the father who sent me witnesses"	3	Jesus/the Jews
8:24	"Unless you believe that I am, you will die in your sins"	3, 4	Jesus/the Jews
8:26	"What I heard from the one who sent me I speak in the world"	1	Jesus/the Jews

Table 23.1 (*continued*)

Verses	Text	Criteria	Riddler/Riddlee
8:31–32	"If you abide in my word, you are truly my disciples, and [then] you will know the truth, and the truth will set you free"	2, 3	Jesus/the Jews
8:38	"I speak what I have seen with the father, and you also should do what you heard with your father"	2, 3	Jesus/the Jews
8:51	"Should anyone keep my word, they will not see death unto eternity"	3, 4	Jesus/the Jews
8:56	"Abraham your father rejoiced to see my day, and he saw it and was glad"	2, 3, 4	Jesus/the Jews
9:2	"Who sinned, this man or his parents, that he should be born blind?"	2, 4	the Disciples/Jesus
9:39	"For judgment I came into this world, so that those not seeing would see and those seeing would become blind"	2, 3, 4	Jesus/the Pharisees
10:1–5	The Parable of the Shepherd and the Strangers	1, 2	Jesus/the Jews
10:34–36	"Is it not written in your law, 'I said, You are gods'? If God said this to those to whom the word of God came, and the scripture cannot be broken, how can you say to the one whom the father sanctified and sent into the world, 'You blaspheme,' because I said, 'I am a son of God'?"	4	Jesus/the Jews
11:11	"Our friend Lazarus is asleep"	1, 2, 3	Jesus/the Disciples
11:23	"Your brother will rise again"	3	Jesus/Martha
11:25–26	"The one who believes in me will live even if they die, and anyone who lives and believes in me will not die unto eternity"	3, 4	Jesus/Martha
12:32	"Should I be lifted up from the earth, I will draw all people to myself"	1, 3	Jesus/the crowd
13:10	"You are clean, but not all of you"	1	Jesus/the Disciples
13:21	"One of you will betray me"	2, 3	Jesus/the Disciples
14:4	"You know the way where I am going"	2, 3	Jesus/the Disciples
14:7	"Now you know him [the father] and have seen him"	2, 3	Jesus/the Disciples

Table 23.1 (*continued*)

Verses	Text	Criteria	Riddler/Riddlee
14:19	"A little while and the world will no longer see me, but you will see me"	2, 3	Jesus/the Disciples
16:16	"A little while and you will no longer see me, and again a little while and you will see me"	2, 3	Jesus/the Disciples
21:18	"When you were younger you girded yourself and went about where you wished, but when you grow old you will stretch out your hands and another will dress you and lead you where you do not want to go"	1	Jesus/Peter
21:22	"Should I desire for him [the Beloved Disciple] to remain until I come, what is that to you?"	1	Jesus/Peter

As Table 23.1 indicates, these four criteria reveal thirty-eight riddles in the present text of FG, three of which appear in more than one saying. Of course, this list may not be exhaustive. Other large sections of FG in which Jesus speaks of his identity and mission, such as chapters 5 and 15, may include statements that FE understood to be riddles but that cannot be identified by the criteria utilized here.

The recognition that the sayings in Table 23.1 are riddles does not necessarily suggest that they represent a primitive tradition and certainly does not suggest that they are authentic to Jesus. What the table does suggest is that the Johannine discourses contain many sayings that may be identified as a widely used oral form, the riddle. This being the case, FE must have been relatively familiar with oral riddles and riddling sessions and therefore probably used some of these sayings orally before their incorporation into the Fourth Gospel. If this is the case, one may speak of a broad oral sayings tradition behind FG's discourses.

This conclusion is strengthened by the fact that the riddles of FG are portrayed in the social contexts in which riddles are typically delivered in oral cultures, that is, in dialogues between Jesus and other characters. As Table 23.1 indicates, two-thirds of Jesus' riddles appear in the major dialogues—at John 2:16–19 (two riddles), 3:1–15 (two riddles), 4:7–15 (two riddles), 6:26–52 (two riddles), 8:21–59 (eight riddles), and 13:10–16:25 (six riddles). The narrative

structure of these dialogues suggests that FE intends to portray them as "riddling sessions," social contexts in which riddles are posed and answered. The
"rules" of FG's riddling sessions are reflected in a consistent underlying narrative pattern. Each time Jesus poses a riddle the person to whom he is speaking becomes confused. Jesus then provides his own, often elaborate, answer.
The answer may introduce another riddle, which again confuses the audience,
and which Jesus again answers. The frequency and extent of this narrative pattern, and the fact that the riddling session is an almost universal cross-cultural
phenomenon, suggest that Jesus' dialogues were sometimes portrayed as riddling sessions in the Johannine oral tradition.

Jesus' dialogue with the Pharisees at John 8:12–29 offers a convenient illustration of a Johannine riddling session.

> *Riddle 1:* "The Father who sent me witnesses about me" (8:18).
> *Confusion:* "Who is your father?" (8:19a).
> *Answer 1:* "You do not know me nor my Father . . ." (8:19bc).
>
> *Riddle 2:* "Where I am going you cannot come" (8:21).
> *Confusion:* "He will not kill himself, will he?" (8:22).
> *Answer 2:* "You are from below, I am from above . . ." (8:23).
>
> *Riddle 3:* "Unless you believe I am, you will die in your sins" (8:24).
> *Confusion:* "Who are you?" (8:25a).
> *Answer 3:* "What have I said from the beginning?" (8:25–26).
>
> *Riddle 4:* "What I heard from the one who sent me I speak in the world"
>   (8:26c).
> *Confusion:* Narrator: "They did not know he spoke about the Father" (8:27).
> *Answer 4:* "When you have lifted up the Son of Man, then you will know that
>   I am . . ." (8:28–29).

The concluding "I Am" saying is presumably a definitive answer to the over-
all exchange up to that point. FG's "I Am" sayings frequently appear within
Jesus' answers to his own riddles, including both the metaphorical—"I Am the
Bread of Life" (6:35, 48, 51); "I Am the Door of the Sheep" (10:7, 9); "I Am
the Good Shepherd" (10:11, 14); "I Am the Resurrection and the Life" (11:25);
"I Am the Way, the Truth, and the Life" (14:6)—and several unpredicated "I
Am" sayings (8:24; 8:28; 8:58). The close association of these sayings with the
riddling sessions suggests that "I Am" sayings were also traditional units in the
Johannine oral archive. This is not to suggest that the present linguistic units
of FG necessarily existed before the composition of that book. It does, however, suggest that the inclusion of "I Am" sayings in the portrayal of Jesus'
answers to his own riddles is characteristic of the Johannine tradition.

Implications: Composition and Community

The prevalence of riddles and riddling sessions in the Johannine tradition has two broad implications for the study of FG. The first relates to the composition of the long speeches of Jesus in FG; the second relates to the social context in which FG was composed.

Riddles and FG's Composition

The prevalence of FG's riddling sessions warns against exegetical approaches that depend on discontinuity in the speeches of Jesus. As riddling sessions, the dialogues evidence a high degree of rhetorical unity, suggesting a careful and conscious composition strategy. The extent and frequency of this narrative pattern suggest that the present version of the major Johannine dialogues, including much of the Farewell (John 13–16), are unified compositions. This observation can have negative implications for a source-critical approach to the dialogues.

As an example of these implications, one may compare a source-critical approach to John 8:12–58, the "Light of the World" discourse, with the reading offered here. The compositional problems associated with this passage are highlighted by Raymond Brown in his Anchor Bible Commentary. Brown notes that 8:21 ("Again he said to them . . .") and 8:31 ("Then Jesus said to the Jews who had believed him . . .") create natural breaks in the discourse by renaming Jesus' audience, but the sequence within each subsection is "far from simple" and often involves "doublets of other discourses." Doublets and parallels with other speeches in the first subsection, 8:12–20, lead Brown to conclude that this passage "is a composite and must have had a complicated literary history before it took its present form." The same is the case with the second subsection, 8:21–30. Parallels between 8:21–22 and 7:33–36 lead Brown to ask, "Can there be any doubt that John has preserved two different forms of the same [traditional] scene?" The genitive absolute at 8:30 ("as he was saying these things, many believed on him") is rare for John, and Brown concludes that it must be "an editor's device." Once this verse was added to "break up the discourse" into "more tractable units," Brown continues, it became necessary to rename Jesus' audience before the speech continued. This was achieved by the composer of 8:31, perhaps "the final redactor" of FG, who made the "believing Jews" of 8:30 the audience of Jesus' subsequent remarks. This person was apparently unaware that "believing Jews" are an oxymoron for John. The same editor may be responsible for the insertion of 8:35, "the slave does not have a permanent place in the household; the son has a place there forever," which Brown believes is "a once independent saying from the Johannine tradition" (all references and quotes from Brown 1966, 1.339–368).

In Brown's view, which is typical of this approach, John 8:12–58 is rife with structural problems that indicate a complex compositional history.

By contrast, the problems Brown highlights disappear when the Light Discourse is understood as a Johannine riddling session. The first two subsections, John 8:12–20 and 8:21–30, which Brown views as particularly problematic, actually follow a clear and coherent outline. All the riddles in this session explore aspects of Jesus' identity, which explains the repetition of themes that Brown detects within the subsections of the dialogue. The passage may be outlined as follows (my translation):

Riddle 1: "I witness on behalf of myself and the father who sent me witnesses" (8:18).
Confusion: "Where is your father?" (8:19).
Answer: "You know neither me nor my father . . . " (8:19).

Riddle 2: "Where I am going you cannot come" (8:21).
Confusion: "He will not kill himself, will he?" (8:22).
Answer: "You are from below, but I am from above. You are from this world, but I am not from this world . . ." (8:23).

Riddle 3: "Unless you believe that I Am, you will die in your sins" (8:24).
Confusion: "Who are you?" (8:25).
No Answer: "What have I said from the first?" (8:25–26).

Riddle 4: "What I heard from the one who sent me I speak in the world" (8:26).
Confusion: Narrator—"They did not realize that he was speaking to them about the Father" (8:27).
Answer: "When you lift up the Son of Man, then you will know that I am. . . . The one who sent me is with me. He will not leave me alone, because I always do what pleases him" (8:28–29).

Riddle 5: "If you abide in my word, you are truly my disciples, and [then] you will know the truth, and the truth will set you free" (8:31–32).
Confusion: "We are Abraham's seed and have never been enslaved to anyone" (8:33).
Answer: "Everyone who does sin is a slave of sin. . . . Should anyone be set free by the son, they are truly free. I know you are Abraham's seed, but rather you seek to kill me . . ." (8:34–37).

Riddle 6: "I speak what I have seen with the father, and you also should do what you heard with your father" (8:38, 41).
Confusion: "Our father is Abraham. . . . We were not born of fornication. We have one father, God" (8:39, 41).
Answer: "If you are children of Abraham, you would do the works of Abraham. But now you seek to kill me, a man who has spoken the truth to you which he heard from God. This Abraham did not do. . . . If God were

your father, you would love me. . . . You are of your father the devil"
(8:39–40, 42–47).

Riddle 7: "Should anyone keep my word, they will not see death unto eternity" (8:51).
Confusion: "Abraham died, and the prophets, and now you say, 'Should anyone keep my word, they will not taste death unto eternity'? You are not greater than our father Abraham who died, are you? . . . What do you make yourself?" (8:52–53).
Answer: "Should I glorify myself, my glory is nothing. It is my father who glorifies me, whom you say is your God. . . . I know him and keep his word" (8:54–55).

Riddle 8: "Abraham your father rejoiced to see my day, and he saw it and was glad" (8:56).
Confusion: "You are not fifty years old, and you have seen Abraham?" (8:57).
Answer: "Before Abraham was, I am" (8:58).

In light of this overall structural unity, evident from an oral model of composition, there is no reason to conclude that this passage is the product of a complex redactional process.

Riddles and the Johannine Community

The Nicodemus episode (John 3:1–15) illustrates a significant feature of FG's riddling sessions.

Riddle 1: "Unless one is born *anōthen*, one cannot see the kingdom of God" (3:3).
Confusion: "How can a person be born when they are old?" (3:4).
No Answer

Riddle 2: "Unless one is born of water and spirit one cannot enter the kingdom" (3:5–8).
Confusion: "How can these things be?" (3:9).
Answer: "We speak what we know . . . the Son of Man must be lifted up" (3:10–15).

The Greek term *anōthen* is intentionally ambiguous, as it can reasonably mean either "again" or "from above." Nicodemus chooses the former, but the correct answer is "from above," which here establishes the difference between "born of flesh" and "born of spirit." But one must question whether Nicodemus could possibly be aware of this nuanced usage of *anōthen* to be able to answer the riddle correctly. It is also doubtful that Nicodemus could understand Jesus' elaborate answer (John 3:11–21). The same appears to be the case in the riddle of the "Good Shepherd" (John 10:1–18). Jesus' brief encounter with the

Pharisees after the healing of the blind man leads him to discourse on various aspects of the livestock industry at John 10:1–5. FE, however, informs FG's audience at 10:6 that Jesus has spoken a *paroimia*, a riddle, which the Jews (10:19) cannot interpret. But if the Jews were confused by 10:1–5, it is difficult to imagine how they could understand anything Jesus offers as the "answer" to the riddle at 10:7–18, a discourse that includes two "I Am" sayings (10:7, 9, 11, 14). The consistent confusion of Jesus' dialogue partners and the complexity of his "explanations" create the impression that it is impossible for his audiences to understand him.

The solution to this problem (i.e., that Jesus' answers are just as ambiguous as his questions), lies in the nature of the special knowledge that Jesus' riddles presuppose. Within the narrative world of FG, Jesus' riddles do not meet the "criterion of solvability" (i.e., the answers cannot be deduced logically from the questions) because they presuppose a belief that Jesus is "from the Father" (John 1:14; 13:1–3) and speaks the words of God (8:37–38). On several occasions Jesus directly informs his opponents that they cannot understand his riddles because they lack this information. Nicodemus, for example, cannot answer riddles that concern "heavenly things" because he is "earthly" (3:12), and at 8:23 Jesus frankly warns the Jews that they are doomed to lose the riddling contest because "you are from below, but I am from above; you are from this world, but I am not from this world." For this reason, although every interaction between the Johannine Jesus and the Jews or Pharisees involves riddling, the Jews are never able to comprehend his words. Surprisingly, this special group knowledge is also hidden from Jesus' disciples, who are also asked to answer riddles on numerous occasions (4:32; 6:5; 11:11, 23; 13:33, 36; 14:4, 7, 21; 16:16) but are no more successful than his enemies. Jesus' riddles cannot be solved by anyone at any point during his earthly ministry.

This situation changes at John 16:25–30, where FE draws a boundary between the Jews and Jesus' disciples. Jesus there admits that "I have spoken to you in riddles," but promises that an hour is coming when he will discuss the Father with them *parrēsia*, "plainly" (16:25). The same terminology is used at 11:14 to introduce Jesus' answer to the Lazarus riddle. "Plain" speech in FG contrasts with Jesus' typical riddling discourse and implies the revelation of an answer to Jesus' enigmatic questions. Jesus explains at 16:26–27 that the disciples will receive this special revelation because of their love for Jesus and their faith. He then reveals that he has come into the world from the Father and is now leaving the world to return to the Father (16:28). This remark is a turning point for the disciples, who affirm Jesus' words by saying that he indeed has spoken "plainly" (*parrēsia*) to them "and you speak riddles to us no longer" (16:29). By 16:30 they have come to understand the full mystery of Jesus' person: "we believe that you have come from God." Belief in this revelation obviously distinguishes the disciples, those who know that Jesus has come from God, from the Jews, who cannot understand Jesus' riddles because they do not recognize who he is.

The boundary created by John 16:30 between Jew and disciple extends beyond the story world. FE's own audience differs from Jesus' audience, whether Jews or disciples, in that they possess the hermeneutical key to the underlying logic of all of Jesus' riddles, his descent and ascent. His words are therefore always plain to FE's audience, a later community that recognizes Jesus as the divine Word of the Prologue. FE assumes this prerequisite knowledge at several points when answering Jesus' riddles in asides. Jesus' first riddle, the riddle of the Temple, was incomprehensible to the disciples until after the resurrection (2:22), an event the audience of FG is clearly aware of already. At 7:39 FE says that the true referent of the "water" riddles became evident only after Jesus' "glorification" and the giving of the Spirit. Those not possessing this hermeneutical key, unbelievers, remain locked in the story world of FG, forever unable to understand Jesus' self-revelatory riddles and damned by their ignorance (1:10–12).

As a social device, knowledge of the correct answers to Jesus' riddles separates FE's audience from Jesus' vanquished enemies within the story and places them in a privileged position. Groups often use riddles in this way to distinguish members by what they know, even when the acquisition of such knowledge relies on group membership rather than individual skill or intelligence. The various characters who encounter Jesus in FG are confused because they seek to comprehend Jesus' words through conventional channels of logic. The logic of Jesus' discourse, however, is a special group logic. The correct answers depend on group knowledge about Jesus' identity; the whole affair remains a mystery to the Jews. Inasmuch as riddles manipulate ideological boundaries ultimately to affirm them, FE uses the riddles of Jesus to affirm the boundary between his subgroup and non-Christian Judaism.

In conclusion, the following points may be stressed in light of the preceding observations. A folkloristic approach to the problem of identifying traditional materials uncovers the presence of a substantial body of riddles in the dialogues of FG. The number and distribution of these units, and the fact that riddles are a widely attested oral form, suggest that at least some of these sayings circulated orally in Johannine circles before FG was written. The fact that these riddles are frequently situated in riddling sessions, the typical environment for riddle performance in oral cultures, suggests that some of FG's larger dialogues may have also circulated orally in a form similar to their form in the current text of FG. If this is the case, it is likely that the Johannine dialogues possess a higher compositional unity than is typically supposed, and further likely that these dialogues emerged from a community seeking to establish its boundaries on the basis of common knowledge.

Part 3

The Fourth Gospel
and Noncanonical Literature

The discoveries of the Dead Sea Scrolls and the Nag Hammadi Library have had a dramatic impact on New Testament studies in the last fifty years. Alongside the research into these new materials, biblical scholars have developed much more refined and nuanced understandings of Q, the hypothetical sayings collection that most believe was a source for the discourse material in the Synoptics. These advances have added depth to our understanding of the background and diversity of early Christian thought and have broadened our perspective on the canonical gospels as sources of information about Jesus. Comparison with the noncanonical materials has highlighted the ways in which Matthew, Mark, and Luke interpreted Jesus for their own purposes. At the same time, certain noncanonical gospels, particularly Q, Thomas, and Peter, are believed by many to contain information about Jesus that is more primitive than that found in the New Testament.

But somehow this wave of interest in the noncanonical writings has left John high and dry. The huge amount of effort to compare the content and ideology of the noncanonical gospels with the New Testament has been focused almost entirely on the Synoptics. The reasons for this preference lie partly in the history of New Testament scholarship. Q, generally considered the earliest written gospel now available, has always been associated with the Synoptics, and very few direct parallels exist between John's discourses and Q materials. The gospel of Thomas, on the other hand, was closely associated with FG in the 1950s and 1960s, under the assumptions that Thomas's second-century "Gnostic" perspective was a further evolution of FE's theology and that some of Thomas's core metaphors and content were drawn from John. More recently, the trend has been to approach the relationship between Thomas and the canonical gospels synchronically, treating Thomas's use of Jesus material as a distinct parallel development to that found in the Synoptics and Q. But the Fourth Gospel has never really come back into the equation, despite the fact that John is, in many ways, more similar to Thomas, Peter, and Q than any of these gospels are to Matthew, Mark, and Luke.

The essays in Part 3 attempt to correct this imbalance by considering similarities and differences between the presentation of Jesus in FG and in noncanonical materials. The authors of these articles do not assume that Q, Thomas, or Peter borrowed material from FG or vice versa, although some do comment on the possibility of dependence. Rather, they treat FG, Q, and other noncanonical materials as parallel developments in distinct strains of early Christian thought. The overarching concern is the way in which the authors of these noncanonical documents have interpreted Jesus and how this informs our understanding of the way John has interpreted Jesus.

24

The Fourth Gospel and Q

CHRISTOPHER M. TUCKETT

The possibility that the Fourth Evangelist (FE) might have known and used one or more of the Synoptic Gospels as sources is a frequently discussed question. The older consensus view that the Fourth Gospel (FG) was entirely independent of the Synoptics has been challenged in recent years (cf. many of the essays in Denaux 1992). Although the reopening of the question has led to a valuable reexamination of these older presuppositions, not all have been convinced by the recent attempts to show FG's dependence on the Synoptics (see the survey in D. M. Smith 1992). At the same time, no one can deny that there must be some kind of relationship between at least parts of the Johannine tradition and parts of the synoptic tradition. Clearly some elements are held in common, for example, the stories of the feeding of the five thousand, the anointing of Jesus, the triumphal entry, and parts of the passion narrative. At the very least, it would appear that there must have been some links between the Johannine and synoptic strands of Jesus tradition at some stage.

It is perhaps surprising that, in the general debate, the possibility has only rarely been canvassed that FG might in some way be related to one of the possible *sources* lying behind the Synoptic Gospels. In one way, this silence is understandable as, for the most part, the precise identification of possible presynoptic sources is a hazardous undertaking. However, there is one presynoptic source whose existence has commanded fairly widespread assent, the so-called sayings source Q lying behind Matthew and Luke. Could there then be any relationship between FG and Q? That question will form the focus of this essay.

Before trying to answer such a question, we should perhaps first define our terms. What do we mean by "FG," or by "Q," in this context? For the purposes of this essay, the terms "FG" and "Q" will refer to the final forms of both texts concerned, though I am fully aware that this assumption begs a number of important questions. I shall not raise the issue of whether or how the present text of FG could or should be divided into tradition and redaction. Thus I shall assume that "FG" refers to the Gospel of John as we have it. (The status of John 7:53–8:11 and John 21 will not be discussed here as there is clearly no possible relationship with Q material in these sections.) I shall be more concerned with the question of where the links between Johannine and synoptic tradition can be located than with the precise composition history of FG.

The same question of tradition and redaction arises in the case of Q. Recent scholarship has been characterized by a readiness to apply a redaction-critical approach to Q, at least in attempting to identify distinctive and characteristic features of the Q material. There has also been strong support for the theory that Q went through a process of steady "growth," so that one should think of stages in the development of Q: from Q^1 to Q^2 to Q^3 (cf. Kloppenborg 1987). For the purposes of this essay, I shall assume that the Q material—roughly the material shared by Matthew and Luke that has not been derived from Mark—did exist in a unified, probably written, form as a Greek text prior to its incorporation into Matthew and Luke. As a corollary, I also assume Markan priority, that Matthew and Luke both used the Gospel of Mark as one of their sources (for further discussion see Tuckett 1996). I am also convinced that the Q material does exhibit a number of distinctive and characteristic features. Hence, it is appropriate to speak of a "Q theology" and perhaps even of a "Q Community," or at least of a group of followers of Jesus who found the contents of Q congenial and reflective of their own ideas. Further, the form of Q as used by Matthew and Luke seems to show the results of an editing process, so that it makes sense to talk of a Q redactor or Q editor. However, I remain less convinced that the available evidence allows us to identify precisely earlier stages in the growth of Q. Thus, I would prefer to think of a more general body of "Q tradition" that has been taken up and used by a Q editor or redactor to produce the version of Q that seems to have been used by both Matthew and Luke. The question before us, then, is whether "Q" in this sense could have been available to FE.

It is not surprising that the question of a possible relationship between FG and Q has not often been raised in the past. This is perhaps due primarily to the fact that, where scholars have identified possible links between FG and the Synoptics, these links have rarely involved Q material on the synoptic side. In fact, there are very few obvious links between FG and Q. There has been a large amount of study of the nature of the relationship between FG and the

Synoptics in the passion narratives, but Q apparently did not have (or certainly cannot be shown to have had) a passion narrative. Other notable links between FG and the Synoptics involve the stories of the feeding of the five thousand, the walking on water, the triumphal entry, and the anointing of Jesus, none of which derive from Q. Links between FG and Q seem to be confined to the story of the centurion's/nobleman's servant/son (John 4); the "Johannine thunderbolt" of Q 10:21–22; and possible parallels between isolated sayings—Q 10:16 (cf. John 5:23), Q 11:9–10 (cf. John 16:23–24), and a possible "anti-parallel" to Q 10:23–24 in John 20:29 (note that all references to Q in this essay use Luke's versification). Each of these possible parallels will be discussed below in order to determine whether FE may have used Q as a source.

Q 7:1–10//John 4:46–54

The story of the healing of the centurion's/nobleman's son has been extensively analyzed in debates about the relationship between FG and the Synoptics. For the most part, the question has been whether FG, or a pre-Johannine stage of the tradition, presupposes the finished Gospels of Matthew and/or Luke. Attention has therefore been focused on possible elements of Matthean or Lukan redaction that reappear in FE's version, under the assumption that, if such elements could be identified, they would indicate that FG's story must be based on Matthew and/or Luke. In other words, if FG's story includes a detail that was added to the original story by Matthew or Luke, FE must have been copying the story from one of these two Gospels.

The identification of Matthean/Lukan redactional elements in Q material is inevitably less certain than in the case of Markan material in Matthew or Luke, simply because we do not have the original Q account to compare with each synoptic version. Thus, any reconstruction of Q will be uncertain, with corresponding uncertainty about possible changes made to Q by Matthew or Luke. The most likely candidates for synoptic redactional elements that reappear in FG may be the note that the child is "about to die" (Luke 7:2; cf. John 4:47) and the note that the boy recovered at the very hour that Jesus spoke (Matt. 8:13; cf. John 4:50–53; cp. the Matthean redaction of Mark at Matt. 9:22; 15:28; 17:18). But neither of these is fully convincing. While Matthew's reference to the "hour" at the end of the story does correspond to similar redactional references elsewhere in his gospel, Matthew is clearly capable of taking up an element of his source material and repeating it (cf. the references to "weeping and gnashing of teeth" in Matt. 8:12; 13:42, 50; 22:13; 24:51; 25:30, probably taking up a single Q reference in Q 13:28 and repeating it). The same may therefore have happened here, with Matthew taking up the Q version at this point.

Luke's note about the boy being "about to die" has been seen as a secondary development of the source, heightening the scale of the miracle. One could argue that the similar note in John 4:47 is due to FE himself, redacting the material in a similar way independently: certainly it is a feature of the Johannine miracle stories that the miraculous side is played up very significantly (cf. the miracle of the water into wine at Cana, or the raising of Lazarus, though this may be due to FE's source, e.g., the Signs Source, rather than FE himself). Alternatively, one could argue that the verb *teleutan* is rather rare in Luke (only here and twice more in Acts). It is thus unlikely to be due to Lukan redaction. Moreover, FE uses the same verb in John 11:39, and hence it is not so clear why FE would have changed it if he found it in a source. In addition we may note that Matthew uses *teleutan* in 9:28 in the context of the Jairus story, which may represent a reminiscence of the use of the verb in Matthew's source (i.e., Q) in the story of the centurion's servant. It is thus at least very uncertain whether FG presupposes either synoptic account here.

What though of Q? Could FE have obtained the story from Q? One attempt to recover the (presumed) common source lying behind Matthew, Luke, and FG is the recent essay of Lindars (1992). Lindars does not specifically raise the question of Q until the very end of his argument when, having reconstructed the alleged source, he asks, "Was John's source Q?" But he responds to this only by saying "that is a question which must be left to Synoptic and Johannine scholars to ponder on future visits to Capernaum." In any case, his argument assumes that all three evangelists are using the same source, which he attempts to reconstruct. Yet his method does not appear entirely satisfactory: he seems satisfied to follow the principle of "majority voting," so that almost any feature common to two of the three gospels is ascribed to the source. Inevitably, the end result is very similar to the "Q" version reconstructed by others on the basis of Matthew and Luke alone. Lindars then simply assumes that any changes to the source were made by the evangelists (mostly FE). But Lindars's reconstruction suggests that FE has done some very complicated editorial work on this common source: the Gentile centurion becomes an ethnically neutral "nobleman"; the conversation between the centurion and Jesus is dropped and transformed so that Jesus becomes the one who issues commands that are instantly obeyed; the note "while he [Jesus] was going" to the man's house becomes "while he [the man] was going" back to his own house; Jesus' marveling at the man's "faith" is transformed by FE into the marveling of others at the miracles of Jesus, who see them as (just) "signs and wonders," leading to the critique of John 4:48. All this is of course possible if FE did have access to the source Lindars reconstructs. But that is precisely the issue! And the huge number of revisions to key elements in the story that have to be postulated here will make others skeptical about the extent and nature of the proposed redaction.

As already noted, modern Q research has been heavily influenced by a redaction-critical approach, seeking to identify redactional elements in Q. We should therefore raise the question of whether Q redactional elements, or at least elements that are significant in Q's overall composition, reappear in FG. If such elements could be identified in FG, this would then be a strong indication that FG did use the version of the story in Q (whether from Q or from a later stage in the tradition). As with the identification of synoptic redactional elements, the isolation of Q's compositional or redactional features is somewhat precarious and uncertain. Nevertheless, some attempt must be made if one is to make any progress in the present context.

The story of the centurion's servant comes in Q just after the Great Sermon (Q 6:20–49) and probably just before the extended discussion about the Baptist and Jesus (Q 7:18–35). Some have seen the placement of the miracle story in Q as based on catchword connections: at the end of the Sermon, Jesus is referred to as "Lord" (Q 6:46), and there are exhortations to obey his "word" (Q 6:47–49); similarly, in the miracle story Jesus is addressed as "Lord" (Q 7:6) with reference to his authoritative "word" (Q 7:7; e.g., Kloppenborg 1987, 117). But this theory does not seem entirely satisfactory, for it makes the connection between the two episodes somewhat arbitrary. Perhaps more to the point is the fact that Q places the healing story just before the material on the Baptist, which culminates in the charge that the hearers have not responded properly to Jesus and John (7:31–35). This is part of a wider pattern in Q, in which the failure of Jesus' Jewish audience to respond positively to his preaching is set in stark contrast to the positive response of non-Jews in similar situations (Q 10:13–15; 11:31–32; 13:28–29; cf. 3:8).[1] In the case of the centurion's servant, the fact that the man is a Gentile and that this Gentile's response to Jesus is used to mount a critique of the (Jewish) hearers gives the Q story its peculiar slant. It also coheres well with other Q material. Thus, while one may not be able to identify specific words or phrases that are Q-redactional, it would seem that the features of the story that are most characteristic of, and distinctive in, Q are those that focus on these elements.

It is striking that none of these redactional features reemerge in John 4. The Gentile centurion is now a "nobleman," and there is no clear reason why FE should have avoided the detail that he was a Gentile ("centurion"). Further, the Q story focuses on the conversation between the man and Jesus about the man's unworthiness to receive his request. This is followed by Jesus' unusual "marveling" at the man's faith (rather than the man marveling at what Jesus has done), which culminates in the comparison between this Gentile's faith and the (comparative) lack of faith in Israel. But any such comparison between Gentiles and Jews makes no appearance in FG. FE does make a comparison between different kinds of faith: note the abrupt saying of Jesus that apparently criticizes the "faith" (or lack of it) displayed so far by the nobleman (John 4:48). It is also unclear in FG when the nobleman comes to true faith: Is it in the note about his belief in verse 53? Or already in verse 50? Or does he display true Johannine faith already in his request to Jesus to come to his house in verse 49? Yet nowhere is a contrast drawn between this man's faith and that of others, at least not directly. The rebuke (if it is such) of John 4:48 is addressed only *to the man* (*pros auton*). So, too, the unusual feature of the Q story, whereby it is Jesus the miracle worker who marvels, does not appear in FG, where all the reaction is implicitly by the man (and others) *to* Jesus: he (and all his house) "believe" as a result of what Jesus has done. In summary, the elements of the story that most likely reflect Q's redactional tendencies find no parallels in FG's version.

In fact, in some respects FG's story seems to be more primitive than the Q version. The reaction to the miracle is the more typical positive response to the miracle worker, rather than Q's highly unusual version where it is Jesus who "marvels." So, too, the Q story seems to need the centurion to be a Gentile in order to make its critique of Jewish responses to Jesus. But this does not surface at all in the Johannine version, where the ethnicity question simply does not arise and the story seems to remain more closely tied to the miracle itself. All in all, it would seem that there is little evidence to justify the theory that FG's account is specifically based on the Q version of the story. Rather, the links between the two streams of the tradition seem to lie further back in the tradition history of the story.

Q 10:21–22

The links between the saying in Q 10:21–22 and the Johannine tradition have often been noted:

> I thank you, Father, Lord of heaven and earth, because you have hidden these things from the wise and the intelligent and have revealed them to infants; yes, Father, for such was your gracious will. All things have been handed over to me by my Father; and no one knows who the Son is except the Father, or who the Father is except the Son and anyone to whom the Son chooses to reveal him.

This saying has been termed a "Johannine thunderbolt" precisely because there are clear Johannine parallels to many of its key aspects. Certainly, the very "high" Christology implied in Q 10:22 can be shown to have many parallels in FG. For the claim that "all things have been given to me by my Father," compare John 5:19–20; 13:3; 16:15. The motifs of the mutual self-knowledge of the Father and the Son, the specific "Son" Christology, and the exclusiveness of the Son as the revealer of the Father are also well known as prominent Johannine themes.

But whether it is fair to call the saying a "thunderbolt" is disputed. The extent to which the saying is an isolated element, either within Q or the synoptic tradition more generally, is debatable. The closest synoptic parallels to the saying do not derive from Q (Mark 4:10–12; 12:1–11; 13:32; Matt. 16:17–19; 28:18). And precisely because it appears to be out of place within Q, the saying has often been thought to be a relative latecomer into Q. Nevertheless, I believe that the saying can be shown to cohere with other parts of the Q material. Verse 22a ("all things have been given to me") may be redolent of Son of Man ideas (cf. Dan. 7:13 where kingship is "given" to the Son of Man), and Son of Man is a key christological category for Q. So too, the apparently exclusive christological statements about the Father and the Son in verse 22 may be, for Q, less christologically oriented and refer rather to any true "son of God," a category which for Q includes all those who are obedient to God and can address him as Father (Q 6:36; also 11:2, 13; 12:30; see Tuckett 1996, 280–281).

One cannot deny that when such language is taken up and developed as it is in FG, the ideas and categories expressed by the same language may be radically changed. Thus FG's use of the category "Son" applied to Jesus may say something very different from the same word used by Q. But whether FE knew this Q saying explicitly is almost impossible to determine. There are no clear Q-compositional or redactional features that one can isolate in the saying to see if they appear in FG. Nor can we necessarily assume that it is a latecomer into Q, and even if it is, there is no way to tell whether it could be an independent tradition taken up by *both* the Q editor *and* FE. *If* FE has taken this saying from Q, then he has clearly developed its terminology into a huge theological edifice in his presentation of Jesus' message.

Other Sayings

As already noted, there are very few sayings common to FG and Q on which to base any theory of dependence. Q 10:16 ("he who receives [(Matt.)//rejects (Luke)] me receives[//rejects] the one who sent me") is similar to John 5:23 (cf. 15:23), but one cannot say more. One may also note the parallel between Q 11:9–10 on asking and receiving and John 16:23–24, though again there are no clear indicators of whether FE knew this saying as mediated through Q. It is possible that the sayings in Q 10:23–24 about the blessedness of the eyes that see the things the disciples have seen is echoed, and perhaps corrected, by FG's risen Jesus saying to Thomas in John 20:29, "Blessed are those who have *not* seen" (though the context is rather different). Further, if (as is usually assumed) Luke preserves the order of the Q material more accurately than Matthew, FG may show parallels to three Q sayings that may have been in the same Q context (Q 10:16; 10:21–22; 10:23–24). But because some of the parallels are uncertain (cf. above on Q 10:23–24 and John 20:29), one cannot place too much reliance on this possibility. Further, none of the parallels here seem to involve elements that have a significant place in the compositional structure of Q.

One must also say that, if FE knew Q, he has omitted an enormous amount from Q. The vast majority of the Q material finds no parallel in FG. On the other hand, there is a great deal of other material that FG shares with the Synoptics that is not Q material.

Conclusion

The results of our probe have been largely negative. In the one extended passage where there seems to be a degree of substantive overlap, the miracle story of Q 7/John 4, FG shows no signs of the characteristic features of the Q version, or of those elements that would fit with Q's general compositional profile. Hence there is no real basis for claiming that FE knew Q. The other points of contact are too few in number to support a substantial theory, and there seems to be little positive evidence for a link between the two strands of the tradition.

If we cannot establish any literary connection between FG and Q, might it still be possible to identify other similarities that would be fruitful for study of either FG or Q? That there are similarities at a number of levels seems undeniable. Q focuses attention primarily on Jesus' teaching and appears to have omitted the passion of Jesus. FE has a passion narrative, and it is clearly very important to him as the "hour" when Jesus is finally "glorified," his being "lifted up" in glory being equated with being lifted up on the cross (see especially John 12:32–33). Yet FE, like Q, places tremendous stress on Jesus' teaching: Jesus' "word" that he has spoken is the power by which the disciples are already "clean" (15:3). Indeed, the Johannine Jesus himself *is* "the" Word (1:1–14).

Q is also famous for sayings that portray Jesus as one of the envoys of Wisdom (7:35; 11:49–51; probably also 13:34–35). Some have argued that Q 10:21–22 advances to the stage of identifying Jesus with Wisdom herself, a step probably taken by Matthew, though it may be that in Q Jesus is still thought of as the messenger of Wisdom. In FG, some kind of equation between Jesus and Wisdom is made: the Prologue, as many have observed, is full of wisdom motifs. Thus FG certainly seems to share a significant, and distinctive, christological trajectory with Q, even if FG may be further "advanced" along it.

It may be that in their attitudes to Judaism, FG and Q also share some things in common. Q's posture toward Judaism has been much debated, with some arguing that the Q Christians had broken completely with their Jewish neighbors. On the other hand, I have argued that Q seems desperate at all costs to maintain the links with Judaism and not to cut the Christian community off (Tuckett 1996, 196–207, 425–438). The same may be true of FG. FE's highly charged polemic against "the Jews" is well known. Yet despite the presence of such polemic, there is clearly still a strand of FG that remains thoroughly positive about "the Jews" and Judaism. Thus salvation is still "of the Jews" (John 4:22), and many of Jesus' actions and teachings show the true fulfillment (without necessarily the abolition) of Jewish scripture and Jewish hopes. Even in the dramatic culmination of FG's account of Jesus' trial before Pilate, where the Jews appear to utter a final cry of self-condemnation ("we have no king but Caesar"; 19:15), it can be argued that they are driven and goaded by Pilate to say what they do. For FE, any separation between Christians and Jews has an element of real tragedy about it.

It is clearly the case that, at least by the time of the present version of FG, Christians and Jews had separated socially: Christians are now excluded from Jewish synagogues (cf. John 9:22; 16:2). Yet perhaps for FE, this is not a matter for rejoicing but an occasion of deepest tragedy. To use the scholarly jargon, Johannine Christians may have been forced to become "Jewish Christians" at the social level, but this is not of their own making; they are still "*Jewish* Christians" and perhaps would have wished to remain "Christian Jews." The situation of the Q Christians may not have been as extreme as that of Johannine Christians. They do not appear to have suffered much direct active persecution (despite the strong language from the Christian side), and they still appear to be struggling to maintain a social position within the Jewish community. But perhaps they too are striving at all costs to remain "Christian Jews" and to avoid the temptation—or the pressure—to become a group of "Jewish Christians." In FG (at least by the time of the present version of the text), the situation has deteriorated and Christians have evidently been driven out of the Jewish community. Nevertheless, there may be sufficient parallels between FG and Q to see both struggling with similar situations and to see both as motivated by a concern to maintain social bridges as well as religious identity in a context of perceived hostility.

Note

1. The precise significance of these texts in relation to Q's own situation is disputed. Some have argued that these passages act as a justification for a Gentile mission by Christians (Kloppenborg 1987, 148). Others have pointed out that most of these texts relate to the past (Q 10:13–15; 11:31–32) or the future (13:28–29), with no real indication that the centurion whose son is healed acts as a prototype for Gentiles in the Jesus movement. Hence, it may be more likely that these texts serve more as a means of intensifying the polemic against a Jewish audience, rather than acting as an apologetic for the existence of a Gentile one (Tuckett 1996, 201–207).

25

The Fourth Gospel
and the Synoptic Sayings Source

The Relationship Reconsidered

EDWIN K. BROADHEAD

This investigation will explore the relationship between the Fourth Gospel (FG) and the Synoptic Sayings Tradition, usually designated "Q." Following a brief sketch of how this relationship has been perceived, the question will be reconsidered in light of recent research. Analysis of John 12:44 13:33 will shed new light on the connection between FG and the Sayings Tradition. While a developing oral tradition certainly lies behind Q, I shall use the terms "Sayings Tradition" and "Q" interchangeably throughout this essay to refer to the *written* collection of sayings that lies behind the Synoptic Gospels.

Previous Research

The perceived relationship between FG and the historical Jesus has moved through various stages. In the precritical view a direct connection was seen between the historical Jesus and the Jesus who walks the pages of FG. The logic behind this position goes like this:

> The real Jesus is the Jesus found on the pages of the canonical gospels;
> and John is the primary gospel for the church;
> therefore, the Johannine Jesus of FG is the true Jesus.

This precritical view represents not simply a stage in the history of research but a way of interpreting the text—a hermeneutic. In terms of its endurance

and popularity, this is still the dominant mode for understanding the relationship between Jesus and FG.

The onset of critical approaches to scripture that occurred in the aftermath
of the Renaissance, the Reformation, and especially the Enlightenment produced a radically different model. Four major steps in this process may be
identified.

1. Because the Gospel of Mark is understood to be the oldest and most
primitive of the canonical gospels, the Jesus of Mark was taken to be the historical Jesus. This affirmation meant a huge step away from the Johannine portrait of Jesus. Among the results of this new focus was the liberal quest for the
historical Jesus that dominated the nineteenth century.

2. The advents of form criticism and then of redaction criticism showed that
the Gospel of Mark is also a theological portrait, composed from sources
under the influence of special interests and needs.

3. Attention to other ancient sources confirms that none of the canonical
gospels gives a straightforward portrait of the historical Jesus. Chief among
these sources is Q, whose portrait of Jesus is more primitive even than that of
Mark. Attention to the Nag Hammadi texts demonstrates the variety of movements and understandings of faith in this period. Some parts of the Gospel of
Thomas suggest a primitive connection to Jesus.

4. Renewed attention to Judaism shows that Jesus was not a Christian but
a Jew. Christianity arose as an alternate, messianic form of Jewish faith. Whatever else the historical Jesus may be, he is thoroughly Jewish.

The accumulative weight of these four factors generates a stark verdict on
the relation of FG to the historical Jesus. The evidence looks like this:

> If the Gospel of Mark is the oldest and most authentic of the canoni-
>   cal gospels;
> and if the primitive gospel tradition predates Mark and differs from
> Mark in significant aspects;
> and if the Sayings Tradition Q and some parts of Thomas are impor-
>   tant witnesses to the life of Jesus;
> and if Judaism provides the key to understanding Jesus;
>   then FG stands at a greater distance from Jesus than the Synoptics,
>   and perhaps also further than some New Testament epistles such as
>   James and Hebrews.

Critical scholarship has thereby reached the conclusion that FG stands far
from the historical Jesus in the material it presents, in its style of presentation,
and in its theology. Because of this position, FG has been more and more
excluded from the discussion of the historical Jesus. While earlier scholarship
defined this distance through the contrast between FG and Mark, recent attention has also focused on the distance between the Johannine Jesus and the por-

trait of Jesus in the Synoptic Sayings Tradition. In their presentation of Jesus, FG and Q are often perceived to be absolute strangers.

The time has come to take a second look at this relationship, particularly in light of recent research on the historical Jesus. Our task here is to reconsider in a specific way the connections between the Sayings Tradition and FG. It will be helpful to look again at previous conclusions that have now become accepted generalizations. It will also prove useful to look at this relationship under a more powerful microscope—that of the renewed focus on pre-Markan traditions, Thomasine traditions, and Q. Our conclusions, however, must be limited to the relationship between Q and FG.

The Relationship Reconsidered

We will first look at general similarities and differences between FG and Q. Then, under a closer lens, we will identify specific points where Q and FG may be connected. Having identified these contact points, we will look at how the Q connections are generally appropriated in FG. In the final section we will look at specific cases where FG represents a development of material found in the Sayings Tradition.

Similarities and Differences

Many general similarities are evident between FG and Q. While FG and Q were once considered to be examples of different genres, the distinction is breaking down. Since the Gospel of Thomas is a sayings collection that claims to be a gospel, many scholars now broaden the concept of the gospel genre to include two types of texts: narrative gospels and sayings gospels. Both FG and Q, then, may be called "gospels."

A greater similarity exists in the matter of form. Like all other gospels, FG employs sayings to describe the ministry of Jesus and to define his identity. Like the other canonical gospels, FG weaves these sayings into narrative scenes. One category of Johannine sayings exhibits a strong relation to the pattern of the Sayings Tradition. The "I Am" sayings of FG require no specific context and are largely interchangeable. As such, they become key vehicles for Johannine Christology. The form of the "I Am" sayings of FG is akin to that of many Q sayings, particularly those that focus on the Son of Man.

The focus and task of the Johannine sayings are shared to a great degree with those of the Sayings Tradition. In each, the reader is to understand that Jesus is the unique point in which God's work has come to the human sphere and that one's response to Jesus' message or revelation is decisive for the future. In both FG and Q, the Synoptics' use of miracle traditions has been limited.

On the other hand, the differences between FG and the Sayings Tradition Q should not be underestimated. One is a canonical gospel attached to the name of an apostle and providing key theological codes for the developing church. The other is a reconstruction of a sayings collection that had a limited circulation at the most primitive level of church history. FG has subsumed ethics into belief and brotherly love and has replaced eschatology with glorification. The life of the Johannine Jesus is painted against the backdrop of cosmology and eternity. In contrast, the Sayings Tradition knows Jesus as the decisive messenger in whom God's final word of salvation has arrived shortly before the collapse of history. Further, FG is thoroughly messianic while Q never refers to Jesus as the messiah. The Passion of Jesus is his exaltation in FG while Q apparently has no passion story and understands the suffering of Jesus as a prophetic trait. Q is deeply rooted in Jewish ideas and concepts. Whatever the Fourth Evangelist (FE) means by "the Jews," he is thoroughly anti-Jewish.

John/Q Connections

When one looks beyond the general traits of these two texts, more precise connections may be seen between them. Notably, a significant part of what has been reconstructed as Q may be found in some form in FG. Table 25.1 demonstrates the breadth of these interconnections. Note that the Q passages are identified by the Lukan chapter and verse numbers. A detailed examination of this list shows that three of the sayings from Q (3:15, 16–17; 6:39–40; 10:16–20) appear twice in FG, and two more Q sayings appear three times (10:21–22; 11:5–13).

This list of connections between Q and FG is impressive in scope, but other texts should also be considered. A significant part of the "triple tradition," or sayings present in all three of the Synoptics—Matthew, Mark, and Luke— also appears in FG. Some parts of the triple tradition may actually originate in Q, but present source-critical methods cannot distinguish this material. The same may be said of L and M—material found only in Matthew (M) or Luke (L): some parts may originate in Q. Some traditions from L and M also appear in FG.

This catalog of links with the double tradition (Q) and possible ties with the triple tradition, L, and M shows that Q and FG are interconnected. But more important is the question of how Q-type materials are appropriated in FG.

Table 25.1

Q	Fourth Gospel	Description
3:1–4	1:3	The arrival of the Baptist
3:15, 16–17	1:24–27	John's preaching
3:21–22	1:32–34	The baptism of Jesus
3:15, 16–17	1:33b	John's preaching
10:21–22	3:35–36	Revelation
7:1–10	4:46–54	Healing the centurion's son
11:16, 29–32	6:30	The sign of Jonah
10:21–22	10:15	Revelation
14:25–27; 17:33	12:25	Jesus' disciples
10:16–20	12:44–45	The authority of the messenger
6:39–40	13:16	Servants and masters
10:16–20	13:20	The authority of the messenger
11:5–13	14:13–14	Prayer
6:39–40	15:20a	Prayer
11:5–13	16:23–24	Servants and masters
10:21–22	17:1b–2	Revelation

Appropriation of Q-Type Material in the Fourth Gospel

The fact that the same materials appear in Q and FG does not demonstrate that FE used Q as a source. The connection may rather signal a common linguistic field of operation, and it may show that Q and FG both drew from a common pool of tradition. Close attention to these texts shows that, in most instances, the connection between Q and FG is a very loose one. Two examples may be noted from the list above. First, Q 10:21–22 is found in almost identical wording in Matthew 11:25–27 and Luke 10:21–22. The things hidden from the wise ones have been revealed to babies; in a similar way, God has chosen to reveal all things through Jesus. This saying is appropriated at three points in FG (3:35–36; 10:15; 17:1–2b). In each instance, FG uses the saying to emphasize the unique tie between Jesus and the Father. The contrast between the wise ones and the babies is absent. Second, Q 11:29–32 also appears in Matthew 12:41–42 and in Luke 11:29–32. While the order of the two sayings is reversed in Matthew and Luke, the content is identical with the exception of one noun and its pronoun. Passages such as this represent the strongest evidence of the existence of Q. John 6:30, with its request for a sign, represents a loose appropriation of this tradition.

A clearer picture thus emerges. Looking beyond the general traits, one finds an extensive line of interconnections between FG and the Sayings Tradition. For the most part, however, the Q-type material has been reshaped and appropriated into a distinctly Johannine view of the world.

Johannine Development
of Traditions Central to Q

The way that FE has developed traditions central to Q may be demonstrated in an important stretch of Johannine narrative, John 12:44–13:33. While in some instances this material seems to be drawn from the Sayings Tradition, in most cases FG and the Sayings Tradition Q seem to be drawing on a common pool of early Christian tradition. In either case, the relationship of FG to the Sayings Tradition in terms of ideas, concepts, and framing is illustrated in this passage.

John 12:44–45

Two key traits from the Sayings Tradition Q are exhibited here, one formal and the other conceptual. First, the Johannine saying exhibits a parallelism of form built around two "whoever" sayings:

> Whoever believes in me
>   believes not in me
>   but in him who sent me. And
> Whoever sees me
>   sees him who sent me.

A similar pattern is found in diverse regions of the Synoptic Tradition, though a contrast or comparison is usually involved. The triple tradition of sayings employs this structure at several points: Mark 3:28 and parallels; Mark 4:25 and parallels; Mark 9:37 and its Lukan parallel; Mark 10:11–12 and its Lukan parallel; Mark 10:43–44 and parallels. The same rhetorical structure is also found in several Matthean passages that seem to reflect Matthew's distinct version of Q: Matthew 5:19, 22; 5:31–32; 10:41. One may also note here Matthew 23:12, which appears in the special material found in Matthew alone (M). Beside the Lukan passages reflecting the triple tradition and the Sayings Tradition Q, this pattern is also found on three occasions in the special Lukan material (L): Luke 3:11; 16:10; 20:18.

This "whoever . . . whoever" rhetorical pattern occurs most frequently in the Synoptic Sayings Tradition Q, as seen in the following texts: Q 6:46–49; 10:16; 11:23; 12:8–9, 10; 13:30; 14:11 (18:14b); 14:26–27 (as found in Matt. 10:37–38); 16:18; 17:33 (as found in Matt. 10:39); 19:26. A few examples will demonstrate the appearance of the pattern in Q. Q 12:8–9 reads, "*Everyone* who acknowledges me before others, the Son of Man will acknowledge . . . and *whoever* denies me before others, will be denied" (italics added). Q 14:11 says, "*Everyone* who exalts self will be humbled, and *whoever* humbles self will be exalted." At Q 17:33 (as found in Matt. 10:39), Jesus says, "*Whoever* finds their life will lose it, and *the one who* loses their life for my sake will find it." Of these instances from Q, a few build the "whoever" contrast distinctly around the way one relates to Jesus (Q 6:47–49; 10:16; 11:23; 12:8–9, 10; 14:26–27; 17:33). Notably, Gospel of Thomas 82 employs this same form: "*Whoever* is near me is near the fire, and *whoever* is far from me is far from the kingdom."

The second connection between the Sayings Tradition and John 12:44–45 is conceptual: in both, one's response to Jesus is one's response to God. This concept lies at the heart of the theology of the Sayings Tradition. The central idea in Q is that one's response to the message of Jesus is decisive. Nonetheless, Q also makes the response to Jesus himself decisive: "Everyone who acknowledges me before others, the Son of Man will also acknowledge . . . ; but whoever denies me before others, will be denied" (Q 12:8–9); "Whoever is not with me is against me, and whoever does not gather with me scatters" (Q 11:23). John 12:44–45 has an almost exact parallel in Q 10:16 as expressed in Matthew 10:40: "Whoever welcomes you welcomes me, and whoever welcomes me welcomes him who sent me."

In light of these formal and conceptual parallels, one may conclude that John 12:44–45 seems to draw directly on a pattern that is central to the Sayings Tradition. This pattern is repeated at John 13:20: "Whoever receives one whom I send receives me, and whoever receives me receives the one who sent me." The Johannine transformation of this primitive tradition is noteworthy. While the Sayings Tradition presents Jesus as the one who is to be heard and welcomed and followed, FE transforms these behavioral responses into terms of faith, revelation, and identity. In FG, one is called to see and to believe Jesus and thus to see and believe God.

John 12:47

An important phrase from the Sayings Tradition appears here. Hearing the words of Jesus but not doing them is a key component of the Sayings Tradition, as demonstrated in the Sermon on the Mount (Matt. 7:26) and the Sermon on the Plain (Luke 6:49). In both sermons a contrast is created between "whoever hears and does" Jesus' words and "whoever hears and does not do" them. In Q, the one who "hears and does not do" is compared to a foolish builder who built upon sand. But in John 12:47–50, the one who does not keep the words of Jesus will be judged in the last day by Jesus' words, which he has spoken at God's command. In this way the ethical admonition of Q, which is based on a wisdom tradition that links hearing and doing, has been transformed into a Johannine pattern of eschatology and judgment.

John 13:13–16

An extensive connection to the Sayings Tradition may be seen here. While the Greek term for "Lord" (*kyrios*) is frequent in FG (forty-five occurrences), terms for "Teacher" are less common (nine occurrences). Six of the nine occurrences appear in a direct address: on three occasions Jesus is called *Rabbi* or *Rabboni* (John 1:38; 3:2; 20:16); in three other contexts he is called "Teacher" (John 8:4; 13:13, 14). But nowhere in FG does the combination "Teacher and Lord" appear, *except* in John 13:13–14. This combination of terms seems to derive from the Sayings Tradition (Q 6:40), especially as found in Matthew 10:24–25: a disciple is not above the teacher, nor a servant above the lord (master). In the Sayings Tradition, the Teacher and Lord connection is expressed in two sets of parallel lines:

> A disciple is not above the teacher,
> nor a servant above the master;
> It is enough for the disciple to be like the teacher,
> and the servant like the master.

A connection to the Sayings Tradition seems to be confirmed by John 13:16. Here the parallelism of Matthew 10:24–25 is picked up, but with a Johannine perspective:

> A servant is not greater than the lord;
> nor is the one sent greater than the one who sent him.

While John 13:13–14, 16 seems out of place in FG (the combination of Teacher and Lord; the form of the saying as parallel comparisons), these traits may be explained as natural extensions of a pattern found in the Synoptic Sayings Tradition.

John 13:20

In a pattern already observed in John 12:44–45, the saying at John 13:20 picks up two central elements found in Q: the "whoever . . . whoever" rhetorical structure and the concept that one's response to Jesus indicates one's response to God. While 12:44–45 uses two versions of a two-part sequence (believe me = believe God; see me = see God), John 13:20 contains a three-part sequence: receive one whom I send = receive me = receive God. This three-part sequence is crowded into a single parallelism in Matthew's version of Q 10:16:

> the one receiving you receives me, and
> the one receiving me receives the one who sent me. (Matt. 10:40)

Luke has conflated the form, seeking to create a contrast between hearing and rejecting while maintaining a three-part sequence:

> Whoever hears you hears me, and
> whoever rejects you rejects me, and
> whoever rejects me rejects the one who sent me. (Luke 10:16)

It is noteworthy that FG maintains both aspects of Q 10:16. The three-part "receiving" sequence of Matthew 10:40 is retained in John 13:20, while the three-part "rejection" sequence of Luke 10:16 is retained in different form in John 12:48. These connections demonstrate that central forms and concepts known to Q have been taken up and transformed along the Johannine trajectory.

John 13:31

A further connection between FG and the Sayings Tradition can be seen in the use of the title "Son of Man" in John 13:31. This title is a central component of the Sayings Tradition, where it is associated with the future judgment. Human reactions to Jesus and his message in the present serve as the basis for this future verdict: the one who acknowledges Jesus now will be acknowledged then by the Son of Man, while the one who denies Jesus now will be denied then (Q 12:8–9). Thus the Sayings Tradition identifies Jesus in his earthly ministry as the Son of Man whose present work determines the future verdict.

FE also uses the Son of Man title, but gives it a radically different function. In FG, "Son of Man" is connected to two clusters of terms. The term for "lift up" or "exalt" is used in FG only in connection with the Son of Man title. The term for "glorify" is used mostly in connection with the name Jesus or with the Son of Man title. Because FG interprets the death of Jesus as his exaltation, the synoptic idea of a future reappearance of the Son of Man falls away. Thus, FG has collapsed the death of Jesus and his subsequent exaltation into a single event and associated this exaltation with the title "Son of Man." John 13:31–32 is typical of this pattern. In these two verses the term for "glorify" is used five times in connection with the Son of Man title from 13:31. Further, the mutual glorification of the Son of Man and God is typical of FE's theological concerns.

These five passages from John 12:44–13:33 demonstrate that major components of Johannine thought are constructed from elements common to the Synoptic Sayings Tradition. While some of these elements may represent no more than a common linguistic world and others may draw from a wide stream of early Christian tradition, the number of shared elements and the specificity of some components suggest possible lines of dependence on the Sayings Tradition. At the same time, these passages also demonstrate the distance between FG and Q. Each of these five elements has been reformulated and transformed to serve the Johannine worldview. The unique portrait of Jesus that emerges stands in stark contrast to that of the Sayings Tradition.

Nowhere is this distance more evident than in the Johannine view of Judaism. As seen in John 13:33, Jesus sets himself and his followers over against "the Jews." This pattern is widespread in FG, where the Jews are blind and unbelieving, while Jesus and his followers are on their way to eternal life. A reader of FG could easily forget that Jesus and his earliest followers were Jews and that the earliest Christian traditions were framed within a Jewish worldview; a reader of the Sayings Tradition could not.

Conclusion

We have sought here to reconsider the general consensus that there is little in common between FG and the Synoptic Sayings Tradition. A closer analysis shows extensive sayings material shared in some form by FG and Q. Other possible connections were identified. While the appropriation of Q-type material was seen to be heavily influenced by Johannine interests, a look at John 12:44–13:33 gives a sharper picture. Five components from this passage demonstrate parallels between FG and Q, yet this material also highlights the distance between these two texts. More importantly, John 12:44–13:33 demonstrates the profound difference in how Jesus is understood in Q and FG. Since Q is likely the most primitive account of Jesus available to us, the distance between Q and FG may be interpreted as an even greater distance between FG and Jesus.

This treatment of the sayings of Jesus is typical of FE. FG represents an ongoing negotiation between traditions about Jesus and the Fourth Evangelist's worldview. The traditions about what Jesus did and said are filtered through the grid of Johannine thought. This hermeneutic has had an impact on all of his story. The emergence of Jesus from shadowy origins in Galilee has been transformed into a cosmic preexistence as the Logos; the pithy parables and sayings of Jesus have been transliterated into Johannine pronouncements; the Jewish Jesus has become the judge of "the Jews"; salvation has been transformed into eternal life; exorcisms have been reformulated as a struggle between belief and unbelief; resurrection and eschatology have been collapsed into glorification. FE stubbornly refuses to abandon either his contact with the Jesus tradition or his own distinctive worldview. He insists instead on a dialectic that transforms and transfers the story of Jesus into the world of FG.

A closer look shows that FG and Q are not wholly unrelated. Important images of the historical Jesus filter through the Johannine story. While specific lines of dependence may or may not exist, FG and Q certainly root in the same pool of primitive Christian traditions. At the same time, these two texts offer a radically different understanding of God's work in Jesus. The relatedness of Q and FG makes their differences even more stark. In contrast to earlier assumptions, Q and FG are not total strangers; they are estranged cousins.

In FG, the Jesus of the early tradition (to which Q is central) has been transformed into a Johannine Jesus. While echoes of the historical Jesus remain, those echoes have been transposed into a new mode. The image of Jesus as a Jewish prophet who speaks little of himself and much about God, and who invites the least and the lowest into the Kingdom, is a stranger in the Johannine world. Instead this Jesus has been replaced by a preexistent savior who brings eternal life for those who see and believe in him and eternal condemnation to those who do not. While rooted in common traditional ground, the ideological distance between Q and FG could hardly be greater.

26

John Rivals Thomas

From Community Conflict to Gospel Narrative

APRIL D. DeConick

This article is not the first attempt to discuss the relationship between the Gospels of John and Thomas. There is already a formidable amount of literature on the subject, most of which tries to establish direct literary dependence between the two books or the use of common sources (see DeConick 2001). The present essay, however, will explore the connection between these two texts on the community level rather than the source level. The Fourth Gospel (FG) and the Gospel of Thomas (Gos. Thom.), like other religious texts, address the particular needs of their respective communities and express special theological and soteriological positions. As community documents, each has its own *Sitz im Leben*: its own geographical location, its own community history, and its own religious traditions. Moreover, like other religious texts, both were written with the express purposes of polemicizing, persuading, and propagating a particular belief system.

Traditio-rhetorical Criticism: A Method for Studying Traditions

To approach this topic, I will appeal to a theoretical model which I call "traditio-rhetorical criticism," a model that defines the territory that allows us to examine the relationship between texts on the community level. It is a historical-critical approach to literature that focuses on reconstructing the exchange and modification of religious traditions as they were discussed, evaluated, and textualized by the communities that used them.

The hyphenated prefix "traditio-" refers to the traditions that express the self-understanding of a community of people: their sense of the past, their system of religious belief, and their manner of conduct. These traditions are transmitted from generation to generation in the form of stories, sayings, myths, creeds, liturgical statements, and hymns. At certain moments in the history of the community, their traditions may be textualized, moving this material from an oral environment to a written one. This process solidifies the community's traditions at a historical moment, which means that the written texts will reflect one particular stage in the development of the community's overall ideology. The suffix "rhetorical" defines the way in which the language of the text creates and communicates this traditional ideology. As Robbins has noted, the term "ideology" "concerns people's relationship to other people. But, ideology does not just concern people; it concerns the discourse of people" (Robbins 1996, 110). Taken together, traditio-rhetorical criticism is a hermeneutic that seeks to understand the discourse that elicited both the creation and modification of a tradition and also the textualization of that tradition as a new ideology. It attempts to understand the ways in which a particular author developed a particular ideology through dialogue with other ideological positions, how a community's traditions were modified by this dialogue, and how the extant texts reflect this process. In terms of early Jesus traditions, it seeks to identify conflicts between Christian communities and the textualization of these conflicts as gospel narratives.

Three horizons or contexts are defined in the traditio-rhetorical model: the "religio-historical context," which is the general religious environment in which the author and his community lived; and the author's and the opponent's "traditio-religious contexts," the Christian heritages of the communities engaged in discourse with one another. For example, in a study of the Johannine tradition, one might consider a) the broad religious environment of the Greco-Roman world in which the Johannine Community lived; b) the specific heritage and faith traditions of the Fourth Evangelist (FE); and c) the specific heritage and faith traditions of FE's opponents, for example, the "Antichrists" of 1 John 2:18–19. These three horizons meet at the "point of discourse," the problem that occupies the center of the dialogue between the two communities. The actual point of discourse may not be explicitly stated in the extant texts, since it is often articulated on a symbolic level. In other words, the author of a text may choose to address issues in the conflict with her opponents indirectly, without specifically naming the opponents or the issues themselves. This means that features of the intercommunity dialogue may appear in the text as symbolic acts and events.

The individual author's response to this intercommunity dialogue can be varied. In writing a text, an author might choose to ignore or condemn her opponent's position while defending her own ideology, or might simply build a case to maintain the status quo. The author might also try to conceal material that would support the opponent's position. The author might attempt to reinterpret her previous position and construct a synthetic endpoint, a newly fashioned ideology that brings some resolution to the conflict. As will be seen, in the case of FG the last option seems to have been adopted: some of the peculiar features of FE's ideology seem to have developed in reaction to an opposing ideology that must have been similar to that promoted by the author of the Gospel of Thomas.

Actual conflicts between religious communities of the past were often fictionalized and recorded as dramas rather than related in terms of verbatim dialogue. This means that stories of conflict in the gospels can be viewed as dramas created to represent and record actual dialogue between later religious communities. The record of an intercommunity dialogue may therefore appear in the form of a hidden rather than an open controversy, in which case the author will not explicitly mention his ideological rival (Hirshman 1996, 126). Given this situation, we must examine religious texts thoughtfully, recognizing that some portions may contain valuable information for understanding the development of the author's theology in relation to other contemporary religious texts. In other words, the characters and situations in the texts may reflect events from the author's own experience of ideological conflict rather than actual "historical" events involving those characters.

John and Thomas: A Mystical Conflict

Elsewhere I have argued at length that the Gospel of Thomas contains logia that reflect a knowledge of Jewish mystical traditions, especially sayings 15, 27, 37, 50, 59, 83, and 84 (see DeConick 1996; DeConick and Fossum 1991). The presence of these sayings suggests that the community that produced Thomas advocated a mystical experience of God. This belief is most evident in statements such as Gospel of Thomas 59, in which Jesus specifically commands the reader to seek a vision of God: "*Look* for the Living One while you are alive, lest you die and seek to *see* him and you will be unable to *see* [him]" (my translation and italics). The vision quest promoted by this saying is a premortem one, an experience that may anticipate death or an eschatological journey but which must be achieved in the believer's lifetime.

What happens to the believer during these premortem spiritual journeys? The answer appears in various forms in the Jewish mystical texts. She ascends through layers of heaven, encountering angelic guards along the way who interrogate the soul (cf. Ascen. Isaiah 10:28–29; Apoc. Ab. 13:6; 3 En. 2, 4, 5). Because these angels were believed to administer life-or-death tests to the seeker, she needed to memorize passwords and hymns in order to appease the guards and ensure her unencumbered journey to God's throne (Apoc. Ab. 17–18; *Hekhalot Rabbati* 1:1; 2:5–5:3; 16:4–25:6). Such beliefs set the broader religious context against which the sort of questions and answers found in Gospel of Thomas 50 should be understood ("If they say to you, 'Where have you come from?' say to them. . . . If they say to you, 'Is it you?' say. . . . If they ask you, 'What is the evidence?' . . . say. . . ."). Sayings of this kind most likely represent the fragments of Christian ascent lore, in which Jesus instructs the believer regarding her anticipated interrogation during the heavenly journey. The etiquette for these ecstatic visionary experiences is found in Gospel of Thomas 15: "When you see the one who was not born of woman, prostrate yourselves on your faces and worship him. That one is your Father." Such advice is consistent with the Jewish mystical portrayals of the divine throne room, in which God's manifestation or *kavod* is often depicted as seated on a throne in the midst of an entourage of angels. It is common in such literature to find descriptions of the mystic entering the throne room and prostrating himself before the divine King (cf. 1 En. 14:24; 2 En. 22:4).

The Thomasites lived a severely ascetic lifestyle in preparation for this ecstatic encounter, repudiating the body so that the spirit could ascend to God. In order to receive a vision, one had to purify oneself by withdrawing from the world and by observing the sanctity of the Sabbath: "If you do not fast from the world, you will not find the Kingdom. If you do not observe the Sabbath as Sabbath, you will not see the Father" (Gos. Thom. 27; see DeConick 1996, 126–143). According to logion 37, a vision of Jesus cannot happen until the believer has stripped off her human body and "tread upon it," thereby renouncing it (DeConick and Fossum 1991, 123–150). The Thomasites believed that the mystical ascent and vision of God was a transformational experience. Note, for example, Gospel of Thomas 108: "Jesus said, 'Whoever drinks from my mouth will become like me; I myself shall become that person, and the hidden things will be revealed to him" (see also 19b, 22, 84).

Paradoxically, FG is sometimes characterized as the "mystical" gospel in the New Testament, yet it clearly condemns the Thomasine notions of heavenly ascent and celestial vision (John 1:18; 3:13; 5:37; and 6:46). In fact, FG includes several statements in which Jesus explicitly proclaims that his disciples will *not* be able to be follow him to "the place where I am going," heaven (7:33–34; 8:21; 13:33; 13:36). These sayings climax in John 14, where Jesus explains that he is leaving to "prepare a place for you"; only then will he "come again and will take you to myself, that where I am you may be also" (14:3). Yet remarkably, while on the one hand FE carefully crafts a polemic against pre-mortem mystical ascent and vision, on the other hand he frequently appro-priates Jewish mystical concepts into his own ideology (Dunn 1983; Kanagaraj 1998). He seems particularly well versed in the mystical concepts of heavenly ascent and the *kavod*, the enthroned manifestation of God that often bears God's divine name (cf. 1:1–18; 1:51; 2:11; 11:40; 12:23, 28; 13:32; 17:4, 15, 20–26). This paradox suggests that the Fourth Evangelist was in some way connected with Jewish mysticism: we may say that this was one of his religio-historical horizons. At the same time, he appears to have been aware that other Christian groups had appropriated Jewish mystical traditions into their ide-ologies to construct their views of Jesus and discipleship.

FE, however, could not accept the position of those who advocated a pre-mortem ascent and visionary experience of Jesus as the heavenly Glory. This conflict is reflected in the narrative of FG in two ways: in FE's emphasis that the character Thomas misunderstands Jesus; and in FE's attempt to charac-terize the Thomasine view of soteriology as a competing traditio-religious horizon that must be corrected (DeConick 1997, 2001). According to John, the disciple Thomas misunderstands Christian soteriology, believing that it is necessary for one to seek the "way" to Jesus as a path of ascent to heaven (John 14:3–7) and a vision of Jesus (20:24–29; cf. 14:20–23). FE's criticism of Thomas specifically among the disciples is probably not arbitrary given the fact that the Gospel of Thomas promotes a type of vision mysticism. Following the tenets of traditio-rhetorical criticism outlined above, it is likely that FE's stories about Thomas are dramatizations of an actual dialogue in which the Johannine Community was engaged with the Thomasine group. The point of discourse seems to have been whether or not the ascent and visionary experiences were salvific or even necessary for Christians. From the Johannine perspective, the answer to both of these questions was "No."

The Johannine Response:
Constructing a Synthetic Endpoint

As noted earlier, in some instances the author of a religious text responds to conflict by modifying a previously held position and then constructing a syn-thetic endpoint that represents her revised position. In the present case, FE's conflict with the Thomasine perspective has forced him to revise and recon-struct his own theory of mystical experience. In so doing, he creates a new the-ology. But what can we discover from the Fourth Gospel about FE's new theology, his interpretive trajectory? First, he argues that faith replaces vision as the vehicle of transformation: "Blessed are those who have not seen and yet believe" (John 20:29). In this way he salvages the basic underpinnings of vision mysticism but also transfigures them into something of value for his community: a salvific mystical experience centered on faith rather than ecstatic vision. Second, FE retains elements of the visionary experience but limits this experience to a special moment in history, the moment when Jesus as the preexistent Glory descended to earth and was witnessed by human beings. This ideological synthesis has in turn had a significant impact on FE's presentation of Christ.

Pretemporal Existence of Jesus

In the Prologue, FE stresses not only that Jesus was "with God" prior to his incarnation (John 1:1) but also that Jesus "has seen God" while he was with the Father in heaven (1:18). Hence, "no one has ever seen God" except the Son who was in "the bosom of the Father" (1:18; 5:37; 6:46). It appears that here FE is articulating his own christological views while distancing himself from the ideology of his broader religio-historical horizon. He writes of a preexistent Logos figure who cohabited with God and was given the sole visionary experience of that God. This pretemporal visionary experience makes this entity, Jesus, special. Jesus is not only the only one who has truly seen and known the Father (1:18); he also participates in and embodies the deity: "the Word was God" (1:1).

Jesus as the Historical Manifestation of Divine Glory

Once the Logos has descended from heaven (John 3:13; 3:31–32; 7:29; 8:23; 17:5) and "tabernacled" with humans (1:14), he, as Jesus, can claim that "the Father and I are one" (10:30) and can urge people to "believe me that I am in the Father and the Father in me" (14:11). As the *kavod*, the divine Glory, he has been given God's name and thus is one with God (17:11; see Fossum 1995). Such statements reveal FE's strategy for creating theological synthesis in the wake of his conflict with Thomasine mysticism. In FG, the Jewish mystical traditions about the Glory enthroned in heaven have been merged with traditions about the historical manifestation of Jesus. The Johannine usage of *doxa* ("glory") is notable here. The glory of Jesus is visible in his person (1:14), his signs (2:11; 11:40; 17:4), and his crucifixion (12:23, 28; 13:32; 17:1, 5). In 1:14, for instance, FE claims that "we have seen his Glory, the Glory as of the only-begotten from the Father." Clearly here the mystical background of the term "glory" has been historicized by connecting it to the historical Jesus, who is the visible manifestation of God (1:18). FE elsewhere further implies that Isaiah's vision of "the Lord" in Isaiah 6 was actually a vision of Jesus as the divine Glory (12:41).

One of the best-known passages in FG claims that God sent his son to earth out of love, so that the world might be saved through encountering him (John 3:16–17). This theme is expanded in 17:20–26, where Jesus is identified with the Glory who has been sent to earth out of God's love. By seeing Jesus the Glory, the disciples will experience a mystic union with the Father through him, because the Glory is the Father (17:21). This Glory or divine essence can then be transferred to the disciples: "The Glory which you have given to me, I have given to them, that they may be one even as we are one, I in them and you in me, that they may become perfectly one" (17:22–23). Such a transformation is possible through the mechanism of the visionary experience. Thus Jesus prays for the disciples "to see my Glory which you [the Father] have given to me in your love for me before the foundation of the world" (17:24). As God's Glory, the human Jesus makes the Father known to the world and makes available the opportunity for union with him (17:25–26).

In the Johannine tradition the deity has been manifested historically. Ascent to heaven and visions of God are unnecessary for personal transformation and the achievement of life, because the divinity has come to earth and has brought this mystic experience with him. FE emphasizes that the vision of Jesus on earth substitutes for the vision of the Father in heaven (John 14:9), and that those who see Jesus shall live (14:19). This revelation of Glory was completely achieved at Golgotha (12:32). FE thereby challenges the Thomasine interest in flights to heaven by insisting that such mystical experiences can only be achieved in the historical encounter with Jesus.

The Absence of Jesus and the Continuing Vision

FE's theological synthesis of tradition and Glory was functional for those who actually witnessed Jesus while he walked on earth. But if God's Glory was manifested in the historical Jesus, how could those who did not see Jesus gain the divine vision and, thereby, eternal life? FE develops several themes in response to this question.

First, the Paraclete, the Holy Spirit, replaces Jesus in his absence (John 14:17; 14:22–26; 15:26; 16:7, 16; see Draper 1992, 14). Although the experience of the Spirit is not a theophany per se (it cannot be because the Spirit does not have a visible form), the community will "know" him nonetheless. The Paraclete will be manifested as the divine love of Jesus for his followers, a love that is mutually shared between the members of the Johannine Community. Furthermore, the true disciples of Jesus will be identified by this mutual love: "By this all people will know that you are my disciples, if you have love for one another" (13:34–35). This means that the fulfillment of Jesus' command to love is the visible evidence that Jesus as the Paraclete dwells within the Johannine Community (14:21–24). Even though later followers will no longer be able to "see" Jesus, they will be able to "know" him as the Paraclete, who will mediate God to them. Visionary ascents are not necessary because the Paraclete has come down to earth in Jesus' absence.

Second, FE responds to the problem of Jesus' absence by repetitively linking the concept of faith in Jesus to the visionary experience. In this way he communicates with his broader religio-historical horizon by preserving the trappings of vision mysticism while simultaneously distancing himself from this horizon by transforming the visionary experience into a faith experience. Faith and vision thereby become correlative concepts: vision accomplishes nothing unless accompanied by belief. It is therefore possible to eat miraculous bread yet not "see signs" of divine glory (John 6:26; see also 1:34, 45–51; 6:36, 40; 11:40; 19:35). In some instances the faith experience entirely displaces the visionary experience. Noteworthy is the allusion to the story of the serpent in the wilderness at John 3:14–15. According to Numbers 21:8, those who *look* will live: Moses is instructed by God to "make a fiery serpent, and set it on a pole; and everyone who is bitten, when he sees it, shall live." In FG the image has shifted: "And as Moses lifted up the serpent in the wilderness, so must the Son of man be lifted up, that whoever *believes in* him may have eternal life" (my italics). By making such an alteration, FE suggests that faith has replaced vision. Similarly, in the climactic story about Thomas in John 20, Jesus blesses those who believe without having seen (20:29). Before the redactional addition of chapter 21, FG ended with the statement "and that [by] believing you may have life in his name" (20:31). According to FE, then, the person of faith need not worry about achieving the sort of mystical visions advocated in the Gospel of Thomas.

Finally, the faith mysticism FE develops to accommodate the absence of Jesus from the community has influenced his presentation of the sacraments. I support the position that the encounter with the Spirit, according to the Gospel of John, is available through the sacramental experience, initially through baptism and continually through the Eucharist. In John 3:5, Jesus speaks of being reborn "of water and spirit" in order to enter the Kingdom of God. There must be a baptismal reference behind this statement, for the Nicodemus dialogue is immediately followed by a story that discusses the baptismal activities of Jesus and John the Baptist (3:22–36). It is plausible that 3:5 reflects the idea that the baptismal experience brings the initiate into the presence of the Spirit. This experience is one of birth into the sacred: "that which is born of the Spirit is spirit" (3:6ff.). The heavenly mystical encounter has been brought to earth first through Jesus' descent and historical presence, and then for believers after his ascent through the sacramental encounter with the Spirit. Thus Jesus stresses to Nicodemus that only the Son of Man has descended from and ascended into heaven (3:13) so that eternal life can be given to the believer (3:15). Through baptism, Jesus as Spirit becomes present to the faithful.

This initial encounter with the divine presence is perpetuated by participating in the Eucharist meal. In John 6, Eucharistic references are behind Jesus' claim to be the "bread of life" who has "come down from heaven" (6:35, 41, 51). This bread is his "flesh" and if the faithful consume it, they will live forever (6:51). The reference is then expanded to include Jesus' blood, which must be drunk by the faithful in order to obtain life everlasting (6:53–55). Participation in this ritual brings about a mystical encounter with Jesus and eternal life because the incorporation of the sacred food allows the believer also to incorporate the person of Jesus: "He who eats my flesh and drinks my blood abides in me, and I in him" (6:56). FE makes clear that Jesus is not speaking of eating the flesh and drinking the blood of his historical body but of an action made effective through the presence of Jesus' Spirit in the elements (6:63). Thus the faithful can encounter Jesus through their participation in the Eucharist even though Jesus is no longer physically alive.

In conclusion, it appears that ascent and vision mysticism was a popular soteriological scheme in the late first century. The mystical approach was apparently advocated by that community out of which the Gospel of Thomas grew. The Fourth Evangelist shows an awareness of the Thomasine position (whether or not he was actually aware of Thomas or the Thomasine Community) and polemicizes against it. This polemic was achieved by altering and expanding the Jesus traditions from FE's own community in response to the type of soteriology represented in the Gospel of Thomas. In so doing, FE creates a new understanding of salvation that may be called "faith mysticism," and he develops a new Christology in which Jesus is seen as the earthly *kavod*, the manifestation of God's Glory in history.

27

The Johannine Jesus in the Gospel of Peter

A Social Memory Approach

ALAN KIRK

[O]ne point emerges very clearly: that the way memories of the past are generated and understood by given social groups is a direct guide to how they understand their position in the present.

(Fentress and Wickham 1992, 126)

Every true community is a community of memory. "Social memory" is a constitutive element in group formation, cohesion, and continuance. A shared past, perpetuated in a group's collective memory, creates and sustains the identity of that community (Fentress and Wickham 1992, 25–26, 201; Hobsbawm and Ranger 1983, 12; Nora 1998, 626, 636). "As individuals acquire knowledge of the past through forebears, common memories endow successive generations with a common heritage, strengthen society's temporal integration . . . and promote consensus over time" (Schwartz 1998, 67). The past of a group, in particular archetypal remembrances of community origins ("constitutive narrative"), penetrates its present and shapes its conceptions of contemporary experiences and challenges (Burke 1989, 103–104; Schudson 1989, 108–113). "Far from being simply the first in a series of irretrievable events, then, social beginnings can infuse the present and occupy space within it" (Schwartz 1982, 395). The struggle for American independence is an obvious example. Another instance is the following: "In Britain, the inhabitants of the coalfields of South Wales and Durham . . . have a very clear sense of the past as struggle, and it constitutes a memory that goes back at least a century. . . . The General Strike

313

of 1926 is a common touchstone, and for many miners the strikes of 1972, 1974, and 1984–5 simply replayed the experiences of 1926, with the same dramatis personae in each: the community, the employers, and the police" (Fentress and Wickham 1992, 115–116). For early Christianity the events surrounding the death of Jesus assumed this kind of archetypal significance.

Such extraordinary events are singled out, and the memory of them is both celebrated and perpetuated, by acts of commemoration (Schwartz 1982, 377). Ritual constitutes a crucial mode of commemoration: prototypical events are re-presented to the community in acts of ritual performance and reenactment. A problematic gap exists between crucial events of origins and a community's ongoing historical existence. Commemorative ritual fills this gap with celebration of memory: "[In commemorative ritual] a community is reminded of its identity as . . . told in a master narrative" (Connerton 1989, 70). The creation of textual artifacts—inscribing versions of the community's archetypal stories—is another form of commemorative activity. Similarly to ritual (or in tandem with ritual as liturgy), such literary productions both perpetuate and shape collective memory: "these records are not innocent acts of memory, but rather attempts to persuade, to shape the memory of others" (Burke 1989, 101). Moreover, by bringing the community's archetypal past into its present, ritual and textual artifacts of commemoration create the predispositions under which the group interprets its present realities in light of patterns supplied from its past (Fentress and Wickham 1992, 51, 74).

Equally, a community constructs its past in accordance with the exigencies of its present, and it is this constructed past which constitutes a group's social memory. "Recollection of the past is an active, constructive process, not simply a matter of retrieving information. To remember is to place a part of the past in the service of conceptions and needs of the present" (Schwartz 1982, 374). "But sacred history, inherited as a patrimony and endowed with a fixed, universal reference, turns out, in fact, to be subject to permanent negotiation, constantly readjusting itself to the local surroundings and experiences, to a policy of memory. This policy could however only be organized along the paradigms of religious tradition" (Valensi 1986, 291). Hence through analysis of a community's commemorative activities a great deal can be learned about its social identity.

Examples of this phenomenon are numerous. Medieval Muslim historians did not treat the Crusades as paradigmatic events, but in post-1945 Muslim historiography "the Crusades have come to be seen as the primary phase of European colonisation . . . culminating in the foundation of the state of Israel" (Connerton 1989, 15–16). John Cabot was commemorated by early American colonists as "first among the post-Columbus explorers to land on the North American continent. By the time of the Revolution, however, anti-British sentiment transformed Cabot into the 'shadowy agent of the British King.' Simultaneously, Columbus—the agent of a Spanish king (whose successors no longer threatened the colonies)—emerged suddenly as America's ultimate founding hero" (Schwartz 1982, 389–390). In the Song of Roland "the Saracens were substituted for the Basques [the original assailants encountered by Charlemagne] because this fitted better" (Fentress and Wickham 1989, 73). In 1985, tricentennial commemoration in France of the Revocation of the Edict of Nantes celebrated themes of diversity and human rights. "The antiracist group S.O.S. Racisme saw the banished Protestants of 1685 as the historical counterpart of today's victims of discrimination" (Nora 1998, 620). Joan of Arc was constructed as an "unfortunate idiot" by Voltaire; as prefiguring "the heroic rising of the Third Estate" by nineteenth-century French republicanism; and as a protoproletarian "born into the poorest class of society" by French socialists, while Vichy France commemorated Joan's resistance to the English. Common to all these examples is the construction of paradigmatic events and heroes of the past in accordance with the present social identity of the commemorating community.

The death of Jesus was an originating event for early Christian communities and accordingly was commemorated in Eucharistic ritual and literary productions of the passion narrative. The passion narrative came eventually to exist in discrete versions beside the canonical versions, including that of the Gospel of Peter. In this essay we shall explore the differences between the respective tellings of the "Legs Not Broken" episode in John 19:31–36 and Gospel of Peter 4:1–5. It will emerge that Peter's version is a retelling of the Johannine pericope that embodies the "social memory" of a second-century community, constructing this archetypal story in accordance with specific contours of its own social identity. The determinative feature of this social setting is religious rivalry and competition with Jewish communities. The respective passages from FG and the Gospel of Peter are presented in Table 27.1.

We shall assess the Johannine version of this story first. The request of the Jews to Pilate in John 19:31 that Jesus' legs be broken is linked to purity concerns. Deuteronomy 21:22–23, prescribing burial by nightfall for an executed criminal, though not cited, is implicit. Attention is drawn to the holiness of the following day (beginning at sunset). However, the evangelist intends that the request also profile the malevolence and the cruelty of the Jews, for though hastening death, the *crurifragium* (breaking of the legs) was brutal. Moreover, this request to Pilate parallels the earlier request that the cross inscription be modified, a request frustrated by Pilate's refusal (John 19:21–22). The Jews, with their subsequent request that Jesus' legs be broken, want to hasten his removal and hence his association with the offensive sign that proclaims him "King of the Jews." So in this regard also they are animated by hostile intentions (Brown

Table 27.1

Comparison of "Legs Not Broken" Episode

John 19:31–36	Gospel of Peter 4:1–5
[31]Since it was the day of Preparation, the Jews did not want the bodies left on the cross during the sabbath, especially because that sabbath was a day of great solemnity. So they asked Pilate to have the legs of the crucified men broken and the bodies removed. [32]Then the soldiers came and broke the legs of the first and of the other who had been crucified with him. [33]But when they came to Jesus and saw that he was already dead, they did not break his legs. [34]Instead, one of the soldiers pierced his side with a spear, and at once blood and water came out. [35](He who saw this has testified so that you also may believe. His testimony is true, and he knows that he tells the truth.) [36]These things occurred so that the scripture might be fulfilled, "None of his bones shall be broken."	[1]And they brought two criminals and crucified the Lord between them. But he himself remained silent, as if in no pain. [2]And when they set up the cross, they put an inscription on it, "This is the king of Israel." [3]And they piled his clothing in front of him; then they divided it among themselves, and gambled for it. [4]But one of those criminals reproached them and said, "We're suffering for the evil that we've done, but this fellow, who has become a savior of humanity, what wrong has he done you?" [5]And they got angry at him and ordered that his legs not be broken so he would die in agony.

1994, 1175–76; Schnackenburg 1987, 3.287). In this as in the earlier request, however, the Jews are frustrated in their desire to control the execution; in fact, their request recoils on them. They fail to cause Jesus' death through the *crurifragium*, for Jesus has sovereignly given up his life prior to the soldiers' arrival. Moreover, the actions of the Roman soldiers transform the episode into an epiphany: Jesus, legs unbroken, is revealed as the Passover Lamb (Exod. 12:46; Num. 9:12) and the Innocent One (Ps. 34:20), while the Jews are forced to "look on the one they have pierced" (Schnackenburg 1987, 287, 292; Barrett 1978, 590; Brown 1966, 2.952–953). The breaking of the legs (forestalled) and the resultant piercing of the side become christological revelations; the Johannine Jews, far from being the agents of Jesus' death as they intend, are portrayed as benighted, impotent dupes of God's sovereign plan being revealed in Jesus' death. The evangelist's perspective on these Jews is not unremittingly harsh, however. The statement "they will look on the one they have pierced" occurs in the context of the salvific blood and water flowing from Jesus' side and hence seems to encompass a recognition entailing either salvation or judgment (Schnackenburg 1987, 3.293–94).

The Gospel of Peter episode parallels that of FG insofar as Jesus' legs remain unbroken, but it features a number of differences. Here the Jews, appearing as Jesus' executioners, order that Jesus' legs not be broken, "so he would die in agony." In John the Jews' influence is exerted, in vain, through indirect agency, for Pilate must authorize their request, and it is Roman soldiers who carry out the order; moreover, the specific request itself is not fulfilled. Hence in John the Jews are depicted as clearly not in control of events. In Peter, by contrast, the Jews are direct agents actively causing Jesus' suffering and death, involved in all the scenes of the Passion, from Herod's condemnation of Jesus at the trial through to the Jews drawing the nails out of Jesus' corpse. The nonbreaking of Jesus' legs is thus told in such a way as to cohere with this narrative leitmotiv of direct Jewish responsibility for the killing of Jesus. Thus while the Johannine Jews are indirect agents in the death-by-*crurifragium* attempt, and failed ones at that, the Petrine Jews order that Jesus' legs not be broken, "so he would die in agony." Their malevolence and cruelty, implicit in John, is here explicit and intense. The Johannine Jews' failure to become (in place of Pilate) Jesus' executioners by virtue of Jesus' sovereign expiration is here the Petrine Jews' successful infliction of the torture of an extended, agonizing crucifixion intended to culminate in Jesus' death. The Johannine Jews act from benighted incomprehension; the Petrine Jews act out of stubborn obduracy, in response to the thief's open proclamation that Jesus is the "savior of humanity."

The purity concerns of the leading Jews are crucial to initiating the Johannine pericope and function as a plausible motive for their attempt to cause Jesus' swift death. Moreover, the concern of the Johannine passage is not really to bury the corpse before sundown but to link Jesus' death with the ritual slaying of the Passover Lamb. So the Johannine Jews' purity concerns, once having fulfilled the function of getting the episode under way, drop out of sight (though they set up the ironic reversal that Jesus' corpse, in the Jews' view a virulent pollutant menacing the purity of the imminent holy day, is in fact the holy Passover Lamb).

How is the purity issue addressed in the Gospel of Peter? The motif at first sight appears to be absent from the episode, where we find the "Legs Not Broken" introduced instead by the "Thief's Rebuke" to Jesus' Jewish executioners (4:4). Peter's tight configuration of these two episodes functions, as noted, to depict Jewish obduracy and is indissolubly linked with attribution to the Jews of direct responsibility for killing Jesus. The purity motif is not absent, however, but is distributed throughout the entire narrative where it likewise serves to pin responsibility for Jesus' death on the Jews. The regulation of Deuteronomy 21:22–23 prescribing burial of a malefactor before sundown, implicit in John 19:31, is cited twice (Gos. Pet. 2:3; 5:1) and accordingly is uppermost in the Jewish executioners' minds throughout the narrative. Their obdurate, infuriated response to the thief's rebuke leads them to rule out swift death by *crurifragium*, "so he would die in agony." But mistaking the onset of preternatural darkness for sundown, they seek some other means of swiftly dispatching Jesus and getting him off the cross and buried (5:15). "And one of them said, 'Give him vinegar mixed with something bitter to drink.' And they mixed it and gave it to him to drink. And they fulfilled all things and brought to completion the sins on their heads" (Gos. Pet. 5:2–3; see Dewey 1990, 10; Kirk 1994, 580). Jesus' death follows and the Jews—able now to fulfill Deuteronomy 21:22–23—disengage Jesus' body from the cross; accordingly, they are relieved when the sun returns (6:2–3). In short, Gospel of Peter uses the purity regulation as the narrative motif that drives the sequence of events that culminates in the Jews' murder of Jesus. Thus it appears in service to Gospel of Peter's generative redactional concern to construct the Jews as the agents directly responsible for Jesus' death.

The production of the passion narrative and its use in ritual and other contexts was central to the commemorative activities of the early Christian communities. Commemoration entails the construction of a community's archetypal past within the framework of the community's present social situation. Peter's passion narrative emerged from a social context characterized by intense religious rivalry and competition with Jewish groups, and it displays certain features that point in particular to the mid-second century.

We saw that the generative dynamic of the Gospel of Peter's telling of the "Legs Not Broken" episode, and correspondingly of the entire Passion, was attribution to the Jews of direct responsibility for Jesus' death. We find the Romans all but completely exculpated, indeed, absent from Calvary altogether, and the Jews acting as Jesus' torturers and murderers. Though a tendency to elaborate Jewish involvement in Jesus' arrest and trial is a feature of the first-century passion accounts, the motif of direct Jewish involvement in Jesus' execution, such as we see in Peter, is characteristic of second-century sources, such as *Peri Pascha* (Melito of Sardis), Epistle of Barnabas, *Kerygma Petrou*, and Acts of Pilate. This indicates a social setting characterized by intensely acrimonious relations with Jewish groups and the reconstruction of the archetypal past accordingly.

P. M. Head has demonstrated that martyrological motifs characteristic of second-century Christian sources (noting in particular the Martyrdom of Polycarp) pervade, in a formative manner, Gospel of Peter's narration of Jesus' trial and sufferings. These include, among others, silence and apparent insensitivity to pain: "But he himself remained silent, as if no pain" (Gos. Pet. 4:1). The martyrological topos of "dying in agony" appears in the segment of the text we chose for close analysis above (4:5). Head states, "There is evidence to suggest that this 'Christology of martyrdom' was widespread among Christians in the second century. In other words, we have a widespread genre in which insensitivity to pain and silent acceptance of real suffering can be juxtaposed, in reports which use Jesus' death as the basic paradigm. If reports of martyrdoms could be shaped by the paradigm of Jesus' passion, it is not difficult to assume that the accounts of Jesus' death could be shaped by the martyr theology" (Head 1992, 213). Second-century Christian communities were characterized by consciousness of vulnerability to martyrdom, even if actual deaths occurred only sporadically. In accordance with the phenomenology of social memory we would expect to see this consciousness appear in commemorative activities and artifacts, and this is what we find in Gospel of Peter's passion narrative. Though the extent of Jewish involvement in Christian martyrdoms is exaggerated by Christian sources, there is evidence that Jews occasionally played a role in denunciations. Christians were executed during the Bar Cochba Revolt (132–135 C.E.), and so tensions between the two communities would have been particularly high in the mid-second century, when memory of this would have been fresh.

Evidently, then, bitter religious rivalry between the Jewish and Christian communities in the second century is the generative social context for the Gospel of Peter and for its appropriation of the "Legs Not Broken" pericope from the Gospel of John. Correspondingly, Peter tells us a great deal about the trajectory of Johannine tradition (synoptic tradition also) into the second century. This last assertion, however, carries with it the obligation of responding to John Dominic Crossan's most recent argument for the priority of the primitive "Cross Gospel" allegedly preserved in Gospel of Peter. Crossan has shown little enthusiasm for engaging the redaction-critical analyses from various quarters that have called into question the existence of the Cross Gospel and his assigning of it to the mid-first century. Instead he has chosen to rest his case on what might be called his "mother of all arguments" for the priority of Gospel of Peter, an argument he considers so unanswerable that it effectively trumps all critiques. Naturally this strategy carries risks: if this argument turns out to be specious, we can write the epitaph of the Cross Gospel.

Crossan argues that Gospel of Peter is less "anti-Jewish" than the Synoptic Gospels and FG. If true, this would undermine one of the major arguments for placing Peter in the second century, and would also serve to place the Cross Gospel at the beginning of a trajectory of increasing so-called anti-Jewishness traceable in the synoptic and Johannine passion narratives. Crossan acknowledges that Gospel of Peter 1:1–6:4 makes the Jewish people directly responsible for Jesus' death. But in 8:1–4 the amorphous Jewish crowd who crucified Jesus split into two groups: the "people" who, affected by the supernatural signs, express second thoughts ("If his death produced these overwhelming signs, he must have been entirely innocent!"), and the Jewish authorities who, fearing a mutiny, place a guard on the tomb to secure the body, and, when this fails of its purpose, arrange to suppress the truth of a resurrection that they themselves have witnessed (see Gos. Pet. 11:5–7). Crossan's argument pivots on this "split between Jewish authorities and Jewish people." "My reading of the Gospel of Peter, therefore, is that it is more anti-Jewish with regard to the authorities than any of the canonical gospels but also more pro-Jewish with regard to the people than any of them" (Crossan 1998a, 496–498; see also Crossan 1998b, 27–28, 39). Moreover, Crossan asks, if Peter is so anti-Jewish yet also dependent on the canonical gospels, why does it pass over Matthew 27:25: "[H]is blood be on us and on our children" (Crossan 1998b, 29)?

Crossan's case for the pro-Jewishness of the Gospel of Peter erodes on scrutiny of this last argument. Peter's passion narrative is nothing if not an extended, vivid dramatization of Matthew 27:24–25: unlike Pilate, the Jewish people refuse to wash their hands (Gospel of Peter 1:1); they crucify and murder Jesus (1:2–6:4). So Crossan's adducing of this argument turns out to discredit his own proposal. The Gospel of Peter hardly stands prior to Matthew; rather it belongs somewhere along the Matthean trajectory. The argument appealing to the "split" between the Jewish authorities and the Jewish people, already damaged by the failure of its corollary, also breaks down. These are the same people whom Peter has just vividly depicted tormenting and killing Jesus. None of the first-century passion accounts goes so far. The Jewish people's subsequent doubts and inclination to reconsider, though a narrative development certainly requiring explanation, do not suffice to cancel this fundamental characterization and therefore cannot render Peter's depiction of the Jewish people "good" in comparison with the synoptic and Johannine accounts, as Crossan would have us believe.

Furthermore, the situation depicted by the Gospel of Peter, in which "the Jewish people [appear] ready, willing, and able to accept Christianity if only the Jewish authorities had not lied and misled them" (Crossan 1998b, 39), fits best in the second century. Crossan's assumption that such a complex depiction of the Jews can only belong early in the first century rests on the superannuated view that makes 70 C.E. the point of decisive breach and irreparable alienation between the Christian and Jewish communities. Recent research has demonstrated that the trauma of the Bar Cochba Revolt (132–135 C.E.) was in fact the decisive factor contributing to the eventual break between Christianity and Judaism, and that a good part of the second century (up to 170 C.E.) was a time of considerable complexity in Jewish-Christian relations, a time of still permeable boundaries and continued engagement between the two communities, albeit an "engagement" characterized by antipathy (but perhaps not always and everywhere), rivalry, and competition (see especially Wilson 1995; also Stark 1996, 49–72). The communities frequently existed in proximity, with the Christians feeling themselves the oppressed minority vis-à-vis established Jewish communities enjoying protected status. As two "Judaic" groups existing in proximity, Christians and Jews competed for recruits. Christians attempted to convert both Jews and Gentiles, but the traffic also went the other way, with Christians defecting to the synagogue (Wilson 1995, 34, 167, 263–265, 300).

Positing this second-century context, characterized by acrimony yet competitive engagement, permits us to reconcile the Gospel of Peter's attribution to the Jewish people of direct responsibility for killing Jesus with its subsequent distinguishing of the Jewish people from the Jewish authorities, and its singling out the latter for particular denigration. In effect, Peter claims that indeed the Jews are responsible for killing Jesus, but their subsequent failure to convert after the resurrection is because the Jewish people are dupes of their dishonest leaders who deliberately conceal from them the truth of the Christian proclamation. The Jewish authorities acknowledge among themselves the wrongfulness of their killing of Jesus (7:1); they witness the resurrection (9:1ff.); yet in a self-serving manner they conceal from their people the truth of what they have seen (11:5–7). This portrayal must be seen as a propagandistic attempt to discredit the leadership of the synagogue. The Gospel of Peter accordingly serves several purposes in the context of second-century religious rivalry. It rationalizes the limited Jewish response to the Christian proclamation ("their leaders keep them in ignorance of the truth of the resurrection") while at the same time makes a case to Jews as to why they should leave the synagogue and join the church ("your leaders are untrustworthy and are deceiving you"). The same propaganda served to hinder defections to the synagogue.

We have seen how the retelling of the Passion in the Gospel of Peter opens a window onto the social identity of a second-century Christian community. Social memory analysis also has permitted us to trace the trajectory of a Johannine pericope, the "Legs Not Broken," into the second century and to make sense of its transformation in that setting. The Gospel of Peter has taken the multifaceted Johannine composition and used it for rather one-dimensional propaganda purposes. As historians of Christian origins we will find Peter a crucial source for understanding second-century Christianity; from another perspective we can have few regrets that Bishop Serapion terminated its career.

28

The Prologue to the Fourth Gospel and the World of Speculative Jewish Theology

STEPHEN J. PATTERSON

The mysterious language of the Prologue to the Gospel of John (John 1:1–18) is at once beautiful and puzzling. Its beauty makes it among the dearest texts of the New Testament. But its distinctive language and conceptuality make it also one of the most difficult texts to understand. And because it is so dear, the discussion of how properly to understand its genesis in the religious world of antiquity has often been highly charged. Conservatives have fought to keep the Prologue within the bounds of orthodox Christianity and Judaism, while scholars pursuing the religious diversity of the period have found in it the strains of what would become "heterodox" to both of these traditions: Gnosticism.

This battle for the Prologue has been present as an undercurrent ever since Rudolf Bultmann startled the theological world with his proposal that John 1:1–18, as well as the discourses of Jesus in the Fourth Gospel (FG), were produced in a religious environment that he called "oriental Gnosticism" (Bultmann 1971, 30; also 1925). He further argued that it was Christianity's origins in John the Baptist's movement that could account for these ideas. The most extensive parallels to the Prologue's distinctive concepts are to be found, he argued, among the texts left behind by the Mandaeans, a Gnostic group claiming roots in the preaching and baptism of John the Baptist. It was in these works that one could most readily find the concept of a preexistent divine savior, who descends from the heavenly Place of Light into the hostile world of darkness. The darkness assails him but does not overcome him. The savior calls out into the world, and some hear his words of truth. For them he prepares the way back to the Place of Light, reascending to the heavenly realm to make a place for them. In the Mandaean texts, one such savior is John the Baptist. This is why, Bultmann argued, the Fourth Evangelist (FE) chose to insert verses 6–8 and 15 into the Prologue, as a pointed reminder to his readers that these poetic words were to be applied to Jesus, not to John the Baptist. Originally, the Prologue had been a Mandaean hymn to John (Bultmann 1971, 17–18).

Bultmann was by no means the first to notice the affinity between FG and Gnosticism. But the elegance of his solution, together with his compelling theological exposition of FG, forced this question to the forefront of Johannine scholarship, where it remains today—one might say, "remains stuck" today. For in trying still to answer Bultmann, much of the discussion remains mired in the presuppositions Bultmann himself brought to the text, presuppositions that have become highly questionable. The debate surrounding the Prologue to the Gospel of John stands in need of a good airing out. The outmoded assumptions that have long dominated this discussion need to be exposed and discarded. When we do this, we might be surprised to find new life in some very old proposals.

Trade-offs and the Problems of the Prologue

The debate over the religious background of FG's Prologue has been structured around a series of contrasts born of dubious assumptions. The first is the common trade-off between *Gnosticism or Jewish Wisdom theology*. Many of the ideas Bultmann traced to "oriental Gnosticism" can be found also in Jewish Wisdom texts such as the Wisdom of Solomon, or in the works of Jewish Wisdom theologians like Philo of Alexandria. Bultmann himself had pointed this out in his earlier work on the Prologue (Bultmann 1923), and many of his opponents— even today—argue that this is a more proper solution to the question.

But today we can see that the extensive overlap between Jewish Wisdom literature and Gnosticism does not mean that we must make a difficult choice between two very similar worlds of thought. Rather, it seems more accurate to say that these are not alternatives at all, but essentially the *same* thought world. Bultmann sensed this and considered Jewish Wisdom theology and oriental Gnosticism to be different branches from a common root. More recently, Hans-Martin Schenke has provided a more apt description of them as different points on a continuum of thought, one end of which lies in the very optimistic strains of court-sponsored *sapientia*—proverbial wisdom—and the other in the utterly pessimistic view one might think of as typical of classical Gnosticism (H. M. Schenke 1978). FG hovers in that between ground occupied by "speculative Wisdom" on the one hand and "primitive Gnosticism" on the other—if we may use these outmoded categories one last time. If FG were not the center of contention on precisely this point, we might see it as one of the key texts that calls into question the validity of these categories in the first place.

Bultmann thought of Gnosticism as coming essentially from the Hellenistic world. His opponents have argued that FG ought rather to be located in the Jewish world of thought. Here is the second tradeoff: *Hellenism or Judaism*. But it hardly needs to be stated that Hellenism and Judaism are not alternatives from which one must choose in trying to understand early Christianity and its texts. As Hengel and others have shown, the Hellenization of Palestine and of Judaism generally, which began soon after Alexander's conquest of the Mediterranean basin, was by FE's day a centuries-old process (Hengel 1974). With baths in Jerusalem, Cynics in Gadara, and Euripides playing on the stages of Galilee, we can hardly assume that placing FG firmly in "the Jewish world" means that various "Hellenistic" ideas are thereby to be ruled out. The very case of Gnosticism itself, as we know it today from the texts of Nag Hammadi, has contributed to this change in perspective. For a number of tractates found in the Nag Hammadi Library are the product of Sethianism, a specifically *Jewish* form of Gnosticism. Thus, one can no longer speak as though Judaism and Gnosticism were alternative explanations for the peculiar language and thought of FG's Prologue. In fact, some have begun to argue, on the basis of these Sethian texts, that the origins of Gnosticism itself lie precisely in early heterodox Judaism (e.g., MacRae 1970).

One more assumption running through much of this debate is a little more difficult to identify because it usually operates tacitly, so much so that it is scarcely even noticed. This is the assumption that *the more abstract, speculative, and complex a theology appears to be, the later it must be*. This assumption has worked to some extent in the dating of FG. While there is no reason to date FG any later than Matthew (and perhaps some good reasons for dating it earlier), it is commonly dated later. But this assumption works even more strongly on the discussion of the religious milieu of Johannine thought. As speculative, mysterious and abstract as FG is, it pales by comparison to the Mandaean texts and the theological tractates from Nag Hammadi. To many, this makes these texts simply "feel" later than FG. John may therefore stand in the same trajectory, but at an earlier point in its development. Assumptions of this sort make it easy for critics to dismiss the relevance of these various heterodox and speculative texts on the grounds that they are "late."

The ideas we find in Mandaeism, Gnosticism, and speculative Jewish Wisdom texts are indeed often complex and highly developed. Whatever this might mean, however, it surely does not mean that they are necessarily of a "late date." This much we may easily conclude from Philo, whose highly speculative work predates most of the New Testament and must certainly have antecedents. Philo shows that the sort of speculative theology we find echoed in FG was going on within Jewish circles long before Christianity emerged. Moreover, its use among the people Paul addresses in 1 Corinthians 1–4 shows that Christians were attracted to this sort of thinking very early on as a way of understanding Jesus and his fate (see Horsely 1998, 39–77). With Platonism, magic, mysticism, and the speculative mythological schemes of the mystery religions all present in the cultural soup from which Christianity emerged, one can reasonably expect almost any belief at any time.

Gnosis and Wisdom were not distinct alternatives within the religious world of early Judaism. Neither are Hellenism and Judaism to be considered alternatives, generally speaking. And given the religious and cultural complexity of the Hellenistic world, one cannot assume that every simple idea is early, and every complex idea is late. These old assumptions, around which the debate over John's Prologue has been structured for more than fifty years, should be given up. When they are, the question of how to account for the ideas found in John 1:1–18 seems not so difficult to answer. What are the texts and traditions that would have been current in the late first century in Palestine and Syria that show an interest in the kind of speculative theological ideas we find in FG, especially in the Prologue? We need not look for FE's sources. What we really wish to know about is the religious thought world from which FG (and possibly its sources) emerged. And for this, we have plenty of extant texts with which to work.

Parallel Perspectives

The Gospel of Thomas is an obvious and important parallel to FG. Both originated in Palestine and Syria in the late first century C.E. (Patterson 1993, 113–120), and, more important, of all the early Christian gospels it is Thomas that lies closest to FG in terms of theology. Both are steeped in the speculative Hellenistic Jewish theology that marks the overlap between Wisdom and Gnosticism. In both Thomas and FG Jesus appears as the redeemer come to earth from heaven to sojourn here for but a brief time (see John 7:33–34; Gos. Thom. 38). He has come to summon his followers out of this hostile and alien world (John 15:18–19; Gos. Thom. 56, 110) back to their heavenly home (John 14:2–4; Gos. Thom. 49). But there is a problem. The savior comes into the world and takes on "flesh" (John 1:14; Gos. Thom. 28:1), but people do not recognize him. John's Prologue laments, "He was in the world, and the world was made through him, yet the world knew him not. He came to his own home, and his own people received him not" (John 1:10–11). This, in a sense, is the whole unfolding story of the Gospel of John in a nutshell. It is also key to understanding the Gospel of Thomas: "Jesus says, 'I stood in the middle of the world, and in flesh I appeared to them. I found them all drunk. None of them did I find thirsty. My soul ached for the children of humanity, for they are blind in their hearts and cannot see'" (Gos. Thom. 28:1–3a).

How close are these texts and the communities from which they come? We do not know. Helmut Koester has shown that they share some traditions in common, FE weaving into discourses common material that appears in Thomas in the form of discrete sayings (Koester 1990, 113–124). Gregory Riley has shown that the two communities likely argued over the meaning and significance of Jesus' resurrection (Riley 1995). How close were they? Close enough to talk, to share traditions, and to argue. They agreed that the world was an evil and hostile place. They agreed that Jesus was the savior descended from God, now reascended into the heavenly realm of God. They agreed that this heavenly realm was their true home as well, and that Jesus had shown them the way home.

Who else was thinking thoughts like these in Palestine and Syria in the first century C.E.? The Mandaeans. For those familiar with the discussion of the history of FG's Prologue, the reappearance of the Mandaeans may seem at first a strange apparition from the past. Since Bultmann first suggested a connection between FG and these followers of John the Baptist, virtually no one has taken his hypothesis seriously. According to current thinking, the Mandaean texts are late, and the Mandaean reverence for John the Baptist is a late development in the Mandaean religion. With that, Bultmann's hypothesis is usually dismissed without further consideration. Meanwhile, however, a generation of scholarship on the Mandaeans has come and gone, and it stands today in a rather surprising position for Johannine scholarship. Though the Mandaean manuscripts are late, the Mandaean religion itself had its origins in the heterodox Jewish baptizing sects at home in the Jordan Valley before the destruction of Jerusalem in 70 C.E. This is what Kurt Rudolf, among others, has concluded from the distinctive baptismal practices of the Mandaeans, the central role played by the Jordan River in all of their writings, and the Mandaean myth of origins as recounted in the *Haran Gawaita*, which speaks of a great persecution of the community by the Jews, resulting in the destruction of Jerusalem and their own flight to the land beyond the Jordan (Rudolf 1960, 59–255; 1983, 363–364). This places the Mandaeans—or "proto-Mandaeans"—right in the middle of the religious and cultural milieu from which the Gospel of John emerged late in the first century.

To read the Mandaean hymns and liturgies, their mythological narratives and polemical texts, is to step into a world in which the language and concepts of FG are thoroughly at home. Here we find a world divided into light and darkness (see *Right Ginza* 3 and other texts in Foerster 1974, 148–169). Here

it is that the savior comes from the Place of Light, in the name of the Great
Life, descends to "utter a cry to the world," and is attacked by the wicked for
speaking a word of truth (*Right Ginza* 2.3). He is the *vine* of life, the *shepherd*
who loves his sheep, the one by whose *name* the righteous will ascend to the
Place of Light. He is *eternal life*, and he is the *way* to the Place of Light (*Right
Ginza* 2.3; 12.2; Mandaean Book of John 11, 59; also Foerster 1974, 227–234).
He promises, "I will take you out of the world and cause you to ascend . . . and
leave all behind" (*Left Ginza* 2.5; Foerster 1974, 255). It is easy to imagine
Bultmann's amazement on reading these texts for the first time. The parallels
between FG and the Mandaean writings are pervasive; Bultmann assembled
dozens of them in twenty-eight different categories (Bultmann 1925). No
other proposal for understanding the religious background of FG even comes
close. These texts and traditions, more than anything else, illustrate the religious climate within which FG and its mysterious Prologue were composed.
It was a polemically charged climate, in which persecution and alienation had
led to a profoundly negative view of the world. The savior has come into a
world of darkness to save those for whom the light still holds one last hope.
This was the sort of thinking one would have found among disaffected Jews
living in the Jordan Valley in the late first century C.E., practicing the ritual of
baptism.

A third group of Jewish writings in which these ideas come to expression is
the Sethian texts from Nag Hammadi. They, too, focus on a savior figure who
descends from the place of light into a world of darkness. They are called
"Sethian" because in them Seth, the third child of Adam and Eve, sometimes
appears as the descending/ascending savior. Though often considered to be
Gnostic, the Sethian tradition ought rather to be seen as part of that speculative Jewish theological field in which we have placed FG, Thomas, and the
Mandaeans. The Sethian texts are diverse, some falling closer to what might
be considered classic Gnosticism (e.g., the Apocryphon of John), others fitting
better into the category of speculative Jewish Wisdom theology (e.g., the Trimorphic Protennoia). Grouped together as a distinct tradition, the Sethian
texts are another sign that these old categories are an inadequate way of map-
ping the territory of heterodox Jewish theology.

The interest of these texts in the figure of Seth makes them especially interesting for Johannine studies. Seth was a key figure in early Samaritan theology,
which suggests an origin for this school of thought in Palestine/Syria, perhaps
in the region of the Jordan (H. M. Schenke 1974, 171). In the Trimorphic Protennoia, for example, the divine voice invites the reader to accept baptism from
the Baptists and thus to become glorious, "the way you first were when you
were [Light]" (13.45.16–20).[1] Another key text in this cluster, the Three Steles of Seth, carries the pseudonymous authorship of Dositheos, an obscure

character whom we otherwise know only from the pseudo-Clementine writings as a disciple of John the Baptist (*Hom.* 2.23–24; *Rec.* 1.54.3). For now, it is enough to note the relationship of these texts to the Baptist movement and thus their general proximity to the religious environment from which the FG also emerged.

The Sethians first came into the discussion of FG when Carsten Colpe and Gesine (Schenke) Robinson noticed extensive parallels between the Trimorphic Protennoia and FG's Prologue (Colpe 1974, 122–123; G. Schenke 1984; 1990). Here, too, we find the distinctive language of the Prologue in a religious world in which it seems quite at home—again, that world of speculative thought straddling Gnosticism and Jewish Wisdom theology. The parallels between the Trimorphic Protennoia and FG's Prologue are indeed extensive. Protennoia is the first created (13.35.1, 6), through whom everything else came into being (12.38.12–13). She is life (12.35.12–13), who brings light into the darkness (13.36.6); she is the light who enlightens all (13.47.28–29). She appears also as the Son, who is the Word (13.46.4ff.). He is the Son of God (13.38.24–25), the Only-Begotten God (13.38.23). Assessing the significance of these parallels for understanding the genesis of FG's Prologue is complicated by the fact that the Trimorphic Protennoia is a Christian text, or better, a "Christianized" text, wherein the savior (the self-begotten son) has been identified with Christ through a gloss (13.38.22; 13.39.6–7). Many have therefore dismissed its relevance on the assumption that the Trimorphic Protennoia is later than FG, is Christian, and is therefore probably dependent on FG for these ideas. Here all the old assumptions come rushing back into the discussion: the Trimorphic Protennoia is a Gnostic text, and thus it is late, Hellenistic, and derivative in nature. But this assessment fails to take in the fact that the Trimorphic Protennoia is not an isolated text but part of a larger school of thought. It is part of a tradition—a *Jewish* tradition—of speculative theology in which its distinctive language and ideas are at home. One finds these same ideas, for example, in the Sethian collection of hymns known as the Three Steles of Seth. Here we encounter the revealer in three-fold form. As Adamas, he is the preexistent one, who creates (7.119.6, 21–24). He is the light, who reveals the light (7.119.9–11). He is a Word, who comes into the world to save those who would prove worthy (7.119.18–20; 7.120.32–121; 7.121. 11–12). His female counterpart is Barbelo, who also exists before creation. Finally, he appears as "the great male First Appearer" (7.123.5), who appears "in a word" (7.123.10–11). In this form he brings life (7.123.18–19), and truth (7.123.17–18), and salvation (7.123.15–16; 7.123.33–124.1).

These are Sethian ideas. They do not come from Christianity, but from early heterodox Judaism. The texts within which we find them are probably best to be described as speculative Jewish wisdom texts connected with baptizing movements in early Judaism. How early could these ideas have developed within Judaism? The answer must remain theoretical, for none of these texts is easily dated. Three Steles of Seth may be a third-century work (Goehring 1988, 397); Trimorphic Protennoia probably comes from the second century (Turner 1988, 513). The earliest Sethian text we have may be Eugnostos the Blessed, which Douglas Parrott dates to the first century B.C.E. (Parrott 1988). The larger point, however, is that with Sethianism we have a long-developing tradition of speculative Jewish theology that lies geographically and conceptually close to the Christian Gospel of John. Sethianism is not derived from FG, but forms part of that world of speculative theology within which FG and its Prologue are very much at home.

Bultmann Revisited

What can be learned from these texts and traditions that stand so close to FG and its mysterious Prologue? First, John 1:1–18 should not seem so mysterious. Its language and concepts are clearly at home in first-century heterodox Judaism, as the Sethian and Mandaean parallels demonstrate. The Gospel of Thomas shows that the Johannine Community was not alone in tapping into these more speculative strains of Jewish thought in the search for an appropriate way of understanding Jesus and his real significance. But what made this way of thinking seem appropriate to the Johannine Community?

Bultmann argued that although FE makes use of Gnostic ideas, he does not fully embrace them. Especially important is FE's rejection of the flesh/spirit dualism in favor of the concept of the revealer's fleshly incarnation ("the Word became flesh"). In Gnosticism, so Bultmann believed, the revealer does not really enter the fleshly world of humanity but remains aloof, preserved in perfection in the spiritual realm. This idea, known as "docetism," did indeed find adherents among Gnostic Christians of the second century and later. Bultmann took the absence of this distinctive feature of Gnosticism in FG as an indication that FE intended to use Gnostic ideas but correct them. In so doing, Bultmann argued, FE could draw adherents of Gnosticism into the Christian circle by couching his own christology in gnostic terms (Bultmann 1971, 9).

Bultmann's assumption is based on the idea that Gnosticism was *fundamentally* docetic and could not tolerate anything like John 1:14: "And the Word became flesh. . . ." But the speculative theological tradition we have been considering is not necessarily docetic. In Thomas, Jesus also appears "in the flesh." The Mandaeans had no difficulty including the historical figure of John the Baptist as a genuine epiphany of the savior. And Seth is a mythic figure, who exists both in human form and as a heavenly being—not unlike the bargain eventually struck in orthodox Christian theology. Docetism does not appear to be a crucial question in this speculative theological tradition. Rather, what is crucial is that question that always pushed Jewish theology into a more speculative mode in the first place: theodicy. How could the existence of a good God be reconciled with the overwhelming experience of the world as an evil and hostile place—an experience common to both Jews and Jewish Christians in the ancient world? This incongruity is what drives one from the self-assured optimism of proverbial wisdom into the less optimistic quest for meaning that finds expression in speculative Jewish Wisdom. The speculative theologian looks at the world and despairs of finding meaning in it. God, the true good, must lie hidden somewhere, waiting to bring light into the overwhelming darkness, yearning to reveal himself to those who would recognize the good when they saw it.

These aspects of the speculative Jewish theological tradition are not minimized or undercut in FG or its Prologue. They are, rather, at its heart. The world, for FE and his community, has become a hostile place. They have been cast out of the synagogue, ostracized from the Jewish community (John 9:22; 12:42; 16:2). Their experience says that the world hates them; it cannot understand them, nor accept their confession of Jesus as the Christ (15:18–16:4). They are resigned: "And this is the judgment, that the light has come into the world, and people loved the darkness rather than the light, because their deeds were evil" (John 3:19). This experience of the world as an alien place, full of darkness, hostility, and ignorance, is what attracts FE to the tradition of Jewish speculative theology. Here he has found a language and a worldview that adequately captures what he and his community have experienced. Here he has found the words that tell their story.

There is something very interesting about these texts and traditions that seem to stand especially close to FE and his world: they are all related in some way to John the Baptist. The Three Steles of Seth bears the pseudonymous authorship of John's disciple and successor, Dositheos; the Trimorphic Protennoia speaks of going to "the Baptists" to be baptized; the Mandaean tradition is thought to have incorporated the figure of John the Baptist into its texts only late, but their roots in a baptizing movement in the Jordan Valley in the first century put them, if not directly in John's camp, just downstream from him. As for the Gospel of Thomas, the Baptist himself is mentioned only in passing, as in the other Christian gospels, in order to establish the superiority of Jesus and his followers (Gos. Thom. 46). But baptism remained important among the Thomasine Christians, as J. Z. Smith has shown (1965/66). Intriguing also is the appearance of a Thomas-like wisdom theology among the Pauline Christians at Corinth, a theology in which baptism played a key role (1 Cor. 1:11–17). And who likely brought that theology to Corinth in Paul's absence? Apollos, whom we encounter elsewhere only in Acts as a Christian sympathizer who "knew only the baptism of John" (Acts 18:25).

What was Baptist theology like at the end of the first century? How would FE have encountered it in the Jordan Valley or in the surrounding villages of Palestine, Syria, or Samaria in his day? Was there more to it than the apocalyptic summaries we have of the Baptist's preaching in the Synoptic Gospels? Was there also a speculative element? Were the Mandaeans right in claiming John as one of their own? Did Apollos really get his speculative baptismal theology from Baptist circles? Why did the Sethians choose John the Baptist's famous disciple, Dositheos, as the author of their sacred hymns of praise—hymns to be sung as one ascends to the highest heaven to encounter the "truly preexistent one"? And why did FE interrupt his beautiful hymn to the preexistent Logos with a disclaimer to ensure that no one would think that John the Baptist was "the true light, which enlightens everyone" (John 1:6–9)? Could it be that Bultmann was not so far from the truth about FG's Prologue after all—that originally this hymn was sung not to Jesus but to John the Baptist?

Note

1. All references to the Trimorphic Protennoia and the Three Steles of Seth are indicated by their Nag Hammadi codex number, treatise number, and line numbers. For example, the reference "(13.35.1–6)" indicates that the material cited may be found in Nag Hammadi codex 13, treatise 35, lines 1–6.

29

Riddles and Mysteries

The Way, the Truth, and the Life

JOHN ASHTON

It has long been recognized that the riddles in the Fourth Gospel (FG) constitute the main element of what Herbert Leroy (1968) has called the Johannine Community's *Sondersprache*, the special or private language it employed to reinforce its sense of identity and the conviction of its superiority to the outside world. James Kelso notes that "'riddle' is a comprehensive term for a puzzling question or an ambiguous proposition which is intended to be solved by conjecture" (1918, 765). The Fourth Evangelist's (FE) riddles make use of ordinary everyday words to convey a meaning that the outsider can only guess at. It is worth stressing from the outset that the riddle, by its very nature, is a confrontational form, opposing the riddler to the (would-be) solver, although the nature of the confrontation will differ from one case to another.

Most of FG's riddles, like the symbols with which they frequently overlap, cluster around the central motifs of "revelation" ("the truth") and the "life" that acceptance of this revelation ensures. Two of the most important, the "living [or fresh] water" in John 4 and "the bread of life" in chapter 6, make this association explicitly. But one could say the same of other key riddles, such as *anōthen* ("again/from above"), the term that so confuses Nicodemus (3:3), and the more frequent *hypagō* ("depart"), as the answers to these riddles involve the entry of the revealing word of God into the world and his eventual withdrawal from it. In spite of the fact that Pilate's question to Jesus, "What is truth?" (18:38), is the only example in FG of the interrogative form generally associated with Western riddles, *alētheia* ("truth") also belongs to the private language

of FE's community. When the Jews show themselves perplexed by Jesus' declaration that "the truth will set you free" (8:32), their failure to understand concerns the nature of the truth just as much as that of the promised freedom.
"Life" carries the same ambiguity in FG. Clearly, FE prefers the term "eternal life," in which ambiguity is replaced by oxymoron: "eternal life," like "centralized democracy," "realized eschatology," and—as Chistopher Ricks once
wryly observed to me—"literary theory," is a term in which the adjective
appears to conflict with, even to negate, the noun it qualifies. But the word *zōē*
("life") appears often enough on its own in FG, and when it does the reader is
well aware that it carries the same kind of special meaning as, say, *anōthen* or
hypagō.

The overlap between symbol and riddle in FG is not incidental. Life, the
gift of inestimable worth promised to those who accept Jesus' message, is the
Johannine equivalent of the synoptic kingdom of God. And just as the picture
language of the synoptic parables (images especially of growth, light, abun-
dance, and value) describes the Kingdom without ever saying what it actually
is, so the everyday symbols of FG, water and bread, even when they figure as
riddles, are immediately associated with the staples of human life and thus subtly conjoin the natural and the supernatural. This kind of association between
the natural and supernatural is fairly typical of the myths, metaphors, and riddles of many religious groups. The language of the riddles of the *Rig Veda*, for
instance, is drawn from the everyday experience of an Indian dairy farmer, his
tools (the plough, the wheel, the cart), the animals associated with them
(horses and oxen), plus other familiar living things (birds, animals, trees), and
climatic phenomena (clouds and rain). The effect of these riddles is to establish indissoluble links binding the mysterious happenings of the natural universe to the daily life of the farmer, as has been demonstrated in a wide-ranging
article by Walter Porzig (1925) in which he also shows how the Brahmins used
these riddles for the instruction of the young with a view to ensuring the survival of the priestly sect and of its privileged status. The Druids too are said to
have included in the final trial to which they subjected their neophytes the task
of "answering complicated riddles before a committee" (Ashe 1957, 30).

It would not be difficult to provide formal solutions to the riddles of FG.
But a list of such answers would hardly grant us access to the thinking of the
Johannine Community. What FG demands of its readers is what Jesus also
demands of his hearers, and that is not knowledge, but *faith*. Faith is a response
not to instruction but to revelation, and revelation is concerned with myster-
ies rather than riddles. Yet the riddles are closely connected with revelation,
and so we must investigate the nature of the link between them. This means
proceeding beyond the form-critical investigation of the original compositional setting of FG's riddles into a deeper analysis of the mystery in which
they are enclosed.

In order to keep this ambitious program within the compass of a single essay, I will restrict my remarks to the crucially important theme of Jesus' return to the Father, which is signified in FG by the word *hypagō* ("go away/depart"; see Ashton 1991, 191–192, 448–452, 492–493). For practical purposes, I will focus on two passages in which this theme occurs: John 8:21–24 and 13:31–14:6.

John 8:21–24—Life and Death

> Again he said to them, "I am going away, and you will search for me, but you will die in your sin. Where I am going, you cannot come." Then the Jews said, "Is he going to kill himself? Is that what he means by saying, 'Where I am going, you cannot come'?" He said to them, "You are from below, I am from above; you are of this world, I am not of this world. I told you that you would die in your sins, for you will die in your sins unless you believe that I am he (*hoti egō eimi*)." (John 8:21–24)

As the opening of verse 21 indicates ("Again he said"), this is not the first mention of Jesus' impending departure in FG. An earlier statement (John 7:33–36) had provoked a similar (though not identical) misunderstanding on the part of the Jews. Both passages take up the important motif of the quest for Jesus, begun in 5:18, that is one facet of the larger Johannine theme of revelation (Ashton 1994, 168–182).

The form of the ensuing dialogue between Jesus and the Jews, the judicial trial, is closely related to the riddle. In the chapter on riddles in his classic study *Einfache Formen*, Andre Jolles compares the judicial trial with another form closely resembling the riddle, the scholastic examination (1982, 131–132). In the latter case, there is someone "in the know" whose job it is to put questions to the examinee in an attempt to elicit the right answers. In the case of the judicial trial (Jolles is thinking of the system employed in continental Europe wherein the accused is examined by a magistrate), it is the judge or magistrate who needs to know and the accused who has the knowledge (of his guilt or innocence) and poses the riddle. Should the judge fail to solve it, he ceases for all practical purposes to be the judge. In FG, this judicial dialectic is most evident in the trial before Pilate, but it is important to recognize that John 8 is also much more than just a "controversy dialogue," the term Leroy uses to describe even the exceptionally bitter exchange that concludes the chapter (1968, 87). While this may be an adequate categorization of the arguments in the Synoptic Gospels, which typically conclude with a clever rejoinder from Jesus that leaves the Pharisees red-faced and discomfited, the angry confrontations between Jesus and the Jews in FG portray the latter no longer as mere interlocutors, but rather as hostile interrogators anxious to secure an admission that will justify a death sentence. On the other hand, Jesus himself, who in FG always initiates the dialogue, also has no qualms about prophesying the death of his adversaries.

The confrontation in John 8 begins abruptly: "'I am going away, and you will search for me, but you will die in your sin. Where I am going, you cannot come.' Then the Jews said, 'Is he going to kill himself?'" (8:21). Both parties speak of death: first, Jesus: "you will die in your sin"—a direct consequence of the Jews' unsuccessful search; then the Jews: "Is he going to kill himself?"—a crass misunderstanding of Jesus' announcement, which, by an extra irony lost on the Jews, does indeed refer in one sense to his approaching death.

The threat of death in this context is counterbalanced by a promise of life: "Whoever keeps my word will never see death" (John 8:51). An identical promise appears at the beginning of the Gospel of Thomas (1; cf. 18, 19), although there it is made, significantly, not to those who "keep" the words of Jesus but to those who "find the interpretation [*hermeneia*]" of them, that is, who find solutions for his many riddles. Throughout the wisdom literature, "life" is the ultimate prize: "For he who finds me [Wisdom] finds life and obtains favor from the Lord; but he who misses me injures himself; all who hate me love death" (Prov. 8:35–36). In the opening of Proverbs 8:36, the LXX substitutes *hoi de eis eme hamartanontes* ("those who sin against me") for the Hebrew "he who misses me," thus bringing the saying closer to Jesus' threat in John 8:21.

John 8:21 is, in fact, an example of what the Germans evocatively call a *Halsrätsel* or *Halslöserätsel* ("neck riddle"), a riddle so dangerous and threatening that one literally risks one's neck by undertaking to solve it. The best-known example of this is the Greek legend of the Sphinx, but almost equally familiar nowadays is the story of the opera *Turandot*, adapted for the stage by Schiller and Brecht and set to music by Puccini and Busoni. FE's irony is many-layered, for both the threat and the promise (8:51) are cloaked as riddles: neither the death the Jews are risking nor the life that is tantalizingly offered to those among them who keep Jesus' word is quite what they think it is.

Crucial for the understanding of this passage is the recognition that, in this instance, the solution to Jesus' riddle is itself the successful outcome of the quest. To grasp the full significance of the term *hypagō* ("go away"), which covers what later came to be called the "Paschal mystery," is ipso facto to have penetrated the heart of the mystery. For to know where Jesus is going is to have found him.

Like the answer to all riddles, the real significance of Jesus' departure is available only to the initiated, that is, to Johannine Christians. But the life-threatening aspect of this particular riddle entitles us to compare it with the central myths of other societies, those that Joseph Goetz calls "the really great myths, the ones that catch man at the depth of his being." Goetz notes that such myths are generally concealed from outsiders, for history proves that divulging them to the uninitiated either leads to their death or perhaps assumes that they are dead already. The modern interpreter often prefers to say nothing, since it is impossible to explain these myths except to people who have lived them from within. In approaching the myths that are central to a community, "we are right at the heart of the problem of religious communication" (Goetz 1980, cols. 1985–6). Surely FE would say the same.

John 13:31–14:6—The Way of Wisdom

When we turn to the departure riddle at John 13:31–14:6, which refers back directly to the one we have just been considering (8:21), the situation could hardly be more different. Now Jesus is surrounded not by his enemies but by his most intimate disciples.

> "Little children, I am with you only a little longer. You will look for me; and as I said to the Jews so now I say to you, 'Where I am going, you cannot come. . . .'" Simon Peter said to him, "Lord, where are you going?" Jesus answered, "Where I am going, you cannot follow me now; but you will follow afterward. . . . And you know the way to the place where I am going." Thomas said to him, "Lord, we do not know where you are going. How can we know the way?" Jesus said to him, "I am the way, and the truth, and the life. No one comes to the Father except through me." (John 13:33, 36; 14:4–6)

We have already noted that "truth" and "life" belong to the special vocabulary of the Johannine Community. Jesus' hearers fail to penetrate his true meaning either because they are culpably blind to it (the Jews) or because they have not yet been initiated into the inner circle (Nicodemus and the Samaritan woman). At the end of the Book of Signs, after going into hiding for the last time (John 12:36), Jesus commences a new kind of dialogue in the Upper Room. The first-time reader of FG is likely to be surprised by the realization that the disciples, who should be able to grasp Jesus' message without difficulty, exhibit a considerable degree of misunderstanding. This is because a new distinction has now been introduced: the temporal distinction between those who, listening to Jesus during his lifetime, cannot yet bear the full burden of what he is saying (16:12), and those others, paradoxically privileged, who are to be led into the wonderful realm of "the truth" under the guidance of the Paraclete after Jesus is gone (16:13).

In the Book of Signs (John 2–12), Jesus had spoken both of "truth" and "life" but never of "the way." The implication of the statement we are now considering (14:6) would seem, at first glance, to be open and direct. Jesus is the truth and Jesus is the life, both statements that can be readily comprehended by those who know FG. But "I am the way" is a new assertion, and not an easy one, following as it does the initial pronouncement that "you know the way where I am going." At 14:4–5, "the way" refers to the goal of Christian experience. But now in 14:6 "the way" seems to be the journey or experience itself; notably, Jesus drops "where I am going" from Thomas's question and replaces it with "no one comes to the Father, but by me."

In the remainder of this essay, I will argue that the Johannine motif of "the way" originates in the Jewish wisdom tradition and that this understanding enables us to assess its significance for the Fourth Gospel as a whole. The combination of the motifs of "wisdom" and "revelation" that characterizes the wisdom literature was taken over and absorbed by a quite different genre, Jewish apocalyptic. It is to this genre that we now turn for clues to the answers of FG's riddles.

Apocalyptic Wisdom

Michael Stone has called attention to the "Lists of Revealed Things" in a number of ancient apocalyptic writings. In these passages, "the subjects of the lists are far from self-evidently unknowable. Indeed, they are revealed or catalogued or shouted out in praise" (1990, 83). Second Enoch, for instance, claims to have "measured all the earth, and its mountains and hills and fields and woods and stones and rivers, and everything that exists" (40:12). "What song the sirens sang," Sir Thomas Browne famously remarked, "or what name Achilles assumed when he hid himself among women, though puzzling questions, are not beyond all conjecture." But the same cannot be said, surely, of Enoch's measurement of everything that exists. Although many, perhaps most, of the items on the apocalyptic lists would fit comfortably in an encyclopedia of scientific lore, this is not true of all of them, for some involve information that is inherently supernatural in nature and origin.

For example, Uriel—the tough-minded angelic guide in 4 Ezra—has evidently perused a list of "revealed things" and can therefore declare that "those who dwell upon earth can understand what is on earth, and he who is above the heavens can understand what is above the height of heaven" (4:20; cp. John 3:12). Uriel is astute enough to pull this list apart, distinguishing those items that might in principle be possible and legitimate objects of human inquiry from those that cannot be understood short of a revelation from heaven or an ascent to heaven. From the former group he selects three items and transforms them into riddles (Latin *similitudines*; Syriac *matlîn*, reflecting the Greek *parabolai* and Hebrew *mesalîm*, unsatisfactorily rendered by the NRSV and Stone as "problems"). He then challenges Ezra to answer any one of them: "Go, weigh for me the weight of fire, or measure for me a measure of wind, or call back for me the day that is past" (4:5). Ezra, not surprisingly, is aghast, and protests that no mere mortal could be expected to answer any of these riddles. But Uriel retorts that the fire, the wind, and the day (unlike the sea, the deep, the exits of hell, or the entrance of paradise) are "things through which you have passed" and therefore should be well within the seer's competence to discover.

Although the items on the apocalyptic lists are not "riddles" in the Johannine sense (because they are not couched in the equivocal language employed by FE), they function in much the same way by setting the privileged guild of seers over against the rest of humankind, clearly distinguishing the "knows" from the "know-nots." There is something decidedly odd, however, about the knowledge involved in apocalyptic wisdom, as evidenced by the previous examples. How, before the invention of anemometers, does one set about measuring the wind? And would you get the same result every time you did? With what instrument does one "weigh fire"? Notably, when Uriel proudly proclaims his knowledge, he does not say specifically what he knows. Instead, he gives a list of questions to which he claims to know the answers without saying what those answers are. So by a rather circuitous route we have found our way back to the kind of dilemma that confronts us in FG. In both FG and the apocalypses, the answers to the riddles we are concerned with seem much too shallow to justify the revelatory claims implicit in each.

Stone further points out that "many of the elements mentioned in the lists in IV Ezra and in II Baruch are drawn from the important chapters 28 and 38 of the Book of Job" (1976, 421). But those chapters of Job make it clear that true wisdom is not to be found in the parts of the universe Enoch claims to have successfully researched—not in the deep, not in the sea—for "the place of understanding . . . is hidden from the eyes of all [the] living" (Job 28:20–21). And by asking Job who determined the measurements of the earth (38:5), God is implying that this information is unavailable, even by way of revelation, to scientists or seers. So it is Uriel, posing unanswerable riddles to Ezra, who is the true heir to the Job tradition. Stone is right to argue that Uriel's list of questions "amounts to a denial, daring, perhaps even polemical, of the availability of certain types of special knowledge, a denial therefore of a specific part of the apocalyptic tradition" (1976, 420). But this denial is at the same time a reaffirmation of the message of Job, in which God alone understands [LXX, "understood"] the way to wisdom (*autēs tēn hodon*) and knows its place (*ton topon autēs*) (Job 28:23). In 4 Ezra, as in Job, the way of God is the heart of the mystery, different in kind as well as in degree from the natural phenomena that surround it. Uriel, fully aware that Ezra will be baffled and frustrated by the riddles he is setting him, knows perfectly well that unlike these natural things the way of God, his plan for the world, is *inaccessible even in principle* to mere mortals. Like Job, he places God's way at the center of his list of things that the seer cannot be expected to comprehend: "for the way of the Most High is created immeasurable" (4:11, Syriac text). This picks up on Ezra's complaint, toward the end of the previous chapter, that God has not shown anyone how "his way" might be understood (3:31).

We return now to FG. To introduce the theme of "the way" in John 13, FE seizes on the same wisdom tradition and boldly reverses it. The Prologue ended by picturing the Logos, who had tabernacled on earth like "the book of the covenant of the Most High God" (Sir. 24:23), nestling in the lap of the Father (John 1:18). Now Jesus reveals himself as "the way" to God. I have argued elsewhere that the real theme of the Johannine Prologue is not creation but revelation, and that "Logos" refers to God's providential plan for the world, a meaning regularly carried in the Hebrew Bible by the terms for wisdom (*hochma* or *sophia*) and, occasionally, for "word" or "thoughts" (*mahsebôth*; Ashton 1994, 17–31). "The way," as both Job and 4 Ezra show, is an alternative formulation of the same principle.

Toward the beginning of her discourse in Proverbs 8, personified Wisdom, standing "on the heights beside the way" and "beside the gates in front of the town" (vv. 2–3), proclaims that her mouth will utter truth (v. 7), while toward the end of the chapter she announces that whoever finds her finds life (v. 33). Hence, the way to wisdom is concealed from all except God (Job 28:12–23), but the way to God is wisdom. In asserting that he in his own person is the way, the truth, and the life, the Johannine Jesus is giving a marvelously inclusive summary of the benefits and graces that wisdom has to offer.

FG and the Wisdom of Solomon

By choosing to enter the domain of FG through a door FE would have wished to reserve for initiates—its riddling language—we have been able to see how he managed to appropriate for his own purposes the central motifs of the Jewish wisdom tradition and then reapply them, with astonishing boldness, to the person of Jesus. In doing so, he was at the same time laying claim to territory staked out over a century earlier by the author of the Wisdom of Solomon. Whether FE was actually acquainted with this apocryphal work (written, like his own, in the Greek language) cannot now be determined. But the two writings exhibit a number of striking similarities that deserve to be emphasized, for a comparison will shed light on the central purposes of each.

In the first place, both FE and the author of Wisdom of Solomon can be seen to be reflecting directly on the genre exemplified by their respective works (Ashton 1991, 434–437). But whereas FE is working with the quite recent (and quite limited) gospel tradition, the author of Wisdom of Solomon is able to draw on the literary corpus of the entire Hebrew Bible. He is not the first Jewish writer to have acted in this way: the narrative section of Deuteronomy is largely a midrash of Exodus and Numbers; Deutero-Isaiah, working with the preexilic prophetic tradition, was able at the same time to reflect on the essential characteristics of prophecy itself. Our author, whom we might call Deutero-Solomon, standing outside the Hebrew canon but clearly harking back to it, is bolder still, incorporating in his work elements from all the major biblical genres. His last chapter even includes apocalyptic, and an earlier passage is highly reminiscent of Stone's "lists of revealed things" (Wis. Sol. 7:17–20).

In the second place, both Deutero-Solomon and FE use a private language to bolster the pride and confidence of what was no doubt a tightly knit group of fellow believers surrounded by a hostile majority. In the case of Greek Solomon, we may suppose that if his Egyptian hosts had even guessed at the nature and extent of the vilification he was heaping on them they would have reacted with anger and hostility. And whereas the Jewish readers for whom he wrote would have greeted the recasting of the biblical legends in the second half of the book, along with their attribution to a series of unnamed men and women, with delighted recognition, their pagan fellow citizens must have responded with blank incomprehension. They are even less likely to have identified the man who pleased God and was "perfected in a short time" (Wis. Sol. 4:13) as the 365-year-old Enoch, or to have seen in the claim for immortality made on behalf of the righteous man at the beginning of the book (who boasted that God was his father; 2:16, cf. 18:13) an acknowledgment of God's determination to rescue his chosen people from all adversity. Yet the key to all these riddles lies in the Hebrew scriptures.

Third, in both books a reflective section is followed by an extended narrative section, with the figure of Wisdom playing a major role in each. In the first (meditative) half of Wisdom of Solomon, an exhortation to seek Wisdom (6:1–21) is followed by a long disquisition on Solomon's quest for wisdom that culminates in a midrashic version of his great prayer (9:1–18; cp. 1 Kings 8). This intricately patterned passage is punctuated by numerous reminders of hymn-like praises of Wisdom from the earlier tradition: Prov. 8:22–31; Sir. 24:1–21; 2 Bar. 3:9–4:4. The second half of the book begins with a narrative (summarized in 9:18) listing the achievements of personified Wisdom. In FG, the meditative section is restricted to the Prologue, often seen as a hymn to the Logos, Wisdom's masculine surrogate, while the hero of the long narrative that follows (who now has the human name "Jesus") is to be seen among other things as a figure of Wisdom.

Finally, we should remember the place each of these authors gives to the theme of "life," found everywhere in the Hebrew Bible from its first appearance as the tree of life in the garden of Eden, but especially common in the wisdom literature. I suspect that "life" almost always carries some of the extra resonance already discernible in the symbol of the tree of life. This, of course, holds out for human beings the enticing prospect of immortality, an idea taken up directly by Greek Solomon when he promises *athanasia* to everyone who heeds the laws of wisdom (Wis. Sol. 6:15; cf. 1:12, 15; 4:1; 5:15; 6:18; 8:13, 17). The Odes of Solomon, claiming the authority of the same name, add a slightly different nuance by speaking of the "deathless life" that "rose up in the land of the Lord, and . . . became known to his faithful ones, and was given unsparingly to those who trust in him" (15:10; cf. 28:31; 38:3; 40:6). The promises of the Odes are more than matched by FE; there is no need to list the numerous passages in FG that guarantee eternal life to those who believe in Jesus. But John goes further. When Jesus says of his adversaries, the Jews, that they "search for life in the scriptures," he could well be speaking to the readers of Wisdom of Solomon, insofar as this book, as we have seen, sets out to encapsulate the whole biblical tradition. But, declares Jesus uncompromisingly, "*I* am the one to whom they [the scriptures] bear witness" (John 5:40; my italics). The scriptures are the hermeneutical key to Jesus, and Jesus is the hermeneutical key to the scriptures. There could be no more direct expression of the challenge Christianity poses to Judaism.

30

"I Am" or "I Am He"?

Self-Declaratory Pronouncements in the Fourth Gospel and Rabbinic Tradition

CATRIN H. WILLIAMS

In addition to the Johannine metaphorical "I am" sayings (for example, "I am the light of the world," John 9:5), two patterns of usage of the expression *egō eimi* are commonly identified in the Fourth Gospel (FG). Depending on whether or not a predicate can be supplied from the immediate context of the phrase, a differentiation is made between 1) "absolute" *egō eimi* declarations, in which Jesus uses the phrase "I am" without clearly identifying what it is he claims to be ("you will die in your sins unless you believe that I am," John 8:24; also 8:28, 58; 13:19); and 2) those declarations where the phrase is used for self-identification ("I am he," 4:26; also 6:20; 9:9; 18:5, 6, 8). This study will explore whether the Fourth Evangelist (FE) actually maintains a distinction between these two patterns of usage, and how *egō eimi* statements in FG's underlying Jesus tradition may have been appropriated. To assist this exploration, the Johannine evidence will be compared first with the rabbinic use of self-declaratory pronouncements, and then with the rabbis' interpretations of self-declaratory pronouncements from the Hebrew Bible.

The Rabbinic "I Am" as Self-Identification

A variety of traditions indicate that the phrase *egō eimi* can be employed as an identification formula to indicate that the speaker is the person under consideration ("I am that person"). According to 2 Samuel 2:20 (LXX), the question

343

posed by Abner ("Is it you, Asahel?") receives the affirmative response "It is I" (*egō eimi*). Such cases clearly cannot be ignored when attempting to elucidate some of Jesus' *egō eimi* statements in FG. In John 9:9, the blind man's use of the phrase following his neighbors' question ("Is this not the man who used to sit and beg?") identifies him as the person whose identity is being discussed ("I am that beggar"; cf. Mark 14:62; *Testament of Job* 29:4; 31:6). The Samaritan woman's remark, "I know that Messiah is coming," leads Jesus to announce: "I am he, the one who is speaking to you" (*egō eimi ho lalōn soi*; John 4:25–26). Jesus gives the same response to the posse during the arrest scene when asked if he is "Jesus of Nazareth" (18:5–8). It is certainly appropriate, at least in formal terms, to interpret Jesus' response, both to the woman and to the arresting party, as affirmation that he is the figure in question: "I am he; I am the person you are talking about."

Rabbinic traditions provide a number of illuminating parallels to this syntactic pattern. One such tradition (*b. Ketubbot* 63a) describes the return of Rabbi Aqiba to the town of his father-in-law twenty-four years after the latter had made a vow that his daughter would not benefit from his estate after she became secretly betrothed to Aqiba. Without recognizing his son-in-law, the old man asks the now well-respected rabbi to invalidate this vow, thus prompting Aqiba to ask, "Would you have made your vow if you had known that he [your son-in-law] was a great man?" When the father-in-law concedes that he would not have established it had he known this, Aqiba declares, "I am he" (Aramaic: *'ana' hû*), and his father-in-law falls to the ground, kisses his feet, and gives him half his wealth. In this case, the phrase attributed to Aqiba undoubtedly serves to disclose his identity, and its antecedent can be easily identified ("I am he, that 'great man' we were just talking about"). Admittedly, this and analogous examples appear in rabbinic materials that cannot be dated before the Amoraic period (second–third century C.E.), but it is unlikely that such declarations represent a linguistic phenomenon that only entered general parlance during the second or third century C.E. (Williams 2000, 185–186). This pattern is, indeed, already attested in biblical Aramaic, for one of Daniel's dream interpretations leads him to identify the king with its central image: "The tree that you saw, which grew great and strong . . . that is you (*'ant hû*), O king!" (Dan. 4:20–22 [17–19]).

The well-documented use of *egō eimi* (and its Aramaic counterpart) as a vehicle for self-identification in a variety of Jewish traditions raises the question of the use of this expression in the traditional material available to FE. This is particularly the case because several source-critical analyses have sought to identify pre-Johannine material behind at least three passages where Jesus pronounces *egō eimi*: in his encounter with the Samaritan woman at the well (John 4:26); in his discussion with the disciples in the boat after walking

on the sea (6:20); and in his arrest in the garden (18:5). As seen in the following discussion, in each of these cases Jesus appears to use the phrase "I am" as
a form of self-identification. The question to be asked for each is whether FE
borrowed the phrase from the sources or traditions behind each story or
inserted the phrase into those traditions.

> The [Samaritan] woman said to him, "I know that Messiah is coming"
> (who is called Christ). "When he comes, he will proclaim all things to
> us." Jesus said to her, "I am he, the one who is speaking to you." (John
> 4:25–26)

It is possible that the "I am" statement at the conclusion of the story of the
Samaritan woman is drawn from an earlier tradition in which Jesus affirms his
messiahship (Bultmann 1971, 180; Link 1992, 283–291). If this is the case, in
that tradition *egō eimi* was the means whereby Jesus identifies himself to the
woman as the Messiah who will "proclaim all things to us" (John 4:25), that
is, "I am that Messiah." This is also a plausible interpretation of Jesus' response
in its present context in FG.

Many interpreters, however, draw attention to the statement's climactic
role as the conclusion to the encounter at the well (John 4:7–26). Its form (*"egō
eimi* the one who is speaking to you") closely parallels the wording of Jesus'
earlier challenge to the woman to grasp the identity of "the one who says to
[her]" (*tis estin ho legōn soi*), 'Give me a drink' " (4:10). Since these two remarks
hold the entire conversation together (Schapdick 2000, 245–247), Jesus' *egō
eimi* statement at the end encompasses all he has hitherto revealed to the
woman about himself. In other words, Jesus does inform the woman that her
messianic expectations are being realized in him, but he also transcends such
expectations. He offers the living water that quenches all thirst and leads to
eternal life (4:10–14), and the worship of the Father in Spirit and truth is made
possible in and through him (4:23–24). Jesus' first *egō eimi* pronouncement in
FG, therefore, discloses the true significance of his identity as the one who
"proclaims all things" (4:25). He enjoys this status not only due to his extraordinary knowledge (4:29) but because he uniquely reveals God and makes
available his offer of eternal life. Because the "I am" saying at 4:26 plays a key
role in FE's christological presentation here, it is difficult to determine
whether he borrowed the saying from the tradition or composed it himself.

> When they had rowed about three or four miles, they saw Jesus walk-
> ing on the sea and coming near the boat, and they were terrified. But
> he said to them, "It is I; do not be afraid." (John 6:20)

While the view that traditional material lies behind John 4:25–26 must
remain a hypothesis, there is scholarly consensus that the account of the sea

crossing (John 6:16–21) is derived from an already existing source. The literary independence of the Johannine narrative in relation to its synoptic parallels, especially Mark 6:45–52, is strongly suggested by the significant degree of variation between them in terms of vocabulary, narrative perspective, and outcome. There seems to be a core tradition underlying both the synoptic and Johannine versions that described the stormy conditions experienced by the disciples, their fear when they encountered Jesus walking on the sea, and his words "It is I; do not be afraid" (*egō eimi mē phobeisthe*; Mark 6:50; Matt. 14:27; John 6:20). The fixed status of Jesus' declaration in all the accounts confirms its pivotal role, but while *egō eimi* was probably understood in the broader tradition as an identification formula only ("It is me, Jesus"), it is possible that its epiphanic overtones were already recognized in the traditional version received by FE.

But several clues indicate that FE has shaped the traditional material in such a way that Jesus' words in FG cannot be interpreted simply as a recognition formula. In the Synoptics, the disciples' initial fear stems from their suspicion that the figure whom they see is a ghost (cf. Mark 6:49; Matt. 14:26), but in FG they are afraid because they actually recognize Jesus as the one who approaches the boat across the sea (6:19). If *egō eimi* does not serve here as a statement of identity ("It is I, Jesus"), its purpose must be to explain the significance of Jesus' act of walking on water, for *egō eimi* is the vehicle whereby he makes himself manifest as the one exercising the power that the Hebrew Bible attributes to God alone (cf. Job 9:8; 38:16; Hab. 3:15). Self-revelatory declarations such as "I am the Lord" and "I am God" figure prominently in a variety of biblical traditions, but the pronouncement of *egō eimi* by God in its bipartite form occurs only in Deuteronomy 32:39 and Isaiah 41:4; 43:10; 46:4 (cf. 45:18; 52:6). In each of these cases, the LXX translators have used *egō eimi* to render the Hebrew expression *'anî hû* ("I am he"). A closer examination of FG's sea-crossing account suggests, in fact, that Jesus' words in the underlying tradition were interpreted by FE in light of Isaiah's use of *egō eimi* as a divine self-proclamation, often accompanying the formula "do not fear" (see Isa. 41:10, "Do not fear, for I am with you, do not be afraid, for I am your God"; also 41:4, 13; 43:1, 5, 10). The description of the sudden arrival of the disciples' boat on the land "to which they were going" (John 6:20) demonstrates that Jesus' self-revelation makes the sea crossable for his disciples and leads them ashore. This can be compared to the promise that God will bring about a new exodus by making a way for his people through the sea (Isa. 43:16; 51:10) and the assurance of his personal presence ("When you pass through the waters, I will be with you. . . . Do not fear, for I am with you"). Isaiah's image of God's presence with his people may even have been the inspiration for the comment, phrased in characteristically Johannine language, that anticipates both the imminent drawing near of Jesus (John 6:19) and the momentous effect of his presence: "It was now dark, and Jesus had not yet come to them" (6:17bc). In the hands of FE, Jesus' walking on the turbulent sea becomes the occasion for divine self-manifestation ("I am; do not fear"), thus enabling the disciples, by means of his presence, to move from the darkness (cf. Isa. 42:16) and reach the safety of the other side.

Since Jesus' pronouncement in the sea-crossing account can be confidently ascribed to traditional material—subtly modified by FE in the light of OT usage to accentuate its theophanic significance—there are good reasons for viewing it as an important source, if not the basis, for the absolute *egō eimi* declarations that follow. Most commentators agree that the Johannine presentation of *egō eimi* as the object of belief (John 8:24; 13:19) and knowledge (8:28) finds its closest parallel in Isaiah 43:10, where Yahweh calls on Israel to act as witnesses "so that you may know and believe and understand that I am" (LXX *egō eimi*; MT: *'anî hû*). But other aspects of the use of *egō eimi* in Isaiah can also illuminate the significance attached to this expression in FG. The Septuagint translators of Isaiah sometimes distinguish between the two first-person pronominal forms used in the Hebrew text by rendering *'anî* as *egō* but *'anochî* as *egō eimi*. The latter translational device is applied on two occasions to divine statements where the phrase "I, I am he" (*'anochî 'anochî hû*) is rendered *egō eimi egō eimi*, "I am, I am" (Isa. 51:12; cf. 43:25). This distinctive doubling of *egō eimi* may well have prompted FE to interpret its second occurrence as a divine name: "I am 'I Am'." It would lead, moreover, to further reflection on other *egō eimi* passages from Isaiah that convey Yahweh's uncontested claim to be the only true God.

Several thematic and structural parallels can also be identified that strengthen the case for arguing that FE has consciously reflected on both the setting and significance of *egō eimi* as a divine self-declaration in LXX Isaiah. Whereas Isaiah's trial speeches are a popular vehicle for Yahweh's assertion of his unique divinity (*egō eimi*) over against the pagan gods (cf. 41:1–5; 43:8–13), the juridical setting and language of these speeches find significant echoes in scenes from FG where Jesus pronounces *egō eimi* during confrontations with "the Jews" (John 8:24, 28). In addition, some of the arguments presented in Isaiah by Yahweh as proof that he alone is God bear striking resemblance to the context of Jesus' *egō eimi* declarations in FG. Yahweh, "from the beginning" (Isa. 43:13), is the eternally active God (41:4; 48:12), the one whose timeless and absolute existence is accentuated in the Septuagintal rendering of his claim as *egō eimi*. With this compare John 8:58: "Before Abraham was, I am." Further, Yahweh's sovereignty is confirmed by his unique ability to foretell events before they take place (Isa. 43:9–10; 46:10–11), a motif applied to the Johannine Jesus when he predicts his imminent betrayal: "I tell you this now before it occurs, so that when it does occur, you may believe that I am" (John 13:19; cf. 18:1–11).

"I Am" in Rabbinic Exegesis

As we've seen, some of the *egō eimi* passages in FG appear to depend on the LXX rendering of the divine self-declaration *ʾanî hû*. Rabbinic traditions that cite or expound the OT passages in question can therefore yield considerable insight into later interpretations of this Hebrew expression (Williams 2000, 114–178). Indeed, because of the status of biblical *ʾanî hû* declarations as unequivocal expressions of monotheism, they are singled out in several midrashic traditions as decisive proof texts in defense of God's unity. These rabbinic usages may, in turn, shed light on FE's appropriation of the same language in those sections of FG that include "I am" sayings.

Two similar versions of a particularly illuminating tradition are recorded in the *Mekhilta de Rabbi Ishmael* (*Shirta* 4 and *Bahodesh* 5). The midrashic argument is set out as follows. The divine name appears twice, both in Exodus 15:3 ("*The Lord* is a warrior; *the Lord* is his name"; italics added) and in Exodus 20:2 ("*I am* the *Lord* your God"), because God can make himself manifest in a variety of guises. At the sea he appeared as a mighty warrior (15:3), but at Sinai he appeared as an "old man full of mercy" (24:10). The aim of this line of argumentation (with further proof adduced from Daniel 7:9–10) is "not to give an opportunity for the nations of the world to say, 'There are two powers.'" In other words, the objective is to show that the repetition of the divine name does not indicate God's being is somehow double. A series of exegetical elaborations and scriptural proof texts follows, presented as God's own defense of his own unity.

The second midrashic tradition, which appears at *Bahodesh* 5, reads,

> I, in Egypt; I, at the Sea. I, at Sinai. I, in the past; I, in the future to come. I, in this world; I, in the world to come. As it is said: "See now that I, I am he" [Deut. 32:39]. And it says: "To old age I am he" [Isa. 46:4]. And it says: "Thus says the Lord, the King of Israel, and his Redeemer, the Lord of hosts, I am the first and I am the last" [44:6]. And it says: "Who has acted and worked? The one who calls the generations from the beginning. I, the Lord, am the first, and with the last, I am he" [41:4].

This rabbinic passage, presented as an innovative divine endorsement of the argument for the unity of God, has been carefully crafted. Seven parallel formulations, which highlight the all-encompassing presence of the one God, correspond numerically to the seven occurrences of the divine "I" in the cited portions of the proof texts. The value of Deuteronomy 32:39 as a proof text is attested by the fact that in its context the initial doubling of 'anî is immediately followed by a monotheistic assertion (32:39b: "there is no god besides me"), while the parallels from Isaiah (46:4; 44:6; 41:4) act as a prophetic explication of the twofold "I" by accentuating God's eternally active presence. A vigorous demonstration of divine unity is thus used to confront those who embrace a "two powers" heresy. The actual identity of the heretics in question is difficult to establish, but the tradition's intricate exposition of certain biblical theophanies (Exod. 15:3; 24:10; Dan. 7:9–10) suggests that Gentile Christians or Jewish apocalyptic-mystical groups are among those targeted. The Tannaitic dating of this tradition has been convincingly demonstrated, so that, before the middle of the second century C.E., rabbinic exegetes were citing biblical declarations that contain 'anî hû as expressing God's own claim to exclusiveness.

A further examination of the midrashic use of Deuteronomy 32:39 and analogous statements from Isaiah reveals that some rabbinic traditions interpreted God's utterance of 'anî hû as the vehicle for his eschatological self-manifestation. An exegetical tradition, probably of Tannaitic origin, in *Mekhilta de Rabbi Ishmael* (*Pisha* 12) establishes the following innovative correlation:

> In similar manner you interpret: "Then the glory of the Lord shall be revealed, and all flesh shall see it together, for the mouth of the Lord has spoken" [Isa. 40:5]. And where did he [God] speak? "See now that I, I am he" [Deut. 32:39].

God's self-declaration as the "source" of Isaiah 40:5, due in all likelihood to its formal resemblance to Isaiah's 'anî hû statements, "I, I am he" is interpreted in this midrash as a self-revelatory formula linked to the future universal disclosure of God's glory. The eschatological perspective adopted for this divine pronouncement is then substantiated in *Pisha* 12 by linking together Isaiah 25:8 and Deuteronomy 32:39c ("I kill and I make alive" [LXX: *zēn poiēsō*]), both widely cited in rabbinic sources as resurrection proof texts.

Biblical traditions in which God declares 'anî hû evidently served as important proof texts in rabbinic sources from a relatively early period. The midrashic citation of these divine pronouncements must, nevertheless, be assessed against the use of this Hebrew phrase and its Aramaic counterpart in other rabbinic traditions. As noted in the previous section, the phrase 'anî hû can be applied for the purpose of self-identification, with the antecedent to "he" provided by its immediate context (see *b. Ketubbot* 63a). And in one of the rare rabbinic cases where 'anî hû is attributed to God in an interpretive statement rather than a scriptural citation, the expression is not self-contained, although the antecedent in question is none other than the tetragrammaton: "'The Lord, the Lord' [Exod. 34:6]. I am he before a man sins, and I am he after a man sins and repents" (*b. Rosh ha-Shanah* 17b). Such examples indicate that the decisive factors when attempting to determine the meaning and significance of *'anî hû* in rabbinic traditions are the way the expression is employed and the content of the claim(s) it seeks to convey. What the available rabbinic evidence does demonstrate is the lack of support for the theory that *'anî hû* was regarded by early sages as an exclusively theophanic formula, too sacred to be pronounced, or even as the Ineffable Name of God. This is not to deny that when the bipartite expression does occur in divine speech, either in a scriptural proof text or innovative exposition, it is recognizable as God's forceful assertion of his unique and eternal sovereignty.

Determining the meaning and function of self-declaratory pronouncements is also of decisive importance for understanding the Johannine use of *egō eimi*. While Jesus' utterance of *egō eimi* to the Samaritan woman (John 4:26) and to his disciples (6:20) could, on one level, be viewed as corresponding to its everyday purpose of self-identification ("I am that person"; cf. 9:9), perceptive readers or hearers of FG will recognize the various clues already provided on those occasions that point to the revelatory character of *egō eimi* to convey Jesus' true divine identity. This interpretive strategy, which amounts to an effective interplay of the possible meanings and import of *egō eimi*, becomes particularly apparent in the series of debates about Jesus' origin, destiny, and authority at John 8:21–59. The high concentration of misunderstandings in this episode accentuates the polarity between Jesus and his interlocutors (cf. 8:23), and it is the various levels on which Jesus' *egō eimi* pronouncements can be understood that accounts for the shift in the Jews' response from one of bewilderment (8:25) to a violent attempt to kill Jesus (8:59).

Early in this episode, Jesus confronts his dialogue partners with the decision of accepting or rejecting his claims: "You will die in your sins unless you believe that I am" (John 8:24). Those who respond positively to his self-revelation (*egō eimi*) will pass from death to life. But Jesus' interlocutors do not grasp the real force of his words. Their question, "Who are you?" (8:25a), indicates that they only adopt the surface meaning of *egō eimi* as a statement of mere identity, which they view as incomplete ("I am . . .") or as possessing an unidentifiable antecedent ("I am he"). Their rootedness in "this world" means that they miss the deeper significance of Jesus' self-declaration. His immediate reaction to their question (8:25b) is obscure, possibly intentionally so (Robert 1988, 282–287), although Barrett's proposed rendering "[I am] from the beginning what I tell you" (1978, 343) does accord with the theological claims that Isaiah associates with *egō eimi* (41:4; 43:10, 13) and anticipates Jesus' climactic words in John 8:58.

"The Jews" at first fail to comprehend that the key to Jesus' assertions about his identity is his unique relationship with God (John 8:26–27), thus leading him to offer further clarification: "When you have lifted up the Son of Man, then you will realize that I am, and that I do nothing on my own, but I speak these things as the Father instructed me" (8:28). The "lifting up" of Jesus, whereby his oneness with God is truly made manifest, will demonstrate that he speaks and acts in complete obedience to the Father who is constantly present with him. This unit of dialogue concludes abruptly with the remark that "many" believed in Jesus (8:30), surprising in view of the repeated cases of misunderstanding (8:22, 25, 27). The next unit opens, however, by stressing that true disciples are those who continue in Jesus' word (8:31), whereas the immediate appeal to descent from Abraham reveals the unwillingness of Jesus' interlocutors to accept his offer of freedom (8:33) and his word (8:37, 43).

It is Jesus' own appeal to the patriarch, the witness who recognized that his hope of eschatological salvation was being realized in Jesus, that prepares the ground for the final claim: "Very truly, I tell you, before Abraham was, I am" (8:58). This pronouncement is so distinctive in its form and content that a Jewish audience cannot fail to recognize its significance as a divine self-proclamation. The impossibility of identifying a predicate for *egō eimi* confirms its absolute meaning, and the adopted clause sequence echoes the poetic technique of "swapping" encountered in Isaiah's *'anî hû* declarations and adopted in their Septuagintal renderings (cf. 46:4: "To old age I am he"). Jesus thus lays claim to a timeless, absolute form of being (cf. John 1:1–3), contrasted with the time-bound existence of Abraham, who "was born" (*genesthai*). So now, at the end of this extended discourse, "the Jews" are finally confronted with the real implications of Jesus' use of *egō eimi*, and they denounce it as blasphemy (8:59). In his self-declaration they perceive God's own claim to exclusive divinity and eternal sovereignty as attested in Deuteronomy 32:39 and Isaiah, passages which in later decades would be cited in rabbinic traditions as incontrovertible proof of the unity of God.

The interplay of the two-level significance of *egō eimi* finds its most dramatic demonstration in the narrative of Jesus' arrest (John 18:1–14). This episode contains Jesus' last two *egō eimi* pronouncements in FG (18:5, 8), both of which could reasonably be interpreted as everyday expressions of self-identification ("I am he, Jesus of Nazareth"). But the first utterance, which may have been drawn from traditional material (Dodd 1963, 75–76; Fortna 1988, 150), is then highlighted by FE in a manner that suggests that the unexpected response of the arresting party (falling to the ground) results directly from Jesus' self-disclosure, *egō eimi*. This first declaration, by means of its formidable effect, exposes the utter powerlessness of the captors and of Judas, who "was standing with them" (18:5). Jesus could have resisted arrest, if that were his desire. It is Jesus' second utterance of *egō eimi* that reveals the real purpose of his earlier demonstration of divine power, namely to secure the freedom of his disciples (18:8). But this intervention possesses more profound significance, as indicated by FE's remark that it fulfills Jesus' word, "I did not lose a single one of those whom you gave me" (18:9). Since two of the sayings echoed here announce that Jesus' own will not be lost but will receive eternal life (6:39–40; 10:28), the physical deliverance of the disciples is intended as a symbolic anticipation of Jesus' ability to give life. This scene in the garden therefore displays Jesus' sovereign control over the events leading to his death and the salvific mission he is destined to accomplish in obedience to the Father's will (18:11). Indeed, Jesus' twofold pronouncement of *egō eimi* during his arrest serves as a powerful exemplification of the claims he has made with the aid of this expression in earlier Johannine narratives and discourses, for it encapsulates Jesus' unique identity as the one in whom God is revealed and his saving promises are fulfilled.

Conclusion

New Directions

Tom Thatcher

This book, and the individual essays contained within it, have not attempted to write the definitive history of Johannine source criticism. Indeed, it should be obvious that the current volume has not aspired to be a "history" of any sort. Neither has it attempted to represent all the major voices on established issues, nor to promote one particular perspective or approach. Rather, the essays' have pointed out that the many and complex problems associated with the composition-history of the Gospel of John are critical to its interpretation and therefore deserve renewed attention. Old questions must be approached in new ways; new questions must be asked and answered. This book is not offered as a review of the past but as a guidepost to the future.

The individual essays in this volume have highlighted the diversity of methods and perspectives that inform current study of the Johannine Jesus tradition and the composition history of the Fourth Gospel (FG). When viewed as a group, however, they also reveal broad contours of common concerns. These common concerns may be described in terms of five questions that underlie current attempts to reconstruct the composition-history of the Gospel of John. The answer to each question locates the study under consideration at a particular point on a spectrum between two interpretive options, some of which involve methods of study and some of which involve conclusions. In the sections that follow, I will briefly describe the issues involved in each question, the limits each places on current study of the Gospel of John, and means by which these limitations may be overcome in future research.

A Diachronic or a Synchronic Perspective?

The first underlying question is, Should the Johannine Jesus tradition be approached from a diachronic perspective or a synchronic perspective?

The terms *synchrony* and *diachrony* describe two broad perspectives from which a researcher may choose to view data. A *synchronic* approach treats pieces of information as *chronologically contemporary*, with a focus on comparison and contrast. This procedure tends to generate an analytical spectrum on which specific phenomena may be located. A *diachronic* approach, on the other hand, looks at items of data in terms of the *chronological sequence* in which they occurred, with a focus on the development from one thing to the next. This procedure tends to generate a time line that shows the evolutionary relationship between items of data. For example, a synchronic approach to the causes of the American Civil War might attempt to contrast the variety of perspectives on issues such as abolition, states' rights, and American foreign policy in the period from 1800 to 1860. A diachronic approach to the same issue, however, might attempt to show the evolving tension between the northern and southern states in the same period by looking at the sequence of historical events that led to the outbreak of the war. Both approaches are legitimate and produce valuable insights, but both also have limits.

Historically, Johannine source criticism has taken a diachronic approach to issues relating to the composition history of FG. For this reason, studies of FG's sources, the Fourth Evangelist's (FE) relationship to the historical Jesus, and the history of the Johannine Community often take the form of time lines or stages of development. This approach has generated the many debates over dependence, where the major concern has been to demonstrate that FE did or did not use other extant works as sources, or that other authors did or did not use FG as a source. As a result, a vast array of extremely sophisticated answers have been offered for several obvious questions: Which gospel came first? Who copied whom? Which author got what from where? The diachronic approach assumes that relationships of dependence must be proven or disproven, and that the current text of FG is the product of an evolution of Johannine thought within the framework of FE's (or the Johannine Community's) experiences.

While the diachronic approach cannot be discarded entirely, several essays in this volume have shown that synchronic approaches to the Johannine Jesus tradition can also have fruitful results. For example, because it is ultimately impossible to know for certain whether FE actually used the Synoptics as sources for FG, what can be gained by studying FG and the Synoptics together as parallel phenomena? In other words, if all four canonical gospels are treated as roughly contemporary, what similarities or differences are evident in the way each has adapted Jesus material, and what does this comparison and contrast highlight about the ways FE used *whatever* tradition was available to him? As the essays in Part 3 have shown, the same questions can be asked when comparing FG with noncanonical documents. What happens if one abandons the notion that Thomas borrowed material from John (or vice versa) and chooses instead to compare and contrast the ways these two gospels present Jesus? The answers to such questions may then be incorporated into the more specific historical concerns of the diachronic approaches. Ultimately, future studies that combine the synchronic and diachronic perspectives will produce deeper understandings than those that remain fiercely committed to one position or the other.

The Perspective of Jesus or John?

A second underlying question is, Do specific segments of FG reflect the perspective of Jesus, or does the entire document represent the perspective of John?

Since the days of Clement, biblical scholars have tended to treat John as a "spiritual gospel" that presents the Christ of faith rather than the Jesus of history. John's presentation is subjective, not objective; mystical, not literal; reflective, not realistic. FG should therefore be treated as a theological treatise rather than a source of historical information. This assumption has had a dramatic impact on biblical scholarship in the last two centuries: by appealing to this principle, scholars can dismiss all of FG from the data pool on Jesus in a cursory fashion, or can wax eloquent on Johannine Christology with little discussion of the historical Jesus. As a result, the historical Jesus of contemporary scholarship is a composite of the Jesus of the Synoptics and Q, with Thomas and Peter drawn in occasionally where they evidence close parallels with those documents. This composite Jesus is seen to be quite different from the Johannine Jesus, a fact that, through circular logic, reinforces the notion that John should not have been included in the database in the first place. Several of the essays in this volume, however, have demonstrated that the issues surrounding the relationship between the Fourth Evangelist and Jesus are too complex to be treated so casually, and that it is time for this relationship to be explored in a much more sophisticated way. For if even a small portion of the neglected material in FG reflects the historical ministry and teaching of Jesus, dramatic revisions will be required both to the contemporary understanding of the historical Jesus and to the nature and development of Johannine Christology.

The essays have revealed that two broad sets of concerns must be addressed in order to move forward on this issue. In the first place, it is necessary to establish more clearly what FE might have understood "the historical Jesus" to be. To what extent was he self-conscious in his presentation of Jesus, and what sense of "history" did he have? In order to address such questions, it will be necessary to describe more precisely how FE understood the relationship between Jesus, Jesus tradition, the Paraclete, and his own "witness." In the second place, questions concerning the relationship between the Johannine Jesus and the historical Jesus have not been, and perhaps cannot be, answered by the conventional "criteria of authenticity" on which contemporary Jesus research is based. These criteria—indeed, the entire disciplines of New Testament form and source criticism—were developed through and for the study of the Synoptic Gospels and are therefore inherently predisposed to find little authentic in FG. It should be obvious that criteria such as "multiple attestation" and "dissimilarity" can say very little about John, the first because FG has few real parallels with other extant gospels, the second because John's theology and historical setting are so complex that it is difficult to determine the "norms" against which to make judgments. But the difficulties in applying such criteria to FG do not indicate problems with the text of the Gospel of John; rather, they indicate limitations in the criteria themselves. The relationship between John and the historical Jesus deserves renewed attention and requires new methods and approaches that are sensitive to the fact that FG is not one of the Synoptics.

Traditional or Johannine?

A third underlying question is, Are specific segments of FG "traditional" or "Johannine" in origin?

This question is closely related to the second. The word "traditional" is one of the most often used and seldom defined terms in the vocabulary of contemporary biblical scholarship. Every person who uses this word seems to know what it means, but this assumed meaning is rarely articulated. In any case, many scholars assume that material that is "Johannine" in its content or style must not be "traditional," a doctrine that is further complicated by the fact that the definition of "Johannine" is also rather vague. The consensus view seems to be that "Johannine" means that FE, or someone close to him, "made up" the material under consideration, so that it could not have been drawn from a broader Jesus tradition. For all practical purposes, "Johannine" generally means "late" when speaking of Jesus traditions and is therefore the opposite of "primitive," which generally means something like "closer to Jesus." Therefore, material that is "Johannine" cannot really be "traditional." The problems inherent in such vague terminology are obvious.

Biblical scholars have developed sophisticated analytical instruments to detect layers of traditional material in the Synoptics, Q, and noncanonical gospels such as Peter and Thomas. These research tools allow us to distinguish primitive Jesus tradition even in sources that took their present form sometime in the second century. How is it, then, that no such tools have been developed to perform a similar operation on FG, to distinguish "traditional" material within "Johannine" material? If we recognize that the terms "Markan" and "Thomasine" are somehow opposed to "traditional" but we work to overcome that problem, why can we not do the same for FG? Several of the essays in this volume have pointed toward the means needed to achieve this task, but much further development is necessary in this area.

Oral or Written Sources?

A fourth underlying question is, Were the Fourth Evangelist's sources primarily oral or written?

Johannine scholars have shown interest in both oral and written sources when discussing the composition-history of FG. Some have focused primarily on oral traditions, some on FG's possible dependence on the Synoptic Gospels, and some on FG's use of noncanonical writings like the Signs Gospel. In many cases, the nature of the Johannine tradition has been approached from an "either/or" model: either eyewitness testimony or the use of sources; either written or oral sources; either the Synoptics or other documents; and so on. Recent developments in folkloristics and ancient literacy have demonstrated that the relationship between writing and orality was dynamic in FE's time. Most people could not read or write, but FG is a written document. One therefore cannot assume that FE would have used written sources in the way we would, nor that his oral traditions had developed in isolation from written texts. The interplay between texts and voices was complex in this period, and this should be taken into consideration when attempting to reconstruct the composition history of all ancient gospels.

Canonical or Noncanonical Perspective?

The fifth and final underlying question is, Does the Johannine Jesus tradition reflect a canonical or noncanonical perspective?

When the discovery of the Nag Hammadi documents led to a serious reconsideration of noncanonical gospels in the 1950s and '60s, it was widely assumed that these works were dependent on the Synoptics and John. In some circles this assumption has been reversed, so that Thomas and Peter are seen to contain materials that are more primitive than the Synoptics and FG; materials contained in these books may, in fact, have served as sources for the canonical gospels. The essays in Part 3 of this volume, however, have shown that a synchronic approach to the relationship between FG and the noncanonical literature raises new possibilities and new avenues of investigation. In order to pursue these avenues, it will be necessary to set aside the question of dependence and the distinction between "canonical" and "noncanonical" documents. From the perspective of the canon, the Gospel of John is one voice against the unified perspective of Matthew, Mark, Luke, and to some extent Paul. But consideration of the noncanonical literature creates a broader picture of the diversity in early Chris-tian thought and shows that the Johannine view of Jesus was one of many competing for dominance in the ancient church.

Three points in the relationship between the noncanonical documents and the Johannine Jesus tradition seem worthy of further investigation. First, it is clear that John's Christology and presentation of Jesus are in some ways more similar to that found in noncanonical documents than to the Synoptics. This would suggest that FE may have used traditional materials in the same way that Thomas, Peter, and other noncanonical authors used Jesus tradition. A close analysis of the use of Jesus tradition in these gospels, irrespective of its source, may therefore shed light on the ways FE used whatever traditions were available to him. Second, it is possible that FG and the noncanonical books used strains of Jesus tradition that Matthew, Mark, and Luke either did not know about or chose to ignore. Third, many scholars believe that the Fourth Gospel was produced in the context of the Antichrist crisis described in 1 John. Since the Antichrists seem to have held beliefs that are reflected in some of the noncanonical writings, it may be possible to use these writings to understand the type of thought that FE hoped to refute in FG.

The question of the Johannine Jesus tradition and the composition-history of the Fourth Gospel is too complicated to be resolved in a single volume. We hope this book has generated new interest and opened new paths for the future study of this important issue.

Works Cited

Abbott, E. A. *The Son of Man*. Cambridge: Cambridge University Press, 1910.

Abrahams, Roger D. "The Complex Relations of Simple Forms." In *Folklore Genres*. Ed. Dan Ben-Amos. Austin, Tex.: University of Texas Press, 1976.

Anderson, Paul N. *The Christology of the Fourth Gospel: Its Unity and Disunity in the Light of John 6*. WUNT II. Tübingen: J. C. B. Mohr (Paul Siebeck), 1996.

———. "The *Sitz im Leben* of the Johannine Bread of Life Discourse and Its Evolving Context." In *Critical Readings of John 6*. BIS. Ed. R. Alan Culpepper. Leiden: E. J. Brill, 1997.

Ashe, G. *King Arthur's Avalon: The Story of Glastonbury*. London: Collins, 1957.

Ashton, John. *Understanding the Fourth Gospel*. Oxford: Clarendon Press, 1991.

———. *Studying John: Approaches to the Fourth Gospel*. Oxford: Clarendon Press, 1994.

Bacon, Benjamin Wisner. *The Fourth Gospel in Research and Debate*. New York: Moffat Yard, 1910.

Bar-Ilan, Meir. "Illiteracy in the Land of Israel in the First Centuries C.E." In *Essays in the Social Scientific Study of Judaism and Jewish Society*, vol 2. Ed. Simcha Fishbane and Stuart Schoenfeld with Alain Goldshläger. Hoboken, N.J.: KTAV Publishing House, 1992.

Barrett, C. K. *The Gospel according to St. John*. 2nd ed. Philadelphia: Westminster Press, 1978.

Bauckham, Richard. "For Whom Were Gospels Written?" In *The Gospels for All Christians: Rethinking the Gospel Audiences*. Ed. Richard Bauckham. Grand Rapids: Wm. B. Eerdmans Publishing Co., 1998.

———. "John for Readers of Mark." In *The Gospels for All Christians*.

———. *God Crucified: Monotheism and Christology in the New Testament*. Grand Rapids: Wm. B. Eerdmans Publishing Co., 1999.

Beasley-Murray, G. R. *Jesus and the Future*. London: Macmillan & Co., 1954.

———. *Jesus and the Kingdom of God*. Grand Rapids: Wm. B. Eerdmans Publishing Co., 1986.

———. *John*. WBC. Waco, Tex.: Word Publishing Co., 1989.

Becker, J. *Das Evangelium des Johannes*. TKNT. Gütersloh: Mohn, 1979–1981.

Ben-Amos, Dan. "Solutions to Riddles." *Journal of American Folklore* 89 (1976): 249–254.

Berger, K. *Im Anfang war Johannes: Datierung und Theologie des vierten Evangeliums.* Stuttgart: Quell, 1997.

Beutler, Johannes. *Martyria: traditionsgeschichtliche Untersuchungen zum Zeugnisthema bei Johannes.* Frankfurter theologische Studien 10. Frankfurt am Main: Knecht, 1972.

———. *Habt kein Angst. Die erste johanneische Aschiedsrede (Joh 14).* Stuttgart: Katholisches Bibelwerk, 1984.

———. *Studien ZU den johanneischen Schriften.* Stuttgarten Biblische Aufsatzbände 25. Stuttart: Katholisches Bibelwerk, 1998.

———. *Die Johannesbriefe.* RNT. Regensburg: Pustet, 2000.

Blomberg, Craig. "Miracles as Parables." In *Gospel Perspectives*, vol. 6. Ed. David Wenham and Craig Blomberg. Sheffield: JSOT Press, 1986.

———. *The Historical Reliability of the Gospels.* Downers Grove, Ill.: InterVarsity Press, 1987.

———. *Interpreting the Parables.* Downers Grove, Ill.: InterVarsity Press, 1990.

———. "To What Extent Is John Historically Reliable?" In *Perspectives on John: Method and Interpretation in the Fourth Gospel.* Ed. Robert B. Sloan and Mikeal C. Parsons. Lewiston, N.Y.: Edwin Mellen Press, 1993.

———. "The Globalization of Biblical Interpretation—A Test Case: John 3–4." *BBR* 5 (1995): 1–15.

———. "The Legitimacy and Limits of Harmonization." In *Hermeneutics, Authority, and Canon.* Ed. D. A. Carson and John D. Woodbridge. Grand Rapids: Baker Book House, 1995.

———. *Jesus and the Gospels: An Introduction and Survey.* Nashville: Broadman Press, 1997.

Bock, Darrell L. *Blasphemy and Exaltation in Judaism and the Final Examination of Jesus.* Tübingen: Mohr, 1998.

Boismard, M. E. "Un procédé rédactionnel dans le quatrième évangile: la Wiederaufnahme." In *L'Evangile de Jean. Sources, redaction, theologie.* Ed. Marinus de Jonge. Leuven: Leuven University Press, 1975.

Borgen, Peder. *Bread from Heaven.* Leiden: Brill, 1965.

Borig, Rainer. *Der wahre weinstock. Untersuchungen ZU Jo 15, 1–10.* Studien Zum Alten und Neuen Testament 16. München: Kösel, 1967.

Broadhead, Edwin K. "Echoes of an Exorcism in the Fourth Gospel?" *ZNW* 86 (1995): 111–119.

Brodie, Thomas. *The Gospel according to John.* Oxford: Oxford University Press, 1993.

———. *The Quest for the Origin of John's Gospel: A Source-Oriented Approach.* New York: Oxford University Press, 1993.

Brown, Raymond. *The Gospel according to John.* New York: Doubleday & Co., 1966.

———. *The Death of the Messiah.* New York: Doubleday, 1994.

———. *The Community of the Beloved Disciple.* New York: Paulist Press, 1979.

Bruce, F. F. *The Gospel of John.* Grand Rapids: Wm. B. Eerdmans Publishing Co., 1983.

Bultmann, Rudolf. "Der religionsgeschichtliche Hintergrund des Prologs zum Johannes-Evangelium." In *EYXAPISTHPION: Festschrift fuer H. Gunkel*, vol. 2. Ed. Hans Schmidt. Göttingen: Vandenhoeck & Ruprecht, 1923.

———. *The Gospel of John: A Commentary.* Trans. G. R. Beasley-Murray, R. W. N. Hoare, and J. K. Riches. Philadelphia: Fortress Press, 1971. This translation is based on the 1966 German edition. The citations by Caragounis are from the first German edition of 1941.

———. "Die Bedeutung der neuerschlossenen mandaeischen und manichaeischen Quellen fuer das Verstaendnis des Johannesevangeliums." *ZNW* 24 (1925): 100–146.

Burge, Gary. *The Anointed Community: The Holy Spirit in the Johannine Tradition.* Grand Rapids: Wm. B. Eerdmans Publishing Co., 1987.

———. *Interpreting the Gospel of John.* Grand Rapids: Baker Book House, 1992.

Burke, Peter. "History as Social Memory." In *Memory: History, Culture and the Mind.* Ed. Thomas Butler. Oxford: Basil Blackwell Publisher, 1989.

Burkett, Delbert. *The Son of Man in the Gospel of John.* Sheffield: Sheffield Academic Press, 1991.

Burns, Thomas A. "Riddling: Occasion to Act." *Journal of American Folklore* 89 (1976): 139–165.

Caragounis, Chrys C. *The Son of Man: Vision and Interpretation.* WUNT 38. Tübingen: Mohr, 1986.

———. "Kingdom of God, Son of Man and Jesus' Self-Understanding." *TynB* 40 (1989): 3–23; 40.2 (1989): 223–38.

———. "The Kingdom of God in John and the Synoptics: Realized or Potential Eschatology?" In *John and the Synoptics.* BETL 101. Ed. Adelbert Denaux. Leuven: Peeters, 1992.

———. "Kingdom of God/Kingdom of Heaven." In *Dictionary of Jesus and the Gospels.* Ed. Joel Green, Scot McKnight, and Daniel Reid. Downers Grove, Ill.: InterVarsity Press, 1992.

Carson, D. A. "Current Source Criticism of the Fourth Gospel: Some Methodological Questions." *JBL* 97 (1978): 411–429.

———. *The Gospel according to John.* Grand Rapids: Wm. B. Eerdmans Publishing Co., 1991.

Cartlidge, David R. "Combien d'unités avez-vous de trois à quatre?: What Do We Mean by Intertextuality in Early Church Studies?" In *Society of Biblical Literature Annual Seminar Papers.* Ed. David J. Lull. Atlanta: Scholars Press, 1990.

Casey, Maurice. *Is John's Gospel True?* London: Routledge & Kegan Paul, 1996.

Charlesworth, James H. *The Beloved Disciple.* Valley Forge, Pa.: Trinity Press International, 1995.

Clanchy, M. T. "Remembering the Past and the Good Old Law." *History* 55 (1970): 165–176.

Cohen, Abner. "The Social Organization of Credit in a West African Cattle Market." *Africa* 35 (1965). Cited from Finnegan, Ruth. *Literacy and Orality: Studies in the Technology of Communication.* Oxford: Basil Blackwell Publisher, 1988.

Colpe, Carsten. "Heidnische, Juedische und Christliche Ueberlieferung in den Schriften aus Nag Hammadi III." *Jahrbuch für Antike und Christentum* 17 (1974): 109–125.

Connerton, Paul. *How Societies Remember.* Cambridge: Cambridge University Press, 1989.

Couch, Carl J. "Oral Technologies: A Cornerstone of Ancient Civilizations?" *Sociological Quarterly* 30 (1989): 587–602.

Crossan, John Dominic. *The Historical Jesus: The Life of a Mediterranean Jewish Peasant.* San Francisco: Harper San Francisco, 1991.

———. *Who Killed Jesus?* San Francisco: Harper San Francisco, 1995.

———. *The Birth of Christianity: Discovering What Happened in the Years Immediately after the Execution of Jesus.* San Francisco: Harper San Francisco, 1998.

———. "The Gospel of Peter and the Canonical Gospels: Independence, Dependence, or Both?" *Forum* (new series) 1 (1998): 7–51.

Cullmann, Oscar. "The Meaning of the Lord's Supper in Primitive Christianity." In *Essays on the Lord's Supper.* Ed. Oscar Cullmann and F. J. Leenhardt. Atlanta: John Knox Press, 1958.

Culpepper, R. Alan. *The Anatomy of the Fourth Gospel: A Study in Literary Design.* Philadelphia: Fortress Press, 1983.

Daube, David. *The New Testament and Rabbinic Judaism.* London: Athlone Press, 1956.

Davies, Margaret. *Rhetoric and Reference in the Fourth Gospel.* Sheffield: JSOT Press, 1992.

Davies, W. D. "Reflections on Aspects of the Jewish Background of the Gospel of John." In *Exploring the Gospel of John.* Ed. R. Alan Culpepper and C. C. Black. Louisville, Ky.: Westminster John Knox Press, 1996.

DeConick, April D. *Seek to See Him: Ascent and Vision Mysticism in the Gospel of Thomas.* Leiden: Brill, 1996.

DeConick, April D., and Fossum, Jarl. "Stripped before God: A New Interpretation of Logion 37." *Vigiliae Christianae* 45 (1991): 123–150.

Denaux, Adelbert, ed. *John and the Synoptics.* BETL 101. Leuven: Peeters, 1992.

Dewey, Arthur J. "'Time to Murder and Create': Visions and Revisions in the *Gospel of Peter.*" *Semeia* 49 (1990): 101–127.

———. "The Passion Narrative of the Gospel of Peter." *Forum,* n. s., 1 (1998): 53–69.

Dewey, Joanna. "Oral Methods of Structuring Narrative in Mark." *Interpretation* 53 (1989): 32–44.

———. "Textuality in an Oral Culture: A Survey of the Pauline Traditions." *Semeia* 65 (1995): 37–65.

———. "From Storytelling to Written Text: The Loss of Early Christian Women's Voices." *BTB* 26 (1996): 71–78.

Dodd, C. H. *The Parables of the Kingdom.* Rev. ed. London: William Collins Sons & Co., 1935.

———. *Historical Tradition in the Fourth Gospel.* Cambridge: Cambridge University Press, 1963.

———. *The Interpretation of the Fourth Gospel.* Cambridge: Cambridge University Press, 1968.

Dunn, James. "Let John Be John: A Gospel for Its Time." In *Das Evangelium und die Evangelium. Vorträge vom Tübinger Symposium 1982.* Ed. Peter Stuhlmacher. WUNT 28. Tübingen: Mohr, 1983.

Duprez, A. *Jésus et les dieux guérisseurs: A propos de Jean V.* Cahiers de la RevBibl. Paris: Gabalda, 1970.

Edwards, Viv, and Thomas J. Sienkewicz. *Oral Cultures Past and Present: Rappin' and Homer.* Cambridge, Mass.: Basil Blackwell, 1990.

Fanning, B. M. *Verbal Aspect in New Testament Greek.* Oxford: Clarendon, 1990.

Fentress, James, and Chris Wickham. *Social Memory.* Oxford: Basil Blackwell Publisher, 1992.

Finnegan, Ruth. *Literacy and Orality: Studies in the Technology of Communication.* Oxford: Basil Blackwell Publisher, 1988.

Foerster, Werner. *Gnosis: A Selection of Gnostic Writings.* Oxford: Clarendon Press, 1974.

———. "What Is Orality—if Anything?" *Byzantine and Modern Studies* 14 (1990): 139–149.

Foley, John Miles. *The Singer of Tales in Performance.* Bloomington, Ind.: Indiana University Press, 1995.

Fortna, Robert T. *The Gospel of Signs: A Reconstruction of the Narrative Source Underlying the Fourth Gospel.* Cambridge: Cambridge University Press, 1970.

———. *The Fourth Gospel and Its Predecessor: From Narrative Source to Present Gospel.* Philadelphia: Fortress Press, 1988. Also Edinburgh: T. & T. Clark, 1989.

Frey, J. *Die Johanneische Eschatologie.* Tübingen: Mohr, 1997–1998.

Fuller, Reginald H. *The Mission and Achievement of Jesus*. SBT. Naperville: Allenson, 1954.

Gardner-Smith, P. *St. John and the Synoptic Gospels*. Cambridge: Cambridge University Press, 1938.

Glazier, Jack, and Phyllis Gorfain Glazier. "Ambiguity and Exchange: The Double Dimension of Mbeeree Riddles." *Journal of American Folklore* 89 (1976): 189–238.

Goehring, James. "The Three Steles of Seth: Introduction." In *The Nag Hammadi Library in English*. 3rd ed. Ed. James M. Robinson. San Francisco: Harper & Row, 1988.

Goetz, J. "Mythe." In *Dictionnaire de spiritualité ascétique et mystique, doctrine et histoire*. Ed. M. Viller et al. Paris: Beauchesne, 1980.

Goody, Jack, and Ian Watt. "The Consequences of Literacy." In *Literacy in Traditional Societies*. Ed. Jack Goody. Cambridge: Cambridge University Press, 1968.

Graham, William A. *Beyond the Written Word: Oral Aspects of Scripture in the History of Religion*. Cambridge: Cambridge University Press, 1987.

Haenchen, Ernst. *Das Johannesevangelium: Ein Kommentar*. Tübingen: Mohr, 1980. English translation, Philadelphia: Fortress Press, 1984.

Harbsmeier, Michael. "Writing and the Other: Travellers' Literacy, or Towards an Archaeology of Orality." In *Literacy and Society*. Ed. Karen Schousboe and Mogens Trolle Larsen. Copenhagen: Akademisk Forlag, 1989.

Hare, Douglas R. A. *The Son of Man Tradition*. Minneapolis: Fortress Press, 1990.

Harris, William V. *Ancient Literacy*. Cambridge, Mass.: Harvard University Press, 1989.

Harvey, A. E. *Jesus on Trial*. London: SPCK, 1976.

Havelock, Eric. *Preface to Plato*. Cambridge, Mass.: Belknap Press, 1963

———. "Oral Composition in the Oedipus Tyrannus of Sophocles." *New Literary History* 16 (1984): 175–197.

Head, P. M. "On the Christology of the Gospel of Peter." *VC* 46 (1992): 209–224.

Heekerens, Hans-Peter. *Die Zeichen-Quelle der johanneischen Redaktion*. Stuttgart: Verlag Katholisches Bibelwerk, 1984.

Hengel, Martin. *Judaism and Hellenism*. Philadelphia: Fortress Press, 1974.

———. *The Johannine Question*. Philadelphia: Trinity Press International, 1989.

———. "Das Johannesevangelium als Quelle für die Geschichte des antiken Judentums." In *Judaica, Hellenistica et Christiana: Kleine Schriften II*. Ed. Martin Hengel. WUNT 109. Tübingen: Mohr-Siebeck, 1999.

Hiers, R. H. *The Historical Jesus and the Kingdom of God*. Gainesville, Fla.: University of Florida Press, 1973.

Horsley, Richard. *1 Corinthians*. Nashville: Abingdon Press, 1998.

Hunter, A. M. *The Work and Words of Jesus*. Rev. ed. London: SCM Press, 1972.

Jeremias, Joachim. *Die Gleichnisse Jesu*. Zurich: Zwingli, 1947. English trans., *The Parables of Jesus*. New York: Charles Scribner's Sons, 1963.

———. *The Rediscovery of Bethesda*. Louisville, Ky.: John Knox Press, 1966.

Jolles, Andres. *Einfache Formen: Legende, Sage, Mythe, Rätsel, Spruch, Kasus, Memorabile, Märchen, Witz*. Tübingen: Niemayer, 1982.

de Jonge, Marinus. "The Radical Eschatology of the Fourth Gospel and the Eschatology of the Synoptics." In *John and the Synoptics*. BETL. Ed. Adelbert Denaux. Leuven: Peeters, 1992.

Kanagaraj, J. J. *"Mysticism" in the Gospel of John: An Inquiry into Its Background*. JSNTSup. Sheffield: Sheffield Academic Press, 1998.

Käsemann, Ernst. "Sätze heiligen Rechtes im Neuen Testament." *NTS* 1 (1954–1955): 248–260. Rpt. in *Apocalypticism*. Ed. Robert Funk. JTC. New York: Herder and Herder, 1969. All citations of this essay use the page numbers from Funk's translation.

Kelber, Werner H. *The Oral and the Written Gospel: The Hermeneutics of Speaking and Writing in the Synoptic Tradition, Mark, Paul, and Q*. Philadelphia: Fortress Press, 1983.

Kelso, J. A. "Riddle." In *Encyclopedia of Religion and Ethics*. Ed. James Hastings. Edinburgh: T. & T. Clark, 1918.

Kirk, Alan. "Examining Priorities: Another Look at the *Gospel of Peter*'s Relationship to the New Testament Gospels." *NTS* 40 (1994): 572–595.

Kloppenborg, John S. *The Formation of Q*. Philadelphia: Fortress Press, 1987.

Koester, Helmut. *Ancient Christian Gospels*. Philadelphia: Trinity Press International, 1990.

Küchler, M. "Die 'Probatische' und Betesda mit den fünf stoai (Joh 5,2)." In *Peregrina Curiositas: Eine Reise durch den orbis antiquus*. Ed. A. Kessler, T. Ricklin, and G. Wurst. NTOA. Freiburg: Freiburger Universtitätsverlag, 1999.

Kümmel, Werner George. *Promise and Fulfilment*. 2nd ed. SBT. Naperville, Ill.: Alec R. Allenson, 1961.

———. *Introduction to the New Testament*. Trans. Howard Clark Kee. Nashville: Abingdon Press, 1975.

Kysar, Robert. *The Fourth Evangelist and His Gospel: An Examination of Contemporary Scholarship*. Minneapolis: Augsburg Publishing House, 1975.

Ladd, George Eldon. *Jesus and the Kingdom: The Eschatology of Biblical Realism*. London: SPCK, 1966. Rpt. as *The Presence of the Future*. Grand Rapids: Wm. B. Eerdmans Publishing Co., 1974.

Leon, Domingo Munoz. "Es el apostol Juan el discipulo amando?" *Est Bib* 45 (1987): 403–492.

Leroy, Herbert. *Rätsel und Missverständnis: Ein Beitrag zur Formgeschichte des Johannesevangeliums*. Bonn: Peter Hanstein, 1968.

Lewis, Thomas, Fari Amini, and Richard Lannon. *A General Theory of Love*. New York: Random House, 2000.

Liddell, Henry George, and Robert Scott. *A Greek-English Lexicon*. 9th ed. New York: Oxford University Press, 1996.

Lindars, Barnabas. *Behind the Fourth Gospel*. London: SPCK, 1971.

———. *The Gospel of John*. NCB. London: Oliphants, 1972.

———. "Capernaum Revisited: Jn 4,46–54 and the Synoptics." In *The Four Gospels 1992: Festschrift for F. Neirynck*. Ed. F. Van Segbroek et. al. BETL. Leuven: Peeters, 1992.

Link, A.. *'Was redest du mit ihr?' Eine Studie zur Exegese-, Redaktions- und Theologiegeschichte von Joh 4, 1–42*. Biblische Untersuchungen. Regensburg: Friedrich Pustet, 1992.

Lord, Albert Bates, ed. *Serbo-Croatian Heroic Songs*. Cambridge, Mass.: Harvard University Press, 1979.

Lundstrum, G. *The Kingdom of God in the Teaching of Jesus*. London: Oliver and Boyd, 1963.

MacRae, George. "The Jewish Background of the Gnostic Sophia Myth." *NovT* 12 (1970): 86–101.

Mandilaras, B. G. *The Verb in the Greek Non-Literary Papyri*. Athens: n. p., 1973.

Maranda, Elli Köngäs. "Theory and Practice of Riddle Analysis." *Journal of American Folklore* 84 (1971): 51–61.

———. "Riddles and Riddling: An Introduction." *Journal of American Folklore* 89 (1976): 127–138.

Martyn, J. Louis. *The Gospel of John in Christian History: Essays for Interpreters*. New York: Paulist Press, 1978.

———. *History and Theology in the Fourth Gospel*. 2nd ed. Nashville: Abingdon Press, 1979. The first edition of this work was published in 1968.

Matson, Mark A. "The Contribution to the Temple Cleansing by the Fourth Gospel." In *Society of Biblical Literature 1992 Seminar Papers*. Atlanta: Scholars Press, 1992.

McKay, K. L. "The Perfect and Other Aspects in New Testament Greek." *NTS* 23 (1981): 289–329.

———. *A New Syntax of the Verb in New Testament Greek: An Aspectual Approach*. New York: Peter Lang, 1994.

Miller, Robert J., ed. *The Complete Gospels: Annotated Scholars Version*. Rev. ed. Sonoma, Calif.: Polebridge, 1994.

Moloney, Francis J. *Belief in the Word*. Minneapolis: Augsburg Fortress, 1993.

———. *The Gospel of John*. Collegeville, Minn.: Liturgical Press, 1998.

Morris, Leon. *Studies in the Fourth Gospel*. Grand Rapids: Wm. B. Eerdmans Publishing Co., 1969.

———. *The Gospel according to John*. Grand Rapids: Wm. B. Eerdmans Publishing Co., 1995.

Nagy, Gregory. *Pindar's Homer: The Lyric Possession of an Epic Past*. Baltimore: Johns Hopkins University Press, 1990.

Neirynck, Franz. "John and the Synoptics." In *L'Evangile de Jean: Sources, Redaction, Theologie*. Ed. Marinus de Jonge. BETL. Leuven: Leuven University Press, 1977.

Neyrey, Jerome. *An Ideology of Revolt: John's Christology in Social-Science Perspective*. Philadelphia: Fortress Press, 1988.

Nichol, W. *The Sēmeia in the Fourth Gospel: Tradition and Redaction*. NovTSup. Leiden: Brill, 1972.

Nora, Pierre, "The Era of Commemoration." In *Realms of Memory: The Construction of the French Past*, vol. 3. Ed. Pierre Nora. Trans. Arthur Goldhammer. New York: Columbia University Press, 1992.

O'Day, Gail R. *Revelation in the Fourth Gospel: Narrative Mode and Theological Claim*. Philadelphia: Fortress Press, 1986.

———. *The Gospel of John, Introduction, Commentary, and Reflections*. NIB. Nashville: Abingdon Press, 1995.

Ong, Walter J. *Orality and Literacy: The Technologizing of the Word*. New York: Methuen, 1982.

Painter, John. *The Quest for the Messiah: The History, Literature, and Theology of the Johannine Community*. 2nd ed. Nashville: Abingdon Press, 1993.

Pamment, Margaret. "The Son of Man in the Fourth Gospel." *JTS*, n.s., 36 (1985): 56–66.

Parrott, Douglas. "Eugnostos the Blessed and the Sophia of Jesus Christ: Introduction." In *The Nag Hammadi Library in English*. 3rd ed. Ed. James M. Robinson. San Francisco: Harper & Row, 1988.

Patterson, Stephen J. *The Gospel of Thomas and Jesus*. Sonoma, Calif.: Polebridge Press, 1993.

Pepicello, W. J., and Thomas A. Green. "Wit in Riddling: A Linguistic Perspective." *Genre* 11 (1978): 1–13.

———. "The Folk Riddle: A Redefinition of Terms." *Western Folklore* 38 (1979): 3–20.

Perrin, Norman. *The Kingdom of God in the Teaching of Jesus*. Philadelphia: Westminster Press, 1963.

———. *Jesus and the Language of the Kingdom*. Philadelphia: Fortress Press, 1976.

Perry, John M. "The Evolution of the Johannine Eucharist." *NTS* 39 (1993): 22–35.

Phillips, Gary A., and Danna Nolan Fewell. "Ethics, Bible, Reading as If." *Semeia* 77 (1997): 1–21.

Plumer, E. "The Absence of Exorcisms in the Fourth Gospel." *Bib* 78 (1997): 350–368.

Porter, Stanley E. *Verbal Aspect in the Greek of the New Testament with Reference to Tense and Mood*. New York: Peter Lang, 1989.

Porzig, W. "Das Rätsel im Rigveda: Ein Beitrag zum Kapitel 'Sondersprache.'" In *GERMANICA: Festschrift Eduard Sievers*. Halle an der Saale: Niemayer, 1925.

Radloff, Wilhelm. "Samples of Folk Literature from the North Turkic Tribes." Trans. Gudrun Böttcher Sherman and Adam Brooke Davis. *Oral Tradition* 5 (1990): 85.

Ridderbos, Hermann. *The Coming of the Kingdom*. Philadelphia: Presbyterian and Reformed Publishing Co., 1962.

Riley, Gregory. *Resurrection Reconsidered: Thomas and John in Controversy*. Minneapolis: Fortress Press, 1995.

Robbins, Vernon K. "Oral, Rhetorical, and Literary Cultures: A Response." *Semeia* 65 (1995): 75–91.

Robert, R. "Le malentendu sur le nom divin au chapitre viii du quatrième évangile." *RThom* 88 (1988): 278–287.

Robinson, John A. T. *Twelve New Testament Studies*. London: SCM Press, 1962.

———. *The Priority of John*. London: SCM Press, 1985.

Rohrbaugh, Richard L. "The Social Location of the Marcan Audience." *BTB* 23 (1993): 114–127.

Ruckstuhl, Ernst. *Die literarische Einheit des Johannesevangeliums, der gegenwärtige Stand der einschlägigen Erforschung*. Studia Friburgensia new ser. 3. Freiburg: Paulus-Verlag, 1958/1987.

———. "Johannine Language and Style: The Question of Their Unity." In *L'Evangile de Jean: Sources, Redaction, Theologie*. Ed. Marinus de Jonge. BETL. Leuven: Leuven University Press, 1977.

Ruckstuhl, Eugen, and Peter Dschulnigg. *Stilkritik und Verfasserfrage im Johannesevangelium: Die johanneischen Sprachmerkmale auf dem Hintergrund des Neuen Testaments und des zeitgenöössischen hellenistischen Schrifttums*. Göttingen: Vandenhoeck & Ruprecht, 1991.

Rudolf, Kurt. *Die Mandäer*. Göttingen: Vandenhoeck & Ruprecht, 1960.

———. *Gnosis: The Nature and History of Gnosticism*. San Francisco: Harper & Row, 1983.

Rydbeck, L. *Fachprosa, vermeintliche Volkssprache und Neues Testament*. Uppsala: Almqvist & Wiksell, 1967.

Sabbe, Maurits. "The Arrest of Jesus in John 18, 1–11 and Its Relationship to the Synoptic Gospels: A Critical Evaluation of A. Dauer's Hypothesis." In *L'Evangile de Jean: Sources, Redaction, Theologie*. Ed. Marinus de Jonge. BETL. Leuven: Leuven University Press, 1977.

Sanders, E. P. *Jesus and Judaism*. Philadelphia: Fortress Press, 1985.

Sanders, J. N., and B. A. Martin. *A Commentary on the Gospel according to St. John*. London: Adam & Charles Black, 1968.

Schapdick, S. *Auf dem Weg in den Konflikt: Exegetische Studien zum theologischen Profil der Erzählung vom Aufenthalt Jesu in Samarien (Joh 4, 1–42) im Kontext des Johannesevangeliums*. BBB. Berlin: Philo, 2000.

Schenke, Gesine. *Die Dreigestaltige Protennoia (Nag-Hammadi-Codex XIII), herausgegeben, uebersetzt und kommentiert*. Texte und Untersuchungen. Berlin: Akademie-Verlag, 1984.

———. "The Trimorphic Protennoia and the Prologue of the Fourth Gospel." In *Gnosticism & the Early Christian World: Essays in Honor of James M. Robinson*. Ed. James Goering et. al. Sonoma, Calif.: Polebridge Press, 1990.

Schenke, Hans-Martin. "Das Sethianische System nach Nag-Hammadi-Hand-schriften." In *Studia Coptica*. Ed. Peter Nagel. Berliner Byzantinische Arbeiten. Berlin: Akademie Verlag, 1974.

———. "Die Tendenz der Weisheit zur Gnosis." In *Gnosis: Festschrift Hans Jonas*. Ed. Barbara Aland. Göttingen: Vandenhoeck & Ruprecht, 1978.

Schnackenburg, Rudolf. *God's Rule and Kingdom*. New York: Herder & Herder, 1963.

———. *The Gospel according to St. John*. Trans. Kevin Smith. HTKNT. New York: Herder and Herder, 1968. The citations by Broer are from the 1971 German edition (Freiberg: Herder and Herder). The citations by Kirk are from the 1987 English reprint (New York: Crossroad). The citations by Culpepper are from the 1980 English reprint (New York: Seabury).

Schnelle, Udo. *Antidocetic Christology in the Gospel of John*. Minneapolis: Fortress Press, 1992.

Schwartz, Barry. "Postmodernity and Historical Reputation: Abraham Lincoln in Late Twentieth-Century American Memory." *Social Forces* 77 (1998): 63–103.

———. "The Social Context of Commemoration: A Study in Collective Memory." *Social Forces* 61 (1982): 374–402.

Schweitzer, Albert. *The Quest of the Historical Jesus*. London: A. & C. Black, 1910.

Schweizer, Eduard. *Ego eimi . . . Die religionsgeschichtliche Herkunft und theologische Bedeutung der johanneischen Bildreden, zugleich ein Beitrag zur Quellenfrage des vierten Evangeliums*. Göttingen: Vandenhoeck & Ruprecht, 1939.

Scott, James C. *Domination and the Arts of Resistance: Hidden Transcripts*. New Haven: Yale University Press, 1990.

Segovia, Fernando. *The Farewell of the Word: The Johannine Call to Abide*. Minneapolis: Fortress Press, 1991.

Slotkin, Edgar. "Response to Professors Fontaine and Camp." In *Text and Tradition: The Hebrew Bible and Folklore*. Ed. Susan Niditch. SemeiaSt. Atlanta: Scholars Press, 1990.

Smith, D. Moody. *The Composition and Order of the Fourth Gospel: Bultmann's Literary Theory*. New Haven: Yale University Press, 1965.

———. *Johannine Christianity: Essays in Its Setting, Sources, and Theology*. Columbia: University of South Carolina Press, 1984.

———. *John among the Gospels: The Relationship in Twentieth Century Research*. Minneapolis: Fortress Press, 1992.

Smith, Jonathan Z. "The Garments of Shame." *HR* 5 (1965/66): 217–238.

Smyth, Herbert Weir. *Greek Grammar*. Cambridge, Mass.: Harvard University Press, 1984.

Stark, Rodney. *The Rise of Christianity*. San Francisco: HarperCollins, 1996.

Stibbe, M. W. G. *John: A Readings Commentary*. Sheffield: Sheffield Academic Press, 1993.

Stone, Michael E. "Lists of Revealed Things in the Apocalyptic Literature." In *Magnalia Dei: The Mighty Acts of God: Essays on the Bible and Archaeology in Memory of G. Ernest Wright*. Ed. F. M. Cross, W. E. Lemke, and P. D. Miller. Garden City, N.J.: Doubleday & Co., 1976.

———. *Fourth Ezra: A Commentary on the Book of Fourth Ezra*. Minneapolis: Fortress Press, 1990.

Stoppard, Tom. *Arcadia*. London: Faber & Faber, 1993.

Temple, Sydney. *The Core of the Fourth Gospel*. London: Mowbrays, 1975.

Thatcher, Tom. *The Riddles of Jesus in John: A Study in Tradition and Folklore*. SBLMS. Atlanta: Scholars Press, 2000.

Thiessen, Gerd, and Annette Merz. *The Historical Jesus*. Minneapolis: Fortress Press, 1998.

Thompson, M. B. "The Holy Internet: Communication Between Churches in the First Christian Generation." In *The Gospels for All Christians: Rethinking the Gospel Audiences*. Ed. Richard Bauckham. Edinburgh: T. & T. Clark, 1998.

Tuckett, Christopher M. *Q and the History of Early Christianity*. Edinburgh: T. & T. Clark, 1996.

Turner, John. "The Trimorphic Protennoia: Introduction." In *The Nag Hammadi Library in English*. 3rd ed. Ed. James M. Robinson. San Francisco: Harper & Row, 1988.

Twelftree, Graham H. *Jesus the Exorcist: A Contribution to the Study of the Historical Jesus*. Tübingen: Mohr, 1993.

———. *Jesus the Miracle Worker: A Historical and Theological Study*. Downers Grove, Ill.: InterVarsity Press, 1999.

Valensi, Lucette. "From Sacred History to Historical Memory and Back: The Jewish Past." *History and Anthropology* 2 (1986): 283–305.

Vansina, Jan. *Oral Traditions as History*. Madison: University of Wisconsin Press, 1985.

von Wahlde, Urban C. "A Redactional Technique in the Fourth Gospel." *CBQ* 38 (1973): 520–533.

———. *The Earliest Version of John's Gospel: Recovering the Gospel of Signs*. Wilmington, Del.: Michael Glazier, 1989.

Wallace, D. B. "John 5:2 and the Date of the Fourth Gospel." *Bib* 71 (1990): 177–205.

Westcott, B. F. *The Gospel according to St. John*. London: John Murray, 1908.

Williams, Catrin H. *I Am He: The Interpretation of 'Anî Hû' in Jewish and Early Christian Literature*. WUNT. Tübingen: Mohr-Siebeck, 2000.

Willis, W. *The Kingdom of God in 20th-Century Interpretation*. Peabody, Mass.: Hendrickson, 1987.

Wilson, Stephen G. *Related Strangers: Jews and Christians 70–170 C.E.* Minneapolis: Fortress Press, 1995.

Witherington, Ben, III. *The Christology of Jesus*. Minneapolis: Fortress Press, 1990.

———. *John's Wisdom*. Louisville, Ky.: Westminster John Knox Press, 1995.

Wright, N. T. *Jesus and the Victory of God*. Minneapolis: Fortress Press, 1996.

Index of Ancient Sources

NEW TESTAMENT

NONCANONICAL CHRISTIAN LITERATURE